ASTROLOGICAL ASPECTS

Also by Jeanne Avery

THE RISING SIGN: YOUR ASTROLOGICAL MASK

Jeanne Avery

ASTROLOGICAL ASPECTS
Your Inner Dialogues

A DOLPHIN BOOK
DOUBLEDAY & COMPANY, INC.
GARDEN CITY, NEW YORK
1985

Jeanne Avery has a private practice in New York City and is the publisher of a newsletter, *Healing in the New Age.*

Library of Congress Cataloging in Publication Data

Avery, Jeanne.
   Astrological aspects.

   "A Dolphin book."
   Includes index.
   1. Astrology. I. Title.
BF1708.1.A9   1985   133.5   84-21086
ISBN 0-385-18857-9

To the youngest and very precious members of my family
Charles and Stephanie

A dedication and thanks for a book about astrology must necessarily go far back into the past to thank the many people, known and unknown, who have influenced my study. It must include the very wonderful individuals who have written to me, given me feedback, and helped me in ways beyond what could have been expected. I am terribly grateful and do not forget small things that have made a difference in my ability to focus on this task.

I am grateful for the existence of my Camelot, the Scorpio island of Ibiza, for that is where I have been so well nurtured in the past year and a half. The original thanks go to Malou Argilaga for pointing me toward that spot in the Mediterranean. Then to Gus and Leah, who even did my food shopping so that I could write uninterruptedly. To the Hotel Hacienda and all the wonderful staff for giving me friendship and aid and to all the special, wonderful new friends who so kindly allowed me to tell their stories.

I give special thanks to a marvelous agent and friend, Lynn Nesbit. Gratitude goes to my editor, Loretta Barrett, for suggesting this book in the first place. As always, I have a special place in my heart for Ferris Mack, my astrological angel, who originally encouraged my books. And the pure joy of working with special editor Nan Grubbs, so attuned to my working habits, thoughts, and feelings that the path was smoothed in a thousand ways, can find no real expression in words.

And finally, for the loving encouragement of my therapist friend Marion Weisberg I give special thanks. I feel deep gratitude to the many therapists who have been my clients and recommended their clients to me, and who have helped me forge ahead into uncharted territory. Last, but far from least, to my three children, who have shown special understanding about my need to concentrate on writing, but who are there for me with their love, consistent and unfailing.

CONTENTS

I. WHAT IS AN ASPECT?
AND HOW TO FIND YOUR OWN   13

II. THE SUN   31

III. ASPECTS TO THE MOON   43
MOON-SUN

IV. ASPECTS TO MERCURY   61
MERCURY-SUN
MERCURY-MOON

V. ASPECTS TO VENUS   83
VENUS-SUN
VENUS-MOON
VENUS-MERCURY

VI. ASPECTS TO MARS   109
MARS-SUN
MARS-MOON
MARS-MERCURY
MARS-VENUS

VII. ASPECTS TO JUPITER   141
JUPITER-SUN
JUPITER-MOON
JUPITER-MERCURY
JUPITER-VENUS
JUPITER-MARS

VIII. ASPECTS TO SATURN   175
SATURN-SUN
SATURN-MOON
SATURN-MERCURY
SATURN-VENUS

SATURN-MARS
SATURN-JUPITER

IX.   ASPECTS TO URANUS   215
URANUS-SUN
URANUS-MOON
URANUS-MERCURY
URANUS-VENUS
URANUS-MARS
URANUS-JUPITER
URANUS-SATURN

X.   ASPECTS TO NEPTUNE   271
NEPTUNE-SUN
NEPTUNE-MOON
NEPTUNE-MERCURY
NEPTUNE-VENUS
NEPTUNE-MARS
NEPTUNE-JUPITER
NEPTUNE-SATURN
NEPTUNE-URANUS

XI.   ASPECTS TO PLUTO   325
PLUTO-SUN
PLUTO-MOON
PLUTO-MERCURY
PLUTO-VENUS
PLUTO-MARS
PLUTO-JUPITER
PLUTO-SATURN
PLUTO-URANUS
PLUTO-NEPTUNE

INTRODUCTION

It is hard to pinpoint an exact moment when life changes and heads in a different direction, but I firmly believe that one small incident may be the cause of a whole new life. One such incident came when I met Marion Weisberg, a psychotherapist practicing in New York City. I discovered a kindred spirit and a person willing to explore alternative methods of healing. Marion and I began our work together much as an experiment, to see if astrology could facilitate the delicate task of the therapeutic process. We explained to the participants in our first group that indeed the session was somewhat of a departure from traditional group workshops, but these participants seemed eager to explore the possibilities with us. After our first daylong workshop, which had been carefully prepared by us in advance, we both felt that a great deal had been accomplished. In particular, the time involved in the therapeutic process seemed cut in half. We accomplished in one day what might have ordinarily taken two days to complete. But that was not the really important point. It seemed that the energy stimulated by our joint endeavor was particularly potent. To me, it is clear that the astrological chart is a profound and exact tool for the pinpointing of underlying patterns. It cannot heal by itself, for it is not a belief system or process. It is the road map, the psychological profile, and the blueprint of the individual energy system.

By working with Marion, I was able to find new language to describe these complex energies that make up the human system. My caring about people and curiosity about what makes them tick has been endlessly satisfied. By reducing subtle variations on the human theme to key words, descriptions, and analogies, I have hoped to make crystal clear to my clients who they are, why they think the way they do, and what they can begin to do about it.

I didn't start out to be a healer. It became obvious, however, that with this tool and combination of astrology and psychotherapy, people were facilitating changes in their lives rather dramatically. So the responsibility of being a healer was unavoidable. The joint practice of psychotherapy and astrology has taken us to conferences for therapists and astrologers. We have not begun a true research program, as such, and yet it has been an unstructured wish that we could dig deeper to correlate information on a more scientific level. Perhaps if time and proximity permit, we will indeed be able to do just that in the future, for as even Carl Jung readily admitted, that kind of study could be incredibly valuable.

In the meantime, on a nonscientific level, I have chosen to present some variety of examples of how a specific aspect can manifest in the life of an individual. Astrology is not unlike a language in symbolic form. If one astrologer says to another, "Mars square Saturn," for example, there is no need for further explanation. For the millions of people who are beginning to show an interest in learning the language, I hope to convey an interpretation in such form of examples that will make meanings clear. In astrological symbology, one word can convey thousands of words of explanation and depth perception. In Spain, a very common and wise phrase is *"poco a poco,"* little by little, step by step. Here's to the possibility of stimulation of constant new awareness, inner development, and resultant kindness of people to each other. With deeper understanding, compassion, generosity of spirit, and love, we can heal our planet.

*Learning about aspects
is like developing X-ray vision.*

WHAT IS AN ASPECT?

AND HOW TO FIND YOUR OWN

ASTROLOGY IS A SYMBOLIC LANGUAGE. IN EARLY TIMES, mankind no doubt began to relate what he observed in nature around him to what he observed in the sky. Fishermen may have noticed that the waxing and waning of the Moon related to the movement of the tides. Shepherds must have affirmed that the heat of the Sun was strongest at midday, when the Sun was at its zenith, and that the strength of that heat changed according to the seasons of growth. Little by little, associations as well as attributes came to be ascribed to the Sun, the Moon, and the planets. Astrologers are still doing just that—observing external conditions and relating those matters to what is known of the patterns in the heavens. As life has become more sophisticated, so has astrology. More planets and asteroids have been discovered, more points that are not visible in the heavens are taken into consideration, and the interpretation of an astrological chart has become infinitely more complicated and deep.

A new preference in astrological circles is the humanistic approach to the subject. That approach describes the relationship of astrology to human behavior and has a natural association with psychotherapy. An astrological chart is truly effective in pointing out psychological predilections. Many humanistic astrologers are also psychologists, and many psychotherapists, whether psychologists or psychiatrists, are using the services of astrologers in conjunction with their healing. Astrology has come a long way from being only a tool for the prediction of events. Astrologers are now counselors, using another formula for determining an individual's underlying psychological makeup.

Whether an astrologer chooses to use his expertise in terms of counseling people or in tracking down cycles in business or politics, there are certain basic rules that are used to set up an astrological chart. There are mathematical formulas to observe for accuracy.

The astrologer must master the technical side of astrology before he can get a clear picture of the patterns that emerge. He may choose to vary the kind of graphical chart or a particular system of house divisions, but certain mathematical facts remain consistent. A circle will always have 360 degrees. Planets fall into specific degrees within that circle according to the date, time, and place of birth, and the mathematical relationship of one planet to another is described according to the placement of the planets at that date, time, and place. This relationship of one planet to another is termed an *aspect.*

The technical side of learning about aspects is simply to discover how many degrees apart a planet lies from another in a chart, but the interpretation of the meaning of those aspects is quite another matter, for it is the interpretation of the relationship of one planet to another that describes human behavior. We can think of each planet as signifying a quality of energy or a voice within. Two planets describe a conversation; all ten planets including the Sun and the Moon considered together can be related to a committee meeting. The relationships of all those planets to each other characterize the effectiveness of that group meeting or the quality of dialogue going on within us. Some people have quite simple and harmonious inner dialogues, but other people may have a riot going on inside.

The first step in learning astrology is to analyze the basic meanings of the planets. Each planet can be associated with a specific word. Depending on the experiences of the astrologer, the descriptive language will change, but there are still key words that represent the qualities, attributes, and energy connected to a planet. After that, a beginning astrologer learns the meanings of the houses (the sections of the chart). Each house is associated with a different department of life. Again, there are basic words all astrologers would agree on to qualify these divisions. The third step is to learn basic mathematical formulas to determine where each planet falls in the individual chart. For this process, an astrologer begins to use an *ephemeris,* or table that gives the astronomical placement of the planets in the heavens for each day of each year.

The final step in the art of interpretation is the awareness of the relationship of one planet to another and what that might mean as a qualifying agent. This is where aspects come in. Since an aspect literally means the mathematical distance of one planet from another, each degree of distance describes a quality of manifestation in the life of the individual. At this point, the interpretation of a specific chart becomes complex.

Each day, planets are moving at differing rates of speed. Therefore they form new relationships to each other depending on the day of the year. Since each planet is in a different place each day of each year, it follows that there will never be two astrological charts that are exactly alike, unless two people are born at exactly the same time on the same day and year and in the same place. If this does occur, we call them astrological twins. The planets in the chart will make exactly the same relationship to each other, describing exactly the same kind of psychological programming.

If we use the analogy of a kaleidoscope, the patterns in an astrological chart can change with a twist of the wrist. Minutes make a difference. There are some planets, however, that move quite slowly. These are what we call "heavier" planets. The difference in their daily movement is so minute that people born within a certain time frame will have these heavier planets in the same relationship to each other. Therefore certain general preconditioning will be evident. For instance, people born around the time of the Depression have the same three planets at odds with each other. The psychological manifestations may differ in the lives of the individuals, but the basic programming of anyone born at that time of financial pressures will be caution, rather than frivolity. In this way, the astrological chart reflects the social conditions around the individual at the time of his birth.

The wheel of the chart turns so that a different sign of the zodiac rules each house, depending on the time of birth. These positions of the wheel describe the varieties of general outlook on life from individual to individual, as well as perspective about external conditions and programming in specific areas of life, and therefore the survival patterns the person begins to develop. When we begin to add planets to that wheel, new dimensions occur. Whenever a planet or planets falls in a house, a qualifying situation will be described. If, for instance, more than one planet falls in a particular house, more attention, energy, and focus will occur in that specific department of life.

The placement of the planets in the various houses and the rotation of the wheel according to the time of birth give the individual chart a basic structure. These structures can have meaning within themselves as described by the kinds of patterns they form. If the planets seem to be bunched together in two separate clusters, they form a seesaw. That seesaw appearance also describes the major pull in the life of the individual between two distinct factors. Sometimes all planets fall within a few houses, describing a tremendous focus of energy in one direction. Sometimes the planets fall indiscriminately throughout the whole chart. This may indicate a scattering of attention, or a proclivity to investigate all sides of life. Perhaps the planets form a bucket or umbrella. It may be a "finger of God chart," with a specific planet pointing The Way. Sometimes the planets seem to form a square, or box, indicating a tendency toward stagnation and restriction. In his book *A Handbook for the Humanistic Astrologer,* Michael Meyer describes these formations in detail. Simply by looking at the diagram of an individual chart, information can be gleaned about the way a person uses his energy or directs his attention.

In *The Rising Sign; Your Astrological Mask,* I discussed only the *outer* personality, or the individual outlook on life, but the next step is to look at the inner quality by examining aspects. Sometimes an individual is aware of his inner dialogues, whether agreements or arguments, but in many instances, a person is unaware of what his conflicts are and where they come from. The aspects indicate whether things are easy to resolve or difficult. It is essential to avoid the use of the words "good" and "bad." In dealing with astrology from a humanistic point of view, what appears to be "good" or easy may not produce growth, whereas "hard," or difficult, aspects direct a person to accomplishment or at least resolution of those conflicts. It is only by the examination and reconciliation of various qualities of energy and dialogue that a person can begin to accomplish what he is truly capable of. We may indeed be able to grow only through pain.

Life brings about constant opportunity to resolve all those inner issues. It seems that just as a person has solved one set of problems, more creep up to take their place. In fact, according to Carl Jung, a person may actually create external conditions to challenge him to his full potential. Jung said that any unrealized energy or potential will manifest or exteriorize as fate or destiny. Another way of saying the same thing is that life may only reflect an image, in the form of external conditions, to mirror what it is an individual needs to tackle next to facilitate growth. If one adopts the perspective, on a daily basis, that life *only* presents conditions that will facilitate growth, one can begin to change by taking responsibility for one's own actions. Astrology, as well as therapy, encourages one to begin to create more-productive situations by pointing out unconscious patterns that may block full expression. When a person has been kicked by a horse every time he walks behind that horse, he learns to go around another way. Every individual makes choices about the life route he wishes to take. An astrological chart can indicate those road conditions in advance. In that way, it is like a map, but ultimately, the individual must make the choices himself.

The total quality of combined energy indicates the makeup of a person. If we liken an individual to a complex computer or electrical system, we might imagine an incredible maze of wires and transistors that feed into a larger wiring system, the brain. It is possible that during birth or at time of stress later on in life, a wire may come loose or a connection has a flaw in its hookup. Any missing link would stop the flow of electricity so that energy becomes backed up or repressed. Decisions might not be as productive as usual, life might not flow so smoothly. Ultimately, it would be important to check out the wires, make the corrections where possible, seal the leaks, find the blocks, and restore the balance. If we were able to take a look at that complex system from above, we might see only a tangled web of crossed wires and transistors. A look at the blueprint could give some clarity as to where the trouble might lie.

An astrological chart describes that underlying structure and can clarify where blocks occur. When an individual is in touch with his own unique blueprint, he learns how to operate his system at a higher level. Each planet represents a type of message going to the brain. Some voices are louder than others. Some are more important at specific times. It may be necessary to encourage a weak voice to speak out, or look past what another voice seems to be saying, to determine what is really going on. If a person has an explosive temper, he simply reacts whenever his frustrations build to a certain pitch. If he can understand *why* his temper is triggered, he can begin to gain more control over his reaction. He may eventually be able to change the conditions of his life to be rid of the very frustrations that triggered the outburst in the first place. It can make all the difference to walk outside ourselves to observe objectively what we cannot see subjectively.

Imagine one man living with ten women. Each woman has a quality that is most attractive to him, so if he were to try to find a preference, he would have a hard time making a choice. Each one is important to him. One woman is strong, a leader, and exhibits a dramatic ability that is quite appealing. Another woman is especially sensitive and nurturing. The third woman is very intelligent, can analyze situations and handle details. Another is extremely beautiful, gracious, and kind. One woman is a ball of energy and exudes sexuality and vivacity that are hard to resist. She may be a fighter for the whole group. A contagious enthusiasm makes the next woman irreplaceable, whereas the seventh is serious, but especially reliable and responsible, willing to take on much of the hard work. Woman number eight may be the free soul, have a musical talent, and be very inventive. The ninth is the visionary, poet, idealist, and can uplift everyone else. The last member of this community is quite powerful, effective, and magnetic. Her charisma is especially strong.

Together these ten women are a phenomenal group. Their combined talents and attributes cover the whole range of what is needed in this community. As long as each lady is aware of what she can best contribute and is willing to express her best traits, harmony reigns in the small kingdom. The man is able to function in his own right even more efficiently by being surrounded by such exceptional women. But suppose these women begin ganging up on the man and on each other. They start to ignore their own best qualities, become jealous of one another, and become balky. Perhaps three of the women get along quite well, but don't like the others. Perhaps one lady decides she has nothing whatever to say to anyone else in the group and maintains a stony silence. Lines of battle form and the clamor is enough to drive the poor man to drink. He tries his best to pacify everyone, but the waste of his own time and energy prevent him from handling his higher responsibilities to the group endeavor. The result is pure chaos and lack of productivity.

The man in this case represents the higher self, the oversoul observer, or the masculine, dominant factor. The female members of the group represent the manifestation on earth of the higher self, or the receptive, expressive. (They are not masculine and feminine in the sexual sense.) The dialogues between these women, whether productive or chaotic, are indicative of aspects in an astrological chart. Suppose the lack of cooperation becomes extreme, a war begins within the kingdom, and the man hides his head under the covers and refuses to listen to anyone. The observer closes his eyes. The female members of the group have no choice but to go outside, into the neighborhood, and create a distraction that will bring help. They may set a fire, do something bizarre in public that will bring attention, or scream out their problems. Eventually, the disturbance brings help. If our higher self refuses to acknowledge the inner dialogue that may need resolution, external conditions are created to force a look, and therefore, eventually, we make progress toward the solution of problems. We may get sick, create intolerable pressures, or antagonize the very people we love. Eventually, our higher self must listen and take action. Pinpointing the problems, pain, or blockings of energy can show the way toward resolution. Then greater harmony and joy can reign.

In writing about astrology, it is important to describe patterns and conditions in such a way that individual lifestyles can be considered. Each aspect, for instance, has a basic description that indicates energy or how a person feels. But the way in which this aspect is manifest in the life of an individual can be quite varied, even if similar in its basic concept. After all, each individual has a choice about how he uses his own energy. Any interpretation of aspects must allow for different lifestyles. As an example, let's say that two children are born in a hospital at exactly the same moment. The children have aspects in the charts that describes a need and tendency to take on a stronger sense of financial responsibility. One child is born to a wealthy family, the other is born to a poor family. The mutual aspect describes the *fact* of the sense of responsibility, but not how it will be manifest in the daily life of the individual. The child born to the wealthy family may feel a weight on his shoulders to protect the family fortune, whereas the child born to the poor family will have an additional determination to build a stable financial future. The decisions about expenditure and management of funds will be similar, but with differing outer conditions to work through. The focus of financial attention will be directed toward the same goal and funds will be earned through quite similar projects or activities, but perhaps on different levels. Imagination and freedom of choice must be considered.

The reading of that astrological chart as well as participation in therapy would help both individuals to reevaluate ideas about financial matters. Both methods enable them to see where their ideas or concern about funds began. The astrological chart can pinpoint the underlying structure and situation, whereas therapy helps the individual work through his fears, insecurities, or inhibitions. Both tools will enable the individual to upgrade the quality of his decisions about financial matters.

A person who is working on a higher spiral of evolution will have different external experiences from someone who has no prior knowledge of his creative ability or patterns. If an individual has been on the path of enlightenment through reading, meditation, therapy, or his own methods of inner search, he will react quite differently to external stimuli than someone who has no prior experience in such matters. The evolved person can more easily transmute difficulties into growth, and mitigate and resolve inner conflicts or dialogues. His path may be far easier than that of someone who is blindly plowing his way through life. Desire is the prerequisite to change and growth. Yet synchronicity works here too, for the astrological patterns can indicate when the individual is ready to attain greater awareness or growth. When the student is ready, the teacher appears.

When we begin to look at the specific aspects in an individual chart, it is difficult to isolate one factor from another. A person is a combination of his emotions, intellect, need for security, and drives, for instance. Each of these elements conditions the others; the areas of a person's life interweave and overlap. Yet it is necessary to try to separate these inner dialogues, or aspects, in order to fully understand specific issues. Differing shades of interpretation will occur according to the *positions* of these aspects in the chart (the house or houses involved) and the *sign* of the zodiac of each planet.

A description of the quality of energy that is associated with each planet is a starting place. Dr. Zipporah Dobyns, a prominent psychologist and astrologer, has described these qualities as an alphabet. They may also be viewed as a number system. The number one relates to the first sign of the zodiac, or Aries, and also the planet Mars, ruler of Aries. So planets and aspects in the first house, or in the sign of Aries, or associated with Mars, will have similar characteristics—intense drive, ambition, and resourceful energy. Number one wants to be first in line. An Aries quality represents a pioneering need for action, cutting down trees to make a trail for everyone else. The first house describes individualization, personality, the "I."

Number two is descriptive of the second house, and the Taurus or Venus (the planet that rules Taurus) quality. Financial ability or desire to secure and collect goods and the fruits of the earth and to enjoy pleasure comes early in life after the full awareness of the individualization of self. Young children begin to develop an acquisitive urge. The third house describes an expansion into communications, interaction with siblings, other relatives, and neighbors. Number three relates to Mercury, the planet of communications, the adult ego state, and the beginning of collection of information. It describes the intellectual activity. The third house relates to Gemini qualities. This first quarter of the chart is most strongly emphasized from birth through the teens.

The fourth house, or number four, the sign of Cancer and the Moon quality, describes the need for creating a home. It describes emotional needs, feelings about the environment, family, and shelter. The fifth house describes creative expression and children, and relates to the sign of Leo and the Sun. Its energy can be associated with dominance, inner strength, and to the gambling urges. It directly relates to the need for recognition from someone else, whether in love areas or with expression of talent. The number six describes the kind of work we do. The sign of Virgo is the sign ruling this house and, again, relates to the planet Mercury. This time Mercury, or the adult ego state, is not just collecting data, but analyzing methods and systems for more efficient ways of doing a job. Number seven brings in partnership. Libra, the seventh sign of the zodiac, is the sign that needs balance, companionship, and the pleasure of cooperative effort; Venus, ruler of Libra, is the planet associated with harmony. Number eight is a financial number. Scorpio is the sign of that natal house, and Pluto is the ruler of Scorpio. That energy is related to getting one's needs met. Since it is also the transformation in life, it describes the death of the old self and the birth of the new, the phoenix rising from the ashes. Eighth-house emphasis, or Plutonian energy, can relate to drastic changes in life as well as ultimate growth and the use of power. The ninth house relates to the sign of Sagittarius, the planet Jupiter, and philosophical concerns. It describes any expansive tendencies, whether involving distances or in development of the higher mind through education. It describes distribution, publishing, and matters that teach others.

The number ten describes the need for building a stronger public image. Capricorn is the tenth sign of the zodiac, with Saturn the ruler of that house and sign. Saturnish qualities are those of responsibility, parental dedication, and image-consciousness. Number eleven relates to the sign of Aquarius. The Aquarian energy is humanitarian, unique, and spontaneous. The planet Uranus, ruling that sign, describes inventiveness and healing. The Aquarian personality is a friend and one who allows freedom in association. The eleventh house describes relationships with friends and groups. The last number is twelve, relating to Pisces and the planet Neptune. The twelfth house is the hidden house, describing the subconscious, and secret thoughts. Neptune describes idealism, the right brain (the creative mind), and the ability to be conceptual.

In looking at aspects, it is necessary to simplify the terminology of each energy and find a description of how the energy manifests in the life. Mercury will always describe the thought process, for instance, but if Mercury is aspected to Uranus, the thoughts will be more unique. Venus will always indicate the quality of energy associated with the love nature, the social consciousness, and the need for peace and harmony. Yet if Venus is aspected to Saturn, for instance, it may not be easy for the individual to express the need for love or get his or her needs met in love areas.

Another factor that is necessary to consider when discussing aspects is whether the aspect is harmonious or inharmonious. Astrologers lump aspects into two major categories. Easy, or harmonious, aspects are called *soft aspects*, whereas difficult, or inharmonious, aspects are called *hard aspects*. (Conjunctions, discussed below, can be either soft or hard depending on the energy of the planets involved.) For the sake of simplicity, the discussion below deals with only the major aspects, or those most commonly known.

First is the *conjunction*, describing planets that occupy the same longitudinal degree position. Two or more planets in the exact degree position, or in very close proximity to each other (see discussion of *orb* later), intensify the quality of energy or the dialogue that each planet represents. The result can be something like a married couple who begin to look alike after many years of marriage. Conjunctions are actually neutral in expression of action, unless the planets involved indicate action or intense energy or the conjunction is set off by another planet or planets that act as a bombarding agent. The *sextile* describes planets that are 60 degrees apart, and the *trine*, planets that are positioned 120 degrees apart. These are both soft aspects and indicate harmonious dialogue and interaction. The energies are primarily supportive of each other, yet these soft aspects may not produce as much energy as the hard aspects.

The discussion of each and every aspect is necessary for the student who is in the process of learning astrology either for pleasure or as part of the training to become a professional astrologer. There are books on all levels that deal with descriptions of all aspects. However, in trying to understand deeper patterns of human behavior that emerge when a specific aspect is present, only the hard aspects reveal problem areas or conflicts that indicate major growth. These two categories of aspects, soft and hard, are analogous to the curriculum offered to a student when he enters a university. When he sees the whole catalogue of classes, he must make choices of subjects that will prepare him for his future. He may want to take only art and music classes, but unless his major is related to those subjects, they might just be diversions or the way he includes pleasurable courses in a difficult work schedule. If his major relates to higher mathematics or science, he may have to tackle advanced calculus or nuclear physics. These courses will demand hard work on his part, but at the end of his years at the university, he will be rewarded with a diploma, or at the least, knowledge wrested from hours of study. He will have grown mentally to a vast degree.

In this book, we are aiming for growth and the diploma; therefore, we will deal only with conjunctions and hard aspects. These stronger dialogues seem to indicate situations that simply *must* be resolved. It appears that we grow through pain, rather than ease, so the more tensions and conflicts in the chart, the more interesting and dynamic the life of the individual. The primary hard aspects are the *square*, describing planets that are 90 degrees apart, and the *opposition*, or planets that are 180 degrees apart, opposing each other. Oppositions describe energies directly in conflict with each other. They form exactly opposite points of view. However, oppositions can be reconciled. Each point of view has a validity and if used in balance can enable one to arrive at a conclusion from dialoguing the two sides of the question. The square, or 90-degree aspect, describes energy that fights for the right to be heard. This quality of energy is not as easy to resolve, as each voice is saying, "I'm right. Listen to me." Neither voice seems to want to give in.

There are other aspects that are less well known and are sometimes ignored. One is the *semisquare*, or 45-degree angle of energy. Another is the *sesquiquadrate* (or *sesquisquare*), or 135-degree angle. In general, these aspects are descriptive of energy that seems irreconcilable and frustrating. They produce tension, so they can be lumped under the category of hard aspects. A *semisextile* is an easy aspect, an angle of only 30 degrees, and the voices are harmonious. The perspective is so similar it can produce easy agreement, but not a lot of dynamic interchange.

The *quincunx*, or *inconjunct*, has an angularity of 150 degrees. This aspect has been described as one of tremendous frustration but producing the greatest growth of all. Bruno and Louisa Huber, psychologists and astrologers who reside in Switzerland, feel that the quincunx is especially important in a chart. It can be likened to reaching out, like a rubber band that is being stretched to its breaking point. Energy so stretched will produce growth, of necessity, rather than as a result of conflict. John Addey, in developing a system called Harmonics, discovered two other aspects especially indicative of talent in a natal chart. They are respectively fifty-six and seventy-two degrees apart. I suggest leaving that subject to the masterful work of our beloved and late John Addey. His book *Harmonics in Astrology* describes the findings of his research and discoveries. Fortunately, Charles Harvey, of England, conducts teaching seminars at Cambridge University and is continuing with John's work.

The basic difference between the types of hard aspects is the level of intensity of dynamic energy produced. These could be related to the level of decibels of sound volume, for instance. The square might have the loudest voice due to the quality of friction. Next in line would be the sesquiquadrate and the semisquare, both of which might sound like major squeaks, with a somewhat less strident sound coming from the inconjunct. Although the opposition might be quite loud, as if two people were shouting at each other, when the two viewpoints are eventually reconciled, the volume or intensity can result in harmonious tones somewhat like those produced by notes an octave or two apart.

Rather than focus on the subtle differences of each one of the aspects throughout the book, since that can seem somewhat like reading a telephone book and become quite tedious, I have used a variety of examples of hard aspects. It should be easy for the reader to bear in mind that differences in similar aspects can be seen in the varying stress levels of the outer manifestations in life. The foregoing analogy of decibels can be helpful, as well as realization that some hard aspects are more easily resolved than others.

I have also taken the liberty of breaking a tradition of describing all the Sun aspects, then all the Moon aspects, Mercury aspects, Venus aspects, and so on down the line, because I feel it is far more important to be aware of how the heavier, *higher-octave* planets modify the Sun, Moon, Mercury, and so on. Planets seem to have their own kind of hierarchy. Faster-moving planets seem to describe energy that is lighter or that has less long-range effect. Slower-moving planets describe a quality that is deeper, more internal. We describe the planets that move in a slower cycle than Saturn as the higher-octave planets (Uranus, Neptune, and Pluto). They seem to indicate energy that is transpersonal or is less easily seen, touched, or felt. Perspective about life, or the scope of one's concerns, is indicated on an ever-spiraling level as planets slow down. Higher octave planets deal with more ephemeral matters, concepts, and senses, whereas faster moving planets describe mundane everyday matters. It is as if each quality of energy lives on a different floor of an apartment building. The view that is seen from the twenty-fifth floor is more breathtaking than the one seen from the fifth floor. The individual living on the fifth floor may not believe the description of the view from the higher level, because he has not seen it for himself. Yet each floor has its value and function. Without the base of floors one through five, floor twenty-five could not exist. For instance, both Mercury and Neptune describe mental functions, yet Neptune is more visionary, right-brain-oriented. Mercury describes intellect, or left-brain activity. Neither can live without the other, yet if intellect interferes with vision, perspective is limited. If an overall concept enables one to have greater overview, yet the individual cannot translate his dreams into practicality, he is hampered. With the combination of right-brain and left-brain activity, a person can accomplish miracles. Alice Bailey described the concept merely through the title of one of her books, *From Intellect to Intuition.* Neptune lives on a higher floor than Mercury.

Consider the natural progression of the planets, as well as their productive and nonproductive energy. The progression is as follows: Sun, Moon, Mercury, Venus, Mars, Jupiter, Saturn, Uranus, Neptune, and Pluto. The Sun represents vitality and ego, and the Moon, emotion and sensitivity. A person who is operating on a purely egocentric level, the quality described by the Sun, is completely overshadowed by an individual with compassion, an attribute connected to the Moon. But the person who deals only on an emotional plane is instantly leveled by someone who is rational and thinking, energy described by Mercury. Clear observation of events (Mercury) is a natural antidote for overreaction (Moon). Love (Venus) modifies analysis. The heart center (Venus) is higher in the body than the solar plexus (the seat of the emotions). Love can outweigh and mitigate argument or too much analysis of a situation. Action (Mars) takes care of any tendency to inertia (Venus) and is more productive than passivity. Enthusiasm (Jupiter) is far more enriching than blind frustration, undirected ambition, or anger (Mars). Practicality (Saturn) can accomplish what a Pollyanna attitude (Jupiter) cannot. Blind faith (Jupiter) can keep one wandering on an endless search, but structure (Saturn) produces results. Spontaneity and openness to new ideas (Uranus) are like letting go of the trunk of the tree (Saturn, security) to walk out to the end of the limb. For it is in working through the scare and taking risks (Uranus) that exciting new conditions exist. Yet vision (Neptune) is important to prevent a total scattering of energy (Uranus). Finally, power of attunement to the universal, divine plan (Pluto) reaches out to the ultimate, cosmic level and describes the greatest degree of effectiveness. Obviously the trick is to utilize the quality of energy associated with each planet in the most productive manner.

HOW TO FIND YOUR OWN ASPECTS

The first step in finding the relationship of one planet to another in an individual chart is to determine the position of each planet in the zodiac on a specific day of the year. The exact placement of each planet within the 360-degree band of the zodiac can be found in an ephemeris, the astronomical tables of calculations used by all astrologers and astronomers. The degree and minute as well as sign placement are listed for each day of the year. These tables may be found in any astrology bookstore, or may be ordered from the list of publications available through the American Federation of Astrologers, P.O. Box 22040, Tempe, Arizona 85282. The easiest way to ascertain both the planetary positions and the aspects the planets make to each other in an individual chart is to order a copy of a natal chart from a professional astrological computer service. Astro-Computing Services provides a printout that is accurate, clear, and inexpensive. A natal chart costs approximately five dollars. The address is P.O. Box 16297, San Diego, California 92116. (Write in advance to find out the exact cost and the information you need to provide.) This service saves a great deal of time and work. The mathematics involved in erecting a chart and calculating each planet's position and its aspects can become quite complicated and can sometimes be very confusing. If an individual is interested in learning this complicated procedure, I highly recommend *The ABC of Chart Erection*, by Lynne Palmer. Lynne has devoted an entire volume to the step-by-step rules as well as many examples to help the student.

If you choose to use an ephemeris, you must determine the angular relationship of one planet to another. If that angle is to be calculated, it is essential to consider the shortest distance between any two planets. For calculation of the aspects, subtract the sign and degree of one planet from another. For instance, if Mars is found to be placed at 26 degrees of Scorpio and the Moon is posited at 10 degrees of Aries, they form an angularity that is called a sesquiquadrate. The Moon, 1 sign (Aries) 10 degrees is subtracted from Mars, 8 sign (Scorpio) 26 degrees. As each sign accounts for 30 degrees, the distance between them in degrees is 226 degrees $1 \times 30 + 10$ (40) subtracted from $8 \times 30 + 26$ (266). But the circle is only 360 degrees, so the accurate count, going the shortest way, is found to be 134 degrees. The angle of a sesquiquadrate is 135 degrees. The extra allowance of degrees beyond the accurate count of an aspect is called an *orb*. For stronger aspects, the orb allowance is greater than for lighter aspects. (The stronger aspects are the conjunction, square, trine, and opposition). Astrologers tend to disagree about the number of degrees of orb allowed for each aspect. The tighter the orb, the stronger the interaction between the two planets. As the orb is widened, the quality of energy is weakened and the voices are not as strong. As a general rule of thumb, however, it is permissible to allow a 10-degree orb between the stronger aspects. Allow only 4 degrees for a semisextile, semisquare, sesquiquadrate, and inconjunct. An allowance of 8 degrees is permissible for a sextile. With more advanced study, each person begins to decide for himself the degree of orb allowance he prefers.

Certain aspects are not possible between some planets due to the paths of these planets through the zodiac. For instance, Mercury is never more than 28 degrees from the Sun. Consequently, these two planets can form only a conjunction or no aspect at all. Venus is never more than 48 degrees away from the path of the Sun. Thus it is possible for these two heavenly bodies to form only a conjunction, a semisextile, or a semisquare aspect. When aspects between two planets are observed, the faster of the two planets is said to be making the aspect. Aspects are said to be *applying* or *separating*, that is, coming toward each other or going away from each other. Applying aspects are stronger.

Each aspect has a symbol to indicate the number of degrees between them:

Conjunction	☌	0 degrees	(neutral)
Semisextile	⚺	30 degrees	(soft)
Semisquare	∠	45 degrees	(hard)
Sextile	✶	60 degrees	(soft)
Square	□	90 degrees	(hard)
Trine	△	120 degrees	(soft)
Sesquiquadrate	⚼	135 degrees	(hard)

Inconjunct π 150 degrees   (hard)

Opposition $\nearrow$ 180 degrees   (hard)

After all the aspects have been discovered in the individual chart, it is possible to comprehend the variety of dialogues within oneself indicated by each specific aspect. Rather than present an interpretation that limits the possibility of an individual's realization, it is my hope that by the description of the way in which hard and neutral aspects have manifested in the lives of others, the reader can be stimulated toward deeper self-examination. It is the integration and assimilation of those inner conflicts that produce outer conditions. If, with more awareness, a person learns how to upgrade his life through the process of making better choices, he can become more attuned to his highest potential in life. The first step is the understanding of his patterns. The next step is taking action to change conditions, rather than living under burdens of guilt and judgment. It is my aim to point the finger, even if at times it is somewhat painful, so that each individual can give himself permission to observe his actions through the mirror of outer circumstances. If he can understand his natural predisposition and his early programming, and begin to reflect, there exists a greater potential of harmonizing inner conflicts. There also exists the potential of the ultimately creative life. Thought produces change. Choices do exist. A basic choice is either to grow or to remain static. Perhaps the greatest growth potential is to make the very real connection between the inner, higher self and the here-and-now personality. Here's to a happy realization of that higher state of balance.

THE SUN

THE SUN IS THE BRIGHTEST LIGHT IN THE SKY. IT REP-
resents the brightest light within the complexity of the human being, for it relates to the ego, the sense of self-worth and pride. It
describes the earthly perspective of that spark of divinity brought
down into materialization. It describes the soul quality of mankind.
Each sign placement of the Sun is merely a color, or hue, contained
within the human rainbow. The self-identification with a particular
sign of the zodiac is merely a facsimile and symbol of an individual
nature. Qualities described by each Sun placement in the zodiac can
be a key or tool for greater self-awareness.

In the five volumes of *A Treatise on the Seven Rays*, Alice Bailey
relates planets, sign placement, and forms in a natal chart to the
unseen levels of evolutionary progress. Particularly the soul quality, described by the sign placement of the Sun, can give an individual greater understanding of his task on earth and the best way in
which he can shed his own inner light outward, toward the rest of
mankind. A stronger development of true ego or self-worth is essential if an individual is part of the light force that connects people to
each other. Personality qualities and early-life decisions are what
keep us separate from each other; on an inner level, the brightness
of the soul light is the beacon that illuminates the path all mankind
must eventually travel. The Sun energy does nothing of itself. It
simply is what it is.

Modern psychology, as well as new forms of awareness groups,
stress the need for ego evaluation. The *EST* Training urges that the
individual get in touch with that sense of being using the Latin
word for "is," *est*, to confirm that approach. Transactional analysis
urges that individuals give themselves "strokes" for a job well
done. It is clear that mankind can learn to transmute early negative
conditioning to positive results, perhaps by much hard work, but it
is also clear that one cannot change the inner quality of beingness.

What is important, and in fact essential, is to recognize that inner quality, glory in the brightness of the soul energy, and find the ultimate use for the sharing of the light energy.

Many books have been written about the values and qualities associated with each Sun-sign placement of the zodiac. But the special quality of each sign of the zodiac is a specific refraction of light and energy. For simplicity's sake, the Sun can be called ego. That word has many modern-day connotations. It is important to go beyond the concept of a swelled head or a puffed-up exclusivity to the concept of *individualization*. For broken particles of light, shining around an obstacle in its way, is still light. Although the rays of energy and specific ego may be refracted by being lowered into a dense (human) body, particles can still shine through openings in the vehicle. Eyes, in particular, are said to carry the light of the soul. Indeed, if one is fortunate enough to look upon the countenance of a master or holy man, the eyes are seen to be exceptionally brilliant.

Perhaps the greatest task for mankind is to enable the vehicle, the form, the body, to become translucent so that the light of the soul may show more clearly. That process of allowing the true energy to emerge may take a lifetime or many, but primary recognition of the true sense of the word ego may be the first step. Another step to take is to look beyond form, words, and appearance in other beings, to see even the tiniest glimmer of light within. In that way, one can recognize himself reflected in the being of another. That process may take many paths. Self-expression of the creative energy can be diversified into a myriad of activity. It is interesting to note that an actor, a writer, or even a businessman is reflecting a tiny part of the overall light. The more an individual allows himself to find his specific way to identify the energy of another, the more he allows his own light to increase. The only "sin" is the separateness that comes with a negative identification of ego. With an inverse sense of self-worth, the individual becomes "puffed up," thereby cutting himself off from the rest of humanity. When he ceases to recognize himself reflected in the eyes of others, yet stops the process of individualization, the pride becomes a negative force of energy.

The aspects to the Sun describe additional qualities attracted by that pure soul energy in this particular lifetime or manifestation.

The Sun may have been traveling through the sign of Aries at the time of birth, let's say, but if the Sun is conjunct Uranus, an additional quality of energy becomes apparent. It is like putting on a filmy garment of Uranian quality on an inner level. The original soul quality does not change, but takes on another dimension. Like cutting a diamond, the more facets or dimensions that are carved, the stronger the possibility for brilliance. Since the outer life is a reflection of all the combined inner lights, the more refractions there are, the more exciting are the possibilities of the outer conditions.

When the Sun is found ruling or placed within the first house, the strength of that ego light is seen overtly. It can describe a dignity and regality, no matter what the sign of the Sun in the zodiac. The individual comes into life to express the dominant qualities, as well as leadership, executive ability, and strength. His sense of self-worth is manifest in the external vehicle more strongly than in other placements of the Sun. He shows his light immediately. He has no need to hide his soul quality within layers of obscure material or activity. He is born knowing who he is. If he has primarily positive aspects to the Sun, he has a strong ability to accept the role of the leader. He can be sure of himself, with no need to hide his quality of energy. When he walks into a room, he takes charge and is allowed to take charge. He has many avenues of self-expression open and available to him. If the Sun aspects are not positive, for some reason, it is important to the individual to hide his value and ability to be dominant. Survival somehow depends on not letting that strength be known.

When this positive quality of energy is found ruling or placed in the second house, of income, financial success can depend on that sense of who he is. He may not be able to wait for other people to give him permission to value himself by material scales. He must take charge of his own income by expressing his leadership potential. His pride has to do with earning capacity. It may be that, through his financial potential, he sheds his own inner light out to others. The outer manifestation of success in material means may be his way of valuing himself. With a well-aspected Sun in the natal chart, he gives himself permission to manifest his energy in positive ways on the material plane. If the Sun has difficult aspects, his evaluation of his inner strength and worth may not be positive; he tends to limit his light, limit what he manifests for himself, and go through the motions of less than satisfying financial situations.

The third house in the natal chart describes the interaction with siblings and other relatives, as well as the beginning efforts to communicate, which determine the overall ability to learn. Transactions in early life predetermine school years. The ability to do well in school gives confidence in later negotiation skills. When the Sun is found in this sector of the chart and is well aspected, the individual has a pride and sense of well-being in connection with his communications with others. He expresses strength, confidence, and energy in those areas of life. He may have been the dominant sibling, or "photographed" (made mental images of) his brothers and sisters, as well as relatives, as having great strength, dramatic appeal, and energy. He will be proud of his extended family. It may be that he comes from a family of note, in which recognition gives him an innate sense of pride, identification, and self-worth. If the Sun is not well aspected in his chart, he may experience lack of pride, even embarrassment, in connection with family and siblings. He may feel that his brothers or sisters do not recognize who they are or who he is. He may not like the identification with his particular extended family. School years may be painful or lacking in recognition and may take energy he does not possess. He may not get strokes from his teachers and fellow students. He may feel, even on a subconscious level, that it is to his advantage to hide his light in school and later in connection with communications, discussions, and negotiations.

The fourth house in the horoscope describes the conditions of the relationship with the parent of the opposite sex, as well as the kind of homelife that is appealing to the individual. When the Sun rules this sector of the chart or is placed therein, the individual can be especially proud of this parent. His inner identification and sense of self-worth is modeled after that sense within the parent. In the case of a woman with this aspect, her pride is connected to her father. She identifies with his strength and sees him as the dominant parent. If the Sun is well aspected, that parent may have held a prestigious position in his life, attracted honor and recognition. He may have been dignified, regal, and strong.

In the case of a man with the Sun in this position of his chart, the mother might have been the dominant parent, with a tendency to show more of her animus qualities than anima. If the Sun is well aspected, the mother may have been especially strong, expert in her ability to be a leader. If the Sun is not well aspected, the mother may not have identified with the strength that was really character- istic of her personality. In either case that parent of the opposite sex may have lacked in ego stroking in his or her life or may have neglected the leadership capacity. He or she may not really have known an inner identification with the strength of the light quali- ties. He or she may have resisted any opportunities to take charge in external affairs and may have not encouraged ego strength in the child. Messages may have been such as "Don't get a swelled head" or "Don't think too much of yourself." The individual with this placement will either make sure he has a home reflective of his sense of self-worth or will not make the effort to establish a home worthy of him. He may not value himself enough to warrant a home of which he can be proud. He may establish a home to give himself ego strokes that are lacking in his life. He may value himself only in relation to his lifestyle.

When the Sun is placed in or rules the fifth house of self-expres- sion, it is in the natural position in the chart when Aries (the first sign) is placed at the first house for the Sun rules the sign of Leo, which is the fifth sign of the zodiac. That fifth house indicates the gambles in life. It is a gamble to express personal creativity, a gamble to fall in love, have children, play the stock market, or give a party. When the fifth house is examined in the light of Sun energy, a strong sense of self enables a person to create those refractions of himself with ease. When he is aware of his strength, his "light" energy, he can express that quality in many ways. He will be proud of his children, others he loves, and areas of creativ- ity. In love areas, for instance, he will be attracted to someone he can identify with on an ego, self-esteem level. He may be attracted to a person who has a strong sense of self-worth, or someone who expresses the dominant part of her or his personality.

If the aspects to the Sun in the natal chart are primarily positive, the indication of a healthy ego allows him to attract other people with healthy egos. He can be attracted to and recognized by one who has a quality of strength that may also bring about recognition. The individual with this placement of the Sun needs no one else to give him permission to express creative energy. If the aspects to the

Sun are not positive, he may have to develop a stronger sense of his own inner worth by his creative products. He may have children who reflect his own creative energies and make him proud. He may need to learn to give himself ego strokes, and permission to express his inner qualities and to have pride in himself. He may need to reaffirm his pride in his children as well.

The sixth house describes vitality, energy, and health. The specific qualities associated with the sixth house give an indication of the kind of work to which the individual is attracted. They also describe the way in which the person attacks his work. When the Sun rules this house or is placed within that sector of the chart, the individual needs work that will allow him to express the dominant part of his personality. He can easily be the leader. When the Sun in the natal chart is in harmonious aspect to other planets, he can take charge without undue effort, give himself permission to express a dramatic quality, and work in areas that bring recognition or inner reward. Health is strong due to positive energy flowing from the heart center, or center of vitality.

When the Sun is not well aspected in the chart, a lack of ego may also have a reflection in a lack of energy. The heart is the area affected when the Sun rules this sector of the chart. The individual with this placement of the Sun, if difficult aspects are shown in the chart, may look to other people to give him permission, ego strokes, and a go-ahead in connection with work projects. His sense of pride may be at stake in connection with his job. He may not be able to attain the status of control, leadership, and executive ability he would like. He can have his toes stepped on in connection with work. Lack of vitality hinders advancement in his job as well.

When the Sun is related to the seventh house of partnership, the individual may look to another person to express the dominant qualities. He can be attracted to a mate who is vital, full of energy, and with a strong inner sense of self. He can easily find a partner— whether in marriage or in business—who reflects how he feels about himself. He has the potential to attract another individual who is easily able to claim a fair share of the spotlight, win recognition, and have achievements that bring more ego strokes. The individual may win his own ego strokes through the accomplishments of his mate and partner. With positive aspects to the Sun, he can enjoy the acclaim given to his partner or mate. When the Sun is not well aspected, lack of ego can make such a partnership difficult. He may resent dominance exhibited by a partner or mate and feel a sense of inferiority when the spotlight is on the other person and not on himself. He may pick a mate, therefore, who is not in touch with her or his inner sense of self-worth, and then feel a basic lack of pride in his choice of partner. The partner or mate may have such a low self-esteem that he or she is in constant need of ego stroking to feel valued.

The eighth house can describe a major transformation that takes place in life. When the Sun is in this sector of the natal chart, the individual may get his needs met by a show of strength, drama, or strong sense of self-worth. If his needs are not met, he may feel as though he has been slighted on an ego level. If the aspects to the Sun are predominantly positive ones, the needs of the individual may have been easily met in childhood, leading to a strong security about the continuation of such availability of aid, income, or inheritance. He is then easily able to send out energy through his personal vitality that may give other people permission to be strong, show leadership qualities, or develop an inner sense of ego. Since the Sun is associated with "making a name" for oneself, the attainment of such recognition may place the person in a position to act as a leader for people. His greatest gift may be associated with sending out that quality of energy to humanity. He becomes a beacon for mankind. He may first have to attain a level of accomplishment that will give him a chance to show strength of self and leadership.

When the Sun is in this position in the chart and has difficult aspects from other planets, early restriction in childhood may have conditioned him to a lack of ego. He may not have easily had his needs met. Ego strokes may have been lacking and vitality robbed. He may suffer from low self-esteem when his needs are not met. He may value himself by the degree of ease with which he obtains things or aid from other people. He may not recognize his ability to send light to aid other people. He may have, as the greatest transformation experience in his own life, the reevaluation of who he is in relation to the universal light energy. Once he becomes aware of his soul qualities of strength, the "little" ego of pomp and drama can give way to the inner source of strength. By his own experiences, lack of self-identification, he may then enable others to find that inner soul quality.

The ninth house describes activities that bring recognition or that indicate wide areas of promotional efforts and publicity. It describes the "higher mind" or higher education. It can indicate the ability to reach out to distances, whether that be through distribution or through travel. It describes areas of expertise in importing and exporting as well as anything related to legalities and diplomacy. It can indicate international affairs. When the Sun is well aspected and connected to this area of the natal chart, recognition comes as a result of any activity connected with widespread release of energy. The individual may have strong potential as an executive in an advertising agency, win personal recognition through publicity that brings him to the attention of people on a wide level, or make a name for himself through diplomatic fields or with legal activity. A strong sense of inner worth quite naturally leads to activities of such a leadership level that recognition comes as an afterthought. If, however, the Sun is not well aspected, the individual may have an ego need to win recognition in any way possible. Sometimes any recognition is better than none at all. He may even become notorious. He may suffer a lack of self-esteem in countries away from his place of birth or dislike travel because of a lack of identification with people in other areas. He may need to give himself permission to reveal the positive strength, energy, and dominance in connection with promotional efforts or dealing on a more international, or universal, level.

The tenth house describes career activity, the quality of energy expressed in public, and the feelings about social life. When the Sun is placed in this sector of the chart or is ruling this tenth house, public life brings energy, greater confirmation of strength, and an opportunity to express strong leadership, executive traits. Since the tenth house in a chart describes the relationship with the parent of the same sex, the attraction to public life or career can be strongly influenced and identified by that parent. The inner quality of self-esteem has been programmed by that parent and leads to activities that will bring public pride and recognition. If the Sun is well aspected, the parent of the same sex may have been very strong, dominant, and aware of leadership potential. The individual can have a great feeling of pride in connection with that parent, leading to activity in his own career that will bring ego strokes and recognition from that parent. Those ego strokes are probably easily given, conditioning the individual to receive a similar quality of ego strokes from his public later on. He will certainly find the kind of career that will enable him to express leadership qualities. He can make a name for himself in connection with his chosen public activity or career. He may even be "recognized" in public areas or in social situations.

When the aspects to the Sun are not easy ones, the possibility of lack of ego may be a motivating force in the choice of career. The individual may have "photographed" or have a visual image of the parent of the same sex as lacking in strong leadership capacity, with a lack of ego, vitality and strength. That parent may have been motivated by the possibility of recognition; he or she may have worked to gain attention from others, rather than expressing dominant energy because of the desire for such activity. The person with this placement of the Sun may not have received the recognition he deserved from that parent and may choose career activities as a means of reaffirming his own, inner sense of ego. When that affirmation is not forthcoming, he tends to value himself by the strokes he does not receive, just as he devalued himself in his relationship to his parent of the same sex. If he felt inadequate in the interaction with that parent, he may have to work very hard to overcome those same feelings of inadequacy in connection with his career. He may have to give himself permission to be involved in public activities that he is really interested in, instead of trying to please that parent.

When the Sun is connected to the eleventh house of friendships, group activity, and associations, the individual may be proud of his friends. His inner sense of pride can attract strong people to his side and bring about a sense of identification with his associations. He can retain his sense of self-worth in group activity and be proud of the recognition he receives from friends and organizations. If the aspects are beneficial ones, his inner sense of self-worth brings additional ego strokes and acclaim from those associations. If the aspects to the Sun are not harmonious and he has a lack of ego vitality, he may not be able to work within the framework of groups or with organizations without losing strength. He may attract people in associations who put him down or who will not recognize a quality of strength and vitality. He may choose to associate with people of whom he can never feel completely proud. He may recognize his real qualities only if he is given strokes by friends or associates.

The twelfth house describes the subconscious process, the "hidden" sectors of the chart, and the qualities expressed when the individual is alone. When the Sun rules this part of the natal chart, the person may need a great deal of time alone in order to recoup energy, get in touch with inner qualities of strength, and reaffirm his connection with himself on an inner level. Overt or public activity may be wearing, debilitating, and enervating. The individual may need even a few moments of time alone in the middle of a busy day to reattune himself, to make an inner connection that will restore inner vitality. On a subconscious level, he is aware of his strength, leadership, and sense of self-worth. Those qualities of light may not show overtly. If the Sun is well aspected, he can reacquaint himself with the inner qualities of leadership potential. He is easily able to remain by himself and feel a renewed sense of who he is. He can be attuned on a subconscious level to a memory of a lifetime or a fantasy about a lifetime in which he was in a leadership, "kingly" position. Those same feelings of "royalty" are with him on a deeply subconscious level. He may have to learn how to release the strength, dominance, and leadership potential overtly.

If the Sun is found in this sector of the chart and is not well aspected, the need to find time alone may be even more necessary. It is when the individual can go off by himself to lick his wounds that he can restore his inner sense of vitality and ego. He may subconsciously feel caged, unable to relate to life with a quality of strength and self-assurance. He can feel sickness on a soul level if he does not receive ego strokes. Activities that connect him with the occult or the study of energy that is unseen can attune him to his quality of inner vitality and ego once again. It may be that a lifetime of keeping a low profile is necessary for ultimate soul growth.

ASPECTS TO THE MOON

THE MOON HAS BEEN CALLED "THE LESSER LIGHT" IN traditional astrological terms. It is the fastest-moving body in the heavens, circling the zodiac approximately every twenty-seven or twenty-eight days. It moves rapidly through each sign of the zodiac at varying rates of speed, waxes and wanes and shimmers through clouds, lending a beacon of light to the darkness of night. Since the Moon is related to the emotional nature of man, it is easy to understand, by observation of the Moon, the changeable quality of mankind's emotional reactions.

Whereas the Sun has been designated to describe masculine, or animus, qualities, as well as vitality, ego, and sense of self-worth, the Moon relates to women and the anima. It indicates sensitivity, vulnerability, and receptive qualities that have traditionally been ascribed to women. In light of modern-day psychology, those sensitive qualities are now acknowledged as existing for men, too, and indeed, the Moon is found in everyone's chart. The Moon can also indicate a basic relationship to women in the life of the individual, and in particular the relationship to the mother. For the Moon describes mothering, nurturing qualities that are the positive manifestation of the emotional nature.

The Moon indicates a subtle, emotional body that can permeate the ethers and find attunement and identification with other emotional bodies. It is descriptive of the astral plane, the natural habitat of the emotions. That plane has its dark corners as well. Since the emotional nature is so fragile and sensitive, it can be trapped like a veil of silk on a rocky crag, causing havoc in the life of the owner. Until a search is made by the objective mind, and that fragment of life is found and returned home again, the life is off balance. Aspects to the Moon as well as the sign and house placement indicate how easy or difficult it may be for the sensitive nature to be hooked. The Moon is found to be prominent in the charts of writers. It may be that writers have a particular psychic quality that allows them to attune themselves, momentarily, to that quality in other people. They can, as it were, peer into the bank of emotions found on the astral plane, where imagination also flourishes, and find the way to bring into concrete reality information that exists for everyone to tap.

The Moon qualities indicate an easy ability to identify with others, to empathize and sympathize. It indicates how well the individual is attuned to the needs and wants of other people. It can describe a particular identification and response from the public. It also indicates a tendency to rescue (try to help or save others) which can easily backfire. It describes the ultimate projection of the interaction between people, for the Moon, above all, is the mirror of the sensitivities.

The placement of the Moon in the individual chart indicates where a symbiosis can occur in life. The exchange of emotional energy can be so contagious between two people, for instance, that it can be difficult to know where each person's feelings and emotions begin and leave off. It describes the area in life that is most sensitive, painful, and that produces the most vulnerability. It can indicate circumstances a person is likely to take personally, for the Moon is completely subjective, having no objectivity. It can also clearly indicate where a transmutation of emotional reaction can take place, so that the individual more easily expresses the nurturing qualities. When objectivity is engaged, the individual understands the theory of transference. He then begins to find ways to give emotional support without rescuing. Writing or providing a service that will supply the needs of mankind may be objective ways of expressing the Moon energy.

When the Moon rules or is placed in the first house, the tendency toward overreaction can develop almost at the moment of birth. There may have been feelings of abandonment that make the infant particularly vulnerable and needy. He can feel orphaned. He tends to overreact to life, being overly sensitive, easily hurt, and very needy. When he transmutes those feelings into positive action, he has a special pipeline to the trends of the times. It is as if he senses what other people feel, need, and want. He can readily identify with the suffering that is indigenous to mankind. He may be particularly adept at writing, or working in a capacity in which he feeds people.

He has strong mothering instincts, whether that may be with his own children or with the children of others. He may appeal to the maternal instincts in other people. He may mother animals, rescue people in difficult situations, get kicked for it, and then find himself once again feeling abandoned. He may have to work very hard to avoid a tendency to be victimized.

Strong oral needs are apparent as well. He may eat too much, drink too much, or talk with an emotional quality that is lacking in clarity. He can overreact to people and find himself too vulnerable to be logical. He may gain weight almost in tune to the phases of the Moon, for he tends to retain fluids. The shock of birth may actually have displaced his solar plexus, which can damage a healthy ability to diffuse or sort out his emotional reactions. He may also withdraw, protecting his own feelings, rather than expressing a sensitivity for the feelings of others. He lacks the ability to clearly discuss the things that bother him. He holds hurts close to himself. He can be moody and unable to understand why he feels different from moment to moment. Those feelings of abandonment tempt him to hold on to people and situations long after they are valuable or necessary in his life. He may feel a lack of security even when signs of security are obvious. Overall, he tends to be totally subjective and takes things too personally. He can lack healthy objectivity.

When the Moon rules or is placed in the second house of money, vulnerability occurs in connection with income. The individual may have felt abandoned when a financial situation changed in his early life. Some emotional traumas may have occurred to keep him especially sensitive and needy in connection with income. If the Moon is well aspected in the chart, the individual can earn money by "feeding" humanity, whether that is through actual food or some product or information that will nurture on some level. If the Moon is not well aspected, he may have deep-seated fears of losing funds he has accumulated. He may be hesitant to part with money, holding on as to an emotional security blanket. When the transmutation of feelings occurs from self-protection to protection of others, the income can be increased tremendously. The nurturing of others produces a wave of emotional response. He can be particularly attuned to the trends of the times, the needs of people around him.

When the Moon is in the third house of communications, the

person may have an emotional need to communicate. The patterns established early in life in connection with siblings and other relatives may have been on a very sensitive level, either positively or negatively. In some instances, the individual may have felt abandoned in his relationship to a brother or sister, or may have taken on the role of mothering or nurturing. Especially when younger children are born into a family, the individual may feel self-protective or may be easily hurt because of lack of attention.

The next stage of development comes with entry into school. Emotions can be stirred in connection with the learning process. If aspects to the Moon in the natal chart are primarily beneficial, he learns on a gut level. He simply absorbs material very sensitively. If, however, aspects to the Moon are more difficult, he may block learning ability due to overreaction, vulnerability, or hurt feelings. He lacks objectivity in connection with schooling. Interrelationship with children around him can be painful, emotionally charged. He may feel abandoned by people around him.

As these patterns develop, he speaks with a quality of emotionalism that lacks clarity, thereby pushing people away from him even more. Eventually, he learns not to overreact but to observe. The quality of sensitivity connected to communications can be very profound. He develops a need to nurture people with his words. The obvious talent that emerges is in connection with the communications fields, in which he reaches many people. He can then express his feelings and *use* them, transmuting a potential for being hurt by contributing sensitivity and energy that come from an identification of needs of people.

The fourth house describes the kind of home to which the individual is attracted. It can also indicate a basic quality of lifestyle, the way the person behaves in his own home and what he expects from family life. It can also indicate conditions around him in the third portion of his life. It describes a basic relationship with the parent of the opposite sex, as well as the photographs he has in his mind in connection with that parent. When the Moon is ruling or placed in the fourth house, that parent may have been very sensitive or emotional, or may have been orphaned or abandoned. The individual may have felt that he had to protect, or mother, that parent, perhaps at his own emotional expense.

Homelife becomes an emotional haven. It is within the confines of his own home that he can show his vulnerability. He may be very attached to his lifestyle and the people and possessions in his home, for that place of abode may act as a substitute for the nurturing he may have lacked as a child. If the Moon is well aspected in the chart, he may have had a strong symbiosis and gut connection with the opposite-sex parent, which enables him to easily create the environment of comfort he wants. If, however, the aspects to the Moon are not so positive, it may be difficult to find the emotional support he wants in connection with land, home, property, and lifestyle. He may begin to express more of the nurturing qualities he possesses when he reaches the third portion of life. He may write, be attuned to needs of others, or express a talent described by the house placement of the Moon in his chart. He may feel abandoned by his family in the later years, but he will find people from an extended family.

Since the fifth house can describe the gambling instincts, that can mean anything from falling in love to playing the stock market, expressing a talent, or having children. It is the house that describes the quality of romance in the soul. When the Moon rules or is placed in this house, vulnerability occurs in connection with these activities. When the individual is upset, he may be tempted to play the horses or make foolish investments. He may be upset because of love in his life or the lack of it. He easily expresses his need for mothering, but that may be smothering as well.

If the Moon is well aspected and descriptive of this sector of the chart, a creative outlet is an emotional necessity. The individual may be talented in writing or in activities connected to the needs of children and women. In romantic areas, the protective urges emerge. He may tend to fall in love with people he can rescue. He may have potential for investments in activities or with products that satisfy hunger. He may work with the commodities market or otherwise in connection with food. Entertainment will bring emotional security.

If the Moon is not well aspected, he may be overly sensitive to his children, unable to express the true emotional reactions in his relationship with them. He may allow his children to rescue or mother him. Activities connected with entertainment, romance, or any kind of gambles can be upsetting for this individual. Vulnerability and overreaction can be too easily triggered until he begins to release his emotional hold on people he loves. With objectivity and lowered expectations of emotional return from loved ones and from these areas of activity, he can release a flood of creative energy. He may need to write, if only to transmute his feelings of lack of love and to find that objectivity. He may discover a latent talent, to his own surprise.

Health is the primary area described by the sixth house in a chart, as well as work projects. The type of work that an individual is attracted to can be clearly indicated by that sector of the chart. When the Moon rules or is placed therein, the person must be involved in work situations that fulfill him emotionally, or he can be very unhappy. If the Moon is well aspected, the probability of satisfying work is very strong. Emotional balance produces good health and sensitive energy that enables the person to fulfill his duties with great response from co-workers. He may act as a mother in some capacity. At the very least, he will show the nurturing part of his personality. Since the sixth house also describes small animals, work with animals can be very satisfying, for instance. Moon qualities indicate the natural ability to feed people. Involvement with food or restaurants can be productive as well.

When the Moon is not well aspected natally, emotional overreaction can play havoc with health. The areas involved are the stomach, the intestines, and the digestive tract in general. Some overreaction to foods, even milk, can upset a delicate digestive balance. When the individual is upset, he may naturally turn to food. Since his choices are not made from a logical point of view, he tends to cram into his mouth almost anything to stop the ache in his solar-plexus area. He may tend to retain food, upsetting the natural process of digestion even more. Information about diet and health will enable the individual to become more aware of what he is doing. He may even be able to stop himself at the moment of overreaction and write about what he feels, which enables him to be more objective and gain insights that will be valuable to other people. In this way, he fulfills a special service to humanity of which he would not have been aware unless he had suffered somewhat. For the Moon truly does act as the mirror. Whatever an individual feels, may be quite similar to feelings of people in general. When he has worked through his own overreactions and found a solution, he is able to nurture in the highest sense. He may write, open a health-food restaurant, or manage a vitamin store. He may work with animals, either in rescue missions or in healing. When his own health starts to suffer, he may have to acknowledge unfulfilling situations in his own work.

The seventh house describes partnership, whether that is marriage or a business partnership. If the Moon rules or is placed in this house, the individual may look for emotional fulfillment in marriage or joint activity. If the Moon is well aspected, he may be fortunate in finding another person who easily expresses the caring and nurturing he wants. But if the Moon has difficult aspects, he may find a partner or mate who is overly emotional, easily hurt, and overly sensitive. He may not then have the emotional response he really wants. He may have to be careful about rescuing another person through marriage. In Transactional Analysis, there is a concept known as the "rescue triangle." In that triangle, the rescuer rescues the victim, and the victim becomes the persecutor and persecutes the rescuer. Usually, the person who tends to rescue may have been the victim at some early stage in his life. He tends to project onto other people what he felt, rather than work through his own emotional pain first. Only after doing the latter can he resist feeling sorry for another person. His unconscious, unintentional attitude may be "I'm OK, but you're not." If that is the case, the attitude is easily sensed by this mate or partner, who is then naturally resentful. The relationship may not reach a level of true understanding until feelings are examined and objective communication can develop. If the Moon has primarily good aspects in the chart, the individual picks someone who is easily able to express the anima part of the personality no matter what sex he or she is. Fulfillment and nurturing can go back and forth at that point.

Since the eighth house describes the way in which the individual gets his needs met and the true transformation in life, this position of the Moon is an interesting one. In the most positive sense, when the Moon is well aspected, the ability to have emotional fulfillment is very strong. It is then fairly easy for the individual to express this same quality of nurturing toward others. He can appeal to people on a sensitive, emotional level and find open response. His own emotional level is strong, so there is no need to protect himself. He is sensitive to people around him and expresses his caring without any feelings of pity or rescue involved. He is secure about getting what he needs and wants as well.

When the aspects to the Moon are not so positive, emotional reaction can be very strong in connection with getting what he needs and wants. He may have felt abandoned in some way in connection with help, money, or emotional support. Therefore he is not easily able to express his own mothering qualities. He is concerned with protecting his wounded emotional body. He becomes especially upset if he has to ask for anything, being vulnerable and overly sensitive. He may be therefore unconcerned with expressing caring for humanity as a whole. Yet the true gift to the human race is his particular quality of nurturing. He may have to examine the cause of his sensitivity, find his answers, and locate an outlet for the expression of his identification with others. He may write, become a therapist, or find a way to satisfy the emotional needs of mankind.

Travel, legalities, development of the higher qualities of intelligence, and promotional efforts can be described by the ninth house in the natal chart. With the Moon in this position, a deep emotional need can be fulfilled by travel, for instance. Sensitivity toward people in all walks of life and in all countries can bring tremendous response to the individual through any activities such as advertising, publishing, promotional efforts, and lecturing. When the Moon is well aspected, a natural identification with people brings the individual to a point where he must deal with people on a broad scale. Those works of his that express products of the higher intelligence show a sensitivity toward the needs of people. He may be involved in higher education, in legal work, or in social work. He can be fulfilled through a change of scene. If he writes and is published, his audience responds on an emotional level. He reaches them almost intuitively.

When the Moon is not well aspected, the overreaction that he experiences when he is traveling may prevent that activity in his life. He may feel vulnerable or lost in other countries or at a distance from his home base. He can be upset over legal matters, too emotionally self-protective to realize his identity with people, and vulnerable to criticism or bad press. If he were to undertake a task such as writing or lecturing and the response was not what he expected, he could be emotionally devastated. He may be too open on an emotional, gut level to appear in the spotlight in front of many people. Yet when he objectifies his own feelings and reactions, he can be especially attuned to people, especially in countries other than his birth or away from his usual environment. If he lets his feelings travel or reach out to humanity on a philosophical level, he satisfies his own emotional needs. Publishing can be an excellent outlet for his need to feed humanity.

When the Moon is placed in or rules the tenth house of career, the individual finds the kind of career that will enable him to nurture people. The tenth house indicates the quality of the relationship with the parent of the same sex. It describes the way the individual "photographs" the personality of that parent. When the Moon is well aspected, the individual may have developed a strong maternal, protective feeling toward that parent. He may have photographed that parent as having been abandoned or orphaned. His feelings may go so far as to make him feel he was the replacement "mother" to that parent. If he sees his parent as being overly vulnerable or needy, he may withhold his own emotional reaction to give space for the parent to express his or her feelings.

If the Moon is not well aspected, the individual may have felt abandoned by that parent. He may be particularly vulnerable in the relationship and tend to be just as sensitive in connection to his own career. He can overreact in public, or be upset and easily hurt in connection with public life or career. When he allows himself to understand the beginnings of his overly emotional reactions, he can begin to express the nurturing qualities in the career or public arena. He may write, deal with women in particular, and experience a flood of response when he allows himself to show vulnerability. He has a sixth sense about the trends of the times. He may also be so open and sensitive to the feelings of others that he lacks objectivity in his career. In social life, he can identify with many people, but feel abandoned, orphaned, or overly sensitive to the people around him. He may prefer quiet social activity, rather than large gatherings.

The eleventh house in a chart describes the kind of friends an individual attracts and how he feels about them. It can also indicate the quality of the relationship in associations with people. That house also indicates activity with large organizations. When the Moon is placed in this sector of the chart, he may be vulnerable in connection with large group activity or with friendships in particular. He can be overly sensitive to slights, feelings of being left out, or he may tend to hang on to friendships for emotional support. If the Moon is not well aspected, those sensitive qualities are enlarged, overexaggerated, and can be quite painful to the individual. He may fear losing friends and is therefore hesitant to make a strong attachment to anyone. He may be self-protective in connection with groups and appear uncaring and unconcerned. If the Moon is well aspected, deep response from friends and groups can bring greater emotional fulfillment into his life. He may act in a nurturing manner with friends and receive that quality of caring in return. He may have to avoid any tendencies to rescue if his own emotional well-being is not balanced and strong.

The twelfth house in a chart describes the behind-the-scenes processes in life. It can indicate subconscious reactions or simply activities that are conducted away from the view of other people. When the Moon is in this sector of the chart, a natural resistance to the display of emotions is quite obvious. The individual may feel deeply within his own subconscious mind, and when alone, or in relaxed circumstances, allow himself to exhibit some vulnerability. Usually the anima, or feminine, qualities are not fully developed. They are there when it is safe, but not easily exposed to the view of other people. Pride may be strong or he may have had childhood messages about the restriction of feelings. If he was constantly told it was not manly to cry, or that big girls don't cry, for instance, tears could be let loose only when privacy was assured.

If the Moon is well aspected in the chart, deep inner feelings of caring may be expressed subconsciously or on more subtle levels. The individual may easily be able to remain by himself to write, work in hospitals, or express talent in connection with art. He can attune himself on a level of sensitivity and produce works that will win response from people on an emotional level. If the Moon is not well aspected, he may not be able to remain alone for very long. He becomes vulnerable and tends to overreact and imagine things. He needs activity and feedback from others, but may indeed attract the very circumstances that hurt him, that he'd like to ignore and that force him back to vulnerability when he is alone. Since the Moon describes the feelings of abandonment, during his mother's pregnancy he may have felt a sense of abandonment or lack of being fed. He may not allow himself to have deep emotional attachments as a result of that programming, for fear of a continuing lack of being fed. He may not be able to express his nurturing, mothering qualities, since he had no overt photographs of that quality in his childhood. He can feel emotionally deprived until he begins to expose a needy, more vulnerable part of his personality. Once he works through his own emotional pain, he develops great sensitivity toward mankind on that inner, subconscious level.

MOON CONJUNCT SUN

When the two "lights" in the chart are conjunct, or interacting, a quality of integration is apparent in the persona. The animus, or male, dominant, characteristics are side by side with the anima, or feminine, traits. Strength and sensitivity are a powerful combination. Ideally, mankind is composed of masculine and feminine energy in balance and interacting. But, in many people, these qualities are sadly out of balance. Ego, sense of self-worth, and vitality may be watered down by oversensitivity and lack of emotional security. To find a balance between these two energies is rather rare and obviously to be treasured.

Sun energy is also descriptive of executive ability, leadership qualities. The Moon energy is indicative of a special intuition and feeling for mankind and the needs of people in general. One quality, utilized effectively, can be quite potent all by itself, but when the two qualities are harmonized and integrated, the end result is very special. Naturally, the effectiveness of such a combination of energies may be mitigated by difficult or hard aspects from other planets. If, for instance, Saturn is in hard aspect to the combination, the individual would have latent ability and inner judgments about the expression of such a quality.

Helga Philippe was married to the former banquet manager Claude Philippe, known as "Philippe of the Waldorf." Claude organized the internationally famous April in Paris Ball in New York and also planned and produced regular gourmet dinners known as the Lucullus Circle Dinners. These dinners, in particular, were very exclusive and attracted some of the wealthiest and most prestigious men in the world. When Claude died, even though she felt terribly vulnerable, Helga took over the role of planning exotic menus, organizing the wines, and greeting the guests. At many such occasions, she was the only woman present and was required to make an opening address to this highly specialized group. Helga's chart confirmed her capability to continue such elegant dinners. In a way, it was very easy for her. Her Sun and Moon are conjunct in the sign of Scorpio in the ninth house of promotion, publicity, distribution, and international affairs. She is very magnetic, vital, and attractive. High energy enables her to get things done that would overwhelm other, less capable people yet she understands how to "feed" people on many levels. In all her activities, she is clearly the leader, yet she never loses her femininity or sensitivity. She seems in control of all situations yet is always able to sense just what others will respond to. She has been known to her friends as a master diplomat. To plan such menus that would continue to surprise and delight gourmets the world over was simply what she had been doing as Claude's wife throughout the years of entertainment on their lovely New York estate.

Marlon Brando has the Sun and Moon conjunct in his chart in the fourth house of home, ruling the ninth house of publicity, promotional efforts, and recognition, and the eighth house of getting needs met. Marlon exhibited this special quality of dominance and sensitivity in his portrayal of Stanley Kowalski in *A Streetcar Named Desire*. His character was a rough-and-tumble workingman and beer-drinking companion but loving husband. His emotional intensity and feeling for Stella revealed a vulnerability that made his portrayal one of the most memorable screen roles in history. Marlon has expressed this sensitive quality in his own life. After his first son was born, and he was divorced from his wife, he took on the role of both mother and father for a period of time, long before it was fashionable for a man to do so.

Adrienne Landau also has the conjunction of the Sun and Moon in the sign of Scorpio, posited in the tenth house of career. An artist for much of her young life, Adrienne began to find an interest in designing accessories. She began a trend in the fashion world by putting fur tails on handbags. Soon fashion-conscious women were wearing another one of her designs, a scarf made of tails. With a bit more success, Adrienne began creating gorgeous fur coats, so exotic that major department stores began to devote a special fur section to her coats. She has been widely advertised in the most prestigious fashion magazines and has an international reputation. Adrienne manufactures her designs from a loft in the fur district in New York. She is a dynamic executive, enjoying her work with her staff and never losing her feminine quality. Since the Moon describes women in particular, Adrienne's designs have great appeal to women who love the look of glamour. She has a special sense of what women will love to wear.

Karl Marx had the Moon conjunct his Sun in the sign of Taurus, placed in the second house of finance. The Sun rules his seventh house of partnership, with the Moon ruling both the sixth house of work, and the fifth house of creativity and gambles. Marx was a philosopher and newspaper editor, and he studied law. He worked with Friedrich Engels to found the Social Democratic Labor Party and to publish the *Communist Manifesto* and *Das Kapital*. Marx's concern for the material welfare of all led to a theory that might satisfy the needs of mankind and feed humanity on a large scale. Many aspects in his chart indicate a possibility of strong vision as well as political acumen. Although Marx was able to express that sensitivity about the plight of common man, he may not have foreseen the bloodshed involved in putting his idealistic theories into practice. That the seed of the Russian Revolution should have been conceived by a German and then later financed by the German Goverment is a contradiction to the practices of that heavily industrialized country. Marx set in motion turbulence that seems to continue, leading to more and more chaos in world affairs. The Moon, that sensitive part of the self, has no objectivity of its own. It simply indicates reaction to hunger needs of others. When the Moon is conjoined the Sun, as in this instance, pride may also be a factor behind that nurturing, protective urge. It must be quite ego-satisfying to think that one can solve all the problems of mankind with one simple theory.

MOON IN HARD ASPECT TO THE SUN

When the Moon is square the Sun in the natal chart, the anima part of the personality can be in conflict with the animus. Emotional energy may be blocked due to lack of recognition early in life, and that lack of early emotional support can damage healthy development of a strong inner sense of self-worth. When vulnerability and emotions are exposed, strength can be dissipated. Recognition by others may bring an overwhelming energy to a fragile, emotional nature. For if, in early life, ego strokes were withheld by parents or by the overall environment, later recognition can seem intolerable, as that could invalidate conditions that were necessary for the young one's survival. Naturally, when the individual with this aspect becomes aware of that programming, he can begin to allow more of the dominant part of himself to be exposed without becoming overly vulnerable and sensitive about that process. He learns to integrate the masculine and feminine characteristics, becoming more open to true development of the ego. He learns to do things for his own satisfaction, rather than to receive an emotional reaction from external conditions.

Corinne has Moon square the Sun in her natal chart. She described the feeling as one of being out of balance. The Moon is placed in the sixth house of work, also describing health issues. It rules the fourth house of home, and indicates the relationship with her father. The Sun is placed in the tenth house of career, and rules her first house of personality. She described her father's reaction to her achievements in life. "My father thought he was doing the right thing by not telling me he was proud of me. He would talk about my accomplishments in front of the wrong people. He might say something in front of the other children in the family, making them feel out of place. That was not good for my relationship with my middle sister and my brother. I didn't know they resented that until recently. Instead of showing his pride to me, he would always push me to do better. He would say, 'With just a little more work, you could make straight A's.' I didn't want to give up everything and stay at home. I preferred to be more well rounded. And if I did make good grades, he wouldn't say anything at all. I'd only hear from him if I didn't do as well as he expected. Those negative strokes confused me as a child.

"My father was the emotional one of my parents. When he was home, he wanted us all there with him. I don't seem to feel the same equilibrium with my father as I do with my mother. There was definite role reversal, as my mother was the disciplinarian. My mother was very consistent, but my father could be very volatile. My father could get to me on a sensitive level, more than anyone else. I always wanted him to be proud of me. The moment my father hurt my feelings, it would bother me so much I couldn't get anything done. Now I can be vulnerable and sometimes feel out of balance at work. If something happens that hurts my feelings, I really have to confront the situation immediately. I have to clear the air by talking to the person involved and get things out. It's the only way I can get to sleep at night. Subconsciously, I don't like to be out of balance."

Michael, a man who has chosen to devote his life to the development of inner spiritual qualities, has the same aspect in his chart. The Sun is placed in the second house of income, and rules the eleventh house of friends. The Moon, posited in the tenth house of career and public life as well as social life, is also ruling that house. The double-barreled intensity of the Moon in that position of the chart describes a very sensitive relationship with his father. Michael was especially clear in his description of the conflict between energy, ego, and activities connected to public life. He was very aware of the effect of the relationship with his father on early decisions about career. He confirmed a strong symbiosis with that parent. "Oh, yes, I am my father. I was always frightened of him. He was very awkward with his children. He was a distant, authoritarian figure, who I loved, or wanted to love. He was not cruel or mean, just very rejecting. He was sensitive, very shy, and had no real friends. He had been brought up in Victorian England by a nanny who would bring the children in to see their father. They would receive a pat on the head as acknowledgement and that's about all. He wasn't literally abandoned, but he had no relationship with his father. When he went to India at the age of eighteen, his father took him to the boat. My father was astonished to see tears in the eyes of his father. That was the first time he had ever shown emotion to my father. In my own lifetime, I never saw my own father break down or even be angry. He barricaded himself to protect his own feelings.

"I tried to be an executive to please my father. He was a businessman and quite successful. He loved his business. I think he only had a family because that was what you were supposed to do. Basically, that was the wrong thing for his personality. He liked his horse better than he liked us. He carried a picture of his horse in his wallet, not a picture of his family. Since my father was my model, I studied business because he was in business. I don't even know if he demanded that, but it seemed natural. Everything I did in school was to please him, but I would lose interest very quickly. I majored in business administration, but I hated it. I'm really an artist. My father only related to me on 'How are your grades?' terms and later on 'How's the business?' I needed his attention, but the other side of the coin was that I didn't really do the things that would win his approval. I always sat on my strength and watered it down so I never made waves. Once, when I lost my temper and yelled, my brother cheered.

"I used to steal, starting when I was only eight or nine in boarding schools. I would get very close to being thrown out lots of times. I even used to steal from my father. But I don't remember him confronting me. He probably said something to my mother. I'm sure he would be upset about that. Although I might have been trying to get some kind of reaction on a subconscious level, on a conscious level all the other stuff would come up about not making waves. I do remember overhearing my father tell my mother that he was very disappointed in the way his sons turned out. I became involved in metaphysical work, and he didn't understand that at all.

"I don't like to be upset any more, because I get exhausted. I get *really* worn down. I joined an ashram and it became very difficult for me, because all that emotional stuff got dredged up. I was terribly tight about my feelings. I was a mess. I was very shy and pathetic. If a pretty girl walked across the street, I couldn't go on that side of the street. I felt shame all the time, shame in not living up to some model I had. Objective work helped me get over that. I like to write letters, because that's how I clarify my own process. The other person is almost an excuse for it."

The Moon has an identification with what all mankind feels and suffers, rather than enjoying exclusivity. Michael continued, "At the ashram, they could never understand why I would keep going out into the world to be with other people. They all felt a bond with each other that was very exclusive, like 'It's just us!' I have very few one-to-one relationships, because that kind of strangles me. I like to share my love with other people, not in a promiscuous sense, but love in the higher sense. Friendships, to me, represent an ultimate level of real love."

ASPECTS TO MERCURY

MERCURY IS THE PLANET THAT DESCRIBES INTELLECT. It indicates the way a person thinks, what he thinks about, and the way he arrives at a conclusion. It describes the quality of communications and the specific ability to collect data, disseminate information, and make choices. Mercury was the messenger of the gods. He was fast, efficient, and only a bit inclined to gossip. Mercury is a fast-moving planet; the placement of Mercury and its aspects indicate the speed of the mind. Mercury specifically describes the left-brain process. That part of the brain is the analyst, the decision maker, the objective being.

Mercury rules the liquid called by that name. In trying to hold onto a ball of mercury, it becomes obvious that the slippery quality makes it impossible to get a good grip. In an untrained state, the mind can be exactly like that. Mercury is an important planet in the chart to understand, as it helps us identify the varieties and shades of thought processes possible. The pattern of Mercury in the sky is variable. It moves at varying rates of speed. The inconsistency of its track through the skies can easily act as a mirror for the inconsistency of the human mind. Mankind has, above all, choices to make in life. He has the right to change his mind. Edgar Cayce, the mystic, said, "The mind is the builder." So the thought processes pave the way for the events in life. The position and aspects of Mercury indicate precisely the possibility of making creative choices. External conditions in an individual's life exactly mirror the way he thinks. If he has had heavy programming that prevents him from total optimism, the aspects to Mercury will describe those conditions exactly. The choices begin at birth, or so it seems. In spite of external conditions, if the person has a healthful, well-aspected Mercury in his chart, the indications are that he will survive difficulties and retain a positive ability to analyze a situation, observe the choices, and clearly make known, if only to himself, what he decides to do about it.

Mercury describes speech patterns as well as the quality of the voice. If a person has Mercury strongly emphasized in his chart, he must be involved in activity in which the mind is stimulated. He may be a speaker, writer, politician, musician, or business person, yet mental stimulation will be obvious in his life in one way or another. When the mind is not stimulated in proportion to the need, trouble can ensue. For if Mercury is strong in the chart, the individual does not stop thinking. What he thinks about is described by the house placement of Mercury in the chart. The astrological sign in which Mercury is found, as well as the house it rules, also describe the quality of the thought processes. Airy placements of Mercury give a stronger intellectual leaning than earthy placements, for instance. Practical, earth positions of Mercury don't lend the same, compassionate quality of thought as a water placement. And dynamic, fire placements of Mercury indicate a mental quality that is extremely enthusiastic and expansive—characteristics that are not so obvious in the other placements of that planet.

In psychological terms, Mercury can describe the adult ego state. Transactional Analysis indicates that a person has an adult ego state that is developed when the learning process begins. For instance, with school years the child begins to develop an adult awareness of the conditions around him. (He may begin that process much sooner in his life. In regression sessions, it is obvious that the infant is quite aware of his environment and the state of mind of his parents, and in some instances the individual describes a decision he made about his survival.) With that new adult awareness, he begins to make choices. He learns to exercise his mental faculties more deliberately. He collects information, stores that in his computer mind, and can begin to give out facts from his storehouse of knowledge. Children display this ability quite early. They begin to tell other children what to do—obviously a reflection of what they have been told and what they have decided to do in their own lives in their early experimentation. The placement of Mercury and its aspects describes this early development of an adult ego. Sometimes that state is initiated too soon. Children begin to make decisions without all the facts at hand. They can be stuck in a mental process unless they learn how to make alternative decisions through awareness processes of some kind.

Intellectual awareness, ease of learning, and an ability to handle any situation that might arise is a benefit of having a strong Mercury in an individual chart. The power of the mind can cut through many confusing situations in life. It can act like a laser beam to hone hazy plans and ideas. It can be a foundation for the higher state of inspiration described by Neptune in the astrological chart. Neptune describes the powers of intuition and higher awareness connected to the right-brain process. Without Mercury to ground and make practical, the concepts that float can simply keep on their path to the state of illusion. Dreams are made real by their practical application in life. It is Mercury that pins down the ephemeral, wispy, cloudlike concepts that are available to all. The aspects to Mercury indicate how swift or efficient an individual might be in collecting the higher thoughts to bring them earthward.

When Mercury rules or is placed in the first house, the individual thinks about his personal life and need for self-expression. He develops an adult ego state almost at the moment of birth and may decide that he will survive as long as he knows the facts. He strengthens his mental muscle until it is rocklike, impenetrable. He may be tempted to hide behind his mind. He is certainly aware of everything around him and is busy filling his computer with data. He tends to ask questions, make observations, and be more analytical than emotional. He is apt to be mentally sharp, and witty. His manner of speaking depends on aspects to other planets, but by and large he is entertaining, full of information about many things. He may be especially aware of daily events in his particular locale. He can become harshly critical when he is not on safe ground. His powers of observation are strong and a predilection to intellectual activity assured, unless Mercury is badly aspected in his chart. He may talk about himself, think about his plans, and be self-concerned. If a lack of activity is indicated by aspects to other planets, he may simply be a talker and not a doer. With negative aspects to Mercury, he may give advice even when it is not requested or wanted by others. He can easily take care of details, paperwork, and organizational demands, however. He may be the person to make decisions based on a profound ability to do research.

When Mercury is placed in the second house in a natal chart, the thoughts concern financial activity. The individual makes money through intellectual activities such as writing, speaking, researching, or collecting data. He may be able to structure financial schedules easily, make financial decisions, or earn money through his voice. He is mentally stimulated by being involved with the financial world. He may be the record keeper or decision maker in his own financial world or on a larger scale. He will love the attention to detail in connection with income. He thinks and talks about money. If Mercury is not well aspected, the individual may not be clear about his financial goals or may be unable to make decisions that will lead to financial success. His overall financial situation may be the prime subject on his mind most of the time. He may think, talk, and worry about money as an intellectual exercise.

The third house in a chart describes communications in general, and specifically interaction with siblings, relatives, and neighbors. It also describes the ability to learn, the connection with schools, and mental processing in general. In the natural chart with Aries on the ascendant (Aries being the first sign in the zodiac, therefore "naturally" ruling the first house), Mercury rules this house of discussion, and Mercury is the planet of the mind. Therefore, communications fields are doubly stimulating for the individual if Mercury is strong in his natal chart. The individual may be critical of his siblings, a critic in theater or the arts, or a writer. He can be involved with community planning, negotiation of contracts, decision making, research projects, languages, or using his speaking or singing voice in theater or in music. The ability to analyze, discuss and negotiate are especially beneficial when Mercury rules this house, primarily due to the natural affinity for collection of data. Facts are at the fingertips of the person with Mercury ruling this house.

Relationships with family and siblings are dependent on discussion; mental rapport is strong. He may think and talk about them. If Mercury is well aspected, an ability to objectively discuss issues within the family gives practice for later life when that same talent comes in handy. Sportscasters, news commentators, actors, and actresses must necessarily have the ability to learn lines, be observant, and have a pleasant speaking voice, for instance. Mercury might be found especially strong in the charts of people in these occupations. The individual may do his best thinking, talking, and planning while he is driving an automobile or taking short trips, for the third house not only describes interaction with people but also driving a car. Mercury, the messenger of the gods, was constantly on the move, collecting and conveying information from one Olympian height to another.

If Mercury is not well aspected in the chart, the ability to discuss things rationally is obviously impaired. A look to discussions and relationships with family members and especially siblings may give clues to early negative programming. Mental restlessness or a lack of clarity in presentation of thought may be obvious traits. The individual may have a speech impairment or speak in a manner less than clear. He may talk too fast, dart from one subject to another, or find it difficult to focus his mind. He may be bossy, negative, unrealistic. He may have a hard time in getting agreement from other people. He may talk too long and loud in hopes he will get his point across. Conversely, he may be reluctant to speak, express ideas, or make observations.

When Mercury rules the fourth house of home, the most important quality between the individual and the parent of the opposite sex was mental rapport. He may have observed that parent as being particularly intelligent, factual, or critical. He may think about that parent a great deal and be influenced in his own speech and thought patterns by that parent. Since the fourth house indicates the kind of lifestyle the individual desires and attracts, and the particular qualities of the homelife, it is clear that the person with Mercury in this sector of his chart wants intelligent conversation in his home and is likely to attract people into his home who are mental, communicative, and aware of factual information. He may even build a home around a library. He may do his best thinking, talking, and making of plans when he is in his own home. He is mentally stimulated by plans and activity connected to land projects. The fourth house describes the conditions surrounding the individual in the third portion of his life. He may become more literary, intellectually polarized and objective as he grows older. He becomes more like the parent of the opposite sex, perhaps fulfilling that parent's unfulfilled ambitions or talents.

If Mercury is not well aspected in the natal chart, the probability of a lack of good communication with the parent of the opposite sex is indicated. He may have felt criticized by that parent. That lack of discussion may affect the later thought processes, preventing him from expressing himself clearly. The photographs of that parent's decisions and choices will be strong imprints in the mind of the person with this aspect. He may think negatively, worry, or have a lack of clarity or information about essential things. He may not easily come to conclusions. He may be mentally restless, scattered, or easily depressed. He may worry unnecessarily about his home-life, his lifestyle, or his property. He may have difficulty attending to details concerning papers, organization, and routines within his home. He may not choose to think about any outside information as he grows older, becoming very self-involved.

Since the fifth house describes gambles in life, an ability to make creative decisions and take risks with intellectual self-expression is easy when Mercury rules or is placed in this position. The placement is especially descriptive of plans and thoughts about love, investments, children, and self-expression. The person may want a romantic relationship that is primarily based on communication and intellectual camaraderie. He expresses his talent on a mental level, whether that is through writing, speaking, acting, or decisions about investments. His children will be mental, alert, and intellectually inclined. The conversations between parent and child can be especially enlightening and agreeable when aspects to Mercury are harmonious. If the aspects to Mercury in this placement are not harmonious, misunderstandings and lack of agreement can be upsetting to both parent and child. The inability or unwillingness to clarify creative thoughts or participate in creative activity in which the mind will be challenged can result in negative manifestation in the life. Mental frustrations may induce restlessness in activities in which clear thinking is necessary. Creative opportunities may produce arguments or upsets.

The fifth house can describe entertainment, whether that means giving a party, being involved in the entertainment world, or enjoying watching entertainment such as theater, dance, musical events, or sports events. When Mercury is well aspected in the chart, mental stimulation comes with activities that will produce new ideas, combine the ideas of many people, or allow for self-expression. The person with Mercury in this house may enjoy parties at which ideas can be exchanged. He is not interested in merely observing other people, he wants to talk to them or hear what they are saying. If Mercury is negatively aspected in the chart, the individual may not be able to talk or express himself when creative people are present. He may not allow himself the risk of exploring his true intellectual potential in creative areas. He may not be able to risk using his powers of observation to the fullest. He may be very critical of entertainment, showing a negative response instead of enjoyment. He may think about love and romance but not allow the possibility to exist in his life.

When Mercury is connected to the sixth house of work and health, either by house position or by rulership, the individual thinks about his work, his health, and the contribution he can make by serving others. He will seek employment or an occupation in which he can use his mind, express his plans and ideas, and make decisions. He is easily able to discuss work projects, analyze problems in his work environment, and think healthful thoughts. He may be concerned with health fields, such as public health, writing about health foods, vitamins, or new inroads of health products. His own health depends on an ability to think and express himself clearly and to be well-balanced mentally. If conditions around him produce worry, his own health may suffer. Thoughts become very real to someone with this placement of Mercury, as he can see the immediate reaction to his mental processes in his physical condition.

If Mercury is not well aspected in the chart, health problems can be indicated, depending on his choice of work activity. The individual may not allow himself the right to be involved with mentally stimulating work and may worry about work, or be overly involved in details that are nonproductive and nonstimulating. He may use left-brain activity to the exclusion of his conceptual mind, and be argumentative with co-workers. He may not like to think about working at all. He may trap himself in boring situations, in which he is left to deal with bare and uninteresting facts and figures. His lack of creative intelligence may keep him trapped there, simply because he cannot decide to allow himself more mental stimulation. He may take his work to bed with him, creating health problems due to overwork. He may need to learn how to collect data, make decisions, and take action on a more healthful course.

The seventh house describes partnership, whether that may be marital or business; the seventh house can also describe live-in situations in which formal marital agreements are missing. The individual with Mercury in this position wants, most of all, to be mentally turned on in a partnership arena. He looks for someone especially intelligent, conversational, and quick-witted. He may attract someone involved in the communications field. He may think about partners a great deal more than he thinks about himself. He may look for someone else to provide interesting conversation or mental stimulation in his life. He likes to share ideas and participate in plans and discussions with someone else, rather than simply analyze and dissect information for himself. He may attract someone who is basically involved in left-brain, analytical occupations. In a business partnership, he may need someone else to handle details, analyze, and organize. If Mercury is well aspected in his own chart, he is fortunate to find someone with a healthy, well-balanced mind. If Mercury is not well aspected, the greatest trial in connection with partnership may come with trying to find accord on a mental level. An ability to come to good agreements may be lacking in the relationship. He may attract someone who has ideas quite contrary to his own, perhaps so foreign that an even balance is difficult to attain. The partner may be negative, critical, or unwilling to see the other side of an argument or disagreement. Mental stress and turmoil may be characteristic of the relationship, instead of mental stimulation.

It is important for the individual with Mercury in the seventh house to tend to his mental processes, for indeed, this placement augments the theory of mirror personality; that is, a tendency to attract in external conditions or people what we may dislike or repress within ourselves. The external conditions reflect the inner state. What the individual really wants in a partnership relationship is good communication. If Mercury is well aspected in the chart, the probability of attracting a very intelligent person in partnership is quite strong. Levels of communications can be extremely harmonious, stimulating, and informative. He finds the very person who shares his ideas and views of life.

Mercury is a fast-moving planet, so there is always possibility of a great deal of mental stimulation or mental restlessness involved with its placement. It follows the Sun closely as the two planets travel through the signs of the zodiac, but moves at a variable rate of speed. If Mercury is too far ahead of the Sun, it then goes "retrograde," or backward, or so it seems, so that the Sun can catch up again. It is actually like two railroad trains traveling on separate tracks in the same direction. It appears as though the slower train is moving backward when it really isn't. Any Mercury placement in the chart will naturally go through variable phases in the quality of communication and agreement. However, the stimulation of controversy can also act as a challenge. There can be agreement, then distance and objectivity, then renewed agreement. Certainly the individual who has Mercury in the seventh house will not be bored in partnership areas, unless he has a difficult block through other aspects which negate his own thought processes. He will then find someone who is critical, unwilling to talk, express ideas, or share in positive plans for mutual benefit.

When Mercury rules or is positioned in the eighth house of the chart, the individual can be exceptionally good at simply stating his needs, and as an addendum to his personality, talented in giving information to people. In psychological terms, habits are developed early on, that precondition an individual toward a healthy ability to get what he needs and wants from life. If Mercury is well aspected in the horoscope, the person learned early on in his life to be clear and precise about what he wanted from the people around him. Perhaps he was taught to verbalize his wants instead of screaming or crying. (Other planets describing this sector of the chart would naturally indicate a variety of feelings and early ability to attract good things to one's side.) With Mercury in this position, the individual is clear, concise, and adult-like in presenting his desires or requests.

Naturally, if Mercury is not well aspected, the individual has the opposite programming. He may hesitate to ask for anything, for fear he will be rejected. He may have to build up tensions before he is willing to make requests, or he may be excessively diplomatic in the presentation of his needs. He may or may not take care of himself through interaction with people and events.

This sector of the chart can also describe inheritance factors. That inheritance may not be only from parents or family, but from the universal bank. That is, from unexpected sources. If life seems to drop goodies into an individual's lap without much effort or in ways that seem undeserved, a deposit must be forthcoming. The repayment of those special blessings from the universal source is through mental activity, information, or dissemination of facts and figures. The individual can act as a teacher, consultant, writer, or speaker. If the person is unwilling or untutored in making requests for himself, it is possible that he is also unwilling to contribute broadly on the mental level. Some inner reluctance or programming stops up the flow coming into and going out of his mind. He may have to look at his willingness to put himself on the line with ideas, plans, and data that he has accumulated. When he releases the mental block, he releases dammed-up energy that may come back to him in financial benefits or simply in attracting a vibrant exchange of mental energy with people.

Publishing, publicity, travel, and distribution are described by the ninth house in the horoscope. This house can also describe activity on an international level, through diplomatic or legal fields. When Mercury is in this position in a chart, the ideas and plans of the individual can be especially far-reaching. He may have observed productive methods of distribution or have practical ideas about advertising or promotional campaigns. He may be especially adept at lecturing, speaking, or writing information that has wide distribution. His adult ego state gives him a head start in the collection and dissemination of material and data. He can be mentally stimulated by travel, dealings with countries other than that of his birth, and be well received by people on a large scale.

If the planet ruling intelligence and mental activity is not well aspected in the chart, the barrier or blocks to recognition may be reflective about fears or inability to have his plans accepted. He may fear a downfall of popularity, criticism for his ideas, or lack of survival if he dares to try to expand. He may not have developed techniques for clear presentation of plans. He may be misunderstood on a wide level when he tries to suggest a course of action. Learning to develop a better ability to be intellectually precise, to get good agreements, and to be willing to make practical decisions can release tremendous mental energy. The ninth house also describes higher education. If Mercury is well aspected in the chart, the individual utilizes the left brain when in college or at the university. If Mercury is not well aspected, he may not have felt inclined toward higher education. He may also have had some difficulties with areas of intellectual expansion.

Career matters, public activity, and social life are described by the tenth house in a natal horoscope. When Mercury is posited in this sector of the chart, the individual may prefer intellectual stimulation when he is in public places. His social life may command a great deal of his thoughts and plans. He may be in a position to speak, be the decision maker, and make clear presentation of data in connection with his career. If Mercury is not well aspected, he may worry about criticism, feel unable to express himself in public, and dare not allow exchange of words and ideas in social situations.

The relationship with the parent of the same sex seems to precondition the attitude about public life and social situations. With Mercury describing this sector of the chart, the relationship with that parent was primarily on a mental level. The individual may have photographed that parent as especially vocal, intelligent, and mental. If Mercury is well aspected in the chart, those photographs are good ones. Clear, good communication was possible between parent and child. That parent may have been a good person to trust with plans and ideas. The individual with this aspect may think and talk about that parent as he respected the information given to him by that parent. An especially alert mental quality might have been obvious no matter what level of actual education that parent attained.

If Mercury is not well aspected, the preconditioning by the relationship with that parent may have been negative on the level of communication. The person may have seen that parent as basically bright but without the courage or energy to express that mentality. The possibility of criticism from that parent is very strong when Mercury is not well aspected and relates to the tenth house in the chart. Therefore, in the public arena, the individual may adopt a critical attitude or hesitate to express himself for fear of public criticism. If the parent was lackadaisical about the development of mental faculties, the individual may also be unconcerned about expressing the adult part of himself. The left brain may lie undeveloped to some degree.

Friendships, group situations, and organizations can be described by the eleventh house in the horoscope. When Mercury is positioned in this sector, interaction with groups and associates is for intellectual purposes, and he expresses his own mentality and intelligence when he is in their company. The individual may choose friends among people who are especially well informed, intelligent, and who stimulate him mentally. Awareness of events and new data comes to him through friends. He thinks about his associates. He may work with organizations involved with communications. If Mercury is well aspected, these activities and associations are harmonious, informative, and mentally uplifting.

When Mercury is not well aspected and rules or is placed in the eleventh house, activity with groups may be mentally upsetting. The individual may attract friends who are critical. He may find himself in situations in which he is unable to express his views easily. He may disagree with people on the correct way to advance, and tend to be argumentative. He may confine himself to working with organizations in which his ability to collect data is limited. He may not find mentally stimulating situations with organizations or groups.

Since the twelfth house describes the "hidden" sector of the chart, it can relate to secrets or subconscious activity. When Mercury is well aspected and placed in this house, the mind is always active when the person is alone. He may do his best thinking when he has solitude and may think about his need for inner seclusion. He develops *mentally* on a subconscious level and is more clear when he is working on that level than when he is in a conscious state. He may or may not be aware of that fact. For instance, in a state of hypnosis, his left brain is activated instead of his right brain, which is more commonly associated with a hypnotic or conceptual state. He may not easily express himself in intellectual areas other than when he is alone. This is especially beneficial for a writer, for instance. He can easily remain alone and be stimulated from his own subconscious storehouse. He becomes more adult, clear, and mentally alert away from other people.

However, if Mercury is not well aspected and is descriptive of the twelfth house, mental upsets become exaggerated when the individual is alone. He may be mentally plagued by inner restlessness, find himself unable to think things through to a positive conclusion, and be lacking in an ability to rest his mind. He may be unable to stop thinking. It may help him to read or be involved in some kind of mental work when he is alone to avoid thinking about matters that disturb him. He may need to seek more objective information to aid him in making up his mind or coming to conclusions. He may avoid expressing his left-brain potential due to some subconscious or prenatal programming. If he collected data during the time before his birth that, if faced, might make life more difficult, he is likely to avoid using his mind to the utmost potential. He may discover that meditation can help him restore clarity on a subconscious level, for through the focusing of attention, the process of balancing the right brain and the left brain can be achieved. In extreme cases, he may have dyslexia or even physical imbalances that make it difficult for him to clearly convey what he is thinking. (Dr. John Thie, in his book *Touch For Help* prescribes simple exercises that help correct those imbalances and redirect proper flow of energy through the meridians.)

MERCURY CONJUNCT SUN

Since Mercury travels in such close proximity to the Sun, many people have this conjunction in their natal charts. The close association between Mercury and the Sun primarily indicates a sense of pride in connection with intelligence. The ego and the intellect are in harmony and the individual can express himself on the mental level. When these two planets interact, the person needs to be mentally stimulated to avoid fatigue. He is more energetic and vital when his mind is activated. He wants to collect data, learn, and grow on an intellectual plane. He can easily assimilate information and come to conclusions on his own. He declares himself through verbal activity to be intelligent, adult, and mentally alert. He enjoys the exchange of views and ideas. He may view a desire and need for recognition or acknowledgment in some areas, as a stimulation for inner vitality. He can be objective and clear.

When Mercury is conjunct the Sun and is in difficult aspect to other planets, the lack of ego in connection with his mind and mental activity may keep him from growing and developing on that level. He may not have been given permission to think of himself as intelligent and dominant. He may have been given messages as a child to indicate that intelligence, as well as a good, healthful sense of self-worth, is a negative quality. Many women have been programmed to think that if the mind is developed, a good relationship with a man is impossible. Since the Sun is descriptive of the masculine or animus part of the whole, the dominant and positively active quality of intelligence can be negated. The individual hesitates to express himself clearly and with strength, for fear of a negative result. He may not be able to make decisions by himself, needing data and permission from someone else. He can resist the development of a fact-finding part of his mind because of a need for peace, or by being indolent about exercising the mental muscle. He may have a strong natural hookup with his intelligent mind, but lack other factors which might motivate him to a level of pride in connection with mental activity.

MERCURY CONJUNCT MOON

The Moon is an extremely personal planet. It describes emotional reactions that may or may not be apparent on the surface. Since Mercury describes the mind and speech, it seems that when the individual is upset, he may say things emotionally motivated that he later wishes he could retract. Emotions and mentality have a strong hookup that can be activated when the individual is vulnerable. Lack of clarity may be obvious in thought and speech patterns when he's upset. He may not easily think quickly or spontaneously, on his feet. He may be especially sensitive about his thought processes, speech patterns, and ideas. If the person with this aspect in his natal chart can work past emotional pain toward more universal attunement, he becomes a spokesman for many people. He may have a gut connection with the needs of humanity and be able to make decisions in a very sensitive manner that will solve problems for many people. He seems to have a major choice in his life regarding the expression of his feelings. He either turns inward toward overreaction, oversensitivity, and vulnerability, or he stresses the Mercurial quality of the aspect to gain objectivity and reason. When Mercury becomes the stronger emphasis in the patterns of thought, he attunes himself quite easily to the emotional qualities of other people. He senses what mankind suffers, through objective examination of his own emotions and feelings. He attracts a giant wave of identification from people around him by clearly expressing his own views and ideas.

This aspect indicates a special quality of sensitivity in the charts of writers, actors, singers, and public figures. This individual can express himself with great compassion and clarity. He may be able to put into words what other people only sense. He can describe what the public relates to on a feeling, emotional level. Historian Arthur Schlesinger, Jr., was born with this aspect in his chart. Although the conjunction of these two planets falls into the second house of financial ability, Mercury rules the tenth house, describing the relationship and identification with his father and therefore his specific talent or ability in public life and with career. The Moon in his chart indicates relationships with friends and associates, since it rules the eleventh house.

Schlesinger's Virgo ascendant describes a natural objectivity in his outlook and indicates a talent for research and detail. The additional color of the Moon enables him to express great sensitivity along with that strong analytical ability. He is known for a quality of lucidity that is identified with the Moon.

Schlesinger's father was a great historian, known as the dean of that field. Schlesinger's strong emotional and mental bond with his father led him into the same field. He became a professor of history at Harvard University. Since the Moon indicates a bond of feeling connected to first his father and then his public, it is interesting to note that he brought history onto a plane where mankind could relate to information on a gut level. He won two Pulitzer prizes, first for *The Age of Jackson* and then for his widely read book on John F. Kennedy *A Thousand Days: J. F. Kennedy in the White House.* Schlesinger is known for being quite opinionated. That impassioned expression of personal opinion is more easily understood by examination of the Mercury-Moon aspect. Otherwise, he might have retained a cool, analytical, detached manner of objectivity that would not have brought the same response from his public.

Sean Connery was born with this aspect in his chart. The conjunction falls in the eighth house in this case, describing the way an individual gets his needs met. It can also indicate the greatest gift an individual can give on a humanitarian level. The Moon rules the seventh house of partnership, and Mercury rules the sixth house of work, as well as the fifth house of creativity. A combination of sensitivity and objectivity can be seen in the expression of talent in the life of Sean Connery. Romantic marriage can be an emotional necessity and creative need in his life. Sean was divorced in 1971, possibly because of overreaction and oversensitivity from his first wife. He now has what appears to be an ideal relationship, with his second mate.

Sean Connery became identified with James Bond, Agent 007, when he did his first film of the series. Unfortunately for Sean, his career was made and his love for his work stymied; he cannot easily play other screen roles after such a response and identification from his public. However, the aspect describes a creative need to work. It may be that with his acting career pigeonholed, Sean may find his true destiny in writing, working with children, or finding a strong identification with the needs of humanity. At this point in his life, he has been quoted as saying he has felt a lack of growth opportunity in connection with creative work. His attention and nurturing seem focused on the beautiful marriage he now has.

Glen Campbell has the Moon conjunct Mercury in the sign of Taurus in his chart. Taurus rules the throat and can indicate a special quality in the speaking or singing voice. The Moon is placed in the seventh house of marriage, while Mercury falls in the sixth house of work. The Moon rules the ninth house of promotion, recognition, and publicity, describing the flood of emotional attachment from his public. Mercury rules the eighth house of income, getting one's needs met, and residuals or dividends that come in periodically. That mental planet also describes the tenth house of public activity. Glen's rise to popularity was peaked by his own television show from 1960–71. He has written music that is lapped up by his fans, and has starred in many films. It is clear to see that Glen has a popular appeal. Such acclaim enables him to have his needs and wants taken care of quite easily. Royalties from records bring great abundance into his life. As with Sean Connery, the greatest gift in return is to identify with people on a gut level and give out information that will soothe and nurture.

The conjunction of these two planets did not bring such a happy response from the public in the case of Lord Alfred Douglas. His aspect fell in the fifth house of romance, in the sign of Libra. Mercury also ruled that house of gambles and love. Douglas was the homosexual partner in a notorious love affair with Oscar Wilde in the late 1800s. He was only twenty-one years old at the time. His difficult relationship with his father brought the affair to public attention when the father started legal action against Oscar Wilde. Wilde was convicted and imprisoned, and became a broken man. In this instance, the Moon can describe a feminine, sensitive quality that was expressed in romantic attachments. The lack of clear thinking in the expression of emotions brought less than good reward for that investment of his affections. In this instance, emotions took first place over rational thought and objectivity.

MERCURY IN HARD ASPECTS TO THE MOON

Reconciliation between feelings and intellect may be more difficult when Mercury and the Moon are in hard aspect. The vulnerability described by the Moon is in conflict with the powers of analysis, and objectivity described by Mercury. Therefore, nonproductive decisions may be made when the individual is emotionally upset and vulnerable. The individual may say things when he is emotional that he may later regret, or he may periodically be too upset to say what he really means. The lack of clarity connected to this aspect can be likened to trying to read a newspaper under water into which a pebble has been dropped; the swirling tide of feeling interferes with seeing what is correct in a given situation. Such vulnerability can quite easily be connected with early events in life that prevent development of a healthy adult ego state. Abandonment on some level may have altered the existence, tempering thought with overreaction and vulnerability.

Patricia McLaine has Mercury square the Moon in her chart, with Mercury in the first house of self-expression, and the Moon in the tenth house of public life and career. The tenth house also describes the relationship with the parent of the same sex. In Patricia's case, the relationship with her mother was stunted early in her life, preconditioning her outlook toward her future public life and career. Patricia developed an adult ego state early on, feeling safe if she could collect data and give information. A need for verbal expression started very early in her life, yet that very strong need was not encouraged by her family.

"I was a chatterbox as a child. I grew up with my grandfather and uncles in the house and nobody wanted me to talk. My grandfather would pay me a nickel if I would shut up. My first name was Gale, so they used to call me 'Windy.' They would say, 'A gale is a big wind and that's all you are. You're always talking too much.' I hated that, since it took away my dignity. I dropped the name Gale and used Patricia. I was not allowed to express my thoughts at all. If I even made a face, that was disobedience. My mother would wash my mouth out with soap. Once I stuck my tongue out at her behind her back. She didn't see me, but I felt so guilty I went to the bathroom and washed out my own mouth with soap. I began to withdraw and I became really resentful."

The Moon describes feelings of abandonment, and the Moon in the tenth house often describes a need to protect the parent of the same sex because the individual photographs that parent as having been abandoned. In Patricia's case, the abandonment of her mother by her father left her vulnerable, upset, and unable to express herself. Patricia continued, "My mother would do unreasonable things. I felt like I was older than she was because her actions implied she didn't know what she was doing. I developed some sort of protective feeling for her because of her separation from my father. But I didn't want to hear her complaints about him. During the war, she worked as a riveter, so I was boarded at orphanages during the week. There were some other children there whose parents worked, but there were also children with no families or who had been taken away from difficult homes by the county. Although the orphanage was not abusive, it was grim. I also went to some Catholic nursery schools. The nuns wore big caps and were stern. It was a forbidding place for a child, but I didn't protest. I simply turned inward and developed a fantasy life. After the war, my mother boarded me with my stepfather's relatives. They were cold and unloving. They would spank me with a strap. I learned early on that children were to be seen and not heard."

She described her first public activity. "I was afraid to lecture or speak in public, but I was asked to perform in church, so I became an actress. When I was seventeen, I wrote my first play and performed in it as well. I overacted and the critics said I had done an injustice to my own script by appearing in it. That took care of my ambitions as an actress. I just couldn't take criticism. I'm terribly vulnerable, especially if something concerns me personally. I learned to hide behind my mind. I then won a play-writing contest, when I was nineteen. I was able to sell that play independently of the church that sponsored the contest and it is still being performed in high schools throughout the country. My frustration is that I haven't been able to sell anything I've written since that time.

"As I grew older, I began to express myself in a better way. However, I was probably in my twenties or thirties before I really learned how to speak up for myself. I would think of things I wished I'd said. The positive thing about all that is that I did develop a vivid imagination and then picked a career that allowed me to speak my mind." Patricia, psychic since childhood, is involved with metaphysical work. She reads tarot cards for clients throughout the United States. Her famous and well-respected clients attest to the fact that information Patricia gives them is enlightened, informed, and valuable. Through lectures and workshops, in the United States and in Europe, she has discovered a platform that enables her to express wisdom on many levels. Current film scripts she's written are witty, clever, and filled with subtle information that can put a finger on solutions for the human condition. Patricia learned how to attune herself to the needs and wants of people around her, thereby healing her own sensitive nature.

Emotional frustrations seem to be a positive motivation in the lives of many successful people. Philosopher and mathematician Bertrand Russell had Mercury inconjunct the Moon in his natal chart. He received the Nobel Prize in Literature. He wrote as a defender of humanity and freedom of thought. He was prolific and outspoken on subjects that ranged from education to politics to philosophy to sex. The special quality of sensitivity seems to mitigate a cool but clear precision with words. The growth indicated by an inconjunct or quincunx may have impelled Bertrand Russell to express, through his writing and speaking, an especially strong identification with mankind's needs. French poet, dramatist, and novelist Alfred de Musset had Mercury in opposition to his Moon. Mercury ruled the fourth and fifth houses in his chart, indicating homelife, relationship with his mother, and feelings about romance, love, and creativity. The Moon was placed in the fourth house, with Mercury in the tenth house of career. That quality of sensitivity or emotionalism also connected with his sixth house of work. His best poems were in memory of the love he felt for George Sand. He expressed deep character understanding in spite of his upbringing in a totally intellectual environment.

Journalist Bill Moyers has won three Emmy awards for outstanding broadcasts. He published the Long Island newspaper *Newsday* for several years and then became editor-in-chief of "Bill Moyers' Journal." He was the author of "Listening to America" and "A Traveler Rediscovers His Country." Bill has the Moon square Mercury in his chart, with Mercury placed in the fifth house of creative expression, and the Moon in the second house of finance. Mercury rules the fifth house of creativity, and the eighth house of getting what one needs and wants from life. The Moon describes the sixth house of work. The quality of information available for Bill Moyers to give to his audience can be creative, clear, and precise, but obviously an additional level of feeling can relate to children in particular. In creative areas, Bill Moyers may have only scratched the surface of possibilities. Sensitivity to the needs of others and special awareness of his nurturing quality may continue to emerge in his life.

ASPECTS TO VENUS

VENUS IS THE PLANET THAT DESCRIBES BEAUTY OF ALL sorts. It can indicate everything from a desire for peace and harmony to comfort and ease of living. It indicates a need for pleasure, balance, and affection. Venus rules any activity that is connected with art, design, texture, feeling, touch, love, charm, graciousness, and beauty. It can describe law and diplomacy. The most dramatic characteristic is a demand for fair play. Venus is the harmonizer, the pacifist, the balance wheel.

The *placement* of Venus in a natal chart describes what the individual loves. It can indicate areas where he is relaxed, easy, and comfortable. The *aspects* to Venus indicate whether the person *actively* creates beauty and pleasurable comforts, or chooses the easy way out to avoid making waves. The active meaning of Venus is to create, the negative is to avoid. With a well-aspected Venus in the natal chart, an individual will express affection easily and be aware of a need for love; he can also assume a diplomatic quality. He wants to create harmony and balance. With many difficult, or hard, aspects to Venus, the individual may be adept at keeping the peace but at the price of his own pleasure and needs. He can be overly adaptive, overly diplomatic, overly pacifying. He may avoid anything that could disturb the status quo. He may be lazy.

Venus is one of the two so-called *benefics* in the chart. The other benefic is Jupiter. Wherever Venus and Jupiter are placed in the chart, basic good fortune exists. Jupiter describes an ability to create contagious enthusiasm, whereas Venus describes an ability to win through charm, graciousness, good manners, and good taste. A person with a strongly placed Venus in his chart is basically an easygoing individual. He enjoys society, social life, gracious living, good manners, and comfort. He can be pleasant in personality or quite beautiful to look at. Whether his beauty is physical or not, there is a quality of loveliness that is pleasing to the companion or observer. Venus can also describe talent. The individual may be especially artistic or talented in any areas where beauty is part of the end result. He may be an artist, a designer, an architect, or a diplomat. He may express himself through theater, with food, or in connection with beauty products. He may work with flowers, makeup, hair design, clothing, home furnishings, or simply know how to combine people and give good parties. Since harmony and balance are essential he may go into the legal field, become a diplomat, or be a social director. He can be a good negotiator and mediator.

Venus rules both Taurus and Libra. The earthy Venus of Taurus is sensual, pleasure-loving, and sometimes stubborn (to avoid being overly adaptive), whereas the Libran Venus is more airy, or intellectual in appreciation of art or balance. The scale of justice is the symbol of Libra and is an apt image for the Venusian person in general. He needs peace at any cost and will create the balance to achieve it. The highest level of service possible for the Venusian person is to be of service on a universal level, to create harmony for all. The penalty for "too much" Venus is a desire to experience only ease and comfort and to end up totally self-indulgent. That seems to manifest when Venus has many hard aspects in the natal chart. In most instances, that self-indulgence can be negative when the individual refuses to take care of himself properly. He can then be overly adaptive to create a harmony that is actually detrimental to his well-being.

When Venus is placed in the first house, the appearance is always pleasant to observe. The level of attractiveness can range from a pleasant countenance to great beauty. If the actual features are not perfect, the personality of the individual is so gracious and charming that he appears beautiful. Childhood is indicated by the first house. This placement of Venus describes a special quality of love and adoration from family and associates throughout childhood, especially if Venus is well aspected. He may have come into the world feeling that he must be the peacemaker, the balance wheel. His survival can sometimes depend on his being very nice, well behaved, and gentle. He may be overly adaptive and too ingratiating if Venus is not well aspected. Talents lie in artistic areas or in areas connected with beauty. He may be a good cook, an artist, designer, architect, or actor. He can lean toward the legal field or be

a professional "yes man." He may not know how to say no. Artistic
expression is necessary for a person with this placement of Venus.
Otherwise he can feel less than balanced. He may also require
companionship. Without a partner, he is one end of a seesaw up in
the air. He will find ways to surround himself with social life,
artistic projects, or beautiful objects. He cannot remain alone, out
of touch, or without pleasure for very long. He may need someone
to stir up trouble so that he can fulfill his role as the peacemaker.

When Venus rules or is placed in the second house of income, the
financial potential depends on his ability to create harmony, express artistry, or show diplomacy. He may love financial success, be
accumulative, or spend money on pleasure, beauty, and enjoyment.
If Venus is well aspected, he may have great good fortune and ease
in connection with financial matters. He can be especially adept
with income. He loves to make and spend money. He is neither
indulgent nor extravagant. He is rarely, if ever, tightfisted in financial matters. He wants what is fair and right for himself and for
others. He can easily earn money when he is connected with art or
artistic endeavors. Income potential can be especially fortunate
when he's dealing with painting, clothing, or beauty products. He
also gains income from activities connected to legalities and diplomatic pursuits. His pleasure comes with an ability to spend money
on cultural matters, or in creating pleasure with social events. He
may earn funds through theater, dance, art; any kind of design,
architecture, or landscaping; or in connection with color, fabrics, or
textures. He loves anything to do with his financial success. If
Venus is not well aspected, earning and spending money are areas
in which he is self-indulgent or lazy.

Third-house placement of Venus describes a sense of tact in connection with communications. This may indicate an especially diplomatic, gracious way of speaking or a beautiful speaking or singing
voice. Venus describes love and affection. The third house indicates
relationships with siblings, other relatives, and neighbors. With
Venus in this position, the individual's affection for siblings and
other relatives is strong. Graciousness and sociability endear him to
people who are pleasant and harmonious. He may have especially
artistic or lovely siblings or relatives and then continue to surround
himself with beautiful people. The third house also describes the
ability to learn. When Venus is well aspected, the individual derives

great pleasure from learning. With a weak or poorly aspected Venus, the person may have taken the easy way out with schools and learning or in connection with getting agreements. Since the third house also describes the way an individual negotiates or consummates contractual matters, with Venus in that position he can be especially gracious, charming, and fair in all areas of negotiation. If Venus is not well aspected, however, he may tend to give away too many points just to keep peace or feel loved by people around him. He may not know how to take care of himself in negotiations.

The third house may also indicate the way an individual feels about communicating with people in general. It can describe the ability to talk on the telephone, the way one drives a car, the kind of vehicle that the individual prefers. With a well-aspected Venus, the person will love all manner of communications, enjoy driving, and want a beautiful automobile. His need for pleasure will direct him to find beauty in scenery, in associations around him, in neighborhood atmosphere. Unless he has a very badly aspected Venus, a need for harmony in all areas of communications is essential. He cannot deal with arguments or strife. He may be an artist, but in any case, he will express himself with taste in any situation.

The fourth house in a chart describes the relationship with and the characteristics of the parent of the opposite sex. When Venus rules this house, that parent is loving, gracious, artistic, diplomatic, and affectionate. The love between the person and that parent is pronounced, and their relationship is one of special caring. If Venus is not well aspected, the relationship can be less than truly loving. An overly polite attitude is characteristic. The parent may have been artistic in nature but lazy in execution. The individual may feel that the parent let him down by not being stronger in his defense at some time. He may have photographed that parent as being too diplomatic, overly sociable, and not strong in character; the parent's weakness of will or an overly indulgent personality may be apparent.

The fourth house also indicates the conditions in the latter part of life. When Venus describes this house, the conditions become more harmonious, easy, and pleasurable as the individual grows older. He may allow himself more enjoyment in the third portion of his life. He may begin to express an artistic talent or ability that has lain dormant. He may begin to take on the characteristics of the parent of the opposite sex at that point. His need for beauty in home life and in his environment can become even more pronounced. He can relinquish ambition, drive, and resourcefulness in career areas for graciousness in connection with home, property, and lifestyle. If Venus is not well aspected, just the opposite can be true. He may grow lazy, not care about order and tidiness, and adopt a careless way of living. His photographs of the parent of the opposite sex have a profound effect on his choice of environment at that point in his life.

When Venus rules or is placed in the fifth house of creativity, artistic talent is very obvious. The fifth house describes the gambles in life, whether those gambles are with love, children, creative expression, or investments. When Venus is well aspected, one's children are especially talented, beautiful, charming, and loving. One can give especially beautiful parties, including people of all walks of life who will enjoy the companionship and special ambience of the moment. One may be talented in music or art, or simply enjoy special situations connecting him to artistic pleasures. He can easily cultivate, for entertainment purposes, people associated with the arts. He may be an indulgent parent, bestowing great affection on his children. His children will be gentle, artistic, sociable. If Venus is not well aspected, one may be lazy in connection with children, entertainment, and the expression of one's talent. He can be overly indulgent with his offspring. In turn, his children tend to be indulgent, easily adaptive, and nonenergetic. His romantic life may be pleasurable, easy, loving, and affectionate, or he may simply want quiet companionship. He may indulge one he loves, or attract, in love objects, a person who simply wants to be indulged. He may take the easy way out in areas of expression of his love nature.

When Venus rules or is posited in the sixth house of work, the individual must love his work or he will be terribly unhappy with his life. His health will suffer if he is forced into areas that are less than harmonious, artistic, and pleasurable. If Venus is well aspected in his life, he will make sure that he finds work connected with art, theater, or social causes. He can be the balance wheel in connection with co-workers or be involved in creating pleasure through upgrading social conditions or with creating momentary beauty. All areas of artistic work will appeal to an individual with Venus in the sixth house, but in particular, work with food is a strong attraction. The sociability connected with creating beautiful dishes and the proper ambience for enjoyment of food doubly ensures the interest and pleasure of one with this placement of Venus. The range of activities connected with foodstuffs can include cooking food, growing food, gourmet food shopping or importing foodstuffs, owning or working in restaurants, or being involved in the commodities market. Naturally, other artistic pursuits are equally pleasurable. Fabrics, designing clothes, designing furnishings, painting, sculpturing, and any work with theater fall under the category of art.

Since the sixth house also describes health, and sugar is a Venus-ruled food, it is important for one with this placement to be careful and aware of the effect on the body of the intake of sugar. If Venus is not well aspected in the chart, the probability of an allergy to sugar or a tendency to hypoglycemia is more than likely. Diabetes can also be indicated by some aspects to Venus in or ruling the sixth house. Venus also rules the pancreas. For instance, Venus in hard aspect to Jupiter, ruling the kidneys, can indicate sluggish kidneys especially in connection with intake of sugar. There are other parts of the body that are affected when Venus is not well aspected, but the prime consideration is the tendency to be self-indulgent with food intake. That may mean eating the wrong foods, being gluttonous, indulging in rich foods the body has a hard time digesting, or simply being lazy about care of the energy of the body.

When Venus rules the seventh house or is placed in that house, the partnership situation can be extremely loving and pleasurable. The individual would be attracted to another person who is artistic, diplomatic, gracious, charming, handsome or beautiful, gentle, and easygoing. If Venus is not well aspected, however, there is a likelihood of being attracted to someone who is lazy, overly adaptable, too easygoing, patronizing, or weak. The survival of the mate or partner may have to do with being nice or overly polite, or hesitating to make waves. The person with Venus connected to the seventh house is primarily attracted to companionship that is easy, gentle, and affectionate. He could never marry except for love. With a badly aspected Venus in his chart, he may have to examine his particular conception of the meaning of love. Happiness, contentment, and pleasure are associated with his idea of partnership. However, he must be sure that the object of his fascination has the same desires in partnership areas. He may also be attracted to great beauty, only to discover that beauty to be skin-deep. With a well-aspected Venus in the natal chart, the individual can be fortunate to attract a mate with whom he can express special and deep love in partnership areas.

The seventh house also describes business partners. It is especially important to know what to look for in business relationships when love is obviously not an issue. The individual with a seventh-house Venus may need someone else to act as the negotiator, diplomat, charmer, or social contact. If a person with many hard aspects to Venus looks for a partner who is a hard worker and finds that he has attracted someone especially easygoing, for instance, the business relationship will certainly suffer. It can be very important to attract a strong balance in a business situation or at least be aware of what the potential partnership might be. When Venus is well aspected, the relationship will always be pleasant, affectionate, polite, and with a great deal of fairness inherent in the situation. The individual may also attract a business partner who can share and be involved in artistic pursuits.

In psychological terms, the eighth house indicates how an individual gets his needs met. The basis for the specific manner of attracting "things" from others depends on the conditioning of childhood. In the case of an individual with Venus ruling the eighth house, the cheerful disposition, charm, and polite qualities can entice and endear him to people who are quite happy to give him things. He would quickly learn that happy smiles and a pleasant manner would enable him to get his needs and wants met quite easily; he then pursues that manner of niceness throughout his life. If Venus is well aspected, this person can be quite fortunate in attracting nice people and situations. He can feel easy about asking for what he needs and wants and in turn send out an abundance of love, graciousness, sociability, and good will to the people around him. The flow of "goodies" is easy. However, if Venus is not well aspected, he may not expect to get what he needs, and behave in an overly adaptive, overly charming manner that might even border on obsequiousness. A basic lack of self-esteem may tempt him to give away too many "points" or too much of his essence for what he receives in return. There is a lack of fairness in what he gives and gets. Aspects to Venus indicate precisely why he might be overly charming or humble in this instance.

When Venus is placed in or is ruling the ninth house, the desire for pleasure can be connected to travel, situations connected to other countries, or expansion of the higher mind. The individual may be most relaxed and happy in connection with higher education, promotional efforts, advertising, or travel. He can be particularly adept with legal matters or in areas of diplomacy. Since Venus describes moderation as well as pleasure, balance as well as graciousness, an ideal outlet is in fields in which those qualities can be utilized most effectively. The Venus qualities lead a person quite naturally to choose peace, tranquillity, and fair play. He will utilize those qualities on whatever level is appropriate to individual development. For instance, the highest form of that sense of fair play is to create social justice for people in all countries. Therefore international law, diplomacy, or dealings with art can bring about widespread balance. The activities can include owning an art gallery, promoting international projects that will introduce artistic or diplomatic ties, being involved in the United Nations, or importing beautiful products. But he may choose to distribute beauty products on a local level or create advertising campaigns for anything that brings pleasure or harmony. The possibilities are endless when Venus is well aspected in this position in the chart. The underlying activity is to send out the quality of mercy and love to as many people as possible, no matter what the obvious method might be. If Venus is not well aspected, the likelihood exists that pure self-indulgence or personal pleasure is more important than the higher Venusian outlets. The individual may love the idea of travel and expansion artistically, yet be too lazy to set plans in motion. It is through the ninth-house activities that the greatest love and enjoyment can come in life, however. Universal goodwill and love bring a boomerang result.

The tenth house in the natal chart describes career choices, social predisposition, and public life. It also describes the relationship with the parent of the same sex. Much of the programming and social consciousness are due to the photographs of that parent. When Venus is ruling or posited in this house, the relationship with that parent was one of great affection and love. The parent may have been beautiful or handsome, and certainly gracious, charming, sociable, and affectionate. With a well-aspected Venus, the programming from that parent for social consciousness and an ability to be at ease in all social circumstances can be especially strong. The individual will ensure that he includes pleasurable activities and social life in connection with his career. He will find a way to enjoy theater, art, and music in combination with public duties. His choice of career activity may range from involvement with beauty products, design, art, theater, music, fashion, film, or any activity that is connected with bringing or expressing great pleasure. He is loved by his public and is most gracious, easy, and sociable when he is in public areas. Even if he is not so easygoing when behind the scenes, his graciousness emerges in full view of his public. If Venus is not well aspected in the chart, he may not want to make waves. He may be quite overly indulgent in public areas, in social life, and in connection with the parent of the same sex. He may also see that parent as having taken the easy way out in life. He may not have respect for the adaptability of that parent. He may have to examine the relationship very carefully to be sure that he doesn't unconsciously follow in his or her footsteps, repeating what he doesn't admire and respect in that parent.

The eleventh house describes activities with friends, associates, and organizations. When Venus is situated in this house or describes the activities therein, the individual loves his friends. He attracts associates and companions who are gracious people, artistic, loving, and affectionate. He enjoys his connection with theatrical organizations and may be surrounded by activities connected with dance, the art world, or those in which pleasurable associations are paramount. He is relaxed and easy with companions. He wants association with people to be free of pressures or problems. He is charming and gracious when in the company of friends.

If Venus is not well aspected, he may find that he attracts people who are lazy, nonproductive, and overly indulgent. He may waste time and energy with groups when it is less than profitable or truly pleasurable for him. He may be too adaptive with people in general, unwilling to say no. At times he may be less than diplomatic in situations in which too many people are involved. He may not be able to handle diverse energies from many people without feeling pulled from one person or situation to another. He may have a hard time finding the balance or deciding what is fair and correct. In general, involvement with groups, organizations, or too many friends may destroy the peace and harmony he needs to find.

When Venus is in the twelfth house or rules that sector of the chart, the individual may find solace only when he is alone. He may want an inner harmony that comes only in a meditative state. Love and expression of affection may be strong on a subconscious level but not easily expressed overtly or verbally. If artistic projects are part of the life of the individual, it is easy to remain out of sight, alone, creating beauty. He may be especially sociable and loving when he is away from the pressures of everyday life or in places where he can enjoy serenity and beauty. The concept of an oriental garden, full of statuary, beautiful songbirds, and tranquillity, may be in line with his inner sense of peace. If Venus is well aspected in his natal chart, the individual finds those moments of repose quite easily. He gives himself the gift of quiet, peaceful moments in his life, no matter what pressing obligations or responsibilities may be facing him. He understands his inner need for a balance that comes from time spent only with himself. He rejoices in his ability to return to a state of pleasure when he is away from external pressures.

If Venus is not well aspected in the individual chart, the person may not allow himself the quiet times he might crave. He might be lazy about healthy introspection or consider it self-indulgent to want peace and quiet. He may avoid the graceful, creative message of his own subconscious mind. He may tend toward unhealthy inactivity when he finds moments alone. He might not allow himself the true pleasures and joys that he may desperately, but secretly, want.

VENUS CONJUNCT SUN

When the planet of graciousness, charm, and good manners is conjunct the Sun in a natal chart, the inner vitality and ego characteristics described by the sign placement of the Sun take on the additional qualities of diplomacy and grace. Venus conjunct the Sun seems to describe quite perfectly the loving, gentle, and sociable people of the world. Venusian tact and beauty can soften and even modify the strongest character traits associated with other Sun signs.

In all consideration of aspects, it is not enough to simply describe the qualities of a particular aspect, for the overall chart must be considered. But, in particular, Venus aspects can be modified tremendously by other qualities described in the chart. For instance, Venus conjunct the Sun might easily describe someone who is especially artistic, yet few artists have this aspect in their natal chart. A possible explanation might be that Venus can also describe a sense of ease or satisfaction which may modify talent, ambition, or self-expression. Yet if Venus conjunct the Sun is supported by other aspects in the natal chart, it may describe a very dynamic quality of graciousness. The ways in which an individual uses his charm, artistry, and diplomacy can be quite varied.

The pairs of opposite qualities possible in this combination of Venus and Sun seem unlimited. In one person, the softness and gentleness is apparent, while in another, total self-indulgence may be the manifestation. Since Venus rules the natural seventh house of partnership in the astrological chart, it is clear that Venus, like water, finds its own level. Venus adjusts to the circumstances of other people and reacts to environment. This constant shifting to find balance is characteristic of the Venus-Sun combination. This aspect might truly reflect the rest of the natal chart. If the chart is basically strong, dynamic, and active, Venus acts on the Sun as a bright but soft light. If the chart is basically one of passivity, the conjunction augments and confirms the inherent laziness or passivity of the individual.

Marie Antoinette had Venus conjunct her Scorpio Sun. The aspect fell in her fifth house of entertainment, romance, talent, and children. Venus rules that same house, while the Sun rules her third house of communications. Marie Antoinette was despised by her French subjects because of her seeming lack of concern for the welfare of the people. She was accused of careless behavior, extravagance, and a totally self-centered approach to her personal pleasures. It is obvious that she adored her children, however. She was also quite adept in social situations and loved her little theater. In other circumstances, Marie might have become a proficient actress and could have expressed her artistic talent in a positive way. Entertaining at lavish parties, gambling (a fifth-house activity), and enjoying her group of special friends while pursuing her special interests was her way of seeking her own level. Joining Marie in all this, her husband, Louis XVI, was equally interested in living the good life.

In contrast to Marie Antoinette is Joan Sutherland, also with Venus conjunct her Scorpio Sun. Joan Sutherland's conjunction is placed in the seventh house of partnership, ruling her sixth house of work, and her first house of personality. Venus ruling the work sector of the chart indicates involvement with the arts, and with a tie in to the partnership sector describes the working relationship Joan has with her conductor husband, Richard Bonynge. He was her coach and was responsible for encouraging her to develop the thrilling upper register of her voice, which is almost inhuman in its perfection. Venus ruling the sixth house of work, might describe an easygoing attitude toward discipline. This is not so in Joan's case. Hard work is the given in her chosen profession. She is reputed to have health problems, yet her courage and determination keep her in the light of stardom in the most difficult profession imaginable. Strength is the positive manifestation indicated by the Venus-Sun conjunction in her chart. It is obvious that Venus describes not only her great talent, but the love she has for her work.

Diane Keaton, Joanne Woodward, Gina Lollobrigida, and Anita Ekberg all have Venus conjunct the Sun in their natal charts. Diane Keaton, with the Sun and Venus in Capricorn, has the conjunction placed in the second house of income, ruling partnership, career, or public activity, and the twelfth house of the subconscious. Diane won tremendous stardom and public acclaim in her work with Woody Allen. She is talented, almost shy, and the epitome of Venusian characteristics. She is nice, diplomatic, easygoing, and is adored by her fans. She was able to carve a niche in the film world without being temperamental, egotistic, or combative.

Joanne Woodward is another especially talented nontemperamental actress. Venus is conjunct her Pisces Sun in the fourth house of home, ruling the seventh house of partnership, and the eleventh house of friends. The Sun rules the ninth house of publicity, promotional efforts, and recognition or acclaim. Joanne is fortunate to have a marriage of long duration in a profession in which that is almost an impossibility. Paul Newman is aptly described by the Venus-Sun combination in her chart. He is also a gracious, nice, talented, charming actor. Love and pride in their homelife is obvious in their marriage. Joanne is admired and respected by her peers, friends, and public. The Venus-Sun conjunction in her chart brings a graciousness to her quality of being, as well as shoring up the inner strength.

Gina Lollobrigida has Venus conjunct her Cancer Sun. She also has Pluto conjunct Venus and the Sun, which modifies the Venusian aspects in her chart tremendously. In this case, if her basic motivation is for the good of all, the quality of love is especially powerful in her chart. Her talent, graciousness, and gentle power could transform everyone around her. If the motivation in her life is for personal pleasure, personal power, and lavish expression of luxury, she might push away the very love possible in her life. Anita Ekberg has Venus conjunct her Libra Sun, augmenting an already Venusian quality in her persona. Ekberg was known less for her talent than for her abundant curves and gorgeous figure. The talent may have required more direction than she was capable of finding. It is possible in her case that beauty of form strongly limited full artistic expression. She may have taken the easy way out.

Joan of Arc had Venus conjunct her Capricorn Sun. She was indeed the epitome of a loving human being, sacrificing her own life to bring into focus what was fair and right for all. Raphael had Venus conjunct his Aries Sun. The conjunction fell in the fifth house of creativity, in his chart and ruled the ninth house of recognition, the sixth house of work, and the seventh house of partnership. Raphael's art is truly indicative of Venusian qualities. The technical expression of beauty and grace, of color and form, add up to gentle but persuasively glorious work. Singer Anthony Newley has Venus conjunct his Libra Sun. Kris Kristofferson has Venus conjunct his Cancer Sun. Ryan O'Neal has Venus conjunct his Taurus Sun. Robert Wagner has Venus conjunct his Aquarius Sun. Each man has a particular quality of charm and talent that not only brings great success but adoration from women in particular. Their predilection for romance and affairs of the heart may go hand in hand with their special brand of graciousness and charm. The combination is unbeatable in each instance. Billy Graham has Venus conjunct his Scorpio Sun. His manner of gentleness combined with the dynamic Scorpio quality of intensity and power bring him in touch with the great leaders of the world. Diplomacy as well as deep religious conviction are a powerful combination in his life. He uses gentle but honest persuasion to convince people worldwide to tap their inner spiritual potential.

VENUS IN HARD ASPECT TO THE SUN

The paths of Venus and the Sun in the heavens are never far enough apart to produce more than a semisquare, hard aspect. That very dynamic may say something about the nature of love; it simply cannot oppose or square the ego, the basic nature. Love's purpose and essence is to harmonize, not polarize. If Venus and the Sun are in conjunction, it is natural for the individual to express some form of love and harmony. If there is no aspect between the two planets, it is possible that the development of those qualities is limited and the link broken in some manner. The connection can be forged by careful thought and action. If, however, a semisquare exists in the chart, the friction of ego and harmony cannot be ignored. It is a constant reminder that love and diplomacy must be developed in spite of lack of early affection or recognition of a loving nature. In this case, the individual, in seeking his own level, was never given the permission to be diplomatic, easygoing, gracious, charming, and artistic. The going can be rough if the individual looks to the world for recognition of his artistry. He may never be given credit for the love he feels or the affection he craves. He may not allow himself to live the gracious life. He may have to learn social conduct, polite manners, and expression of talent the hard way. He may desperately crave an easier existence without knowing how to find it. His sense of self-worth may seem dependent on a certain quality of charm that can disappear when his ego is damaged. He may have to learn how to love himself first. He can then begin to balance an overadaptability that is connected with a desire for ego strokes. He may have to swallow his pride in connection with affairs of the heart, loving exchange between people, and expression of talent. He may first have to give himself permission and then find the confirmation in external events.

When Venus is in semisquare to the Sun, it may be difficult for the individual to show affection or be demonstrative. The love nature is strong, yet expression of that love or expression of an artistic ability may be especially difficult. An appreciation of beauty is obvious, as well as a desire to live well, yet the reality of attaining a leisurely life may not be in line with the individual's sense of self-worth. He may not be physically lazy, but can be basically lacking in enough confidence to actively pursue talent, artistry, love, or ease of living. If he attains some of his goals in those areas, he may indeed sustain a blow to his pride along the way.

Gustav, an energetic, vibrant man, has Venus semisquare his Sun in the sign of Pisces. Venus is posited in the ninth house of recognition, travel, importing and exporting, and distribution. Gus and his wife began importing furniture and art objects from China when that became possible, in the 1970s. After a successful sale of their business, they moved to an area that would allow more ease of living and comfort. Gus began to take great pleasure in planting a beautiful garden on their hilly estate. He then undertook to build small structures, one resembling an oriental resting spot. He remarked that his creations were merely ego needs. "I must prove that I can do what other people can do . . . maybe not as well, but that I can do it." The Sun in his chart is placed in the tenth house of recognition. That house describes the relationship Gus had with his father. His observations about his father's artistic potential were confirmation that an ego identification with that parent was strong in Gus's life. "In one way my father was a creative man, but he didn't have the time to do just what he wanted to do." His father evidently had never given permission to his son to express a latent artistic talent either verbally or by example.

Venus rules the fifth house in his chart. The quality of the relationship Gus had with his father was identical to the relationship with his children. "I knew my father loved me, but he didn't let it show. I'm a little bit better than my father in that way. I try to express my love by doing things for them. I don't think I have ever said, 'I love you,' to my children since they were perhaps nine years old. I think they would be very surprised if I ever said that to them." The discussion became more philosophical. "As long as my father was alive, I didn't really recognize special things about him. I did not give to my father the very things that I would like to have from my children. Sometimes it is painful if you do things for your children and they don't respond very much. But the very moment it is painful, I also realize that children are not obliged to thank their parents. They didn't ask to be born. I do not expect anything in return from them, but sometimes it would be nice."

When the Sun is in difficult aspect to another planet, the sensitivity or lack of ego may demand permission to act from some outer situation or person; an inner quality of recognition is lacking. The person is simply unable to operate out of a sense of "I'm doing this or behaving such a way because it is what *I* want to do and how *I'm* feeling." The individual is likely to measure himself by the recognition he receives from the outer world. Eventually he learns to measure himself by an inner yardstick, of self-worth.

VENUS CONJUNCT MOON

The Moon describes the specific emotional reactions or overreactions in life. When the Moon and Venus are interacting in the chart, the feelings of love are especially sensitive. Artistic sense is heightened, and qualities of diplomacy are emotionally charged. With such pronounced sensitivity, overreactions are quite possible, especially when a situation is not fair, balanced, or harmonious. The individual may be less than his most charming self when he is hurt. The positive qualities of this aspect give a profound sense of identification with people. Love, social situations, and expression of talent become emotional necessities.

With this Moon-Venus hookup, vulnerability becomes more pronounced when the heart becomes involved. There is a fear of abandonment connected to matters of affection, whether that applies to friendships, family, or romantic love. The individual is especially vulnerable about his artistic expression. He is quite upset by any situation in which there is a lack of fair play, and can be overly concerned if he can't please everyone in a specific situation. He may take things too personally when his heart is activated.

In most instances, childhood brought a feeling of abandonment and a noticeable lack of affection, hugging, stroking. The touch becomes especially sensitive and the need for touch quite profound. In some instances a strong mothering, nurturing quality emerges that is beyond objective necessity. It becomes a way of assuring love in return on a very subconscious level. At times the individual may be hurt when he feels he gives affection but does not receive the same measure in return. When this aspect is turned to positive expression, the individual touches the hearts of humanity through his artistry, sense of fair play, and love nature.

Singer Jenny Lind had this aspect in her chart. Her voice was so beautiful that she was compared to a nightingale. Jenny had Taurus on the ascendant with the Moon giving an additional color to her personality. The conjunction was placed in her sixth house of work, and ruled her fifth house of creativity, and the fourth house of home, father, and later life. Jenny may have felt abandoned by her father, whom she must have loved deeply. In her case, she transmuted her emotional sensitivity outwardly in singing. The emotional reaction from her public was adoration. The beauty she sent forth through her music swept back to her in gigantic waves. Her public recognition knew no bounds. She had international fame.

Phil Donohue also has this aspect in his chart. Phil climbed to the top of a terribly competitive field with his morning television show. He finds controversial subjects and then interviews his guests with piercing questions to expose the truth of a situation. The overall tone of his show is compassion, however, and a real desire to find what is fair and right in a situation. He has a controlled but passionate ability to bring out the best in the guests on his show. The conjunction of Venus and the Moon lies in the eighth house of transformation, in his chart. He obviously gets what he wants in all ways through his sensitive combination of emotion and charm. His overall gift to humanity is to express nurturing concern for the welfare of people and to reveal the truth.

The Moon rules the fifth house of creativity and children, in his chart, whereas Venus rules the third house of communications. One of the most beautifully touching segments on his show was an interview with Dr. Gerald Jampolsky, of Washington, D.C., who works with children who have cancer. Part of his treatment is to teach and encourage the children to use art to express their pain and frustration. They learn to draw a picture of their demon and thereby relate to the cancer directly. Phil's compassion was evident throughout the show. It was a moving experience to hear the dialogue between Donohue, the children (who were also present), and their doctor. Phil Donohue exhibited a very special example of the Moon-Venus quality of nurturing when he went through a court battle to win custody of his own children at the time of his divorce. He set an important precedent for other men who feel strongly about the upbringing of their offspring.

Eddie Cantor also had this aspect. He was a sensitive, loving man adored by his fans. Tom Jones has Venus conjunct the Moon in his chart, as do Desi Arnaz, Jr., and actor Robert Duvall. Composers Jules Massenet and Igor Stravinsky had the same aspect, and effectively expressed that passionate, beautiful quality in their music.

Since the Moon describes such a deeply personal quality, it is not always easy to spot this in behavior. The outer manifestation can come in many ways. One overt characteristic may be a sweet tooth. It is possible that when the individual is upset, he craves something sweet to alleviate that hurt and empty feeling. Yet he may have an emotional reaction to sugar and sweets, even an allergic reaction, since the Moon rules the stomach and Venus describes the pancreas and kidneys. The psychological reasoning behind such vulnerability in love varies from individual to individual.

Muhammad Ali has this aspect in his chart. It comes as a surprise to realize that the pugilist poet is really very vulnerable. His Leo-rising mask effectively shows the drama but hides the sensitivity. However, with Venus conjunct the Moon on the cusp of the seventh house, ruling the third house of communications, and the tenth house of career, the poems he writes can help express his real feelings. He was particularly adamant about major conflicts and refused to fight in Vietnam, for instance. It is also obvious that he has a love for children. Perhaps Muhammad Ali can make a new career of writing his poems to express his concern about fair play for all.

VENUS IN HARD ASPECT TO THE MOON

Herman Leonard is a very successful photographer. At one time, he worked from his own studios in New York and in Paris. A high point in his career came when Herman accompanied Marlon Brando on a working trip throughout Java. Herman's artistic expression found a variety of outlets, but one of his special loves was to photograph jazz musicians at work. He has one of the most extensive collections of the greatest in that field in existence. He possesses a pictorial record of a special time in musical history.

Herman was quite expressive in discussing the Venus square Moon aspect in his chart. The Moon is placed in the eighth house of transformation, whereas Venus lies hidden in the twelfth house of the subconscious mind. Venus rules the third house of communications and the fourth house of home. The fourth house also describes the relationship with his mother. The Moon rules the sixth house of work. Obviously the vulnerability in his makeup concerns getting his needs met in connection with work projects. The contribution he makes to the artistic world can be especially nurturing and sensitive, yet the obvious conflict between artistic expression and feelings can be strong.

Herman commented, "Sometimes I got the emotional response from my clients for my best work, but often I did not. I was never sure of the reason. I reacted by thinking that perhaps my work wasn't as good as I thought it was. I took it personally. That was part of my vulnerability. Perhaps that concern about being good enough has been the overall problem in my life, whether that is in connection with photography or love. I have not been able to be objective. I have been terribly hurt in love. I am easily hurt. I can remember being about five or six years old in summer camp and meeting a little girl. She went off with the other guy and didn't pay any attention to me. My heart was bleeding. A rejection like that could kill me."

Since Venus rules the fourth house of home, Herman shed some light on his desires as far as home life is concerned. He said, "I'm not comfortable unless I have beauty around me in my surroundings. I need harmony. I'm overly sensitive to my surroundings, so my life is directed by a never-ending effort to make my environment comfortable and beautiful. My studio in Paris was pretty, pleasant, and clean. It was probably the nicest photographer's studio in Paris. I had to constantly devote myself to maintaining it, but I needed that beauty and comfort for my work. I am still constantly involved in improving and fixing and putting things away. It never ends. I am never totally satisfied. I have never finished a house or quarters just the way I want it. But now I don't get frustrated about it. I could get quite upset if I let myself."

Venus describes Herman's feelings about his mother. He continued, "My relationship with my mother was excellent. We were very close. I admired and respected her. She was very cultured, a very warm person and very family oriented. Although she was simple and unpretentious, she was very gracious and charming. I think I inherited some of those qualities. However, the easygoing traits can get me into trouble sometimes. My mother wasn't overly mothering.

She wasn't totally open. She probably protected her own emotional feelings. She was very humanitarian, considerate, and understanding. When I was sick, for instance, she took care of me very well and was very warm, but I don't remember a lot of touching. I do recall one instance where my mother hugged me very tightly. It stuck in my memory because it was not a common experience. I remember feeling the softness of her body and being slightly embarrassed about it. I had been physically hurt when I was four or five but I was really alright. She was so relieved she squeezed me. It took me back a bit."

Since Venus describes fair play or give and take, Herman might be especially sensitive about negotiations, or it might be difficult for him to ask for his needs to be met without being vulnerable and upset about it. He volunteered, "It is very important to me to be very fair. My mother was the same way. It was always difficult for me to ask for things, because I was very vulnerable, *extremely* vulnerable. Now I have learned how to get my needs met. I avoid asking people to do things if I don't have to, however. If I ask someone to do something and it is not done the way I want it done, I get upset—first with them, then with me for having asked in the first place and for having made a bad judgment. I'd rather do it myself and have it done right. If someone does something for me and it is done well, I am extremely grateful. I overpraise and overpay. I want things to be harmonious and fair with work."

There is a general feeling of abandonment connected with love when this aspect is evident in an individual chart. The person may fear letting love into his life to avoid the possibility of hurt. He may not have had enough hugging and touching in his early life to make him feel secure about love. He may tend to be overly adaptive, overly nice for fear of losing love. He may feel that if only he were nicer or more handsome (or she more beautiful), love would be strong and secure.

Amy has the same placement in her chart, with Venus describing her relationship with her father, rather than with her mother. She confirmed that she also must have the right environment for her best work. She said, "I am overly emotional and sensitive about my homelife. My environment is very important to my sense of well-being. I am so sensitive to color and decor. I like to have fresh flowers around me. I need nice aromas, because I am very sensitive to smells. I will buy scents, perfume, and flowers or things to make my home beautiful before almost anything else. I abhor seeing newspapers strewn around the house, for instance, and cannot relax unless order is restored. I can be more relaxed by keeping my home in beautiful condition, but then I don't want to change anything. I agonize over the possibility of a move or loss of a home. I become very emotional, because one of my earliest memories was of having to move from a home I loved. I think I blamed my father for being such a gentleman and not fighting for better conditions in my early life. I saw my mother abandoned and almost anticipate that in any romantic situation of my own. I tend to be attracted to men who are charming and easygoing but overly adaptive or lacking in ambition. I can then be quite upset and insecure in the relationship. I feel that I will have to take charge then. I do worry about losing love or friends. I become overly upset if interaction with people is not absolutely fair and right. If someone I care about is upset about something I've done or have not done, I become very vulnerable and will give them whatever they want. It is quite often at my own expense, however. I take care of others instead of myself. I suspect it is to ensure their continuing respect and love. I'm learning not to be so dependent on anyone's feelings about me now. Although I'm very independent in some ways, I care about being loved more than almost anything else. Sometimes I'd rather not be in love, because it is always so painful. I become too emotional and vulnerable. I know that, in a relationship, one person always seems to love a bit more than the other one. I would much prefer to be loved more than I love. I probably protect my feelings that way. When it is the other way around I'm no good to anyone. That love must be returned in full or I am devastated. I watched my mother be so badly hurt in her marriage, I am sure I decided I could never stand that. But indeed, I followed her pattern exactly. I hope I have learned not to be so sensitive in the wrong way. Some objectivity is very important in long-term relationships."

VENUS CONJUNCT MERCURY

This aspect in a natal chart can indicate an especially lovely, warm singing or speaking voice. Harmony in connection with communications can be very important to the individual with this aspect in his chart. The person may not only possess a mellifluous vocal quality, but the manner in which he communicates will be especially gracious and polite. This particular ability to speak beautifully can be essential in careers such as politics, theater, and music. Mercury also describes the thought processes. With this aspect in evidence, upsetting conditions can be very disturbing mentally. The person requires harmonious interchange with other people in order to be mentally well balanced. When external events are disturbing, he may be able to act as a mediator, balance wheel, and negotiator. If other aspects in the natal chart modify Venus to the point of over-adaptability, the individual may not find it easy to express himself with total clarity and precision of thought. He may be compelled to be very diplomatic, sometimes with an inability to get his ideas across.

Julio Iglesias was born with Venus conjunct Mercury in his chart. After tremendous success in his native Spain and throughout Europe, Julio was "discovered" by America. Although his international reputation assures his place in the music world, Julio has chosen to work in the United States. After years of climbing to the top of the musical ladder, Julio is able to enjoy the harmony he desires in his life. Jerry Brown, California's dashing young governor, was also born with Venus conjunct Mercury. The golden tongue that is associated with this aspect is indeed in demand in the politi-cal world. Venus and Mercury lie at the top of his chart, indicating the ability to express himself fluidly through ideas and words. Mercury rules the third house of communications, giving Jerry great diplomatic qualities in negotiations or in presentation of ideas and in discussions. Venus rules the fourth house of home, and the eleventh house of associations. Friends and associates lend ready support to Jerry in order to further his plans and activities.

Actor Paul Newman was born with Venus conjunct Mercury. The soft quality of Newman's voice lends an interesting contrast to the rough-and-ready roles he plays in films. The aspect is posited in the first house of personality, and rules the ninth house of publicity, promotional efforts, and recognition. Mercury rules his fifth house of creativity, and the sixth house of work. The aspect also describes the fourth house of home and the relationship with family, especially his mother. As Paul Newman grows older, the intellectual qualities and diplomatic trends can take him far afield from acting.

A need for mental stimulation is apparent in his chart, but in particular in connection with creative work. The potential for international activity of a peacemaking nature is strongly indicated with the strength of Venus conjunct Mercury in his chart. Ideas concerning balance on an international level are important in the life of someone with this aspect. Concern for the welfare of people everywhere can lead to peace missions. Travel to express ideas about social welfare may be expressed on a wide scale, becoming especially important later in his life.

Since Mercury and Venus travel in close orbit to each other in the heavens, many people are born with this aspect in their charts. Primarily, the combination leads to expression in music, composition, the art world, theater, and politics. Frédéric Chopin had this aspect in his natal chart, as did Johann Sebastian Bach and Richard Strauss. Singers Elvis Presley, Liza Minnelli, Tom Jones, Bob Dylan, Nelson Eddy, and Desi Arnaz, Sr., have this velvet quality indicated by Venus conjunct Mercury.

VENUS IN HARD ASPECT TO MERCURY

Venus is never far enough away from Mercury to be in square aspect, but as with Venus and the Sun, angles of forty-five degrees can exist, creating some less than harmonious activity. Venus in difficult aspect to any planet can describe an inability to be dynamically harmonious and balanced. It basically describes a tendency to take the easy way out, opt for peace at any price, and be overly nice, overly indulgent, and overly gracious. When Venus is not in harmonious aspect to Mercury, the quality of clear, precise expression of ideas, thoughts, and plans can be modified somewhat. The person may not be able to simply say what he thinks. He may resist the expression of ideas verbally until things are really out of balance. He may then say what is on his mind in less than a diplomatic manner. He may find it hard to concentrate unless everything is totally harmonious and easy around him. He may think and speak in less than totally gracious ways.

Guy Lombardo was very successful in the musical world, but love was a different matter. He was married many times. Lack of harmony in his life may have played games with his mental ease. Certainly multiple marriages played havoc with his financial life.

He may have been less than charming with women he loved, causing distress for himself and for the people around him. He had a reputation for less than diplomatic relations with the musicians who worked for him. Lombardo may not have had the quality of leisure in his life that success is hoped to bring.

ASPECTS TO MARS

MARS IS THE PLANET OF ACTION. IT REPRESENTS PHYSI-cal activity, drive, determination, ambition, and resourcefulness. Mars is the planet that rules aggression and competition. Therefore, it describes both war and sports. It is representative of energy that is highly creative and sexual. Mars energy can be related to the pioneering instincts. Its specific quality of movement is both grace-ful and predatory, controlled, directed, and energetic. The ways in which the Mars energy can be used are varied. Mars rules metal. Steel can be honed to forge weapons of war or tools of agriculture; the quality of Martian energy can be descriptive of antagonism and street fighting or redirected toward ambitious goals. It is very prev-alent in the charts of athletes, surgeons, and dancers. If the energy is not utilized, it turns inward to frustration and anger.

Mars energy can be related to the lower *chakra*, which gives the basic grounding of the release of energy throughout the body. There are seven spiritual centers located in the body, which are called chakras. They are batteries of energy, storehouses of light and color, which vibrate in certain patterns and can indicate health in the physical body. If these centers are balanced, they produce an evolved manifestation of energy almost like a fountain of light that is released through the top chakra, at the top of the skull. This process of balance may take one lifetime or many. The starting point must be the proper use of the Mars energy. Therefore if the individual with strong Mars in his chart sits on that energy, he is bottom-heavy. Grounded, yes, but perhaps only ready to work on a competitive level, anxious to express himself in warlike manner, or only interested in his sexual function and activity. Ideally, he learns to move that energy upward through the rest of his energy centers to find higher levels of expression. Ultimately, Mars can become the highest form of creative energy when it is transmuted to merge with Plutonian energy. Then the cycle is complete and man is once again whole and free. Mars rules metals in general, but specifically lead, the metal associated with that base chakra energy, which through spiritual alchemy and transmutation becomes gold and is ultimately released through the top chakra. The golden halo depicted in paintings of saints is the pictorial image of that completed cycle. This is the true meaning of the art of alchemy—turning lead into gold. However, that is a goal that is not accomplished overnight, nor is everyone on earth interested in attempting such a transmutation. But each man does have Mars energy that must be released in some manner to prevent the warlike, negative expression of that energy. When it is simply ignored, it pops out in accidents, ill health, or unexpected violence. Sublimation of the sexual energy only produces more tension and frustration. Healthy release of the energy is quite different.

Mars is the ruler of the first sign of the zodiac, Aries. The Aries quality, or Martian quality, exhibits the same need to be first. There is an impatience about Mars energy that must be given an outlet. Aggravations, temper, annoyance, and arguments can all be outer manifestations and signals that some sublimation of Mars energy is going on. It is too simplistic to expect people with Mars strong in their charts to simply be patient. Patience will come when the Mars energy is properly directed. There are many ways to direct or release this energy. The real problem lies in early programming, when children are told it is not nice to argue, to create friction or strife. They are not told what to do with the energy that caused the problem in the first place.

Mayan civilization was highly evolved. The Mayans had a very sophisticated way of dealing with conflict or disagreements. A game was decreed, with each team being carefully selected. The winning team became the victor in the original disagreement or argument. Perhaps our Olympic teams could perform an even greater function than just to provide entertainment and satisfaction for the participants and the viewers. If our governments put as much money into the training of athletes as into the training of soldiers and manufacture of armaments, we might have teams that would be truly capable of settling international conflicts. War is a highly skilled exhibition of strategy, but it is the common soldier who performs the task. Sports is a reflection of the strategy of the coach, with the performance left to the individual players.

The world is becoming more aware of the necessity of exercise. Heart-attack victims are told to jog, and indeed exercise is a fabulous way of moving the Mars energy throughout the body. Mars also rules the bloodstream. Cholesterol can be reduced by moving the blood through the body, as can any tendency to inertia of the blood vessels. The overall condition and function of all organs are improved by regular exercise. The aspects to Mars in an individual chart can indicate the kind of movement that is preferable to the person, however. If Mars is strongly aspected to Venus, artistic movement is more to the taste than lifting weights, for instance. Dance is an especially good way to work off frustrations, aggravations, and inhibitions.

Mars can describe even more subtle forms of activity. Since even a small needle is a Mars instrument, sewing, knitting, needlepoint, embroidery, and crocheting also release frustrations indicated by Mars in the astrological chart. Typing on a metal typewriter can do the trick as well. Building, working with hammer and nails, and sculpture give release in the same way. In *Flashdance*, Jennifer Beals portrayed a welder turned dancer. Inadvertently, the writers of the script found two forms of Mars activity. Surgery is a very specific form of expression of Mars energy. Designing and working with jewelry is another form of release, as is mining for ore or fuel sources.

Since Mars describes the competitive urges, anyone involved in the entertainment industry must have strong Mars in his chart. It takes physical stamina, a desire for competition, and strong ambition to be successful in theater or in the music world. Musicians have instruments to work with, whether metal horns or drums or guitars with metal strings. Concert violinists must also have strong Mars urges. Actors work with the total body energy. Actors must move well, but also become—whether consciously or not—involved with that metaphysical process of transferring energy from place to place throughout the energy system. It is no coincidence that many actors are also highly connected to their spiritual needs. Even in the competition for roles, however, the person with strong Mars in his chart wants someone who is a worthy adversary. The more evolved expression of the Mars energy is a desire to have balanced conflict. A person with Mars strong in his chart derives no pleasure in walking all over someone. He needs the challenge of someone who is an equal.

Naturally, prize-fighters exhibit a very basic form of the Martian quality. Once he has finished fighting, however, it is not possible for the former pugilist to become passive. He may become quite active in the business world. Kirk Kerkorian, with Mars quite prominent in his chart, was a boxer in his youth. He formed his own airline company and eventually owned Metro-Goldwyn-Mayer, Inc. He then built a huge luxury hotel in Las Vegas called the MGM Hotel. It takes a tremendous amount of ambition, drive, and Mars energy to deal on that highly competitive level of business. Paul Newman, with Mars strong in his chart, races automobiles, another Mars activity. Robert Redford became a film director after achieving stardom in his own field of acting. He has also built (a Mars activity) a ski resort and a "community" for developing the talents of filmmakers, both in Utah. Skiing is a perfect example of expression of Mars energy. His choice of directing is only another manifestation of the strong Mars in his own chart.

Mars energy wants new fields to conquer. The individual with this planet strongly aspected in his chart is a wonderful starter, but not such a good finisher. He is the natural pioneer. He wants to cut down trees and pave the way for others. He never wants to go back over old ground or old experiences. He is willing to risk all for the adventure of new situations. He has a single-minded kind of concentration. He actually may not be able to do two things at once. He is the person to act as a wedge to break the ice. If an individual is not utilizing the Mars energy in a positive way, he can indulge in jealousy. If he ever looks sideways at the achievements of someone else, he can be lost, for the true aim of his attention is toward the new conditions in his own life. He must not remain stagnant or inactive, or a kind of toxemia may set in and pollute his system. The poisons created by frustrations may not only affect physical health, but health of the mind and emotions as well.

The Mars individual is the creator. If he can compare his energy with that of the first season of the year, he can see in nature what he is able to do in his own life. Nature plants the seeds that will sprout with the advent of spring. The pollinization process is quite natural to the Mars-ruled person. Nature plants indiscriminately as the winds blow and the bees buzz. A Mars-ruled individual has the freedom to choose what he wants to plant. He must stay out of his own way, however, until seasons have allowed the seed to germinate. He can act as the initiator of many projects. He may have to learn how to leave things alone while they are growing. Activity well directed can help him do just that.

Since Mars describes the quality of the pioneer, it is no surprise that Daniel Boone had Mars in strong evidence in his chart. Mars energy also describes the reformer. Areas of reform can range from evangelism to the women's movement. Albert Schweitzer may have utilized the strong Mars in his chart in the most positive way possible. He was a missionary, doctor, and author. His courage, daring, and resourcefulness are perfect examples of Mars energy at work. Mars energy knows no fear unless it is blocked by a more cautious planetary quality. Pure, unadulterated Mars energy is the pure, uninhibited sexuality of a child, a mystic, or a savage. The ultimate expression of that quality is the result of programming and conditioning from the environment and people. The mores of society have much to do with repression of Martian drives. Unfortunately, society does not always provide a substitute outlet.

Negative Mars energy manifests in very obvious ways. Whenever a society has reached a point where there is no room left for exploration or competition, where sports are not encouraged and personal initiative is removed, negative expression must become obvious. Hard work is good for the soul, mind, and body. The downfall of Roman civilization was coincidental with orgies, bloody sport, and general decadence. In our own society, permissive sex and excessive drinking are some manifestations of the frustrated Mars energy. Alcoholism can quite often be connected to repressed rage or unreleased frustrations. Perhaps governments might see a useful comparison with the concept of communism. When initiative is repressed, it may be directed into more dangerous areas of territorial aggression, as is demonstrated in Russia's takeover of other countries. Warlike energy is an assumed and obvious manifestation of frustration at home.

It is interesting to note the attempts at balance that are prevalent on a worldwide scale. People in all countries are now advocating exercise, running, proper diet, and health consciousness, along with antiwar sentiments. Since Mars is a primal force that will always find a way out, it is up to the individual to choose the kind of activity that will release the energy in a productive manner. It is an easily directed energy, but it needs a focal point, a starting place, and some adversity or competition along the way. It describes the quality of sexuality that can be released into many other areas of life, translated into higher, more ambitious goals, and directed toward fighting for the rights of others. Mars is the primal force of springtime and indicative of all new beginnings and exploration.

When Mars is ruling or is placed in the first house of personality and self-expression, the physical energy is always strong. Restlessness, impatience, and a need for activity are especially apparent. The individual has a distaste for anything that is slow or passive. He might abhor waiting for anyone or anything. He can be feisty and argumentative. His movements are quick and he may have a hard time sitting still. He fidgets, twists, or drums his fingers. Physical mannerisms such as these can be a dead giveaway. He is sexy, adventuresome, and risk-taking. He will take a dare, loves fast cars, and wants lots of fun. He is the true romantic of the zodiac.

When we consider that the first house describes the conditions of birth, early childhood, and survival issues, it can be clear that impatience is a quality he may have brought in with him. He may have been in a hurry to be born. He would therefore resent any restrictions that would keep him confined or inactive. He may have felt a need to fight to survive as an infant. He may have had a tendency to fevers, accidents, or blood disorders during childhood. He can trip over his own two feet, as he is in too much of a hurry to look where he is going. He can cut himself, burn himself, yet love to repair things, work with tools or machinery. As a child, the need to dance or be involved with sports is obvious. If he has restrictions and frustrations, he may develop a fighting spirit that may get him into trouble. He is not cautious by nature. His physical build is wiry and slim, giving him a natural physique for dance or sports. He needs physical activity to channel his unusually strong aggressive drives.

When Mars rules the second house of income, the individual's fight, drive, and ambition lead to resourcefulness where income is concerned. He can earn money through any Mars activity, whether that be dancing, fighting, surgery or welding. His greatest ambition has to do with financial achievement. He loves the fight for the sake of competitive challenge. If Mars is well aspected in his chart, he will be very innovative or pioneering in financial areas. His spending habits may coincide with energy cycles. When he is able to go forward with plans and projects, releasing energy in a productive manner, his spending habits are regular and constructive, but if he is frustrated or angry, he is liable to spend funds in an erratic manner. He may spend money in destructive avenues or in connection with events that are not positive in the long run. He, in some instances, could spend money on alcohol, drugs or guns if he is in a frustrated or negative mood. He might be lured by activities connected to romance, or in creating a romantic atmosphere in his life. He is attracted to activities that will help release his own energy, such as through sports activities, dancing and driving the latest cars. He may spend money more easily in a competitive situation, whether it is business oriented or personal. He can show a special ambitious quality where financial matters are concerned, willing to take risks to have a challenge ahead of him.

The third house in a chart describes communications, conversations, ways of speaking and learning, and interaction with siblings and neighbors. When Mars is ruling or is placed in this house, the individual will be aggressive in discussions, impatient in speech, and abrupt when forced to talk on telephones or deal with contracts and negotiations. Relationships with siblings and neighbors can be competitive or full of strife unless he is working on the evolved level of Mars energy. He will then be especially resourceful in dealing with people around him and anxious to pave the way for new conditions. Since he learns rapidly, he can be very impatient with people or learning situations in which things are slow-paced. He may love to argue as a way of sharpening his wits. He may have no patience with stupidity. To him it is an unforgivable sin.

The fourth house indicates the basic relationship with the parent of the opposite sex as well as the preference of lifestyle. When Mars is placed in this house in an individual's chart, the association with the parent of the opposite sex may have been full of discord and anger. The possibility exists that the strongest ties with that parent were basically sexual or competitive. In most cases, the difficulty in early expression of those urges and inclinations results in frustrated energy later on. The aspects to Mars ruling or placed in this house can indicate that photographs of that parent were quite strong in early conditioning of sexuality. If Mars is well aspected in an individual chart, that parent may have been easily in touch with his or her own aggressive, ambitious qualities. The child was given permission to express his or her sexuality and ambition. He or she was encouraged to be active and resourceful. He was shown good examples of energy in action. He then grows up to be especially resourceful in his later years. His ambition and physical energy increase with age. A prime focus for drives is in connection with land, property, and home life. He may be involved with mining, building, contracting, or pioneering new land or a new lifestyle.

If Mars is not well aspected when describing the relationship with that parent, the child may have unreleased anger and frustration. In dealing with the parent, he may not have been able to express his natural attraction or have a good, healthy fight. He may have photographed the parent as frustrated, lacking in ambition, or overly angry with the circumstances in his or her own life. The natural trend toward frustration in later life can be mitigated with awareness of that relationship. When Mars rules the fourth house and is not well aspected, the individual must have more activity as he grows older. As long as he is involved in activity within his own home or in connection with property or building, he will be content. Renovation, rebuilding, or simply moving furniture can relieve symptoms of boredom momentarily. What he really needs is a very active life in connection with land reform, property development, or constant new conditions and change of scene.

The fifth house in a chart indicates the creative ability, the gambling instincts, and the romantic nature. That house traditionally describes love, children, entertainment, the stock market, and talent. It is a gamble to fall in love, and a gamble to have children, give a party, or invest in the stock market. Gambles in this context mean a great deal more than going to the racetrack or playing poker. The fifth house ultimately indicates the quality of creative energy that is available to the individual and how he feels about expressing that talent. When Mars rules this house, the gambling urge is especially strong. If Mars has primarily positive aspects, the drive and ambition make it easy to release creative energy. The individual is particularly romantic, loves to dance, and needs a creative outlet more than most people. He may be resourceful in connection with children, and produce sexy, ambitious, energetic offspring. He may be a pioneer in his expression of talent, always seeking some new form for the release of creativity. He can be attracted romantically to someone aggressive, sexy, athletic, or competitive. He can be interested in investments in a primitive state, like undeveloped oil wells, or silver or gold mines. He is able to take risks to satisfy his ambition and urge for accomplishment. A good, healthy fight is right up his alley. When dealing with creative situations, he likes to stir things up a bit and deal with competitive, challenging people.

The sixth house describes work, relationships with co-workers, and desire for service. It is also particularly connected with health. It would seem that satisfying work and good health go together. With an association of Mars to this sixth house, active work is necessary for good health. Sedentary professions will produce a condition that can indirectly reduce the amount of oxygen in the bloodstream. If an individual with Mars ruling or placed in this house is occupied in such a profession, it is essential for him to get outside exercise to rebalance physical energy and health. Ambitious work projects, situations that enable the individual to show resourcefulness, or any activity connected with sports, dance, mining, or work with metals will work off excess aggressive energy.

If Mars is well aspected in the natal chart, the person will naturally be inclined to work where he has a healthy amount of competition and where he is able to pioneer new trends. He can act as a director or initiator of projects, and will be especially effective in any area that has an overtone of reformation. If Mars is not well aspected in the chart, there is a strong possibility that the person will not tap his real ambition. Whether through fear, a desire to take things easy and not make waves, or an inability to direct energy wisely, the person may choose to avoid work that would help release his frustration. He puts his health in jeopardy. Accidents, cuts, burns, fevers, and blood disorders may plague him unless he looks to the source of the problem. He needs something to give him a chance to fight in a healthful way.

When Mars rules or is positioned in the seventh house of marriage or partnership, the most active area of his life has to do with cooperative ventures. He may always need someone else to set things in motion, whether in business or personally. He will naturally be attracted to someone who is aggressive, ambitious, and active. He may inadvertently love the idea of someone who stirs things up so that he can follow behind, even acting as the peace-maker. If Mars is well aspected in the natal chart, the partner will show special romantic inclinations, sexuality, drive, and determination. He or she will happily be the forerunner, the aggressor, in paving the way for others. The dynamic exchange can make marriage or partnership especially exciting, a new and constant challenge.

If Mars is not well aspected and is placed in or rules this house, frustration and strife are the obvious characteristics of relationships. The individual needs, then, to look within for the cause of the original attraction. He may want someone else to do all the nasty work for him and then be ready to criticize the quality of argumentativeness. He may actually need a stimulus in the form of a partner and mate to keep him from going to sleep in life. He may not want to tap his own sexuality, drive, and ambition, picking someone else who may also be so inclined. Competition can be an underlying characteristic to the relationship. He may need to avoid people who are frustrated, aggravated and very impatient, as those may be the very qualities that trigger his own feelings of strife.

The eighth house in a chart is the house of transformation, transmutation, and an indication of a major turning point in life. It describes the early methods of getting needs met and the later quality of energy that is the gift for humanity. When Mars rules this house, the individual may have to do battle to get his personal needs met. That may mean being involved in a competitive situation, in which he must bid against others or be first in line. Competition can give release for a great deal of active physical energy. He may have income derived from drilling, mining, or very original pursuits. If Mars is well aspected in the chart, the individual may not have any problem in the direction of energy toward his own needs. If Mars is not well aspected, frustration may occur in connection with residual income, inheritance, or competitive situations. In this case, he may not want to fight for what is rightfully his. The level of effectiveness in getting individual needs met is in direct proportion to the ease of utilizing energy on behalf of others.

When Mars describes this house, the ultimate gift for others is to show ambition and resourcefulness that will pave the way for mankind. This Mars placement describes a strong ability to be a reformer, fighter for better conditions, or pioneer. There can be no one more resourceful or willing to go to bat for others when Mars is well aspected. If it is not, the individual can have many aggravations within himself about his lack of drive. He may not know where to draw the line in his contributions to mankind. He may have feelings of anger in connection with inheritance, therefore with any contribution he makes to others. Rather than being able to set things in motion, he can feel cheated. He may resent what he has to do in the line of icebreaking, or taking the first step in a situation.

Mars as a ruler of the ninth house can be described only as the individual energy willing to speak out for a cause or project. Whatever touches the heart of the person with this placement of Mars may seem an opportunity to pave the way for others by his own involvement. He can be especially effective in dealing with legalities, issues of reform, or travel projects that are unique. He may be the first person to visit a new territory as an explorer. His drive and ambition lead to projects that are somehow innovative or connected to bettering conditions. If Mars is well aspected, he is easily able to do battle for his particular project. He can publicize, promote, start publications, and show ambitious energy in areas of competition. He must be first in line with philosophical trends.

If Mars is not well aspected, frustration in connection with legalities, travel conditions, or situations around the world can cause him to harness his aggressive energy to fight. Yet it may not be easy for him to do so. He may have blocks about new territory in his life, or show an unwillingness to take the risks that would be natural to him. He may hesitate to take up the sword of truth, unwilling to fight for others, even though he is capable of reform he might settle for stagnation and frustration rather than actively fighting to change conditions. His aggravations can extend to areas of higher learning, publications, and international dealings. He can be very frustrated when he is forced to sit still in an airplane. He is impatient with things that move too slowly on a philosophical, reform level.

The tenth house describes career focus, public behavior, and the relationship with the parent of the same sex. When Mars rules this house, ambition is clearly marked in career areas. The individual is not at all interested in projects or activities that come too easily. He is not passive in the public arena, but very active, ambitious, and aggressive. He may prefer social situations that allow him to move, rather than activities in which he is forced to sit still. He loves the challenge of competition and will handle that kind of activity quite well. He is interested in pioneering new trends. He cares very little for what other people have done before him. He wants to make new contributions in areas of public life.

He may have photographed the parent of the same sex as quite aggressive, ambitious, and sexual. He may have had an amount of competition with this parent and was certainly given clear permission to be ambitious. Arguments and strife in connection with that parent may have created an atmosphere of frustration. He may have to learn how to deal with frustration in his own career attempts. If Mars is well aspected, he will be able to channel ambition into constantly new areas of focus. He is a good starter, not a good finisher. He will fight for bettered conditions in public life. If Mars is not well aspected, he may not know how to channel his energy into competitive areas that would be healthful for him. He can experience too much frustration, in his own career, that causes him to be impatient, aggravated, and annoyed in public life. He needs an active social life or career to release energy.

Friendships, group associations, and dealings with organizations describe the energy of the eleventh house. When Mars is placed in or is the ruler of this house, healthful competition exists in areas of friendship and with group projects. The individual is attracted to people and friends who are active, ambitious, aggressive, and daring. He likes associations in organizations that are connected to pioneering activity and projects. He may have a healthy competitive spirit with his friends, being involved in sports and games in which competitiveness can be released. If Mars is well aspected in the individual chart, he will attract people who are innovative, daring, energetic, and ambitious. If Mars is not well aspected, he may find frustration in friendship areas. With good inner dialogue about his own drives and ambition, the person will be especially resourceful in friendships. He will move furniture, go to bat for a friend when he is in need of help, and generally stick his neck out for an associate. If the individual is not in touch with his need for the expression of his aggressive energy, drive, and ambition, he may not do the very things that would bring him satisfaction in connection with associations.

The twelfth house in a chart describes subconscious processes, prenatal programming, and activities that are largely conducted away from the prying eyes of the public. It describes behavior that is private and different from the personality mask. When Mars rules or is placed in this house, the individual may not be able to express anger, drive, ambition, or romantic inclinations easily; this part of his character, he can show when he is alone or totally at ease in his surroundings. He may have deep prenatal frustrations and anger. His greatest awareness of his ambitions comes when he is alone. When Mars is making harmonious aspect to other planets, he is able to tap his inner sense of direction, knowing just where to place his focus of energy at all times. He is at the right place at the right time. If Mars is not well aspected to other planets in his chart, deep inner frustrations seem to have no release in life. He may suppress his romantic inclinations, work off aggravations by having secret romances, and experience lack of awareness of an inner sense of direction. He may not know how to get out of his own way. He may not easily express anger until it has reached the boiling point. He may try to calm down the rage with less than productive ways of showing aggression.

MARS CONJUNCT SUN

The Sun describes the soul of the individual. That particular energy may or may not be visible within the personality, but it describes the condition of pride, ego. As with any planet in a conjunction aspect to the Sun, the added characteristics of Mars energy combine with the quality of ego and vitality to impart a second color, or hue. When Mars is conjunct the Sun, the inner pride is connected to accomplishment, drive, and ambition, even if the Sun is in a more passive sign. As long as the person has an opportunity to express inner drive, he is centered and balanced. He needs something to fight for. He cannot be passive, inactive. Otherwise, impatience, annoyance, and frustrations take hold on a deep level. Mars is the planet of sexuality. In this instance, a quality of sexual magnetism is heightened. The vitality is wiry, aggressive, focused. The individual is courageous and willing to take risks.

The natural need for Martian energy is to be involved in activity that enables the individual to be, first, a pioneer of sorts. He is willing and able to be the icebreaker in connection with new activity. He is frustrated when he must wait for someone else to give the go-ahead signal. He expresses tremendous initiative and may not be very tolerant of sheeplike people, who only follow or quote other sources. Right or wrong, he must take up the dare of new risks and conditions. He can be impulsive, impetuous, hotheaded, and temperamental, but give him a chance to show his resourcefulness and he shines like an arrow headed toward the Sun. He must have an outlet for his feisty disposition, or he can antagonize people with a display of temper or overly predatory behavior. He cannot sit still or wait for people.

Astronaut John Glenn was born with his Sun in the sign of Cancer, but the additional Mars characteristics are quite obvious when one looks at the kind of activity he chose. Cancer is the sign that is connected with home and hearth. John Glenn took his focus of energy far beyond the confines of earth, into space. He was a fighter pilot, completing fifty-nine missions in World War II. He had ninety combat missions in Korea and then became a test pilot. The placement of Mars conjunct the Sun is in the ninth house of John's chart. Mars rules his sixth house of work, and the Sun rules the tenth house of career. This ambitious placement of Mars-Sun describes activity that would lead to paving the way for better conditions, being on a soapbox, and needing a working occupation that would bring recognition for pioneering activities. John Glenn, in spite of incredible accomplishments and feats of daring, has not fulfilled all his ambitions, or so it would seem. Even though he is an acknowledged hero and has been elected to the Aviation Hall of Fame, he is not content to sit on his laurels. He has become a successful business entrepreneur, is now a United States senator, and in 1984 ran for President of the United States. He is outspoken, daring to say what he thinks, and would obviously be a fighter for reformation of negative conditions in any position he might hold. His life is the epitome of what a Mars-conjunct-Sun aspect might suggest.

Grace Kelly also was born with this conjunction in her chart. Grace is a Scorpio by birth, with her Mars-Sun aspect in the first house of personality, self-expression, and early years. Mars rules her sixth house of work, and the Sun rules her tenth house of career, public life, and describes her relationship with her mother.

Grace Kelly was not content to be the pampered daughter of a wealthy Philadelphia socialite. She channeled her ambitious energy into the world of entertainment, starting as a photographers' model in New York, studying acting, and finally making her stage debut at the age of twenty. She was swept into stardom in less than two years. Focused and directed energy paid off with an Academy Award for her performance in *The Country Girl*, with Bing Crosby.

Everyone knows of the fairy-tale meeting with her handsome prince and the ultimate dream come true of every little girl. She became Her Royal Highness, Princess Grace of Monaco. Mars is the planet of sexuality, romance, and creativity. Grace exuded a cool sexuality and fulfilled her dreams by achieving stardom and the acclaim of her peers with the winning of the Academy Award. Yet how much more romantic is the role of a princess of the tiny principality of Monaco! Grace was never content to be a mere figurehead, though. She was active in many areas of charity. She was concerned about the welfare of her people. She is quoted as saying, "I am a woman of action, which above all means being creative." She exhibited her needlework and flower collages to the Monaco residents. She had also planned to resume her film career. Mars rules impatience, sometimes causing accidents, especially when placed in the first house of physical energy. When Mars is connected to health, also described by the first house, it can indicate a stroke. Grace suffered a stroke while driving her car over winding Monaco roads with her daughter Stephanie. Grace died as a result of her accident. She still had unfulfilled ambitions, however, that are now left to her children to express. She is mourned by millions of people all over the world. The romantic fairy tale of her life is left as a beautiful memory for her family to cherish.

Jill St. John was also born with Mars conjunct the Sun. Jill is a Leo by placement of her Sun at birth. Her conjunction of Mars and the Sun is placed in the seventh house of marriage and partnership. Mars rules the second house of income, and the Sun rules her seventh house of partnership, as well as being placed there. Jill had early signs of obvious sexuality that brought her her first film at age sixteen. But with Mars conjunct the Sun in the house of partnership, Jill's ambitions did not lie with her career. Her first wealthy marriage was to laundry heir Neil Dublin, but since Mars energy can indicate strife, she was divorced thirteen months later. Then she married Woolworth heir Lance Reventlow. Even the obvious benefits of such a wealthy marriage could not tempt her to put up with the strife created in that relationship, and she was divorced about three years later. After one more attempt, to singer Jack Jones, with the third divorce under her belt Jill seems to have backed off from marriage. Her complaint with all three husbands was that they made her extremely nervous. When Mars is in the house of partnership, the individual chooses someone very aggressive, ambitious, or argumentative. Jill may need to work through her own anger, known or unknown, to find a more peaceful, harmonious relationship. She may also need to redirect her own ambition toward activity that will keep her busy, out of her own way. With enough energy diverted into a different kind of partnership activity, she may leave peaceful space to be filled with a romantic relationship that will weather the storms.

MARS IN HARD ASPECT TO THE SUN

The keynote for Mars in a difficult aspect to the Sun is frustration. Drive and ambition can come from a need for recognition. The inner sense of self-worth may suffer to the point that anger is triggered, producing a great deal of energy, albeit not necessarily a smooth flow of it. Conflict can serve as a challenge. It is obvious in looking at the lives of successful people that hard aspects in a natal chart indicate hardships or difficulties that must be overcome, thereby producing external conditions of success. Pain seems to produce growth. So it is with frustration. If a person becomes angry enough about a situation in his own life, he may do something about it. The next step to take is to identify with the same crises or aggravations in the lives of others. The willingness to do something about what may seem a universal condition leads to reform efforts, pioneering activity, and the breaking up of the old to make room for the new. That is what the Mars energy is ultimately all about.

An outstanding example was shown in the life of Aimee Semple McPherson. Mars, in her chart, is placed in the tenth house of career and public life, describing the relationship she had with her mother as well. The Sun is placed in the seventh house of marriage or partnership. Mars co-rules her first house of self-expression, and describes her personality. The Sun rules the sixth house of work, health, and service to others. Aimee's career began with the death of her first husband, in Hong Kong. She was stranded and obviously frustrated, even angry. She landed in Los Angeles with ten dollars and a tambourine. She went to work for God. Crusading is a marvelous outlet for Mars energy. Aimee founded four hundred churches and two hundred missions, a Bible college, and a radio station.

Lest anyone assume that working for God calms down a vibrant temperament, it was reported that Aimee Semple McPherson punched her business manager. It so happens that it was her mother she hit, for her mother had become her manager as well. One look at her Mars aspects indicates that her mother was the root of her aggravations in life to begin with. She may have had cause to thank her mother, however, for stimulating her into a career in which she was known as "the Barnum of religion." It is also obvious that people who are passionate in their service for God are also passionate in their private lives. They seem to be working on two levels at once in an attempt to resolve and transmute the Martian passions. Aimee was no exception. She was said to be kidnapped at one point in her life, when she was discovered in a love nest. She also found time in her busy schedule to personally check out the situation in Paris nightclubs, obviously with the intent of reform.

Two of the most dynamic performers in the theatrical world have Mars square the Sun in their natal charts. Both are redheads, with energy to match. If we could assign a color to Mars energy, it would most certainly be red. Gwen Verdon took her Mars energy into dance and the Broadway stage, and Lucille Ball found television as the medium that exposed her talent to the finest advantage. Gwen Verdon has Mars posited in the first house of self-expression, and also ruling that house. The Sun is placed in the eleventh house of group effort and associations with people, and rules her work. When Mars is ruling the first house, frustrated energy can be an obvious malady unless physical activity is found. Dance is a perfect outlet for that placement of Mars. In Gwen's case, her legs were so badly misshapen and bent as an infant that her doctors recommended breaking them and attempting to reset them. Gwen's mother resisted that drastic measure and started Gwen dancing at the age of two. That therapy not only corrected her legs but set her feet firmly on the path to an illustrious career. Gwen won Tony awards for *Can-Can* and *Damn Yankees.*

Lucille Ball has Mars placed in the tenth house, describing career activity and relationship with the parent of the same sex. Mars also rules that house of public life, intensifying the ambition and drive that led to her phenomenal success for twenty-five years on television. After many films, but not much lasting success, Lucille conceived, produced, and starred in her own life story of marriage to Desi Arnaz. The Sun in her chart is placed in the first house, describing executive ability, and rules the second house of income. She would quite naturally earn money through her leadership qualities, acting ability, and personality. The frustrations of her early years were released through ambition. If she had impatience with waiting for others to spot her talent, it led to her resourcefulness and initiative in finding and creating her own vehicle. Lucy overcame any financial frustrations with her sale of Desilu Corporation to Gulf & Western for seventeen million dollars.

MARS CONJUNCT MOON

Whenever two planets are in conjunction, the two colors and qualities of energy can augment each other or fade into each other, as the case may be. When the Moon is conjunct another planet, the sensitivity that is described by that heavenly body lends itself quite naturally to absorbing the energy of the other planet. The quality of the emotional nature, at that point, may be more in character with the other planet than the sign position of the Moon. When the Moon is conjunct Mars, it is the same as if the Moon were in the sign of Aries. If the placement of the Moon is in a passive sign, the Mars energy will surely overwhelm that passivity and produce a temperament much more colorful. When emotional overreaction is stimulated, the response will be one of anger and impatience. That display of fireworks may be only a trigger response to hide hurt, for temper is one way of getting rid of hurt feelings. These two planets individually can indicate a jealous nature if not channeled positively. When they are conjunct, the jealousy may become the motivation for successful and positive release of energy in life.

The contamination or leakage of energy from one planet to the other in this instance manifests as inappropriate reaction to a spe-

cific circumstance. The individual with Mars conjunct the Moon
may *feel* hurt when he is really angry or impatient, and express
anger when he is really hurt. It seems that he has a faulty hookup
between the emotional nature and the aggressive drives. This may
also mean an overly emotional reaction in connection with ambition
and sexuality. Achievement of high ambitions may be an attempt to
assuage feelings of abandonment or oral deprivation. Sexuality may
be a deeply emotional experience to one with this aspect. Emotional
upsets may easily come with sexual arousings.

The Moon is strongly placed in the chart of an individual who
evokes special response from the public. The Moon is the energy
that describes identification, nurturing instincts, and a gut connection with what mankind feels and thinks. Montgomery Clift has
Mars conjunct the Moon in his natal chart. The placement of this
emotionally frustrated aspect is in the fourth house of home,
describing the relationship with his mother. Mars rules the ninth
house of travel, publicity, public relations, and that house describes
activities and international response from the public. The eleventh
house of group activity and friendship, is ruled by the Moon. Clift
would have been most sensitive on an emotional level to his friends,
his peers, and in any situation in which he may have had bad
publicity. His original frustrations were obviously in relationship to
his mother.

In a positive sense, the Moon's identification with people produced a person aware of the emotional pain in the lives of others.
Clift may have had an overly protective feeling about his mother
and experienced much frustration in trying to make things right for
her. His mother was a person who felt abandoned, whether that was
really the case or not. He may have had a strong sexual attraction to
his mother that no doubt was upsetting to him. Emotional ties with
her were certainly very strong, and arguments may have been the
way of releasing such strong feelings. In addition, Clift may have
been very jealous of his mother, whether he was aware of that or
not.

Montgomery Clift was a brilliant actor. His portrayal of the
young man caught between his feelings for a factory worker and the
ambitious goal of marriage to the boss's daughter in *A Place in the
Sun* brought an Academy Award nomination. He was also nomi-
nated for his role in *From Here to Eternity* and *The Search*. Profes-

sional success didn't bring a great deal of personal happiness, however. The sensitivity of the Moon and the frustration of Mars can
produce alcoholic leanings. Clift was a drinker and drug user. He
was also a homosexual. He may have had deep emotional problems
that were never resolved. Perhaps the symbiosis with his mother
was like the umbilical cord that was never cut. He died of a heart
attack when he was only forty-six years old.

One young girl's life was nearly ruined when she killed her
mother's lover. Cheryl Crane was acquitted by a jury, who gave a
verdict of justifiable homicide. Her statement was "I had to protect
my mother." Cheryl is the daughter of Lana Turner and Stephen
Crane. Her Mars-conjunct-Moon aspect is divided between the tenth
house of career, public activity, and the relationship with her
mother, and the eleventh house of group activity. Mars rules the
tenth house as well, intensifying the frustrated relationship with
Lana, and the Moon rules her personal life, personality, and need
for self-expression. When the Moon rules or is placed in the first
house, feelings of abandonment are very deep. Since the Moon co-
rules Cheryl's tenth house, the deep emotional reaction came from
her frustrated ties with her mother. She may also have photographed her mother's feelings of abandonment and developed an
overly protective urge that was triggered when she saw Johnny
Stompanato in an argument with Lana. There may have been more
connected to that rescue attempt than met the eye. Whether she was
jealous of her mother being with Johnny, or in seeing Johnny involved with her mother, can only be speculated about. Sexual feelings must have been aroused within her that were very confusing to
the nubile fourteen-year-old daughter of a very sexy film star.

Cheryl was living with her mother after running away from
boarding school the previous year. The frustration of not being able
to get the emotional response she needed from her mother may
have provoked first her rebellion about being away at school, and
then the drastic act of stabbing Stompanato. Her mother was given
custody of Cheryl after the trial with the stipulation that the girl
needed psychiatric care. It is clear in Cheryl's case that the anger
and hurt she felt in connection with her mother were not easily
reconciled. She lived with her maternal grandmother for many
years after she reached young adulthood.

Phyllis Schlafly also has Mars conjunct the Moon in her tenth house of public life, career, and relationship with her mother. The Moon rules her third house of communications, however, and Mars rules the twelfth house of the subconscious. Phyllis may have a deep inner motivation about her work that is connected to emotional frustrations. She may or may not be aware of subconscious feelings of anger, abandonment, and aggravation connected to the relationship with her mother. It appears that those upsetting and mixed emotions began even prenatally. She has translated her own ambitious desires into fighting against the women's movement. Phyllis may be touched very subconsciously by the very thought of anything that might threaten the emotional support of her chosen lifestyle. She is obviously campaigning about very personal issues, while translating them into words with which many women identify. Phyllis may have deep scars left by seeing her mother frustrated and, abandoned. At least she uses her personal anger to fight for what she considers the rights of others.

Clare Boothe Luce is another very dynamic lady with Mars conjunct the Moon in her tenth house of career. Mars rules her fifth house of creativity, talent, and gambling instincts, and the Moon rules her eighth house of getting her needs met. This multitalented lady rose from a situation of near poverty to become an international diplomat. She may also have had many feelings of frustration over the relationship with her mother. The feelings of protectiveness conflict with anger, but in Clare's case, she turned them to wonderful creative use. She also fought for the National Woman's Party when she was only nineteen years old. She scattered leaflets of propaganda from an open biplane. She became a writer, a perfect outlet for the Moon, and a magazine editor. After her marriage to Henry Luce, founder of *Time* magazine, she wrote three hit plays. She became a war correspondent and continually fought for her beliefs. Ultimately, after a six-year stint in Congress, she was appointed ambassador to Italy. New careers, conditions, and creative challenges have been strong motivating forces, allowing her to transmute any frustration in her own life into positive action.

MARS IN HARD ASPECT TO THE MOON

When these two planets are in hard aspect to each other, the dialogue between them carries widely differing messages. The Mars voice is one of anger, and the Moon's message is of hurt. Therefore, the mis-hookup between these two energies can be seen quite clearly; wounded feelings or overly emotional reactions to even imagined slights can immediately snap into a temperamental reaction. When the individual loses his temper, he feels guilty and therefore even more vulnerable. And the cycle can begin all over again. He may also contaminate his sexual feelings with a fear of abandonment. He may never feel free to express either emotion or healthy aggression. Any hurt triggers a reaction of frustration that clouds the original issue, even for himself. He may have to dissect and analyze a particular situation to discover what set him off. If the individual can recognize that temper, anger, and argumentativeness may cover a hurt, he can begin to decontaminate these two diverse energies. Ideally, he learns to express hurt when that is appropriate and anger when that is what is really deserved.

Marlon Brando has Mars square the Moon in his chart. It would be safe to say that Marlon's strongest film roles have been portrayals of the angry young man. His brilliant performance as Stanley Kowalski in *A Streetcar Named Desire* is an example of the sexuality, sensitivity, anger, aggressive nature, and intense emotional reaction described by this aspect. Marlon's own character is composed of these characteristics. His ability to draw on his own attributes and translate them into characteristics appropriate to the current role is what makes him a brilliant actor. But the reverse side of the coin is that while infusing those characteristics into a fictional person, the actor, especially Marlon, is able to transmute his own frustrations into a healthful outlet.

In Marlon's natal chart, Mars is posited in the second house of income, and rules his fifth house of creative expression, talent, and gambling. The Moon is placed in the fourth house of home, describing sensitivity and protective feelings toward his mother, and rules the eighth house of getting his needs met. Obviously his sensitivity and feelings have much to do with being paid for his talent. In the early part of his career, Marlon refused to go to Hollywood. He was offered a contract when he was twenty-three years old, but it may not have been lucrative enough to persuade him to leave the familiarity of New York. He may also have been especially sensitive about any restrictions that might have frustrated him. Mars energy must have an opportunity to take risks. Marlon may have even more of a need for risk taking than most, because of emotional overtones connected to having to ask for his needs to be met (Moon ruling the eighth house). His true emotional, sensitive nature has great need to express nurturing and identification with mankind. He needs a home that is a safe place to let out his feelings. Marlon lived in Tahiti for many years. Perhaps he could feel more at ease emotionally with the gentleness and lack of competitive spirit in that country.

Surprisingly enough, Doris Day has Mars opposite her Moon. In her film roles, Doris was always the happy, peppy, exuberant girl next door. But on closer examination there was always a situation in her roles that gave her cause to express temperament or, especially, moral indignation. In Doris' chart, Mars is placed in the third house of communications, and rules the eighth house of getting her needs met. The Moon is placed in the tenth house of career, and rules her eleventh house of group activity. Doris may have experienced frustrations in working with her fellow actors and in film productions, especially if she felt underpaid. Doris was not one of the highest-paid actresses in Hollywood, even though she was one of its shining stars. If she had been able to separate emotions from action, she might have fought for better conditions and income. She may have been too vulnerable and sensitive, or hurt, to do so. Any feelings of abandonment in connection with her mother may have kept her worrying about just such a situation in her career and in the esteem of the public. She did elicit tremendous response and identification from her fans.

MARS CONJUNCT MERCURY

The conjunction of Mars and Mercury describes a mentality of special brilliance. The mind is honed to a razor-sharp edge with a resulting perception that is incredibly accurate. An individual with this aspect can put his finger on the exact spot, the core of importance, in a situation of question. He may forget that the metal tip on the end of his finger, or tongue, can cause wounds that are difficult to heal. He can be impatient, caustic, and sarcastic along with his special ability to be perceptive.

Whenever Mars energy is adjoining other energy, overall pace is quickened. In this instance, speech may be rapid and blunt, but it is, at least, quite to the point. Conversations do not linger and dawdle into areas of subtlety. The positive possibilities of such an aspect are endless, for the individual possessing such a quick mind does not hesitate to go to bat for other people in areas in which a clear head is necessary. He learns, speaks, thinks, and reacts rapidly. He comes to positive conclusions long before other people even grasp the facts. Therefore, the greatest problem comes with impatience in discussions with people who think more conceptually or idealistically. He is not tolerant of stupidity or difficulty in coming to the point. He is ready to race past any situation that demands too much beating around the bush. He is not exactly a prime candidate for a diplomatic post. He is a fighter for rights, however.

Mercury describes basic right-brain thinking. That includes the ability to do research, collect facts, and correlate data. Mars indicates a need for a fight, healthful competition, and ambition. When the conjunction occurs in the natal chart, the individual has a particular need for mental challenges and conquests. He cares about explorative, courageous, or surgical precision of thought. Without embellishment, he clarifies, cuts away, and exposes the grains of fact within. He has no quarrel with truth, but despises a lie or any hazy quality of misinformation. He has no talent for glamorizing a situation. He can become unpopular with people who cannot look into the bright light of reality.

Mars energy is feisty, sometimes angry, always impatient. The individual with this aspect may seem angry, whereas he is really looking for a healthful contretemps on a mental level. He loves argument that is positive. He has no intention of wounding anyone. He wants to heal a situation with his analysis. Frustration occurs when he unconsciously offends someone. Then he can become angry at the stupidity of the situation. He tests and respects the people who can stand up to him on a mental level.

The person with this aspect cannot easily work under someone else. He must be first in expressing ideas, plans, or projects. He may be disposed to many careers during his life, simply because when he has accomplished a particular project, he must keep going. His goals are linear. He wants to penetrate farther along the same path. Mars can rule mathematics. The individual may or may not be mathematical, but his thought processes are mathematical in form.

David Cogan is a very prominent business manager in New York

City. David has fingers in many pies. He has an organization that handles the financial affairs of many well known people, but David also owns a Broadway theater and is a producer in his own right. Needless to say, David is a very busy man. An interview with him may be broken by several telephone calls, yet he is as direct and to the point as if the conversation had not been interrupted. He never loses his train of thought. The conjunction of Mercury and Mars is in the first house of David's chart. Since the first house describes conditions of childhood that program and shape the personality, it is interesting to know David's background. He was born in Romania, with Gypsy midwives attending his birth because his mother's escape from Russia was unavoidably close to the time of his birth. The Gypsies offered to keep him safe in their community because the next step of the trip was across very dangerous ice floes. His mother decided to take the risk of escaping with the newborn baby. The earliest condition in David's life was adventure and risk. He described the excitement of the danger. In his own vision of the incident, he felt the need to be mentally alert to avoid mishap from a very early time in his life. David has confessed that he finds his brusque manner quite effective as a deterrent and safety device. It can seem like taking your life in your hands to have a telephone conversation with David, and can easily relegate thought of any favor to the back of your mind. For David, this manner of speech that does not invite requests is easier, safer, and more familiar than continually saying no.

Mars describes a directorial ability or talent. This aspect can easily be released by involvement in activities that require direction. Mars is usually found in a very prominent place in charts of actors, directors, or producers. The entertainment world in particular offers enough competition and challenge for someone with excess mental restlessness. Dean Martin, Bing Crosby, Ringo Starr, Tom Jones, and Johnny Cash have Mars conjunct Mercury in their natal charts. In each instance, Mars-Mercury energy found release in music, yet the level of expression differs in the lives of these men. Ringo Starr released an aggressive kind of mentality by playing drums. The physical coming together of percussion instruments is Martian in nature. Ringo is not known for temperamental display, although he may express sarcasm in private. Bing Crosby had no such release on an obvious physical-mental level, and was described by his sons as having a terrible temper. His wife, Kathryn Grant Crosby, has vehemently denied the existence of such a temper. In sexual relationships, the mental tensions are released and may not be so obvious as quality of speech. Kathryn may not have born the brunt of Bing's frustration and sarcasm.

Both Dean Martin and Johnny Cash have touched on other characteristics of Mars. Johnny was a rebel in his youth, behaving in such a way as to land himself in jail. In his musical expression he sings about injustice, his frustrating experiences, and hidden anger. Johnny has an additional release through plucking metal strings on his guitar. Metal has a special way of conducting and releasing Mars energy. In the case of Dean Martin, the excess mental frustration is exemplified in excessive drinking. Mars is one planet that can be strong in the charts of individuals who drink heavily. It is the release for frustration in that instance. In an interesting way, people with Mars conjunct Mercury are very romantic in nature. Mercury describes what an individual thinks about. The thought processes are not always angry in this case. Thoughts can range from ambitious ones to creative ones. In that scope lies the sexuality. Tom Jones may or may not think about sex and romance, but the response from his female audiences indicate what their thoughts may be.

Salvador Dalí also has Mars conjunct Mercury. The quality of his art is pioneering, precise, and daring. Dalí was ahead of his contemporaries in the art world. He paved the way for others by daring to express something new. He started the trend toward surrealism. Dalí is also quite well known in connection with his amorous adventures.

MARS IN HARD ASPECT TO MERCURY

In the positive sense, Mars represents courage. When that planet is badly aspected, the negative traits may be a daring that borders on defiance, anger, and an outright refusal to go along with tradition. When Mars and Mercury are in hard aspect to each other, the defiant attitude may come out in speech or in behavior. This can still produce brilliance, yet the release of original thought may come in a more frustrated manner.

This aspect is found in the chart of Princess Margaret of England. Margaret has always been the thorn in the side of her more conservative sister. She began attracting attention by her independent behavior when she was quite young. She was constantly reported in the British newspapers for dancing too late, drinking too much champagne, and keeping fast company. Her clothes were less than conservative and her romantic preferences definitely not traditional. Margaret has Aries on the ascendant. Mars is posited in the third house, describing relationships with relatives and especially siblings. Mercury rules that third house and is posited in the sixth house of work, service, and health. Although there are many aspects in her chart that augment the rebellious quality of her personality, it is obvious that her caustic wit and defiant behavior are no doubt compounded by a frustrating lack of communication with her sister. Margaret seems determined to show her independence from family dictates, yet she is also part of the royal scene when it is important and necessary.

The difference in personality, taste, and outlook between Margaret and Elizabeth was obvious when they were both growing up. Margaret was second in succession to the throne of England until she was seventeen years old. After Elizabeth had children and it was clear that Margaret must be relegated to the background, she began her rebellious behavior. She must have felt a tremendous lack of direction to her life. With high Martian energy, dancing until wee hours and drinking with friends might have been the only outlet for her frustrations. The creative spark was channeled into other areas. Margaret obviously enjoys attending public functions, yet it is also obvious that she gets the leftover duties, rather than ones that are of prime importance. For someone so daring, active, adventurous, and independent, the job of waiting is extremely difficult. Someone with strong Mars energy is not easily able to take second place. Since Mars rules the first house of personality, Margaret's very survival may depend on appearing not to care about her secondary role. Sarcasm, caustic wit, and defiance can be a release for a great deal of anger and frustrated energy. Drinking can also be a way to drown some of that dynamic but impatient spirit. As Margaret grows older, she may be able to discover a more productive outlet for her brilliance and ambition.

Barbra Streisand also has Mars square Mercury in her chart. She also has Aries on the ascendant. The story of Barbra's rise to fame and fortune is well known. It is obvious that early on she had to fight for what she wanted in life. Born in Brooklyn, with stars in her eyes, the high ambition described by her Martian nature found outlet on the Broadway stage. Mars is placed in the third house of communications, with Mercury posited in the first house of personality, ruling the third house as well. Mercury also rules her sixth house of work, service, and health. Her feisty disposition, determination, drive, and courage commanded attention in the competitive world of show business. Then her brilliant talent sustained her in the dizzying rise to the top.

The similarity in the two charts gives a perfect example of an outward expression of energy and a frustrated drive and ambition. In Margaret's case, there was no way to fight for what she wanted. She had a comfortable life, position, and wealth. There were no obstacles to battle, except control by family and public opinion. Barbra had nothing but a fight on her hands from the very beginning. Her sarcasm was accepted and tolerated as part of her exceptional talent. A star is allowed to be sharp, caustic, even temperamental. In her case it was excused and even applauded as part of her sense of perfection. If Mars energy has no battle to fight, it must turn inward to frustration. When it is hooked up to Mercury by a hard aspect, the mental strain is too great unless an outlet is ready at hand. This aspect can be transmuted to energy that paves the way for others. If Barbra Streisand, with neither great traditional beauty nor family background or money, can make it to the top of her chosen field, there exists a possibility for success for many little girls who are not born with the advantages of social status, money, or obvious beauty. Barbra may unconsciously be a role model for many girls who would like to follow in her footsteps. She has the potential of using her wit and caustic manner to go to bat for a special cause. The strong combination of Mars and Mercury is the reformer's aspect.

MARS CONJUNCT VENUS

Mars is the planet that describes not only drive and ambition, but romance and sexuality. It is the planet that might describe pure, raw, fiery energy which leads to the concept of the knight in shining armor. He goes to battle for people less capable than himself and, with victory, sweeps the beautiful maiden into his arms with tenderness and love. He lays flowers at her feet and ensures total devotion from her by his gentleness and passion. Venus is the planet of love, beauty, gentleness, affection, pleasure, and graciousness. When these two planets are conjoined, or conjunct, the individual is extremely sensual, artistic, sociable, gracious, and romantic.

This aspect might be termed the "Casanova complex," for indeed the conjunction of Mars and Venus was found in the chart of the Italian adventurer named Casanova. It is also found in the charts of actors Farley Granger and Peter Lawford, television star Merv Griffin, and playwright Neil Simon. Scottish poet Robert Burns wrote of his passionate love nature described by Mars conjunct Venus in his chart. In extreme cases, this aspect might even be termed hedonistic. Surely it indicates a love of the pleasures in life, whether they take the form of food, fine wines, beautiful surroundings, or lovely companionship.

Madame DuBarry was a famous courtesan in eighteenth-century France. She was a peasant girl who was discovered by Louis XV. He arranged a pseudo marriage for her brother so that she was titled and could be presented to the court. At twenty-five, she was established as his mistress at court. The conjunction of Mars and Venus assures an individual of a quality of charm and graciousness no matter what the circumstances of birth and upbringing. DuBarry was able to establish herself firmly at court. The combination of graciousness and ambition ensured a position for her even after the death of Louis XV. She was able to make many influential friends.

Our modern-day lady at court is Rosalynn Carter, born with Mars conjunct Venus in her chart. Both Madame DuBarry and Rosalynn have Sun positioned in Leo and Virgo in the ascendant. The conjunction of Mars and Venus is in the first house, ruling the second house of income, in Rosalynn's chart. The position of the aspect in Madame DuBarry's chart is similar. Rosalynn Carter was a southern girl swept off her feet by her knight in the uniform of a naval cadet from Annapolis. After serving as governor's wife of Georgia, Rosalynn found herself in the White House as wife of the President. She rose to the occasion and became so comfortable in her role that she has confessed missing politics more than her husband does. She earned the title of a "magnolia made of steel." Her husband called her "my secret weapon." Rosalynn has obviously kept the romance in her marriage. Most of the informal pictures of Jimmy and Rosalynn show them walking hand in hand. For individuals with this aspect, ambitious plans can be most easily achieved through the power of love.

MARS IN HARD ASPECT TO VENUS

When Mars and Venus are in hard aspect to each other, the possibility of overadaptation in love matters is most probable. Venus is described as the peacemaker. When it is not in good aspect, the individual may give in for the sake of peace all too easily. The balance is upset between the drive, courage, resourcefulness, and ambition, and the need for harmony and the status quo. A young man named Phillip described the aspect in his own chart. He said, "I was always curious about my lack of ambition. I was very aware of how my mother's life was conditioned by having inherited money. She and her brothers and sisters were given money all their lives and eventually inherited a great deal. They never had to work. I realized by the time I was very young that it made them irresponsible. I knew when I was thirteen or fourteen that I would never have to work for a living. I'm sure it affected my ambition, because ambition is connected with gain. My mother started giving me an allowance by the time I was sixteen years old. So there I was, a teenager with an income that was big enough to make me lose incentive. On the other hand, if incentive is motivated by just a desire to make money, it is not well placed."

In Phillip's chart, Venus is posited in the fifth house of creativity, romance, children, and entertainment. Mars is placed in the eighth house, which describes inheritance and the way one gets needs met. I asked Phillip about creative expression in his life. He said, "I do have a creative desire and urge. It is absolutely choked and under the carpet. I have built within me, along the way, an inferiority complex. I might have been an achiever, but since I didn't achieve in the way that was recognized and acclaimed, I turned it around and said, 'I'll fail. I reserve the right to fail and that will be my expression.' To accomplish anything would be to deny this role model I've set for myself. I'm optimistic about transcending what is really negative."

It seemed important to talk about romance, since the fifth house

is so strongly aspected in Phillip's chart. We talked about two differing voices—one, easygoing about matters of affection, and the
other, feisty, sexual, energetic, and active. "The tough part of me
sees that I suffer for being easygoing. I get ripped off emotionally
and financially. The tough part says, 'Use these experiences. Don't
let it happen again. If you allow yourself to be easygoing without
protecting yourself, you'll get walked on.' I feel that I have been
misused a lot. I always think, 'What's the catch this time?' At this
point in my life, all the strings and obligations about being with a
woman are just too much for me to consider. I don't even want
flirtations." He continued, "In a worldly sense, I have inherited
energy in the form of money. I feel that money is something to be
dealt with, tended to, and cared for. I don't feel trapped by all that.
I do want to use my energy and resources in a positive way. I
suppose the only answer is to work on the spiritual side of life. I do
know that saints are not passive but active."

It is interesting to note that the aspect describing the conflict
between love and sexuality, passivity and action, adaptability and
ambition, is found in the chart of Sigmund Freud. Freud built his
whole career on the question of sexuality. His astrological chart
indicated the major complex within himself, which was naturally
mirrored in his clients. Marcello Mastroianni has achieved great
success in the film world by playing the weary Italian always entan-
gled with energetic, sexy women dogging his heels. Marcello has
Mars in opposition to Venus in his chart. Perhaps in life as well as
in art, Marcello has a hard time saying no.

ASPECTS TO JUPITER

THE CHARACTERISTICS THAT ARE ALWAYS ASSOCIATED with Jupiter are luck, abundance, optimism, expansion, and joy. High, contagious enthusiasm seems consistent in a person with strong Jupiterian qualities. He can be an expert salesman, an especially fabulous teacher, or just an eternal optimist. He always has a need for new horizons. He may need strong goals to motivate him, because he loves to tackle what is just out of reach. When he has accomplished something or reaches his goal, he must have a new plan before him to act as a stimulant. In most instances, the individual with Jupiter strong in his chart will have a curiosity about the workings of the universe. He may be religious or a nature lover. He has tremendous curiosity about people as well. That curiosity is not expressed in a prying way, but more in an interest about lifestyles, the workings of the mind, and what makes people tick. He wants to excite people about his particular cause or interest and can usually do so quite easily.

The symbology of Jupiter is most revealing. Understanding the quality of a Centaur, the symbol that describes Jupiterian energy, can give wonderful clues to the personal needs of a Jupiterian person or situation. The horse half of the Centaur has four feet firmly placed on the ground, but the man is aiming at the stars. The Jupiterian quality is a marvelous combination of practicality and enthusiasm. The reverse of that quality is disappointment. If the aim is too high and the goals are missed, the individual can be paralyzed by the letdown. Yet he must continue to search for projects and situations that are out of reach. The answer seems to come in his setting many goals, knowing that some are surely bound to fall by the wayside, but that others will come to pass. If he puts all his attention on one project, he blocks his real potential. He must aim for the highest, keep his feet on the ground, and look to the heavens for inspiration.

Due to this natural enthusiasm, he can be labeled anything from Pollyanna to impractical by those people around him who work with a different set of energies. He can be extravagant in taste, whether that is connected to food, clothing, or lifestyle, simply because he wants new experiences. If he has used something too often, or feels that he is in a rut, he may have to discard old conditions, or people, to go on to new situations. Horizons beckon to him. He may have a desire to travel or simply explore with his mind. He can sometimes want what is out of reach, even if that person or situation is nonproductive in the long run.

With the worst aspects of Jupiter, a person may overdo, be indulgent in his extravagant whims, and promise more than he can deliver. He may overestimate time, situations, and people. He may bite off more than he can chew. He may appear to exhibit a quality of grandiosity. His intent is noble, however, for basically Jupiter is indicative of good cheer, a sort of hail-fellow-well-met attitude.

Jupiter has been called the *great benefic*, simply because of the luck connected with this planet. There are really no difficulties where Jupiter is concerned, because the worst that can happen is overexpectation, with the consequent disappointment of letdown. But with Jupiterian energy, the person or situation can bounce back with a *c'est la vie* attitude. Jupiter is the planet that balances Saturn. Since Saturn indicates gravity and Jupiter represents optimism, they form opposite ends of the pole. They are not antidotes for each other, but gently descriptive of heaven and earth. If earth conditions seem too limited and restrictive, a look at the heavens can represent something to strive for.

The tarot card The Fool can give a description of Jupiter energy. On that tarot card, a young man is walking along with a bag over his shoulder, a dog at his heels, and a grin on his face. It appears that he is about to walk over the edge of a cliff without being aware of the danger ahead. However, the deeper meaning of that card comes with a closer look. At the edge of the cliff is a ledge that is partially obscured from sight. The card really indicates that in life there is always one more step one can take to avoid pitfalls or what appears to be disaster. One may have to look carefully to find that extra ledge of security, but it always exists. The message of Jupiter is that there is always hope. With humor and expectancy, an extra step is possible that will save the situation. The placement of Jupiter describes where the ultimate luck factor exists in an individual life.

Whether that luck comes from within or without is a matter of philosophy. It may be that the gods smile on certain people or it may be the quality of contagious enthusiasm that brings luck to a Jupiterian person. The true quality of inner faith and religion has always been described as joyous. Whether that faith comes from a sense of universality or a specific religion seems to have no bearing when it comes to the manifestation of good fortune. Wealth of spirit brings abundance of some kind or other. So it is that Jupiter is the planet that is associated with religion on a universal level.

When Jupiter is placed in or rules the first house, the disposition is noticeably optimistic. There is a quality of expectancy that may have to do with basic survival. The individual must have goals and hope in order to keep going. If the person has problems or difficulties, he is even more likely to adopt a philosophical attitude in order to survive. If he confessed to pressures or tragedy, he would lose the very thing that is part of his good fortune. He may appear especially even in temperament or even altruistic, but in reality this may be only his mask. The person with this aspect tends to live in the future instead of the present. Only goals that are momentarily out of reach are interesting to him. He is especially in need of new horizons to conquer.

This Jupiterian person may not like traditional lifestyles. He becomes bored with conditions that are stagnant. He may want to peer into many kinds of customs to satisfy his curiosity. He is an excellent teacher. He likes to give permission to people and encourage them to be their best selves. He can appear quite content and self-satisfied, even complacent. He may gain weight about the hips, since Jupiter rules that part of the body. Overindulgence in food or drink may be due to disappointment or static conditions. This person may not actually want everything to come to him at once. If he attains all his desires, he has nothing else to strive for. He may therefore not appear too ambitious. He avoids getting stuck in any particular kind of activity unless it promises to lead to new experiences. He can be like the donkey with the carrot in front of his nose. If Jupiter is not well aspected, the quality of grandiosity can be the mask to cover less than fortunate experiences.

When Jupiter rules or is placed in the second house of money, the individual can be quite fortunate in financial areas. He may seem extravagant, but it is simply that he tends to spend money when he is enthusiastic. He develops an easy-come-easy-go outlook even though that may not be the reality of the situation. He prefers to earn income on a sliding scale or with possibility of commissions, royalties, or residuals. He does not like to be fixed to a static income. He must have expectations of money growth, or he becomes paralyzed in his financial attempts. He really doesn't care about money for its own sake. His identification with income is just like his identification with goals of any kind. The expectancy or challenge of bigger and better is what gets him going. When he is most enthusiastic, his financial condition seems hopeful as well. Outlook and ability go hand in hand.

However, he may also tend to be extravagant. At the very times when he may not be affluent, he can spend money that he doesn't have, adopting an attitude of Jupiterian enthusiasm to hide a sense of inner disappointment. He may appear to be wealthy because of his wealth of spirit, whether he has money or not. He will never be without the Jupiterian protection in some way or another, with Jupiter ruling this house. If he is in the chips, he will be very generous. If he is not, he will motivate himself to greater earning potential so that he can express his generosity. He primarily loves the freedom and growth associated with income. He can sometimes go after financial opportunities simply because they are a challenge. He may need to develop a more focused look at where his energies truly lie. He can expect more than is forthcoming, then suffer the paralysis he feels with disappointment. Luckily, he is not down for very long. He may subconsciously set it up to have some letdown in order to have a new challenge. Ultimately he will learn how to set goals in financial areas, avoiding spending the income before it arrives, and then applying his energy to that end. He may always need to allow some discounts in what his expectations lead him toward.

Jupiter ruling the third house or placed therein describes the perennial student. All Jupiterian people are in need of constant new learning to fuel the fires of enthusiasm, but in particular, when Jupiter describes communications, he is enamored of myriads of new information. He is not a gossip, but he loves to explore many interesting facets of life on a philosophical level. He loves to talk with people he thinks are knowledgeable. Mac Adam, with Jupiter in his third house of communications, said he "went through people" rapidly unless they were really interesting, for this is also an area where boredom can set in. If, after expecting much from another person in the way of experiences, he is dull, after all, the Jupiterian person is quite let down.

With this placement of Jupiter in a chart, the individual has a special gift for sales. He may sell tractors or ideas, but if he is enthusiastic about his product or plan, he is irresistible. He may promise more than he can deliver. He is humorous, outgoing, gregarious, philosophical to the hilt. He loves associations with anything concerning nature. He can restore perspective, after even a small letdown, by attunement with anything living. He may love long walks in the woods, or skiing new and unexplored mountain passes. He must read, be well informed and in touch with what is going on in the minds of men. He may never get quite enough information.

The fourth house in a chart describes the kind of lifestyle the person chooses to live. That includes the kind of home, the amount of property, and even the activity and quality of energy within the home. This attraction to a particular way of life seems predescribed by the relationship with the parent of the opposite sex. A female usually relates matters concerning the base of her life with her photographs of her father. A male seems to identify home with mother. Sometimes this is reversed, but, generally speaking, matters concerning the environment are identified in that way. In this case, the parent of the opposite sex may be wealthy, or optimistic, expansive, and with great wealth of spirit. Aspects to Jupiter in the chart usually indicate whether that parent has been able to live up to his or her goals and potential. Therefore, the aspects to Jupiter describe whether, at the end of his life, the individual will have accomplished his goals. Naturally he can change his patterns if he is aware of the kind of photographs he has made of the opposite-sex parent.

When Jupiter is well aspected and placed in this house, the lifestyle will be extravagant and luxurious. The individual may desire more than one residence. He may graduate from one home to another. He may be challenged by the experience of expanding his lifestyle constantly. The size of his home may not be grand and

Jupiterian, but the ambience certainly will be. He likes a free-flowing lifestyle, with eclectic tastes. He may have traveled in his life and accumulated objects that are symbols of his expansive attitude. He is happiest in his own environment. The relationship with the parent of the opposite sex will be joyous, optimistic, humorous, and stimulating. He will be given permission and encouragement by that parent. More than likely, that parent will have been fortunate in life, or especially philosophical and even religious. He or she may have been a teacher. The individual with Jupiter in this position of the chart can look forward to abundance in his later years. His accumulated wisdom and experiences will stand him in good stead as he ages. If anything, his good fortune increases as he grows older. If Jupiter is not well aspected in the chart, the possibility of disappointment is strong. The parent of the opposite sex may not have reached his potential, may have disappointed the person with this aspect, and may have been less than encouraging. The patterns can be changed with therapy, or any form of awareness, in order to facilitate better conditions in life.

The fifth-house placement of Jupiter describes abundant talent. Creative urges are strong, whether to procreate or express qualities of joy through art, painting, and especially teaching. The fifth house might be called the house of gambles. It describes love, romance, children, entertainment, investments, the stock market, and playing the horses. If Jupiter is well aspected in the natal chart, all such gambles and activities will be lucky. Divine protection seems to exist with the expression of creativity. Children will be philosophical, humorous, and nature-loving. Entertainment will be lavish and extravagant, investments will be blessed. Contagious enthusiasm seems to attract a quality of divine protection.

If Jupiter is not well aspected, all these areas can promise disappointment on some level. That disappointment may come from an overly expectant attitude in the first place, however. Expectations can be very high, with a resultant tendency to overdo. If the person is optimistic about something, he may put all his energy into that situation instead of hedging his bet. If he invests all his money in a stock that he *expects* to do well and is let down, his devastation is total. He may need to discount his own enthusiasm somewhat. He eventually learns to do a bit less, expect a bit less, and have a bit less overexpectation. He may expect so much from his children they cannot possibly please him. In romantic areas, he looks for a challenge, someone who appears to be wealthy or optimistic and may discover that the capture of his prize is not as much fun as the chase. He may buy too much food for a party, invite too many people, expend too much energy in frivolity, rather than aiming for the highest expression of his talent.

The sixth house describes the kind of work an individual is attracted to, the way he works, and the quality of his health. When Jupiter rules or is posited in this house, enthusiasm describes his attitude about his job. He is attracted to anything that allows him to give encouragement or express his natural joy. He can be abundantly healthy, with great stores of energy. He loves a challenge with his work. He may be involved in sales, even when that is not apparent. He wants to grow and learn through whatever his occupation might be. His quality of expansion can give everyone around him permission to tap their own life goals. Jupiter rules the hips, thighs, and kidneys. It may also describe the pancreas and the liver. It can also include the adrenal glands. If Jupiter is well aspected, these organs function well, but if Jupiter is not in good dialogue with other planets, those same organs can malfunction. He may overdo, overwork, overeat, and thereby abuse his preordained good health. Disappointment with his work can clearly affect his vitality. He may have a tendency to overindulge in food and drink to compensate for the letdown he experiences. It is very important for him to set goals on his job. He needs to have new horizons to conquer.

The seventh house describes partnership, whether that partnership is a marriage or a personal partnership or a business association. If Jupiter is placed in or rules this house, the attraction is always toward someone who expresses the Jupiterian quality of optimism. The person with this placement may be unaware of his need for wealth on the part of a mate. He may not actually look for material wealth, but the quality that is permission-giving. The partner may be especially philosophical, expansive, or wealthy of spirit. If the mate possesses that true wealth, the probability of material wealth can follow. In fact, disappointment frequently comes when the expectations are for material wealth; the partner may have a façade of grandeur that belies the true facts. Qualities of spirituality may also keep the partner locked in his own visions of universal truths, rather than dealing with matters on the earth plane. He may simply be in love with the wealth of the universe and forget to deal with matters of practicality. Aspects to Jupiter describe the exact quality of the expectations or disappointments in connection with marriage or a business partnership.

When Jupiter is placed in the eighth house or is ruling that house, joyous enthusiasm enables the person to get his needs met easily. The eighth house is the natural Scorpio house. It describes transmutation on a spiritual, psychological level. It is first necessary for the individual to practice getting what he wants from life before he can understand the giving out of that particular brand of energy. A baby is not able to be generous or think of people around him. He is self-involved. Eventually, however, he is grown, saturated (or not, as the case may be) and begins to expand his consciousness. He first expands to his immediate environment and his family, then begins to look to community and the broader plane. The extent of that expansion is of course up to him. With Jupiter describing this house, he is fortunate in getting his own needs met and is therefore more likely to easily look outside his own frame of reference. In fact, his curiosity leads to the giving of himself, his exuberance, or his money. He has great generosity of spirit. The likelihood of inheritance exists. He may also be most fortunate in income that is derived from royalties, commissions, or bonuses.

If Jupiter is not well aspected, it is in this area that disappointment can occur. He may be expectant, let down, and then tempted to run up bills or overextend financially in compensation. Indeed, he may motivate himself to a bigger and better ability to get his needs met precisely by setting himself up for disappointment. In any case, the gift he can express to humanity is encouragement. His greatest talent is to give permission to others, even if he suffers slight letdowns himself. He is the eternal optimist about people and their ability. He may even be more encouraging when things are not going so well in his own life. It is his way of talking himself into a better frame of mind. His way of raising funds, collecting income, or asking favors is to sprinkle any requests with a strong dose of humor and expectancy. He may truly believe that his windfall is just around the corner. He may not intend to mislead anyone or himself. He is simply paving the way for good fortune to follow.

People may have to learn to take his brand of enthusiasm with a grain of salt.

Jupiter rules the natural ninth house in the natural progression of rulerships. Therefore the ninth house describes philosophy, expansion of the higher mind, universal truths, and new horizons. Those rulerships can encompass travel, dealings with foreign countries, or unexplored territory of the mind; they describe publishing, higher education, promotional effort, publicity, and legalities. When Jupiter rules or is placed in this house in particular, curiosity about the workings of the universe is very strong. The desire to explore, expand consciousness, and satisfy longings for the unknown leads the person to travel. Whether that travel is physical or mental really doesn't matter. He is definitely not interested in settling into a preordained kind of thinking or living.

The individual with Jupiter in this house can be attracted to the academic world. The Jupiterian's natural ability to teach can find an ideal outlet in this way. His special curiosity about the workings of the minds of others enables him to have constant new material for his instruction. The changing scene around him keeps him challenged and on his toes. Jupiter is not necessarily a planet of action but, rather, of philosophy. He may satisfy his longing for travel through books and information, rather than through actual experience. He can be especially good at promotional efforts, distribution, and public relations if Jupiter is well aspected. If it is not, he can suffer disappointment in these same areas.

Career matters, social desires, and public behavior seem formed by the identification and association with the parent of the same sex. The tenth house is the sector that describes the quality of energy connected to these areas. When Jupiter rules this house, the enormous store of enthusiasm, joy, and expectation can go into career activity. The parent of the same sex may have imparted a special brand of philosophy, joy, and encouragement that enables this person to express those qualities easily in public areas. He is especially good at sales, encouragement of participation from others, and expression of a philosophical goal. He may be able to minister to others through religion, activities connected to nature, and areas that are constantly expansive. He may not be satisfied with only one career. When he has learned or expressed all he feels he can in one area, he wants to go on to others. He cannot bear static conditions in public activity.

If Jupiter is not well aspected in the natal chart, the person may be constantly overextended in his public activity. He tends to take on more than he can handle, overestimate the response from authority figures, and set himself up for disappointment. That source of disappointment may originally have been connected with the parent of the same sex. His reaction can vary from an unwillingness to set goals in the first place (for fear of a letdown) to overextension. The first step of the antidote is simply to recognize the patterns. He may have to diversify his interests to avoid focusing too much energy on one project. If he puts all his eggs into one basket, he has nowhere else to turn when things go sour. The aim of Sagittarius, the archer, may have to be adjusted to allow for the wind drift. He will never suffer great misfortunes in his public life, no matter what the aspects, however. His natural *c'est la vie* attitude will enable him to direct his attention elsewhere without too much sorrow. Jupiter is, after all, the planet of luck and abundance.

When that fortunate planet is placed in the eleventh house, luck lies in companionship. The individual is blessed with good friends who are optimistic, philosophical, and joyous. He can share laughter, and discussions that are basically philosophical and encouraging. He seems never to lack for association with people. If his natal aspects to Jupiter are not all harmonious, he may have to allow for some letdown from friends. He can give encouragement and feel it is not returned, or simply be overloaded with group activities. He may have too much to do in connection with group endeavor. Yet his natural enthusiasm makes that a natural place for release of joy. He can attract wealthy people or simply people who have wealth of spirit. Great good fortune goes hand in hand with his spirit of friendship.

The twelfth house describes the subconscious processes, matters that remain hidden, and in particular, how the individual feels, thinks, and behaves when he is all by himself. It can describe qualities that are difficult to express openly or in front of other people. Jupiter in this house or ruling this house gives an inner optimism and joy that keeps him challenged no matter what the outer circumstances. Quite often, the personality of the individual with this placement belies the inner spiritual quality and attunement. His feelings about life may be more connected to the nature of things, rather than any identification with a formal type of religion. He may not talk about how he feels or exhibit those qualities, but, as an inner quality of joy is bound to manifest in some fashion, he can seem very calm and centered. When the barriers are down and the individual is safe, his inner optimism will show itself most easily. Humor emerges, and he may be willing to share his deep philosophy about life. If things are not going well for him on a surface level, a long walk in the woods will restore perspective easily. This aspect can describe a quality of strength that will see him through almost any kind of turmoil or trial.

If Jupiter is not well aspected, just the opposite can be true. That inner quality of joy gives way to an inner sense of joylessness or despair. The negative side of Jupiter can indicate a quality of paralysis. Without expectations or goals, the individual cannot express action or challenge himself. Since this aspect may be very subconscious with a twelfth-house placement of Jupiter, it may take a long time to uncover the primal cause of this attitude. His earliest disappointment may have come prenatally. If Jupiter is ruling the twelfth house and Capricorn rules the ascendant, childhood rejection can bring about feelings of despondency or even despair. The inner voice says, "What's the use?" Early disappointments in his life seem to confirm what may be a survival issue. Regression therapy is especially important in this case. It takes a special kind of awareness to tap the wellspring of enthusiasm that is most naturally there. Meditation or any form of inner attunement can enable the individual to reprogram that habit of lowered expectation.

JUPITER CONJUNCT SUN

The qualities of the Sun and its placement in the zodiac are always modified when it is conjunct another planet. Naturally, it is a mistake to identify or characterize a person by the position of his Sun at birth, or the Sun sign, but particularly so when another planet augments what might be the natural characteristic. The Jupiterian augmentation gives a quality of expansiveness and humor that is hard to miss, no matter what the birthdate of the individual. The sense of self-worth is connected to an identification with nature, the universe, and a general feeling of expectancy. Enthusiasm is marked, as is an abundance of high energy. The feeling of the joy of life is rather easily recognized.

The individual quite naturally develops a philosophy and modus operandi that is similar to what might be characterized as the Sagittarian quality. He needs goals to stimulate and challenge him; he is the eternal, or cockeyed, optimist, and perhaps the luckiest person in his own sphere of activity. Erma Bombeck has this aspect in her chart. Her Pisces Sun with Capricorn ascendant seem overshadowed by her Jupiterian humor and *c'est la vie* attitude. Generosity is another characteristic of this aspect. Erma is indeed connected to several charities. Whether that generosity is with money or is simply given in the form of encouragement, it is a special privilege to the recipient. The person with Jupiter conjunct Sun can seem to mitigate any existing shadows in his own life or in that of others by presenting a different point of view. His enthusiasm is contagious, as is his generosity of spirit. Erma is able to express her special gift and brand of encouragement through her books, newspaper columns, and appearances on television.

Sidney Poitier has Jupiter conjunct his Pisces Sun as well. In his case, the placement lies in the fifth house of creativity, and rules the areas describing friendship, group association, and communications. Life may reflect art, but art reflects aspects also. Sidney typified the quality of this aspect in his film *Lilies of the Field*, for which he won an Oscar. It is fascinating to notice that film casting is always in harmony with characteristics that can be identified in an astrological chart. It is unlikely that Sidney would ever play the antihero. Sidney's own life may not have been that easy as a child, since he was the oldest in a family of eight children. Yet he made his own luck. Fortunately, that luck is magnetic. Sidney's talent is obvious. Yet the quality of optimism may have been a major factor in the recognition of that talent. With Jupiter-Sun ruling the house of contracts, negotiations, and communications, Sidney can "sell" anyone anything. In *Lilies of the Field*, that is precisely what his role was all about. Jupiter describes religion. Again, in the film, he was associated with nuns. Even in films such as *The Defiant Ones* and *No Way Out*, Sidney had to emerge with hope and expectancy.

Carl Sandburg was born with this aspect in his chart. The placement of the Sun is in the sign of Capricorn, yet his philosophy is surely optimistic, hopeful, attuned to life's higher goals. Jupiter rules and is placed in the third house of communications, with the Sun in the fourth house of home. The Sun rules the eleventh house of friendship, associations, and group activity. Although the aspect was always there in potential, it was the latter part of his life that brought the greatest gifts to him. He associated with many people who expressed wealth of spirit. Sandburg was very prolific in his writing and won numerous awards for his work.

Juan de Aguirre is a Leo Sun sign with Jupiter in the sign of Virgo conjunct his Sun. Even though these two planets are in different signs and in different houses, the aspect gives the same optimistic, philosophical quality of expression. The Sun is posited in the first house of personality, in Juan's chart, with Jupiter placed in the second house of income. Jupiter rules the fifth house of creativity, investments, and children. Jupiter is associated with religion as well as with mundane ideas of expansion. Juan had the potential of tremendous material wealth in his life, but chose instead to devote himself to religion. He joined the priesthood and was a Jesuit for nineteen years. His Jupiterian need for learning was satisfied through work with what might be the most prestigious educational system and group of teachers in the world. He loved his life, dedicated to study, teaching, and ministering to people, but that life was not without problems. The obvious manifestation was health problems, which forced him to leave his chosen work.

The Jupiter quality has also been associated with "foot-in-mouth disease." The strong Jupiterian characteristics seem to manifest in a rather blunt way of speaking that can sometimes hurt others and cause the individual to regret his brusque manner. Juan described it in this way: "Many of the troubles I had as a Jesuit were caused because I spoke openly. My superiors reacted as could be expected. Before I entered the Jesuits, I was a noisy Leo with a criticizing mind. I said what I thought. My superior said I had a mouth like a surgeon's knife. I became totally honed after becoming a Jesuit. (Juan also has Mercury conjunct his Sun and Jupiter, giving an extra quality of enthusiastic speaking.) I weighed two hundred pounds in those days. I suppose I just couldn't go unnoticed, but it was very subconscious. The dramatic impact is obvious." Jupiterian expansion is also obvious in this manifestation because Jupiter describes the physical appearance in Juan's chart, as well as the personality.

Juan might have gone into the family banking business if he had remained out of the priesthood. He said, "I don't understand finance. I cannot grasp concepts about money. I feel quite happy if, at the end of the year, I have had enough and especially if I find that I have some left over. I'm always absolutely honest and straightforward about financial matters, and I'm also concerned about doing what is right. My assumption is that other people will be ethical also. I can be disappointed, but my usual attitude is 'Let it go, don't worry.' But of course that kind of attitude, a typical Jupiterian one, doesn't work too well with money on a practical level."

Carl Jung said that any unrealized energy, or potential, exteriorizes as fate or destiny. After health problems forced Juan to leave the priesthood, he married a very special lady who shares his philosophy and attitudes about life. Juan and Magdalena have two beautiful young daughters. They are both very happy children, outgoing, optimistic, and a joy to be around. They may well be the ultimate expression of the "luck" in Juan's life.

Since Jupiter rules the fifth house of children and creative ability, Juan also has a special talent. He plays piano, preferring the classics and liturgical music. He has also found a language that can express much of his philosophy; it is not usually associated with religion, but is a study of nature itself. Juan is a tireless student and researcher of astrology. The very symbology of the centaur searching the heavens for new meaning may characterize his life.

JUPITER IN HARD ASPECT TO THE SUN

When Jupiter is in difficult aspect to the Sun, luck does not seem diminished. What becomes more apparent is the tendency to take on too many projects, become involved in too many activities at once, and exhibit somewhat of a grandiose manner. Extravaganzas and excesses of all kinds can be quite natural to one with this aspect. Disappointments may never be known by the outside world. The Jupiterian easy-come-easy-go attitude can cover quite a few letdowns. The individual with such an inner dialogue is always hopeful and expresses that attitude no matter what his real expectations might have been.

David O. Selznick was among the most prolific film producers of his time, producing films over a period of twenty-two years. His greatest work was so extravagant and spectacular that it is still being seen by audiences forty-five years after it was released. The classic epic *Gone with the Wind* was his production, as was *Rebecca*, starring his wife, Jennifer Jones. He won Oscars for those two films as well as many awards for the overall quality of his work. The Sun in his chart is in the sign of Taurus, placed in the tenth house of career and public activity, with Jupiter squaring it in the seventh house of marriage. Jupiter rules his work, whereas the Sun rules his financial house. We can obviously associate the extravagance connected with this aspect in his career and work. We may not know the secrets of his financial life and marriages. More than likely, it could be presumed that he was over budget in his films and may have had overexpectations within the confines of marriage. He may have been so occupied in his work and public life that he caused disappointment on the part of the women he married. This aspect also carries the sting of promising more than can be delivered. Allowances always have to be made for these promises, because the intention is there. Sheer enthusiasm tempts the individual to think he can do more than he actually can. His promises should be taken with a grain of salt. David Selznick's lifestyle and films represent the grandiosity that is associated with difficult aspects to Jupiter.

Johann Sebastian Bach and Benjamin Franklin had Jupiter in opposition to the Sun in their charts. On a personal level it is hard to know what might have been their overexpectations, but the personalities and talents reveal the convivial, outgoing description of Jupiter in difficult aspect. Bach's music is grand and grandiose, Ben Franklin's talent extremely prodigious. Both men may have lacked time enough in life to express all they desired. The religious quality of Jupiterian energy is exemplified in Bach's music; in Ben Franklin's life, the attunement to nature was obvious. His philosophy was key to much of his success in life. Perhaps his greatest accomplishment was his contribution to the Declaration of Independence, a work that gave joy and hope, optimism and encouragement to millions of millions of people. The grandeur and foresight of the future are apparent in the drafting of that great document.

Marianne, with Jupiter opposite her Sun, met an Arab student, married him, and joined his harem. Jupiter rules her first house of personality and personal life, with that planet posited in the ninth house of travel, foreign countries, and international affairs. The natural curiosity about the lifestyles of others may have led her to attempt the difficult transition from America to Saudi Arabia. The Sun in her chart lies in the third house of communications, and rules the eighth house of getting her needs met. Obviously, she must have been disappointed in the amount of time she could spend with her husband and in the expectations of what might be forthcoming. He divorced her with no warning and would naturally have kept their children, according to Muslim law. Luck was manifest in her chart by the winning back of her children through a legal battle that was unheard of in Muslim law. Jupiter describes that house of legalities, in her chart and is actually placed in the strongest position in the chart. We can only imagine the quality of adventure that came her way through that marriage, even though it was contained within the walls of the harem. Jupiter also rules her twelfth house of the subconscious. Marianne may have needed that quality of life to develop her inner spirituality to its highest degree. Overexpectation and disappointment may have led her to the inner search that would not have been possible in any other way.

JUPITER CONJUNCT MOON

The Moon describes the sensitive nature. It is associated with emotion, and identification with women in particular. It can also indicate mothering qualities, nurturing potential, and a special sense of what mankind shares in common. Depending on the placement of the Moon, the specific quality of any vulnerability is surely indicated, the precise way of showing emotional reaction. When it is conjunct and augmented by a Jupiterian energy, it is the same as if the Moon were in the sign of Sagittarius. Humor and joy are a saving grace when this aspect is found in a natal chart. No matter how painful things may be, the person with Jupiter conjunct Moon can laugh about his troubles. He seems to restore his perspective and philosophical viewpoint in that way.

Andrea is an elegant English lady with Jupiter conjunct her Moon in the first house in her chart. That placement of this aspect describes the conditions of childhood and early life, as well as birth survival decisions; the personality development comes as a result of the circumstances at that time. Whenever the Moon is placed in the first house or ruling the ascendant, conditions of childhood are very emotional and traumatic. The feelings of abandonment may have been literal and real, or connected with small incidents that are nevertheless very meaningful to the individual.

Andrea confirmed that by saying, "I was abandoned by my mother when I was four years old. She was a principal soprano with an opera company and took me on tour with her, very much against the wishes of my father and the rest of the family. She obviously neglected me very much. I was left alone at night and must have been very frightened. When I got back home, I had lice in my hair. I can remember that I was never allowed to watch her rehearse, which hurt me very much. I loved watching her. So I was kept away from everything the whole time. I was very frightened of my mother. She was very, very temperamental, very fierce. She had a caustic way of speaking and was very psychic, so she could really get to what would hurt most. Something drastic must have happened, because after I was home again, I had the most fearful horrors at night. I would awaken shrieking and screaming. I was extremely neurotic. She would give me a tremendous beating for looking out the window when I was supposed to be sleeping. I was always supposed to sleep, being bundled away when she was singing or practicing, without even a book to read or anything to play with.

"My mother ran off with her leading man, so my father divorced her, a thing unheard of in those days. I was brought up by an aunt and later on, a stepmother. I have never had a feeling of security, unless I had enough money. I've been so poor in my life, and that gives such an inferiority complex. Money represents freedom. There is no escape unless you have money in the background. Now that my personality is slotted into place, I think I can begin dealing with that issue."

The Jupiter-Moon conjunction also rules the second house in Andrea's chart. It would appear that Andrea has the potential of earning a great deal of money through her personality and self-expression, with Jupiter ruling that house. Financial increase can also come through partnership in her chart, since the aspect also rules the seventh house of marriage or business partnership. However, the feelings of abandonment and disappointment described by this aspect can also relate to finance and partnership. Andrea confirmed that she had been married to someone very sensitive and had been abandoned by him. "I was married to a man whose mother died of alcoholism when he was only eighteen months old. He was brought up by a very strict Edwardian grandmother who had no love in her soul. He became an alcoholic. I absolutely adored him, but I was in such a terrible state myself because he wouldn't give me any money. I had to divorce him to get a court order for support. He was impossible temperamentally. He was brilliant, hypersensitive, moody, and needed mothering. He simply couldn't cope. He was probably latent homosexual." The Moon describes feminine characteristics in an individual no matter what the sex. Andrea may always be attracted to a mate who expresses more of the anima qualities than the animus. When the aspect ruling the first house also rules or describes the seventh house of marriage, the person may want to find his soul mate, or someone who is an exact reflection of himself. In Andrea's case, she would ideally seek the mutual caring and sharing of joy and nurturing. The Moon also describes strong feelings of symbiosis. Andrea's need to mother would bind her to someone who needed that quality. Emotional ties would be strong. Yet the Jupiterian need for a challenge might be denied. Jupiterian energy in marriage in particular demands the space to grow unhampered through constant learning and experiences.

Andrea is now married to a charming, handsome, elegant man. She said, "We both want the space to be ourselves without the other person following you around all the time. Sometimes I go off and leave Brian and he really likes it. Then he goes off and leaves me and I like it. Then we come back together again. The strongest thing we have in our marriage is the spiritual connection. We can argue or have the most fearful rows, but we are on the spiritual path together. Brian told his mother when he met me that he had found his soul mate."

When Jupiter and the Moon are conjunct in the natal chart, especially if there is a connection with the first house of appearance, or the sixth house of health, there may be a tendency to gain weight. That weight gain may have much to do with retention of fluids. The individual can blow up or feel bloated, almost with the phases of the Moon, or so it might seem. When young, Moon children appear very skinny, with spindly arms and legs, yet develop into plump adults, especially after about forty years old. There can also be an extremely strong connection with people on a gut level. The solar plexus seems out of whack, out of line with the rest of the chakras. The Jupiterian enthusiasm can tempt the individual to eat too much. The idea of expansion is there with food and drink as with everything else.

The joyousness can be very apparent when this aspect is prominent in the chart. Sometimes that quality of enthusiasm hides a pack of troubles, however. The Jupiterian optimism can also give an appearance of wealth and elegance when that is in fact not the case. Yet the joy, humor, optimism, can be very magnetic, attracting those conditions on a material level if the emotional part of the duo can be brought under control. The Moon is magnetic, attracting the exact emotional response in other people that is inherent in the personality of the person with this aspect. It would appear that the first step in reconciliation and harmonizing of these two voices is to become aware of the feelings, sensitivity and needs in the lives of others.

Since the Moon describes such an identification with the astral level of feeling, the person with this aspect can be especially sensitive and responsive to emotions of mankind in general. He can sense the trends of the times and know how to nuture people. He may express this quality more easily by learning, first of all, how to avoid taking on the problems of other people. He can be a rescuer, then be doubly hurt when his attentions and ministrations are not appreciated. He may have to work on a less personal level. Jupiter describes a teacher at heart, whereas the Moon describes a writer. This may even take the form of writing about personal experiences in order to give permission to others to survive with joy. The life may be important in particular in order to exhibit the strong natural spiritual tendencies that lift the emotions above the level of circumstances.

Sir Thomas More had this aspect in his natal chart, as did Joan of Arc. Erasmus, Copernicus, and Leonardo da Vinci also shared this conjunction in their charts. Whether the expression of this quality was through religion, as in the case of Joan of Arc and Sir Thomas More, or through gazing at the heavens, as with Leonardo and Copernicus, does not matter. Erasmus expressed his joy through the philosophical message. The irrepressible joy cannot be contained for very long, no matter what the gloomy or difficult outer circumstances might be. Joan of Arc epitomized this quality of joy throughout her life. She seemed able to transcend the pain during her trial and execution in a way that was more uplifting than anything she might have said. Her life was devoted to the giving of joy to others.

JUPITER IN HARD ASPECT TO THE MOON

The difficulty associated with the divergent qualities of these two planets can be intensified when they are in hard aspect to each other. Joyousness seems in conflict with emotional reaction. The paradox may be that once goals are set and optimism is released and aimed, the potential for hurt can be the greatest. With vulnerability and sensitivity, the joy of the challenge is watered down with overreaction. Disappointment then prevents the enthusiasm needed to work up to new challenges. In this instance, the key to the dilemma lies in the antidotes for each quality of dialogue. When the Moon is expressed in a less than productive way, it is essential to analyze what is happening. There is a likelihood that the individual is reacting to transference from other people. He may only be a mirror for the feelings and upsetting events around him. With greater awareness, he can then react less painfully to himself.

When Jupiter is in hard aspect to the Moon, consequent overexpectation can produce such emotional reaction that the disappointment negates the usual joyous, optimistic outlook. Yet, the solution may lie in the awareness of grandiosity on the part of the individual in the beginning. He may have promised more than he could deliver, aimed for targets that were really out of reach at that moment, or failed to diversify his attention and energy in the most productive way. Since Jupiter describes overdoing something, the individual may overwhelm people or the situation with his enthusiasm, leaving the potential for a letdown once he withdraws his energy. He may expect reactions from life situations that are impossible at the moment. With too much of this merry-go-round, the person may make an inner adjustment of resignation that does indeed leave him exposed and vulnerable to the winds of fortune.

Miguel de Cervantes had Jupiter square Moon in his natal chart. His great work, *Don Quixote*, identified with the quality of feeling and disappointment in all of Spain in 1605. His description is still considered to be a portrait of the Spanish character, to some extent. Cervantes himself must have experienced the hurt, disappointment, and frustration in his own life to see so clearly what others felt as well. Petrarch, the Italian poet and humanist, with Jupiter square his Moon, expressed the same mixture of optimism and tragedy described by this aspect. Yet it can perhaps be seen most clearly in the life of Julius Caesar. The aspect between Jupiter and the Moon is inconjunct in his chart. His words (according to Shakespeare) "Et tu, Brute?" express all too well the resigned pain that can be indicated by this aspect.

Marilyn seems to have an especially happy disposition with an ability to shrug off disappointments with a philosophical attitude. But Marilyn has Jupiter square her Moon in the natal chart and that astrological aspect would indicate deep disappointments that she might tend to hide, since her Moon rules the twelfth house of the subconscious. Jupiter rules and is also placed in the fifth house of creative expression, children, and romance. The Moon resides in the eighth house of getting her needs met. One of the biggest disappointments in her life is connected to her children.

"After Andrew and I were divorced, we had joint custody of our two sons. Andrew worked from an office at his home but I had to go out and get a job. The boys were going back and forth and it was really not good for them. Their grades were falling and they were always behind with homework. I finally signed a paper letting them go to live with Andrew. Although they could come and go whenever they liked and I could see them at any time, it really killed me to give them up. I was simply devastated. But Andrew could give them a much better lifestyle than I could. They travel a great deal now, go to really good camps, and if I had them, they wouldn't have gone to Hawaii and to see the Rockies. I actually think they are closer to me than if I had them with me all the time."

She described the hurt and betrayal she felt over the difficulty in getting the child support she was due. "Andrew owed me money constantly. I had really expected that he would take care of the children, but he reneged on me by not paying alimony. He kept cutting back constantly, which naturally hurt the children. Not only did I lose any possible interest, but I would have to pay lawyers' fees every time I was forced to use legal means just to get what had been agreed upon. I would finally just throw up my hands and say to myself, 'forget it.' However, very recently my younger son began to express his sympathy. He said, 'Does Dad owe you money?' When I said yes, the tears started to flow. He said, 'Mom, it isn't fair. You've worked hard all your life. Why don't you kidnap me and put me up for ransom? Dad has everything and you have nothing.' It was the first sign I had that he was even aware of what had happened. He usually keeps things to himself. I realized I must do something so that he doesn't feel sorry for me and mother *me*. Now that I've finally thrown it all out to the universe, I have recovered my philosophy. I have high hopes but I'm working on not putting all my eggs in one basket. Since I have adopted the new attitude, I have not had a letdown. I'll go after some project I really want, but if I don't get it, I'll go after something else. In the old days, I would think of something I wanted very badly, like a particular goal, but I would immediately say to myself, 'I might not get it.' I didn't set goals because if I didn't reach them, it would have hurt too much. Now I know how to cover myself and avoid the paralyzing disappointment."

JUPITER CONJUNCT MERCURY

Jupiterian qualities describe a need for continual learning and growing throughout life. The challenge and quest of knowledge is intensified when this expansive planet is augmented by Mercury. The difficulty lies in the decisions about focus. Mercurial energy is microscopic, attentive to details, knowledgeable on a practical level, whereas Jupiterian growth is far-reaching, toward the horizon. The left-brain activity described by Mercury is concerned with research, accumulation of data, and storing facts. Jupiterian goals lead toward philosophy, universal curiosity, and spirituality. If the individual with this aspect can integrate and harmonize these energies, he has an unbeatable ability to see into the distance while dealing on a practical level of manifestation in the here and now.

A natural outlet for this quality of mentality can be seen in the life and works of William Blake—poet, mystic, and artist who was born in 1757 and died in 1827. He was a master in each field. The expansive quality of his mind made much of his works incomprehensible to the average man. Scholars study Blake's works for many years to uncover the obscure meanings. In his chart, the Jupiter-Mercury conjunction is placed in the fifth house of creativity, ruling the sixth house of work. Mercury rules his twelfth house of the subconscious, and fourth house, describing later years. Blake was able to tap a universal, subconscious source of genius within himself and translate it into language of philosophical mastery.

Carl Sandburg also had Jupiter conjunct Mercury in his chart. The quality of universality and philosophy indicated by Jupiter is obvious in his poetry, prose writing and speaking, which are mental, or Mercurial, activities. Willa Cather, an American author who wrote about nature in particular, used the aspect in a positive manner by focusing on life as she saw it. A man little known in this day and age was John Dee, astrologer to Queen Elizabeth I. His Jupiter conjunct Mercury was also a reflection of his personal viewpoint, which enabled him to give information with great enthusiasm. His counsel was to a queen especially skillful in skirting the practical, political dangers surrounding her. His advice may have helped.

Since Jupiter describes grandiosity, any overexpansive plans, goals, and ideas can lead to danger with this aspect. For the negative side of the Jupiterian coin is great disappointment. The quality of enthusiasm may not have boundaries of practicality. Two people whose lives ended in disaster because of this overwhelming grandiosity were Louis XVI and Napoleon Bonaparte. Luck in original manifestation of goals can tempt the individual to do more and more, without thought of the cost to others. If the practicality of Mercury can focus the far-reaching view of the Jupiterian energy, and the lure of bigger and better things can be kept in perspective, success is evident and long-lasting.

JUPITER IN HARD ASPECT TO MERCURY

Perhaps the most tragic thing to observe in the lives of other people is an incident of broken dreams and unrealized goals that brings an individual to a point of no return. When that quality of joy seems to be buried in a pit of despair and obscured forever beneath a mound of unforgettable disappointments, there seems to be no way to restore humor and perspective. The individual becomes paralyzed on some level. This quality can be associated with Jupiter in hard aspect to Mercury. Originally, there was hope. With each situation that failed to live up to expectations, a tiny drop of despair was etched into the soul. Goals and expectations may lead to more of the same. The *c'est la vie* attitude turns to "What's the use?" To find a positive outlet for this particular quality of energy may be difficult, but it is imperative.

Charles Dickens was born with Jupiter inconjunct Mercury in his natal chart. He wrote about the hopelessness he saw around him at that period of history. The conditions were terrible. Joy seemed something to squeeze out and ration, like a tiny bit of pudding at Christmas. Only occasionally and after much struggle did his heroes and heroines find the light at the end of the tunnel. Robert Burton, born in 1577, inadvertently wrote about Jupiter opposite Mercury, found in his own chart. His book was entitled *The Anatomy of Melancholy*.

Jane Austen, brilliant English novelist, also had Jupiter opposite Mercury in her chart. She wrote about conditions that were hard and life that could be grim. Astrologer-prophet Nostradamus predicted events five centuries into the future. To this day, he is read by many people who seem able to decipher his words and glean understanding about history and the future. He is rarely considered to be a doomsday prophet, yet Nostradamus does not seem to convey the hope that man's free will can transmute and forestall an ultimate calamity. The light at the end of the tunnel is the age of true enlightenment, peace, and tranquillity after the catastrophe. Could it be that Nostradamus saw an atomic war that would indeed wipe out humanity? We can only hope that with Jupiter in opposition to his own Mercury, he would be hesitant to predict hope because of his own experiences in life.

Noelle is an especially talented French astrologer with this aspect in her own chart. As is often the case when Jupiter opposes Mercury, it also opposes the Sun. The travels of Mercury and the Sun through the zodiac are such that these two planets are conjunct in many charts. Noelle's Sun conjunct Mercury rules the tenth house of career, the eighth house of getting her needs met and inheritance, and the eleventh house of friendships, groups, and associations. That conjunction is placed in the ninth house of publishing, travel, philosophy, and the higher mind. Jupiter is in opposition in the third house of communications, and rules the second house of money. Noelle's chart is a "finger of God" chart (one with all the planets on one side of the wheel, with one planet leading the way like a point). Jupiter is the point or release of energy in her chart. It would appear that it is extremely important for Noelle to write, teach, or be involved in communications to release any possibility of disappointment in her own life.

Noelle is familiar with the aspects in her own chart. We talked about the ways in which she has experienced overexpectation. She confirmed that she has had disappointments from friends that have been really devastating. Travel is an activity that is at the top of her list of priorities, but she confessed she has had incredible experiences traveling in less than first-class manner just to get to where she wanted to go. In getting her needs met, Noelle was especially specific. She said, "I did have an inheritance from my father in the last years when he was alive. But it wasn't money I wanted from him. My family couldn't give me what I really wanted. They were always too poor for my taste. But what they didn't give me was something else. I had an image of how I wanted them to be. They didn't have the self-image I needed from them. I wanted much more from life than they could ever offer me. I'm always inclined to ask for less than what I want, rather than more. I feel guilty about asking for things at all."

We discussed the photographs she had taken, in her subconscious mind's eye, of her mother. "My mother suffered a lot. She died when I was thirteen, so I did not get my needs met from her. She had the potential of being the strong, dominant one. She had to take on everything and she was very capable, but she suffered so much. She was dominated by my father; I would have wanted her to be stronger, more capable of saying what she needed and wanted. She was very loving and wouldn't hurt a fly. She had a basic kind of intelligence, but she was a martyr. We never knew what her illness was. She just wasted away."

In Noelle's chart, the Jupiter opposition to the Sun-Mercury conjunction describes her mother. Her despair was in connection to the despair that she saw in her mother's life. She described the tragic events that led up to the time of her mother's death. "She really didn't want to marry my father. But she got pregnant and had to marry him. Then my brother died at birth. Before that, during the war, she was in a concentration camp. All her family were killed. I can't identify with all that suffering. It's like I'm of a different race and live in a different world.

"Of course I feel so guilty about my mother. I suppose I don't quite take charge of my life in that I pick men who may stop me, just like my father stopped my mother. There are areas of my life I feel I cannot handle very well. Money and my profession are especially difficult areas. I have high goals, but I may overwhelm myself with expectations of how things should be. I am ambitious on a philosophical level, not on a worldly level. I feel like a pilgrim climbing a mountain. If I reach the peak, I just have to come down again."

The description of the Jupiterian energy always needing something out of reach seemed appropriate in Noelle's experience. She clarified that a bit more. "I have learned in my life that the disappointment comes when you think you're eating the whole pie. You desire something and you eat it, thinking it is what you really want. Then you realize it is just making you fat. So you want something else, something just a little bit farther on. But everything takes time, all the growing and learning. If you let yourself have everything too soon, maybe there's nothing left to go toward. So you only let yourself have a little bit of the pie. Then you have the whole pie to look forward to. I would really like to be totally me and not let any disappointment in. I know I'm going to reach my goals, but they are always just a little bit farther on." With Noelle's knowledge of astrology and human nature, it seems certain that she will not allow herself to give in to less than joyous expectation of her own future. She knows, as do all true astrologers, that "The fault, dear Brutus, is not in our stars,/But in ourselves."

JUPITER CONJUNCT VENUS

Venus is usually associated with love, art, theater, and any activity that brings pleasure or ease of living. Venus is considered a benefic, as is Jupiter. When these two planets are conjunct, the luck in some area of life can bring great comfort, pleasure, and ease. Since the negative aspects of both these planets can only describe overdoing with pleasure or the love nature, the results are never "bad." However, as is the case with Jupiterian grandiosity, there can be a temptation and a tendency to overdo, have overexpectation and extravagance of pleasures and comfort. The most negative trait associated with Venus is laziness or a tendency to take the easy way out.

Sharon has Jupiter conjunct Venus in her chart, posited in the third house of communications, describing her relationship to siblings. The conjunction rules the first house of personality, self-expression, and outlook on life. Sharon's humor and philosophy were apparent even as a young child. She is outgoing, affectionate, and very beautiful. Graciousness and charm are quite natural attributes. Her relationship with her siblings and other relatives is especially diplomatic, generous, and affectionate. She is often the peacemaker in areas of conflict. Her love of learning was obvious from the beginning of her school years. She never seemed to consider that study was drudgery or anything less than pleasurable. A very special talent was exhibited as a tiny child. Even at the age of one, her ear for languages was exceptional. She never mispronounced a word or substituted baby talk for a difficult sound. Later, when she learned French, her accent was so perfect that she was mistaken for a native Frenchwoman. The Jupiterian need for constant challenges with learning is apparent in her life.

Sharon began working in the communications fields when she was a teenager. She spent a great deal of time commuting around New York City, another third-house activity, juggling schoolwork with a great deal of other activity. Her school grades never suffered. It seems that wherever Jupiter is placed describes a need for bigger and better, more and more. The challenge of many projects is stimulating. Sharon did her first feature film when she was fifteen; however, that film was never released. That Jupiterian disappointment must have been difficult, as there was a great deal of buildup from producers, friends, and well-wishers. The overexpectation connected to Jupiter was obvious then. Although Sharon was offered a generous Jupiterian contract from a major Hollywood studio, she declined. She continued to work in the communications fields, but her original expectations and joy never seemed to be quite as strong after that first experience of disappointment.

With all her interests, Sharon has found a special pastime that presents a constant challenge and brings her constant pleasure. She has become an expert horsewoman. The symbology of the Jupiterian Centaur has become literal in her life. The freedom she experiences in riding provides outlet for the need for a pleasurable challenge. Experiences with nature and animals are associated with Jupiter, whereas the harmony she can achieve is connected to the Venusian concept of balance. She seems to have mitigated any disappointments connected with that aspect.

That special blend of gentleness apparent with Jupiter conjunct Venus is also seen in the creative work of Sissy Spacek. The aspect is placed in her fifth house of creativity, talent, and gambles, and rules the second house of income, the fourth house, describing homelife and relationship with her father, and the ninth house of publicity, public relations, and travel. Within a short period of time, Sissy was able to win recognition for her talent and thereby fulfill the promise of a Jupiter-Venus kind of income. This aspect describes a trend toward extravagance that may be transmuted in her life. She lives modestly. Yet her leanings toward nature, the metaphysical, and the philosophical are a higher octave of that same quality of energy. She expresses a great deal of her need for creative challenge by dancing. She must constantly find the beauty and art of self-expression, whether through dance, theater, or other kinds of artistic outlet.

JUPITER IN HARD ASPECT TO VENUS

When these two planets are in difficult aspect to each other, the negative dialogues describe disappointment and a tendency to overpassivity. Overadaptation can be the end result. What once might have promised to be great shining adventure may now be only a shadow of a memory of expectation. The person with this aspect may hesitate to set in motion any conditions that can bring about more of a letdown. He can be overly diplomatic, unwilling to disrupt the status quo, and hesitant to be totally forthright and precise about a situation. Since Jupiter is associated with grandiosity, psychologically speaking, overdoing with love, diplomacy, or ease of living is quite possible. This aspect can describe a basic tendency toward possessiveness in love. That in itself may bring about disappointment when that kind of love is not returned.

Liv Ullman has Jupiter square Venus in her chart. Jupiter is posited in the eighth house of inheritance, death, and getting her needs met. Venus is placed in the fourth house of home, describing a relationship with her father. Venus also rules that house, with Jupiter ruling the fifth house of creativity, romance, and children. Liv's father was killed when she was only five years old. She was not able to get the love from him that she obviously needed. The devastation of losing that first major love in her life may have tempted her to cling to love after that. She was extremely passive in her relationship to Bergman, for instance, making sure that his privacy was not disturbed and his volcanic personality set in motion. She had a child by Bergman without the benefit of marriage, a love child indeed. She may not have cared about a legal ceremony at that point in her life. Bergman's influence on her acting ability was to hone and perfect her natural talent. She learned to act with mobility and restraint, expressing her special gentleness with strength. With Jupiter square Venus in her chart, Liv may never be satisfied with her own performance. She would surely be in need of constant creative challenges.

When Jupiter is squaring Venus, the general tendency is toward possessiveness. The love nature is abundant, but the quality of the return in affection may always be slightly disappointing. One person may love a bit more than the other one. When this energy is released on a universal level, or the individual learns the meaning of universal love, the disappointment is abated. Abundance of affection and love come pouring in from many people and also from the object of the personal affections. Diversification is necessary, as is the partner's understanding of this need to express the love nature and affection in many ways. Art, creation of beauty, and dealing with social concepts can help with this diversification. Love is very important for one with this aspect in the chart.

When this aspect describes areas of health in the chart, the sweet tooth can be indicative of a tendency toward sugar imbalance. The disturbance to the pancreas may vary from a mild form of hypoglycemia to diabetes, if that disease runs in the family. The obvious psychological implications are that the individual cannot get enough sweetness, or love. The craving may be for carbohydrates in other forms. It is wise to look out for kidney weaknesses as well as liver ailments. Moderation in all things seems essential for the balance and maintenance of optimism and joy.

JUPITER CONJUNCT MARS

Mars is the planet that describes basic energy such as ambition, drive, and aggressive action. It is related to the sexual energy as well as the highest creative urges. Mars energy is forceful, quick, and impatient. When Jupiter is augmenting the quality of that dynamic pioneering tendency, initiative is even stronger. Mars is the ruler of Aries, the first sign of the zodiac. The desire to be first is apparent in pioneering tendencies. The Jupiterian qualities of goal-seeking are very much in harmony with the energy of Mars. High success comes with tremendous drive, resourcefulness, and enthusiasm. The individual can deal with competition with humor and goodwill. He loves the challenge of a healthy skirmish, with the best man winning the prize. He has no desire to enter into a competitive situation unless he can be sure of a worthy opponent. Mars is always strong in the charts of athletes, for the challenge of competition is the basis of sports. The world of entertainment can also present a natural outlet for someone with this energy. New opportunities are ever present for many qualified people to try to usurp the present champion. Since Mars describes sexuality, many stars have this aspect in their charts. The allure of that Mars physicality can be an important part in winning coveted roles.

Hugh Hefner was born with Jupiter conjunct Mars in his natal chart. The aspect is divided between the fifth and the sixth houses, with Mars positioned in the fifth house of romance, creative expression, and the gambling urges. Jupiter is placed in the sixth house of work and health. Mars rules the eighth house of getting needs met, inheritance, income through royalties, dividends, or franchises. Jupiter rules the fourth house of home. Hugh's romantic, creative energy is especially high. He is famous for his romantic involvements, usually with girls who have worked for him. He has built an empire that brings abundance of income through property, home, or investments in land. Hugh's Playboy Clubs throughout the United States are very successful. His own home is lavish, in keeping with the Jupiterian need for opulence and extravagance. The fifth house describes entertainment as well as investments. Hugh combines entertainment with work, fulfilling the description of work and play described by a Jupiter-Mars conjunction. He is known to be very hard working, never satisfied with the status quo. His ambition is prodigious, bringing great bounty in his chosen lifestyle.

One of the most dynamic businessmen in the entertainment world is Kirk Kerkorian, chairman of the board of Metro-Goldwyn-Mayer. Kirk has Jupiter conjunct Mars in the ninth house of travel, legalities, promotional effort, and distribution. Mars rules his eighth house of getting his needs met and income from investments, and Jupiter rules the fourth house of home. Kirk founded his own airline corporation and, in the style of Howard Hughes, became involved with the entertainment world. He managed to overcome many obstacles connected with MGM at the time he took the reins. By selling property belonging to that giant studio and building a huge luxury hotel in Las Vegas, he managed to get the studio out of debt. Kirk's personal lifestyle reflects the grand design of his continuing ambition. As a young man, he was a scrapper, fighting all the time. He became a boxer and was nicknamed "Rifle Right K." He was able to transmute all of that fighting spirit, drive, and ambition into very successful enterprises. Kirk is a pilot and flies his own plane. He is generally never still or in one place for very long. It would appear that in the case of both Hugh Hefner and Kirk Kerkorian, the good fortune associated with Jupiter becomes increasingly better as time goes on.

Marlene Dietrich may well be the epitome of sexuality, still gorgeous and alluring in her eighties. With Jupiter conjunct Mars in her fifth house of creativity, entertainment, and romance, it is no surprise that she was still appearing on stage as a singer when she was in her seventies. Jupiter rules her fourth house of home, with Mars ruling the eighth house of getting her needs met. In Marlene's case, she became a fighter for her homeland. The transmutation of the eighth house describes the ultimate contribution available to be sent out to humanity. When it is connected to Jupiter, Mars describes reform, fighting for better conditions, and ambition on a more philosophical level. After focusing her energy toward building her own lifestyle, with income from the investment of her time, energy, and talent, she began to fight for others. She refused to live in Germany under Hitler's regime, and even though her films were banned in Germany, she fought on a subtle level for freedom for her country by entertaining Allied troops on the front line. Courage is also a characteristic of Martian energy, especially when connected to Jupiterian enthusiasm. She was awarded the U.S. Medal of Freedom and the French Légion d'Honneur. When Jupiter rules or is placed in the eighth house, the message that is sent out is one of giving permission, encouragement. Her contribution to the war effort through her personal initiative, courage, and talent enabled the fighting men to have a symbol of hope and encouragement. The uplifting of morale was obvious. Her strongest message was "Go to it, you can do it." The same message is there for womankind as well. If Marlene can keep her sexuality and vitality throughout her life, there is no reason why women all over the world cannot retain their youth.

JUPITER IN HARD ASPECT TO MARS

When these two planets are in hard aspect to each other, the release of the fighting spirit is more difficult than when they are harmonious and easy. The struggle connected to the two internal messages can also produce great results, but not without continual battle, it might seem. Nothing seems to be easy with this aspect, yet the energy produced by the friction of these two planets can even increase the ambition, fighting spirit, and drive. Goals may continually have to be redefined, because overexpectation is likely. It would seem in this instance that the disappointments in life only intensify the need for ambitious outlet. Sexuality is strong, perhaps never totally fulfilled, and any competitive situation may produce slightly less than expected results. Yet new goals and challenges can always promise the pot of gold at the end of the rainbow.

Eartha Kitt, talented black singer, has Jupiter square Mars in her chart. Jupiter is placed in the sixth house of work and health, and rules the third house of communications. Mars is positioned in the fourth house of home, also describing the relationship with her father. Mars rules the partnership area in her life. Eartha's father, a sharecropper, left home when she was only two, leaving her mother quite deserted and with two children to care for. Her mother died when Eartha was six. Childhood was a nightmare of insecurity, starvation, and beatings. She moved to the New York slums when she was eight and began to learn street survival. The anger she must have felt over her father's desertion and the disappointment may well have acted as an unconscious motivation to succeed in her work. Whatever overexpectations Eartha had in connection with contracts, work, marriage or partnership, and her lifestyle can only be assumed, yet the constant battle enabled her to fight for women's rights after her own success was assured. Her need for constant learning, challenges, and goals has produced an erudite, well-traveled woman who speaks six languages. Her story is another source of encouragement and permission to anyone with hardships to overcome.

One young lady found a unique way to transmute the obvious tensions and disappointments in her own life as indicated by Jupiter square Mars. Jupiter in her chart is placed in the eleventh house of associations and friends, and rules the twelfth house of secret affairs or the subconscious processes. Mars is placed in the eighth house of getting her needs met, and rules her homelife. Strong need for associations seems to bring some kind of disappointment in her life, so secret associations within her own home can compensate for any lack of activity with groups. She expressed a strong sexuality in belly dancing, but ultimately found a course on sensuality conducted at UCLA. She became a sex therapist, acting as a surrogate sex partner recommended by several psychologists. She sees about seven clients a week, usually for a period of four months up to two or three years. She said she considers her work to be healing and teaching. She feels that sexual dysfunction is really a problem with intimacy. Her feeling is that she is very helpful and it gives her satisfaction to provide such a service. Mars in the eighth house indicates a need to pave the way for others, "break the ice," and be a pioneer. Naturally her work is done in her home in the privacy indicated by the twelfth-house placement of Jupiter.

ASPECTS TO SATURN

IN THE EVALUATION OF THE PLANETS, SATURN IS THE heaviest of all, for it describes the area of the individual's breakthrough, in psychological terms. It represents the outer boundaries of gravity that keep a person earthbound physically, emotionally, and spiritually. Saturn represents tradition, duty, responsibility, and anything that keeps one tied to limiting conditions. Saturn is the value judgment inherited and absorbed from the moment of birth. It describes "shoulds," "musts," and "oughts," the guilts that keep us bound. But without Saturn, no one would be able to accomplish anything. Saturn is the testing ground of life and indicates the greatest karmic lesson to be learned.

After the breakthrough of Saturn is accomplished and the restrictions are resolved, the individual begins to work on the higher octave, of Uranus, Neptune, and Pluto, but before one can take flight, the engine must be checked, safety precautions observed, and higher responsibility assumed. If the square of Saturn is never rearranged to form the geometric five-pointed star, and limitation is accepted as inevitable, the individual remains in a static position. There are key times in life when the pressures become so intense that the person may have no choice but to grow. He is squeezed upward onto a new level, blasted out of his rut and forced to take a new look. Growth seems always to be born of pain. If it were not so, mankind would not create such pressures and limitations in outer conditions. The hermit, represented by Saturn, keeps a careful, watchful eye on the progress, step by step, of each soul's growth.

In the positive sense, Saturn describes security, practicality, and parenting. It is the platform of good, solid earth beneath the feet. It has been associated with drudgery, fear, and negativity, however, because of much misunderstanding. It may be that Saturn, along with Pluto, is the most perplexing of the energies described by astrology. Saturn has alternately been called the teacher, the devil, the planet of bondage. The Saturn card in the tarot deck is enough to make anyone want to turn away from anything associated with that planet, for it depicts a great black beast with two tender people chained to it, one in each paw. The overly harsh description of the Saturnian energy needs another look. For it is true that Saturn describes worry, fear, and heaviness, but the discovery of the psychological issue behind those fears can set one free. It is the *why* behind the *what* that is important.

If life is viewed as a laboratory, and Saturn as the major experiment we choose to work on, a new perspective can emerge. Because one chooses to go into that laboratory, he can become an alchemist and transmute leaden fears into gold. It may take a bit of time to learn the secret of that formula. He can be told how to do it, but until he completes the experiment, it remains merely a formula on a piece of paper. Others can lend a hand, give some hints, but no one can do it for anyone else. The problem lies in the resistance to shutting oneself in that room. The darkness of the windowless laboratory makes one long for sunlight and fresh air. One dreams of the beach, the mountains, long walks in the woods, time with his friends. Suddenly the day is over and he has neglected to finish his experiment. Now he must dread the thought of going back into the confines of that space the next day. He must continue to go back into that room day after day until he finally, joyfully, sets out to create what he has chosen to do and completes his experiment. He can then go out beyond that place of limitation. With the recognition of the creativity associated with Saturn, freedom can exist. Only on the earth plane, or in that laboratory, can the practice take place. The sheer weight of Saturn, or gravity, enables the individual to sit on a lower level of vibrational energy to work out the details of the individual experiment. Saturn can seem stronger in the charts of more evolved souls, who have come to the earth for a specific purpose or karmic resolution. Without that heavy ball and chain, the light soul would simply float upward. He, in particular, seems to have to weight himself down. Saturn can be the sandbag that keeps the helium-filled balloon from floating away prematurely.

Saturn operates under the fear principle until greater understanding of that energy is accomplished. It describes seeing a glass half empty instead of half full. It indicates regimentation instead of technology. It describes the boundaries and walls a person erects around himself, the split, the division, the cracks, instead of the wonderful refractions of the crystals of life. The ultimate responsibility of Saturn is seeing the joy of completing the individual experiment which then enables the person to lend a helping hand. He becomes a good parent to himself first; then he can be supportive of others. Pain is transmuted into joy, sorrow into celebration, fears into creativity. Since life is a canvas, the determination to create beauty instead of ugliness is a matter of choosing the right colors and paints. Saturn describes choice, determinism. Saturnian energy is sometimes seen as selfish energy, yet selflessness can come only as a result of the resolution of the ultimate choice to complete the individual alchemical task. Once that commitment is made, the experiment begun, the attention focused, the task can be finalized. The ultimate choice is whether that job is done joyfully or begrudgingly.

The breaking down of the walls of fear, self-righteousness, defensiveness, limitation, and drudgery brings an individual into the Uranian light of humanitarianism, healing, and ultimate freedom. Then his perspective is one of looking down on the limitations or restrictions imposed by the natural gravitational pull of earth, instead of looking out through bars. It is merely another quality of energy that must be handled. To substitute *I choose* for *I must* gives an entirely different perspective to things. Finally the individual learns to choose more wisely until he has reached the point where Plutonian transmutation makes choice unnecessary. Then he can go on remote control, which means that he turns his life over to his higher self, being motivated not by personal gain, but by a sincere desire to want only what is right for all concerned. Then he proves to the higher self, the parent ego, that he is ready. Until that decision is made, the individual can put himself through incredible tests and torments, described by Saturn.

Saturn has been described by the Kabbalists as the "playpen" that Mother Earth puts her children in. We put babies in a playpen to keep them safe, out of harm's way. But eventually the baby must leave the protection of those four walls and learn to take care of himself. We give a child more freedom when we're convinced he will act in a responsible manner. So it is with Saturn. Wherever Saturn lies in the astrological chart is where life presents some limitation, yet protection. It may be a self-imposed playpen comprising messages such as fear, worry, or insecurity. When we convince our higher selves we'll be responsible and good to ourselves, we give ourselves more elbow room. To work past restrictions is simply to take on more—but better quality—responsibility.

In terms of Transactional Analysis, Saturn represents the parent ego state. We develop parental messages inside our own brain by listening to what we have been told by parents or parental figures. We may be repeating those internal messages long after they are necessary for protection. Finally, with reexamination of negative internal injunctions, we begin to take responsibility for unblocking that quality of energy or potential that has been repressed. Transmutation of energy in a person's life simply has to do with the decision to use a particular potential in a positive way, rather than in a negative manner. It may not be easy to let go of fears, insecurities, and overly judgmental messages, but eventually it may be necessary to work past those blocks in the system.

The last analogy for Saturn is related to a tarot card, the six of swords. That tarot card shows a mother, father, and child in a red boat. The card is the card of journey. If we consider that card as representative of life's journey, the mother and child represent the conscious and subconscious minds. Those two figures are sitting down in the boat, with swords or crosses in front of them, so that they are unable to see where they're going. The father is propelling the boat by standing up behind and using a long pole to push clear of the shore. The father represents the superconscious mind, or God-self. If we are piloting our "vessels" from the higher perspective, we will never get too close to the shore or hit a rock. The father takes care of the mother and child. His purpose is to take them downstream to the ultimate destination. He takes care not to damage the vessel; otherwise, mother and child could drown. When we are working from conscious and subconscious levels, we really don't know where we're headed in life's journey. Periodically, we decide to try for security and get close to the shore. Sometimes we hit a rock that has jagged edges and get pulled in by its whirlpool of negative messages. It hooks our insecurities and says, in effect, "Stay here with me. I've found a nice, safe harbor. Don't go downstream, because danger may lurk there." We buy into the restrictive messages, hook up to the rock—which is really just stuck in the mud—and stay until it is no longer possible to get away. Or perhaps at the last minute, we get away as fast as possible before drowning. As we leave, the rock may move a tiny fraction out of its stuck place, simply because the wake of our vessel stirs up enough turbulence to disturb things slightly. Saturn in a chart can represent "rocks" that, because of their own insecurities, give us negative but "be safe" messages. Many times, an individual hooks up to those rocks, uses people to act as playpens, because he needs an excuse to remain in a rut.

When Saturn is placed in or is ruling the first house, the individual is overly cautious, insecure, shy, or judgmental. The feeling of rejection may have been strong in early life, causing the person to adopt an overly judgmental attitude toward himself. He seems unable to see where and why insecurities developed, takes on a rejection complex, and needs desperately to be needed. His early message may have been, "I won't eat too much or take up too much room. Then someone will want me if I'm perfect." Later in life he learns how to upgrade the quality of responsibility. He will always act as the parent figure in a relationship, but may be quite well barricaded behind his own walls.

With a second-house placement or rulership of Saturn, finance is the cause of worry, restrictions, and fear, yet the individual can eventually work past limitation and take on responsibility to earn his own money. This placement can cause a "poor" complex: no matter how much money he or she has, it may never be enough to stop worrying. He may wish to avoid the responsibility of financial matters but must handle details and become financially secure. The placement can represent an early fear or sense of limitation with funds; yet, later on, the individual may find great security in the financial arena by transmuting his worry into learning to structure financial arrangements in a practical way.

A third-house Saturn placement or rulership indicates a specific need to be involved in communications. Early in life, the child has a tendency to be overly hard on himself in connection with schools. He may not be given permission to express himself or can be criticized for his views and ideas. He may have karmic, or "heavy," relationships with siblings, yet, in a positive sense, feel a great responsibility toward or from those siblings. Eventually, an individual with Saturn ruling or posited in the third house must break through barriers with communications and be involved with activities in which he must express himself, working past the fear of not being perfect. His greatest security eventually comes through discussion, negotiation, talking, writing. Learning to communicate effectively will build a platform of security beneath him.

When Saturn is posited in or ruling the fourth house of home, the individual's security lies with land, property, development of real estate, or dealing with matters connected to the earth. Early in life, he may resist an expansive lifestyle, feeling more comfortable with a small living space. Even if the person lives in a grand or lavish manner, he may always want one little corner that he can call his own. He needs a small space to feel secure. These patterns are developed by the relationship with the parent of the opposite sex. He may have felt judgment coming from that parent, or great support. Nevertheless, that parent would have expressed more feelings of caution, insecurity, and limitation than the same-sex parent, and would have delivered the negative or "be safe" messages, depending on the aspects to Saturn.

The fifth house describes the gambling tendencies. It rules such activities or situations as love, romance, creative self-expression, children, investments, and entertainment. When Saturn rules this house, the creative instincts can be repressed or stymied. The individual may have insecurities about his talent. If he learns a technique in connection with creative expression, he can feel on safe ground, but by and large he is not a risk taker. In romantic areas, he may need someone who is always there for him, expressing a strong sense of responsibility, yet may resist finding the romance he really craves. Affairs of the heart may be tinged with a practical streak. His children may be especially serious, responsible, dedicated, yet act like the parent. He may need to be needed by his children to the point of exclusion in expression of his own talent. Yet children become his security later in life.

Saturn ruling or posited in the sixth house describes a need to work, take on major responsibilities with his job, as well as a need to be of service on some level or other. He may avoid working on a level of ultimate responsibility, instead overloading himself with responsibility for too many mundane details. He may work long, hard hours until he has to get sick to get out from under the pressure. Health matters demand attention when Saturn rules this house. Ultimately, the individual must learn to delegate responsibility so that he can work on a level of service that demands much of his true essence. He may avoid working on a high level of responsibility early on, until he has no choice but to work up the ladder to the level where he is really needed.

The seventh house describes marriage or business partnership. When Saturn rules or is placed in this house, the restrictions or security in life are in this area. An individual may look for another person to give him a sense of security and, depending on how Saturn is aspected in the natal chart, can find a lifetime, secure relationship in marriage or feel tremendous restrictions in that area. A person with Saturn not well aspected may attract someone who is insecure, has feelings of limitation, or is hard on himself or herself. Marriage represents the playpen in both positive and negative ways. The marriage or business partner can be the one to assume great responsibility or wish to avoid it. The individual will look for someone conservative in partnership matters. He or she may be looking for a parent. With awareness, the business or marital partnership can provide great security without the restrictions that are possible.

In traditional astrological language, the eighth house described death, yet in psychological terminology, this house represents the ultimate transformation, perhaps including death and rebirth of the self. Another way of describing this sector of the chart relates to the way in which one gets his needs met. After an individual has convinced himself of his ability to get what he needs and wants from life, he then is ready to make his contribution to society and humanity. With Saturn ruling or posited in this house, early in life there may be restrictions in getting needs met. The person with this aspect hesitates to ask for anything at all, in case there are strings attached. To him, the word *obligation* is the dirtiest word in the English language. The final transmutation for the person with this aspect is to find a situation that is so compelling that he overlooks any insecurity in getting his own needs met, as he is dedicated to taking on higher responsibility for humanity as a whole. He may discover that with a higher sense of service he is able to get his own needs met as well.

With a ninth-house placement of Saturn, a strong emphasis yet resistance come with promotion, publicity, and recognition. If Saturn is well aspected, an important focus and security in life comes with travel, higher education, publicity, distribution, legalities, promotional efforts. Early in life, the individual may resist the idea of being in the spotlight. He may dislike the routine of travel, yet be faced with the necessity of dealing with it. As he tackles responsibilities in a stronger way, he builds security through his willingness to expand.

When Saturn rules or is placed in the tenth house, career emphasis is especially strong. Usually, the parent of the same sex represents the ultimate authority figure in one's life. If the parental messages were supportive, the individual builds great security by taking on high responsibilities in public life. If he has had judgmental messages, overly cautious injunctions from that parent, or even rejection, he will take on responsibility in his career, yet overload himself at the same time. Later on, after he has more sense of security with his efforts in the public arena, he begins to take on responsibility for his own company, or to do something that will benefit people on a higher level. His image in public areas will always be one of dedication and high responsibility. He learns eventually to tackle only projects that demand much of him and provide security for others.

The eleventh house describes friendships, groups, organizations, associations. The individual with Saturn placed in this house will find great security in friends or associations that have been in his life for a long time. He may look for conservative people with whom to associate, and can sometimes attract friends or organizations that represent security, yet are actually inhibited and give forth judgmental, overly conservative, cautious messages. He may choose to associate with people who provide a particular kind of stability, yet do not encourage him to express individuality. Their strongest message is "Be like us, don't go downstream." He may eventually have to cut away from negative influences and hook up with associates or organizations that are dedicated to a higher level of operation.

Perhaps the most difficult placement for Saturn is in the twelfth house. This is the sector of the chart that represents subconscious fears, guilts, insecurities. Saturn in this house or ruling this area of mind can indicate a feeling of imprisonment, defeat on a' deep level. Johannes, a German psychiatrist, described this by saying, "I feel as though I've had a shadow on my soul all my life." An inner paralysis prevents the individual from reaching out for opportunity.

It may be that guilts from a previous life or strong subconscious programming prenatally gives the child inner fears or guilts. This placement has been said to describe a karmic, racial guilt that keeps the individual from letting himself have ultimate success or attainment. It is as if he could atone for any sins of omission or commission by refusing to allow himself the greatest success in his own life. The individual may be especially hard on himself subconsciously. Regression therapy uncovers a great deal of subconscious sadness and seems to give the individual permission to express more of his inner longings. This is one of the psychic houses. When Saturn is placed in the twelfth house, a refusal to trust psychic impressions may be due to fears that a monster lurks somewhere in one's past. With some light shed on the subconscious fears, the subconscious areas of inspiration can be safely opened.

SATURN CONJUNCT SUN

Since Saturn describes the greatest area of scrutiny, in this case the ego (Sun) comes under pressure. This aspect describes the true perfectionist, one who is incredibly hard on himself. The degree of perfectionism and self-pressure the individual exerts may be in direct proportion to his degree of procrastination. A deep sense of responsibility makes him serious, dedicated, and highly structured, yet the opposite side of the coin is also true. He has deep insecurities, fears, and worries that may keep him somewhat boxed in. He may doubt his real worth and therefore have to prove to himself and to others that he is really a deserving individual. He may have such a strong sense of destiny that he must keep himself regimented for fear he won't accomplish what he feels he must in life. He may never have had the ego strokes he needed early in childhood. He is an old soul come back to take on high responsibility.

The Sun represents not only the ego and sense of self, but the soul quality. No matter what placement or sign the Sun occupies in the chart, the person with this aspect expresses a Capricornian quality. He has long-range goals, can take only one step at a time, and cannot be pressured or pushed. He pushes himself so much on an inner level that he will be defensive against any external load. He can tend to take on more than is really healthful, yet he thrives under these responsibilities and may use them as a kind of structure to prevent imposition of outside forces. His ego is the vulnerable point. He needs outside permission to feel worthy, and he may not ever get what he deserves. If he is given acclaim, recognition, and responsibility, he may doubt the sincerity of the honor. He may not be able to accept strokes, for those strokes only make him guilty and consequently under more pressure to perform perfectly.

On a physical level, the Sun represents the heart center and the fire element. There can be a restriction around the heart center and a damping of the natural enthusiasm when the pressures are too much. His programming must have included such injunctions as "Be perfect," "Do your duty," "Be a good soldier," and similar messages. He knows no other way of behavior and may have to work very hard to get away from a rigidity and inner closing off around the heart area. He can block a flow of feeling around the heart center and may not allow himself any deviation from his chosen path. Yet, he can avoid the ultimate responsibility of his executive potential by taking on too much of the wrong kind of pressures. He may have a deep karmic guilt about his leadership potential.

He may have an inner sense of self-consciousness that makes him feel cut off, barricaded, even different or isolated from his fellowman. He may desperately need recognition from his peers to know that he really exists. He may pretend that he doesn't want accolades, but his need for ego strokes can sometimes be transparent; his very soul is hungry for the conditions that will make him feel good about himself. He thinks that if he is really at the top of the mountain, he can relax and survey all that he has accomplished, yet the minute one mountain has been climbed, another one looms in its place. He may, sadly enough, surround himself by the very people who will continue to remind him of his imperfections. He can feel quite safe if he can put up his defenses and feel justified in cutting off again. He then only feels more isolated and alone.

He can be controlling, judgmental, parental, and rigid on an inner level, yet not show any of those qualities on a personality level. His judgments and control are aimed mainly at himself. If, however, he is hard on himself, he will expect others to be hard on him and he will also express that even on a subtle level. He cannot handle guilt, yet he may put himself in situations that constantly stimulate guilt feelings. His inner message is "Don't pressure me," yet he will go to the very person who puts him under pressure. His very body may show a quality of rigidity that bespeaks blocked energy flow. Inside, he is as tightly wound as an unreleased spring, even though outwardly he may look at ease. He can be overly proper, overly formal, and very barricaded.

Saturnian energy can be masochistic because of a sense of deprivation. Deep-seated guilts can make it seem essential to be deprived in some way in order to feel OK again. Those conditions of deprivation and the need to repeat them can be far from conscious. Many times, extremely early conditioning leads to the conditions that bring deprivation and pressure over and over again on an entirely subconscious level. If the individual can really confront his need to be deprived, he can break the patterning. Sometimes the sense of deprivation seems necessary to accomplish what the person feels he must; if discipline replaces pressure, the accomplishments may be more productive and easy.

John was able to bring a great deal of information into the open about Saturn conjunct Sun because of his commitment to more understanding about his own energy blockage. John has participated in many forms of therapy, from bioenergetics to Transactional Analysis. During a regression session, John experienced what he had been told about the conditions of his birth and infancy. He was born just after World War II came to a close, but conditions were still quite grim in Europe at that time. His father was a sailor and was never at home, so John rarely saw him as he was growing up. Three weeks after John was born, his mother was taken back to the hospital for an operation and he was taken there to be near her. Yet he was placed in a room where he was completely isolated except for the times when his mother fed him.

John told the following story. "During the regression session, I became aware of what it felt like to be in that room. It was just terrible. I had been around my mother and my aunt at home, in comfortable surroundings where I was held and cared for, and suddenly I found myself absolutely alone. I could have screamed and screamed and no one would have heard me. I felt so totally isolated and so lonely and cold. I could sense myself struggling to get up off my back so that I could see something or do something about the situation, but all I got was an intense backache. I have worked and worked in bioenergetics to get rid of the back pains that still bother me, but I didn't really know how early they started. I would see my mother so rarely, only when I was fed, and then I was put into that room again.

"There was so much blockage of energy at that time that my limbs have been ice-cold many times in my life. I have worked through a lot of that in therapy, consciously learning to let go and release the tensions, but that has not been easy. My sense of isolation continued throughout my childhood, because my brother was born handicapped. Most of my mother's attention had to go to him. I had to consciously set a time during group therapy sessions when I was willing to be helped by the participants. Some of that fear and sense of isolation was helped by allowing people in the group to hold me and touch me. But that horrible feeling of isolation would return when I was put down again. Even in those sessions I could deal with the sense of aloneness more easily than I could deal with the loss and deprivation of touching. Naturally, I picked a cold wife to stay safe. I am no longer afraid of relationships, but I do respect the personal privacy and space of others. My goal is to keep my space but allow other people in."

I asked John about his sense of self-worth as a result of all that isolation. He confirmed a lacking of ego and sense of self. He continued, "First of all, I rarely saw my father and it was from him that I wanted ego strokes. I felt as if I had to set boundaries with my mother and keep her at arm's length in order to build any relationship with him at all. I could feel the tensing around the heart area in connection with feelings for my father. He hardly knew I existed, much less was he able to be proud of me. There is another factor at work here too. I was never told that it is OK to think well of yourself. This aspect is a hell of a job to break."

John had a birthday during the time we were together and we celebrated with a party and silly gifts. It was obvious that he was not easily able to accept the caring and attention that were lavished on him that evening. His natural graciousness and charm enabled him to be sociable, but he was clearly touched on a far deeper level. It was a joy to see the pleasure he felt when the people around him expressed their caring. His natural dignity and prideful bearing would have led other people to expect that he would not care very much for a display of affection; yet just the opposite was really true. John has Saturn conjunct the Sun placed in the tenth house of public life, social situations, and ruling the relationship with his father. Because of strong determination and need, John is able to express natural executive capacity. With the resolution of Saturnian energy, he may have a much stronger destiny in store for him in the public arena.

David Frost has this aspect in his chart. David also has Saturn conjunct the Sun in the tenth house of career, but an additional Jupiter conjunct the midheaven, describing great good fortune and luck in career, mitigates the sense of deprivation. In connection with public activity, however, David is serious, capable, and very shrewd. The focal point of Saturn in his chart enabled him to express the determination to build an important public image very early in his life. Only through the chart is it possible to see the frustrations that must occur in connection with career projects. David will never be considered frivolous or less than serious. In fact, the quality of formality that is associated with a Saturn-Sun conjunction is very apparent. He never quite lets down his own barriers even when he is probing behind the façade of his TV guests.

Arnold Schwarzenegger has Saturn conjunct the Sun in the first house of personality. Although Arnold would not be the typical example of a conservative personality, his determination to discipline his body enabled him to build not only muscles but a worldwide reputation. The discipline necessary to hold world body-building titles is a positive example of the rigidity of perfection connected to this aspect. Ultimate discipline in some area begins to release restrictions.

SATURN IN HARD ASPECT TO SUN

As usual in a difficult aspect, the two voices are more difficult to reconcile. The inner quality of self-esteem may be squelched by outer conditioning but produce a character that is strong and determined. Anyone with such an aspect is a responsible citizen, needing to be needed, determined to accomplish something in life, if only to prove to himself that he can do it. But he may still have the masochistic aspects within himself that ultimately make him fail. He seems not to be able to accept too much success.

John Mitchell has Saturn square the Sun in his chart. He reached a point of prestige in his career when his leadership ability could not be denied. As Attorney General of the United States, he could go no higher unless he sought the office of President. He was Richard Nixon's law partner and climbed with him to the executive pinnacle by first managing Nixon's campaign, then celebrating the fruits of victory. Mitchell has Leo on the ascendant with the Sun posited in the first house. The leadership, the executive quality was doubly strong. Saturn is placed in the tenth house of career, ruling the sixth house of work. No one could accuse him of shirking his duty, neglecting details, or shunning responsibility, until Watergate. But he must never have been given the ego recognition he deserved by his father, or even in his public life. Nixon was always there to be more prestigious. Mitchell may have felt colorless beside him.

John Mitchell ruined the strong reputation he must have worked so hard to build by his connection to the Watergate scandal. He may have been motivated by the possibility of more glory than would have come with another term in office. But it may have been a subconscious way of persecuting himself, to keep himself humble and limited. Jail proved the ultimate deprivation and limitation that Saturn can describe. Self-punishment and masochism reached an ultimate with the international scandal of Watergate and its aftermath.

Some unlikely people have Saturn squaring the Sun in their charts. Two of the most successful comedians, Erma Bombeck and Phyllis Diller, share this aspect. Their humor is based on self-deprecation, however. Nelson Rockefeller had Saturn square his Sun, with the Sun placed in the ninth house and Saturn posited in his house of work. His financial situation hardly required his working, yet with strong parental messages he sought public office. He held the high office of governor of New York State for fifteen years and then sought the highest office in the land by running for President in 1960 and in 1968. He became Vice President under Gerald Ford but never reached the top position in the land.

Two exceptionally brilliant actresses, Diane Ladd and Sally Field, also have this square aspect in their charts, as does Doris Day. Doris became (and still is) the ultimate symbol of the girl next door—but it may not have been the role she really wanted to play, over and over. Sally had tremendous success early in her career by

playing the starring role in *The Flying Nun*, and later success came
with her brilliant performance in *Sybil*, for which she won a TV
Emmy. She worked with Burt Reynolds in *Smokey and the Bandit*
and was dramatically powerful as a social worker in a later film,
Norma Rae, for which she won an Academy Award. Sally's romance
with Burt Reynolds may have been dampened by her tremendous
public success. In her chart, the conflict lies between a need for
personal life and friendship and the demands of her career.

Diane Ladd made major headway in her career by playing the
gum-cracking, tough waitress with a heart of gold in *Alice Doesn't
Live Here Anymore*. But it was Ellen Burstyn who won the Academy
Award. Diane won an award in London for that performance, but it
wasn't very meaningful in sunny California, where only the Oscar
really counts. Diane went on to a starring Broadway role in *Texas
Trilogy*, playing Lou Ann Laverty, the little Texas cheerleader who
grew to maturity in front of the audience's eyes. Not a dry eye was
left in the audience at her final scene and she received a standing
ovation every night. But the show closed after only a few weeks of
performance. Diane went back to the role she created in the television version of *Alice*, but the working conditions were very trying.

Who knows what subtle early conditioning prevents talented
people from achieving their ultimate goals? In Diane's case, she
was always slightly lacking in ego-stroking from her father. A damaged psyche seems to continue to magnetize situations in which
frustrations exist. It may be the manifestation of a continuing need
to be deprived, or second best, or a subconscious way of keeping
the ego in check. The pride must necessarily suffer when other
performers, perhaps less talented, continue to reap the fruits of
success.

SATURN CONJUNCT MOON

When Saturn is conjunct the Moon, the fears have to do with expression of feelings, emotions, and vulnerability. The tendency is to
put up a barricade against those situations or people that could
trigger upsetting reactions. The Moon describes areas where strong
symbiosis can develop, whether that symbiosis is with an individual
or with masses of people. The nurturing instincts could be quite
strong and rescue tendencies pronounced, but the individual has

resistance and fears attached to such strong emotional sensations. Instead, he puts up walls, blocks feelings, and suffers from deep depression. This particular aspect describes symptoms that are especially paradoxical and difficult to resolve.

There may have been deprivation in the oral stage of development. The child cuts off his oral needs as his inner, judgmental, parent ego says, "Don't feel, it's dangerous." If the deprivation had to do with contaminated mother's milk (that is, laced with anxiety, worry, or fear), there may be an inner message of "Don't eat." In his later life those messages persist. Unless he has worked very hard to unblock those emotional areas, he will pick the very person who does not "feed" him and who cares little for his emotional welfare. He can attract and feel safe with someone cold and unresponsive. Then when he receives little support on a feeling level, he goes deeper into depression. He may be totally unaware that he has erected a thick wall to protect himself from hurt. He cannot show his neediness. Therefore he doesn't get his needs met.

His own mothering instincts may be undeveloped as well. He has such a fear of too strong a symbiosis with someone who will not care about his needs in return that he doesn't allow himself to express his caring. He can appear cold and unresponsive. Perhaps just the opposite is true. He is so feeling and caring that he is terrified of those emotions. The fear may be that he will not be able to provide enough nurturing or that his caring will go unheeded and unnoticed. A fear of rejection is extremely strong.

The Moon has been found to be strong in charts of writers. It seems that there is a natural inclination to use writing to work past the emotional blocks. The identification with people in general is so strong wherever the Moon is strong, that there is a natural give and take on an emotional level. When Saturn is "sitting" on those feelings, so that there is no flow, feelings of defeat and negativity prevail. The opposite side of the coin is that once the responsibility to fellowman is awakened and the nurturing is expressed, the response is constant. Taking that first step of opening up is the painful one.

Joseph, with Saturn on his Moon, was a writer for Reuters News Service for many years. He reported on the events in Spain during a time when Spain was in great turmoil. He could protect himself through objective reporting and was diligent in developing his technical proficiency. Then he began to search for a deeper meaning to life and went to India, where he became a disciple of a guru. There he began to open up the feelings that had been blocked. Joseph has his Moon-Saturn aspect in the third house of communications, but ruling the tenth house of the father, and the fourth house of the mother. I asked Joseph about the role reversal that was apparent in his chart. I also asked if he photographed his father as having been abandoned. He said, "Yes, by my mother. I watched her abandon him when he needed her the most, later on in his life." With Saturn in the third house of communications, Joseph might have had a difficult relationship with a sibling. In his case, there was no sibling at all, therefore, there was no one else in the family to divert some of the symbiosis and share some of the painful burdens. Joseph was unable to let down the walls for fear of being swamped by family feelings. The sense of responsibility was too strong, the helpless feelings too great, for Joseph to allow himself to be vulnerable, since there wasn't much he could do about the difficult family situation. In India, however, he began to feel and express his emotions. Now he is writing a children's book that relates to his own experiences in trying to find his teacher. He is expressing the parental quality described by Saturn-Moon conjunction, for Saturn is related to the father, or the parent that disciplines, and the Moon is related to the mother, or the parent that nurtures. In many cases, when Saturn is aspecting the Moon, the quality of writing or nurturing at first takes on more of the technical or judgmental parent and later becomes vulnerable and related to experiences in life that are sensitive. It is that willingness to be vulnerable that brings the response from people, for it relates to feelings that everyone shares.

Socrates also had Saturn conjunct the Moon in his chart in the third house. His depth of feeling was revealed through teaching. In a positive sense, Saturn describes wisdom. Jane Austen had this aspect in her second house of income, but ruling the fifth house of creativity. Jane Austen wrote about oppressive circumstances and financial difficulties. Henry Wadsworth Longfellow also had this aspect ruling the creative areas in his solar chart. The style, depth, and stillness of his poetry are apparent. Charlotte Brontë wrote about melancholy and gloom. She had Saturn conjunct the Moon in her house of work, describing the creative potential. It is obvious that none of these people were less than deep and serious. Frivolity was not part of their nature, yet their contribution to literature and to life was profound.

SATURN IN HARD ASPECT TO THE MOON

With a hard aspect between Saturn and the Moon, the inner messages are even more difficult to reconcile. Sensitivity is pronounced, as well as a strong sense of responsibility. That sense of responsibility can be overburdening, however. The emotional body can just take so much pressure before the Saturnian walls emerge to protect that sensitive, overly responsive energy. The Moon describes rescuing tendencies, which are more insidious than mere mothering qualities. For with rescue comes ultimate punishment, rejection, and persecution. The individual may also have memories of times when his attempts at expressing the nurturing, caring part of himself were rejected. Therefore, at some point, the protective quality of Saturn steps in and says, "Oh, no you don't. Not again. Remember the pain of the last time." The walls go up and the person can appear quite cold and indifferent, when just the opposite is true.

The identification and response to the suffering of mankind is very pronounced with these hard aspects. The feelings of limitation are so overwhelming that the individual feels helpless to solve individual or world problems and so he does nothing at all. He instead protects his own feelings. Marie Antoinette had Saturn square the Moon in her chart. The famous statement attributed to her was "Let them eat cake" when she heard that the starving masses were without bread. Actually, a satirist of the day wrote that the statement was characteristic of what she might be expected to say. It was quickly changed to be a direct quote. She was terribly unpopular, perhaps because she was unable to show her caring. She may have had such deep caring and concern, with the simultaneous fear of not being able to feed everyone, that she appeared indifferent.

Nurie Vidal, with her Moon in the ninth house, squared by Saturn in her sixth house of work, talked about these very feelings. She said, "I feel sorry for so many people that I became very involved in politics in Spain. It was during the time of Franco and feelings of depression were great. I was working in a district, trying to organize people so that they would want new programs. I wanted to make them more aware. For me it was a dream, to make people want more freedom. I had a fantasy of everyone playing and having fun. I suddenly became aware that I was trying to make people do something that was impossible. I felt politics was only a game and I began to see that nothing could be accomplished in this way.

"When I got to the point that I was talking on the radio and having five hundred people turn up for meetings, I suddenly stopped. I didn't want to go ahead with my project. I have always had this identification with people, so it was easy to attract people, but I think the responsibility began to get to me. I worried about being in that position. One day, I was scheduled to talk to six hundred people. I woke up saying to myself, 'I don't want to go.' It came in a flash. I got sick. I felt my throat was closing up and I couldn't talk. I called someone and said, 'I'm not coming.' They said, 'You have to come. The newspapers are here and everything is ready.' I suggested that they read the statement I had already prepared. I got very sick, even running a fever, and I was completely convinced that I couldn't talk. But I knew that I had created the sickness for myself, because I suddenly said, 'What am I doing?' I realized I could not take on the burden of rescuing people or making them want to be different. I stopped any involvement with political issues."

Some very interesting people have had Saturn square the Moon in their charts. Julius Caesar, Cicero, Vergil, St. Augustine, Immanuel Kant, Spinoza, Jonathan Swift, Jean Jacques Rousseau, and Goya. Machiavelli also had Saturn square the Moon. Joan of Arc and William Blake had Saturn inconjunct their Moon, and Napoleon had Saturn in opposition to his Moon. It can seem that the burdens of the world are almost too much for an individual with this aspect. In many instances, overly needy people turned on the very individual who wanted to give help. The sad result is the tendency to go into symbiosis with the very people or person who will not care about the individual's welfare in return.

The individual with this aspect must avoid overly needy people who will drain him until he cannot help them any longer. The tendency is to "take it" far too long, then put up a wall that no one can penetrate. This individual needs to learn that he can give only what he can give and no more. If he ultimately learns to take care of his own emotional reaction, know what he can do and what he cannot, he can be safe in a close relationship. That may take a bit of practice.

SATURN CONJUNCT MERCURY

A person with Saturn conjunct Mercury is the doubting Thomas of the zodiac. His pronounced tendency toward negative thinking is really a wonderful (though perhaps unconscious) excuse for not using his mind in a creative way. Whenever he questions a person or a situation, he really just wants to be convinced. Behind the shield of Saturn lies an inquisitive mind longing to have permission to explore, accept, express plans and ideas. If he is able to go beyond his skepticism and negativity, he takes words, thoughts, and ideas very seriously. He may want to make a contribution through his own mind and can worry that he will be unable to do that in as profound a way as he wants to. He is the perfectionist, the sober observer, the mental conservative.

Ingmar Bergman has Saturn conjunct Mercury in his chart. He observes life through the writing and filming of his own scripts; he is not a person to take life lightly. One of his most potent films, *Scenes from a Marriage*, portrayed all the boredom and painful banality that can come in a union that has outgrown its time. It takes quite a grave sense of responsibility to be willing to point the finger of truth so definitely. In her autobiography, *Changing*, Liv Ullman described what it was like to live with such a man, however. The total commitment to his art and writing kept him from any sense of relaxation or ease. Everything becomes serious with this aspect.

Herman Melville also had this aspect in his chart. His greatest work, *Moby Dick*, is a classic in literature. The careful craftsmanship expressed by Melville is an example of the depth of his talent. Gay Talese, a more modern writer, has the same aspect. He writes very slowly, and with great dedication. His books have a reportorial quality, and it is said that he takes his research most seriously.

Teilhard de Chardin conducted another kind of research. He was a Jesuit priest who achieved tremendous recognition for his work in China and with archaeological expeditions in Asia and South Africa. He was acclaimed for genetic and scientific investigation.

Saturn conjunct Mercury is the aspect of the critic as well as the researcher. George Bernard Shaw had Saturn conjunct Mercury. He was a critic as well as a dramatist and novelist. Mercury rules his Gemini ascendant and the fifth house of creativity. Saturn rules his ninth house of publishing and distribution. The aspect is placed in the second house of income. George Bernard Shaw had a sharp wit and a dour personality. His observations continue to delight many people. His craftsmanship is superb and the underlying point of his stories quite serious, even though covered by a netting of wit. George Shearing, blind pianist born with this aspect, found music early on, but whether George's blindness caused his cautious turn of mind or whether it was merely coincidental is mere speculation. Pat Scheinwold, formerly married to George, attested to her husband's brilliance and dedication but to the fact that his negativity was so strong, it was almost impossible to deal with. It provided a barricade that was most difficult to penetrate.

When the individual with this aspect can observe his reactions and understand why he feels it is so urgent to express caution, he can begin to utilize the positive aspects of this energy. In the laboratory, this is the kind of diligence that is needed. Healthy skepticism is a marvelous safety device against naïveté. From my perspective, this aspect is descriptive of an individual who may have taken grave responsibility to make decisions in a past life on a deeply subconscious level, or in the fantasy of a past life, only to be punished or ignored. He comes back to say, "Never again will I risk such torment by speaking my mind openly." If he can doubt his own intelligence or opinions as well as those of others, he has a mask to hide behind. He won't have to take responsibility to make decisions that can have serious repercussions. He can hide behind the shield of criticism or doubt. But this may be the person who has the most important contribution to make through the undertaking of responsibility. Dag Hammarskjöld had this aspect in opposition. He not only took on the responsibility to head the United Nations, he wrote serious, rather metaphysical treatises about life and its purpose. He eventually committed suicide.

SATURN IN HARD ASPECT TO MERCURY

Two people who figure importantly in their chosen fields are James Taylor, musician, and Mary Wells, advertising executive. Both of these people use their minds to produce work of top quality. Mary

Wells formed her own advertising agency, with her partners, Rich and Greene, and zoomed to the top of her field when small agencies didn't have much of a chance against the giants of the industry. She seized not only the important Braniff airline account, which put her agency in top company, but also the owner of the airline as her husband. With Saturn co-ruling the fifth house of creativity, this dynamic woman would opt for a technical way to express her talent. Mary would need to develop a strong technical know-how to provide a platform of security in connection with her creativity. Saturnish creativity also describes an ability to take on high levels of responsibility. In Mary's chart, Saturn is placed in the fourth house of home, in opposition to Mercury in the tenth house of career. Saturn in connection with the fourth house can also indicate an ability to have or start a corporation or company. Mercury in her chart rules money and friends or group associations. Mary obviously has built a strong base of security in connection with her financial ability and in group associations. A major pull in her life between father and mother has translated into a pull between security in connection with home base and lifestyle, and her obvious brilliance and mental competence in public areas. Mary was able to combine the Mercury-Saturn energy to build a strong public image in the advertising world. Putting oneself under pressure is a fantastic way to experience the energy of Saturn. Mary has proven her ability to work under the nonstop pressure of the advertising world.

James Taylor became a success in the music world as a result, in part, of an incredibly goal-oriented personality. James has Mercury ruling his Virgo ascendant and his Gemini career. Mercury is posited in the sixth house of work. Saturn rules the fifth house of creativity, and is in opposition to Mercury from the eleventh house of friendship, group activity, and associations with organizations. The pull of the opposition can be as strong as the square, yet it can be reconciled by treating it like a conjunction. The two voices that are opposing each other can eventually find a way of reconciliation. James married Carly Simon, the daughter of one of New York's biggest publishers. He may have needed her reputation as a singer to give him permission in his own life. But pressures, many obviously self-imposed, made him look to drugs as a way of unblocking the creativity. On a psychological level, negativity and restrictions imposed by a father figure would be hard programming to break.

With even great success, he may have doubted his real talent without the aid of drugs. Mercury describes left-brain activity, and Saturn describes judgments. If the individual with the Saturn-Mercury aspects can learn to monitor each thought to transmute doubt into less-pressured beliefs, he can take more responsibility to work creatively on a mental level and find balance between left- and right-brain activity.

Saturn in hard aspect to Mercury can also describe a tendency to worry. Nicole is a lovely, warm lady who has a thriving design studio. Although she appears totally soft and easygoing, she is a businesswoman, combining an artistry with a strong business sense. She grew up in Paris, the fashion center of the world, and has early memories of her grandmother designing and sewing clothes. Nicole has always been aware of an ability to do anything in connection with design, fabrics, and silhouettes and has been extraordinarily successful. She designs and imports clothing to New York from Europe and is fast becoming known for her unique styles.

Nicole confesses that she worries about things, even when it is obvious that all is going well. With Saturn posited in the sixth house of work, but ruling the twelfth house of the subconscious, and Mercury placed in that twelfth house and ruling the fourth house of the father and the seventh house of partnership, it is clear that much of her negative programming came from a father figure. In her case, the restriction was connected to her stepfather, not her real father. "My Father was a warm, loving man. It was never necessary to have an obvious display of affection and love because the real love was so obvious it was always there. He was Armenian and expressed constant and deep love. But my adored father died when I was twelve and my life changed drastically. My Mother then married a Frenchman who was hardworking and responsible, but caused many problems in my life. He was like a stranger in a way. We even called him Monsieur, not a 'father' name. He may have tried to take over the role of a father, but my sisters and I rejected him completely. When he tried to tell us what to do, we didn't listen, because he was not our father. He was a typical Frenchman, very conservative on the surface, although very charming, but he was lacking in social graces and in warmth or real caring that I had known with my Father. He was a baker. When I was fourteen, I was taken out of school and made to work in the bakery. Naturally, I hated it. He was very critical and judgmental and I finally left home at the age of seventeen, because the situation was simply intolerable.

"I married someone with a very similar personality, although I certainly didn't know it then. My husband is very critical and judgmental, yet very handsome and charming on the surface. I think he is basically insecure, too. In France, the woman is always made to feel special. She always enters a room first and is treated with special care. Both my husband and my stepfather would push me aside to go first. They are not polite. I was put under the same kind of pressure in my marriage, because no matter what I did, it was never, ever, right and never enough. I was simply expected to do things, not thanked or made to feel good about what I did.

"My husband pushed me to go back to work even when I was pregnant. Soon after our son was born, we separated and then I had to work because of no support from my husband. When we first started our joint business, he worked with leathers and furs and took care of all the paperwork, leaving me free to create and design. Now I have to do all that myself and I find it very tedious. (Mercury rules details, facts, and figures.) I had to take on all the responsibility and it is not easy. Although I do worry, I reach a point where I simply don't care anymore. I am motivated by the need and desire to take care of someone else. At first it was for us, when I was with my husband, but now it is for my child. I am not pessimistic, but I can feel overloaded with responsibilities at times."

It is ironic, of course, that with such hard work as a young girl, Nicole would attract the very situation in marriage that would give the same kind of lack of security, forcing her to go back to work again. With Saturn in the sixth house, the workaholic tendency is hard programming to break. The positive reconciliation of Saturn in hard aspect to Mercury is to work past worry, fears, and insecurities and tackle responsibilities that are on a high level. It seems that Nicole has done just that by handling responsibilities that build security rather than continue to bring feelings of limitation.

SATURN CONJUNCT VENUS

With all Saturn aspects, there is a deep need for and fear about a particular energy. In the case of Saturn conjunct Venus, the need for love, affection, pleasure, and the ease of gracious living is pronounced, yet the individual may inadvertently pick the very conditions that prevent that in his life. Subconscious fears attached to Venus are connected to loss. It may be easier to live with less of the longed-for physical touching, hugging, and affection than to have it and then lose it. The individual can put himself under incredible pressures that prevent self-indulgence, for fear that if he ever experienced total ease, he might never want anything else. It is sad to see cases in which an individual is still bound to parental programming, still denying himself simple pleasures that could make a big difference in his life.

Charles is a handsome, blond man, very dedicated to his work as a physician. Saturn is conjunct Venus in his chart, placed in the tenth house of career and father, ruling the first house of personality and self-expression. Charles's story was so sadly typical of individuals born during or just after the war in Europe. Times were very hard. Charles described walking with his father, who was quiet, shrunken, and withdrawn, and not being able to fathom the story that his father had been big, robust, and jolly before the war. Charles remembered paintings that he had done as a child, for he showed remarkable artistic talent, but he was never encouraged in such frivolous pastimes. He dedicated himself to the serious business of living and did a very good job at it.

He established a lifestyle that included a winter home, a lovely summer home, and security. His wife and his children sometimes resented the stringency Charles occasionally imposed, and could not understand why he would balk at certain small luxuries. His son wanted to play a musical instrument, but there was a great deal of family discussion about whether or not he would pursue music diligently enough to invest in instruments and lessons. Charles went into therapy and learned a great deal about himself. One of the decisions he made was to begin to enjoy the fruits of his labors and allow for those small things for himself and his family that would upgrade daily pleasure.

He decided to begin painting again and made the major decision to make contact with his father. Deprivation of affection, pleasure, and love is very strong with this aspect. The desires, talents, and needs are there, but walls have been erected that must be torn down. Rejection from a parent can be a strong incentive indeed.

The individual steels himself against any future letdown along those lines.

In a positive sense, Venus conjunct Saturn can indicate tremendous dedication to art. Rudolf Nureyev, for instance, with Saturn conjunct Venus in his chart, dedicated himself to dance to such a degree that he was willing to leave his family and country to have more freedom of expression in that medium. His determination has not gone unrewarded. Nureyev was known to dance when he was in great pain, being able to overcome any obstacle to give a great performance. Vanessa Redgrave also has this conjunction. She is a fine performer, a dedicated actress, and an outspoken human being. Venus also describes a need for balance and social equality. Vanessa has been on her platform to take responsibility in areas where she feels things are not fair or balanced.

SATURN IN HARD ASPECT TO VENUS

The tragedy of difficult Venus-Saturn aspects is that love and pleasure seem always tainted by hardship or shadow. If great love is attained, it may be lost. If pleasure is hard-won, it is in danger of disappearing. The balance of Saturn and Venus is the very foundation of life. If Venus is seen as social justice, balance, and fair play, to undertake the responsibility to keep that balance in the individual life seems to be one way of feeling safe. Good, honest choices about the quality of love and pleasure are important in breaking through worries about loss. Venus is the natural antidote for Saturn. Love can mitigate sorrow and hardship. Balance between the two planets is also indicated in acupuncture. Venus rules the throat and Saturn rules the knees. According to famous Aspen, Colorado, healer Margaret Wong, the two areas are related. If you have something wrong with your knees, says Margaret, you will also have a reaction in the throat area. Margaret uses many techniques, but especially acupressure, in her healing massage. She finds the balance between two conflicting energies in her work.

Andy is a charming man with a deep dimple in his chin and twinkling blue eyes. He is sociable, outgoing, and extremely well-mannered. With all the inherent qualities that would attract many ladies to his side, Andy has chosen to remain single after a short and unfulfilling marriage. Andy has Saturn square Venus in his

chart, with Venus ruling and posited in the first house of personality
and personal life, and Saturn placed in the third house of communications and ruling the fourth house of home and the parent of the
opposite sex. Andy was quite open in his willingness to discuss the
dilemma he felt. He had an ongoing relationship with a very beautiful girl, several years younger than he, who matched his personality
and looks in a very distinctive way. Yet Andy confessed that strife
and argument seemed to be the strongest characteristic of their
relationship. He said, "I don't know what to do. When I am not in a
relationship, I can be very lonely and desirous of that special quality of companionship, but the minute I become involved, I feel
squelched, pinned down and almost claustrophobic. I am beginning
to think that a loving friendship is the only thing I can handle. Yet,
when someone as lovely as Francesca declares her love and devotion, I think I am a fool not to let myself enjoy it."

We talked about his relationship with his mother. "I watched my
mother being shut out of any warm, loving relationship with my
father, simply because he was a man who didn't know how to give
anything of himself. My poor mother had very little comfort in her
marriage, and was unable to express much affection to me or to my
brother. I will never forget the feelings of abandonment when she
took me to a boarding school and dropped me off to face unknown
terrors by myself. I was only eight. I suppose I felt I couldn't
depend on her to stand up for me in any situation with my father,
so I cut off and never expressed my love or affection to her, either.
As a matter of fact, my relationship with my brother is not exactly
warm and loving either. I suppose I can accept lack of love and
affection more easily than I can any demonstrations of caring."

Even though Andy was intelligent enough to analyze his programming, it didn't seem to help him reconcile the situation that
caused him such anguish. He consented to a regression session
after Francesca left him for someone more willing to give and receive love. In this session, Andy was able to go backward through
his childhood, relive the circumstances of his birth and then uncover a sense of what a past life must have been. Andy saw himself
as an Egyptian man, dignified, intelligent and well respected. He
sensed that he was fulfilled in almost every way possible in that
"life." He had ease of living, respect from his community and the
love of a special woman. Andy began to show signs of great emotion

during this session and finally allowed great, wracking sobs to escape. With the tears pouring down his cheeks, he confessed that the woman he loved so much was taken away from him by death. He saw himself living in a state of self-imposed isolation and loneliness. It seemed that after a while of this torment, he simply disappeared into the atmosphere.

When he opened his eyes and allowed his objective mind to observe what he had experienced, Andy had some realizations and questions. "I think I committed suicide in that life. I'm sure the woman was my mother in this present lifetime and I can see how that pain was so terrible, I decided right then never to allow love of that depth into my life again. Do you think a decision made such a long time ago could be viable even to today?" Whether the experience was a real lifetime experience or simply a figment of the imagination is totally unimportant. Andy was able to get to a deeper explanation of his two voices. One voice (Venus) says loudly and clearly, "To love is beautiful and the most important thing of all." The other voice (Saturn) says, "The end result of that depth of love is pain." Therefore in the present time, Andy would attract the love he craved, but somehow push it away, squelch it or deny it because of the possibility of loss. Andy decided that he must first heal the relationship with his mother. When they next spent time together, it was clear that a great affection and ease existed between them that was lovely to see. Andy then met another beautiful young woman who expressed her love for him and was willing to work through almost anything to clear away the psychological blocks. Although it was not easy for Andy to simply switch gears and accept the newfound affection in the new relationship, he was determined to give it a chance to build and develop. The story is not yet complete, but it can only be hoped that Andy can allow the two dialogues to be reconciled within himself.

SATURN CONJUNCT MARS

When these two diametrically opposed kinds of energies begin to interact, much confusion can occur within the individual. Mars energy is pioneering, forceful, aggressive, and ambitious, whereas Saturn energy is cautious, fearful, timid, overly conservative, and restrictive. The Mars message is "I want to hurry up," while Saturn says, "Wait, be careful." The end result can be a squelching of energy that is paralyzing. Mars is the basic sexual drive, which can be translated into creative action, dance, exercise, or athletics. If the inner voices are reconciled, the individual with this aspect in his chart learns to consistently direct his energy outward in areas that demand physical courage or ambition. Usually, there have been strong negative messages about the evils of sex or ambition from environmental conditions if not from a specific parent.

Paul, a man of many talents, has this aspect in his chart. Paul was quite clear in his description of early sexual counseling from his mother. He recalled an incident, from when he was about ten years old, in which he spontaneously felt like expressing affection to his mother. She was sitting in a chair and Paul went to put his arms around her waist to give a hug. She responded, "Don't rub that thing against me!" Naturally that led to rather strange messages about the beauty of the sexual energy. Paul said he became quite resourceful about getting his sexual needs met, sometimes in a cold-blooded fashion. This kind of programming does not easily lead to love within the sexual union.

Mars also rules anger and temper when it is unreleased and unresolved. With a Saturn-Mars aspect in the chart, it is not easy to release the temper. Once that inner frustration builds up to the boiling point, it comes out filtered through the Saturnian cheese-cloth and becomes cold-blooded. It is anger through gritted teeth and clenched fists. The tendency is to fear the temper, hold it in until it seems justified. Transactional analysis talks about collecting stamps. This is what happens in many relationships. An individual says to himself, "You [the partner] owe me one." If he can collect enough of those "stamps," he can trade them in for a big payoff, such as having an excuse to break up the relationship. He can feel justified in running off with someone else, ignoring the hurt he causes, because he has been storing events away like the squirrel with his nuts. When the individual takes responsibility to consistently release his frustrations (perhaps through exercise) and his temper (through immediate discussion), he can clear the decks for more productive expression of energy.

Alan describes this aspect in the chart of his wife. Alan is an astrologer and quite familiar with the way the energy works in his married life. He said, "I don't have a very strong Mars in my chart.

It's interesting that I should pull in someone with Saturn conjunct
Mars in her chart. I act like her garbage can and get to clean up her
act, but it is difficult for both of us. She remembers that her father
hit her when he was angry with her, and accidentally hurt her back.
Coincidentally it was just before her first sexual experience. She
used to confuse sex with love. Now she's always bargaining for sex.
I have a hard time with that. I'm always busy. I have clients, I have
to study and practice my music. She needs a lot of time and attention from her mate and I don't. She'll say, 'I'll do this or that for
you if you'll make time for me in your busy schedule, or for us
tonight.' It becomes a constant issue. If I'm too busy, or not in the
mood, she sees it in a competitive way and thinks I don't love her.
She'll take it as a direct and personal issue, or feel as though I was
trying to be cool with her. Fortunately, with therapy we're learning
to work it out. Physically, she sits on her energy a lot. She needs a
great deal of energy release, like exercise. She can be incredibly
resourceful with money. But she is not as conscientious about paying money back as getting it in the first place. I let her do business
deals for us because she is much more hard-nosed than I am. She
tends to get nitpicky about money between us, though. If I buy a
piece of equipment, she will buy clothes whether she needs them or
not, or whether that is rent or food money. It's a little bit like tit for
tat. We have to make agreements about things like that, for it is not
naturally easy."

Sometimes Saturn-Mars aspects can seem sadistic. They describe
a quality of aggression that can be released in a rather cold-blooded
fashion. But the positive manifestation of this energy is a willingness and determination to express the creative energy in a more
natural way. The sexual energy can be transformed into consistent
aggressive action. The aspect describes a determination and drive
that are clearly focused and directed. Ambition can be very strong.
Many actors and actresses have this aspect in their charts, for it
describes a quality that simply won't give up. Alan Alda and Lucille
Ball have this aspect in their charts. Lucille Ball was a well-known
actress but stuck in roles that seemingly would get her nowhere in
the film world. She finally took the bull by the horns, conceived and
produced her own television series with her husband, Desi Arnaz,
and the rest is television history. After twenty years in theater,
Alan Alda achieved stardom in the long-running, extremely popular

series "M*A*S*H." Alan also wrote and directed many of the show's episodes. For Mars can describe a directorial ability; the Mars energy can put the finger on the precise spot that needs attention. When it is conjoined with Saturn, the willingness to assume that role is key to the release and change of blocked energy. This powerful combination of energy can create a platform of security born of high levels of responsibility. Resourcefulness and courage enable a person to pioneer new trends and pave the way for others.

SATURN IN HARD ASPECT TO MARS

The block to the drive, ambition, courage, aggression, sexuality, and activity may be more difficult to resolve when Saturn and Mars are in hard aspect to each other. One voice is saying, "Go to it," and the other voice is simultaneously saying, "Watch out, be careful." It becomes a push-pull situation. The minute the energy is focused and directed toward a single goal, fear sets in, or restrictions occur that can prevent action. A person with such an aspect may unconsciously pick the very circumstances that will keep him from the full expression of his resourcefulness and courage. Physical blocks of energy can be very real with this aspect, because Mars rules the bloodstream, circulation, fevers, and the head and brain. Exercise is very important for an individual with this aspect. Consistency of activity keeps the blood moving throughout the body. If the energy is backed up, it can cause not only lowered vitality, but poor circulation, headaches, and a variety of other physical manifestations.

Prince Albert, consort to Queen Victoria, had Saturn squaring Mars in his chart. Mars is placed in the tenth house of public life and career, and would naturally indicate quite a resourceful, pioneering quality to career activity. Reform can sometimes be connected with such an aspect. Saturn, however, was placed in the house of marriage and describes Queen Victoria perfectly. Albert was constantly blocked in his own career, no doubt, because of the overly conservative nature of his marital partner. Victoria's morality was the basis for a new word in the English language. *Victorian* stimulates many images connected to propriety, conservatism, concealment, old-fashionedness. Yet, supposedly, their marriage was ideal. Albert probably was able to "keep his place." The prince consort is a most difficult role, to begin with, but in this instance, Victoria was a particularly strong woman. Prince Albert died of typhoid fever when he was quite young, only 42. Mars, ruling his eighth house, describes the kind of death that might be expected. His energy must have been almost completely turned inward in frustration.

Jacques Cousteau also has Saturn square Mars, with Mars placed in the tenth house of career, and ruling his seventh house of marriage, and the eighth house of getting needs met. Saturn rules the fourth house of home, and is placed in the eighth house. However, Jacques Cousteau leaves no stone unturned in his efforts toward exploration of the underwater world. He fully expresses his inventiveness and his need to be a pioneer and explorer. His marriages have not been allowed to stand in the way of his career. Yet, Jacques Cousteau may have had to sacrifice the security of a stable homelife, described by Saturn ruling that sector of his chart, to accomplish his mission. The transformation of the eighth house describes the quality of energy that can be sent out to mankind. In his case, he has taken full responsibility to be resourceful and pave the way for mankind in uncharted territory of the sea.

Thomas is a man gifted with a special artistic sense. He established a reputation as one of the top interior and stage designers in his field, working internationally with wealthy and prestigious clients. Thomas decided to leave his thriving business and retire, at an early age. Thomas was quite willing to talk about what might appear to be a lack of ambition. (Saturn is posited in the twelfth house in Thomas's chart, ruling the eighth house of getting one's needs met, as well as the ninth house of higher education, reputation, promotional ability squaring Mars in the tenth house of career, ruling the twelfth house of subconscious processes.) The conflict between the drive and ambition and the responsible nature seemed to be connected to the relationship Thomas has with his father. A strong identification might lead Thomas to resist, subconsciously, any activity that would put him in conflict with his father. "I was never able to engage my father in any kind of conflict. I always thought my father was weak, with no ambition, but of course I now know that is not true. I watched him being dumped on all the time and was really angry that he wouldn't say no or fight back. I was also upset that he wouldn't go to bat for me, or at least not when I wanted him to. I also never felt any sense of direction from my father, other than that of family pressure in general. As far back as generations ago, on my father's side, everyone, but everyone, had a Ph.D. and taught. My father was a physicist and had an amazing mind, so it was just assumed that I would follow in the family footsteps. However, when I got to college, I rebelled completely and went to art school instead."

I suggested that a lot of pressure of a different sort was put on Thomas's shoulders. "I was expected to take on a great deal of responsibility. For instance, my sister was an ugly duckling and I was expected to take care of her. I also had to dance with every wallflower at a dance and do things that weren't much fun but were considerate. When I was a child, I would do things in a sort of slapdash manner. I would start things and then my father would come along and patiently explain all my mistakes. My father was a perfectionist, but that stopped my initiative. I was not given permission, by example, to be daring or courageous. I became so self-critical there was never any point in criticism from other people. It was just totally unnecessary."

He continued, "When I was building the sets for my last production, I kept thinking about my father. I had to make them perfect and they had to work. They couldn't be slapdash. It seems I have come full cycle with my father. I appreciate that all those things he taught me as a child are completely useful. I also see that I can allow myself to be dumped on, and I don't say no or protest. Then of course I am angry at myself. That is just like my father. I'm sure I repress a lot of my ambition and drive for fear I won't be perfect enough."

In many instances, the awareness of the programming of "Be perfect, don't have initiative," associated with Saturn in hard aspect to Mars is enough to stimulate new behavior. It is never easy to change, but in the case of this aspect, consistent action begins to make new imprint on behavior. The mere fact that Thomas can see clearly the source of his own perfectionist tendency and can appreciate just where it is productive and where it is not is half the battle. Like a drop of water on a stone, step by step, awareness eventually produces healthy change.

SATURN CONJUNCT JUPITER

When these two planets are conjunct, the negative expression can indicate a block of the natural philosophical outlook and joy, but when the energies are reconciled and overcautious tendencies are resolved, the outcome seems to indicate a natural good business sense. Ultimate responsibility has to do with assuming the expectancy of success, rather than worrying about the outcome of expansion. In a positive sense, the individual with this aspect has a natural sense of timing about business ventures. He has a built-in safety device of caution that eventually allows him to know exactly how much and when to expand. Jupiter describes goals, challenges, philosophy, good humor, and growth or expansion. With Saturnian energy firmly blocking these qualities early on, the cautious nature by far overwhelms the natural need for new horizons.

Genevieve, an extremely successful therapist, described this aspect in her own chart. Her Saturn-Jupiter conjunction is placed in the third house of communications, and describes the relationship with her siblings. Saturn also rules her sixth house of work and health, with Jupiter ruling the fifth house of love, creativity, children. Genevieve's relationship with her sister was practically non-existent. They were four years apart and, in spite of much time spent in therapy, she has little recollection of having any connection with her at all. However, she had a male cousin who lived with her family and was like a brother. She said she felt safe with her cousin, who was quite shy. Saturn in this case describes the relationship with both children, but one relationship was Saturnish and one Jupiterian. The third house rules grade school and learning ability or potential. I suggested that perhaps Genevieve had not achieved her full potential in her early school years because of an overly perfectionistic tendency. She said, "In lower school, I was scared I wouldn't be good enough. However, the pressures stopped once I went away to the university. Once I left home, I became much more natural and outgoing."

We broached the subject of health. With Saturn ruling the sixth house, health, work, and service are key to a sense of security. But usually the tendency is to overwork, put oneself under too much pressure, and get sick in order to get out from under. Genevieve confirmed this by saying, "Exactly. I discovered through my own therapy that I would put myself under so much work pressure that I would have to get sick to get away from that pressure. When I broke my script, I made a decision that I would never get sick again. I now see my stress level more realistically and I allow more days of rest." Saturn, in its positive sense, describes discipline and routine. Genevieve acknowledged that she takes very good care of her diet and does specific exercises every morning so that she can keep her health in balance. Her particular forte and success in therapy has to do with healing. She has had great success in helping people restore health through a variety of forms of therapeutic techniques. She is very much associated with transactional analysis, which primarily focuses on communications. Contracts are negotiated in daily activity. Genevieve's business sense is terrific when it comes to negotiating her own contracts.

But perhaps the most important aspect of the extremes between the Jupiter and Saturn energy is high expectation, then a consequent depression when disappointment sets in. Genevieve was able to shed particular light on that area of highs and lows. She continued, "Before my therapy and breaking my script, I was always expecting things from people and I would always be let down. I expected people to be the way I am or to feel the way that I feel. Naturally that was unrealistic. I don't expect anything anymore. I don't mean that in a negative way at all. I now let people do things their way. I feel that I have made the last jump in that area and I'm very happy that I've come to the point where I can let things be as they are. I have had some very severe disappointments that have helped me reach that conclusion. But now, even with love relationships, I don't project or expect. I just live each moment as it comes." Genevieve's sunny disposition and extraordinary capability of bouncing back gave testimony to what she said. Especially in her work, the encouragement and enthusiasm she projects enables many people to heal themselves. Her success record makes her a very busy and productive therapist.

John Glenn was the first American astronaut to orbit the earth. John has Saturn conjunct Jupiter at the very top of his chart. Jupiter is placed in the ninth house, with Saturn in the tenth. The aspect describes his personality and financial ability as well as career potential. Jupiter describes a need for goals. Usually, an individual is never content with just one level of success. When he has achieved something great, he must have new challenges. John showed this characteristic by becoming an executive with Royal Crown Cola and then by becoming a U.S. senator. In 1984, he was a contender to be the Democratic party's presidential candidate.

Emperor Hirohito has this conjunction in the first house of personality, ruling the twelfth house of subconscious-mind activity. He was personally against militarism but was Emperor at the time of World War II. His decisions led to Japan's entering the war. Before that time, the Emperor of Japan was considered to be a reincarnation on earth of divinity. After the Japanese defeat, he renounced that claim of divinity and became merely a *symbol* of the state of divinity. Jupiter describes not only philosophy but religion. Perhaps with the realization that he was a mere mortal on earth, Hirohito was able to relieve himself of some personal pressures. The painful lessons associated with this aspect are quite evident in his case, however. On a purely subconscious level, the person with this aspect may not know when to stop a level of high enthusiasm until he creates external conditions that will act as a natural deterrent. He can then live a more peaceful existence by learning personal limits without external conditions to dictate them. With such an aspect, the person wants more and more until he is somehow stopped by life and the people around them. The business sense comes with a combination of high enthusiasm and goals, and the practical ability to structure time and energy in order to achieve his high aims. Balance is the key to success.

SATURN IN HARD ASPECT TO JUPITER

When these planets are in hard aspect to each other, a sense of natural caution can be equally as strong as a desire to attain goals, but Saturn may have a heavier brake than when these two planets are in conjunction. There can be an innate fear of trusting to luck and a lack of spontaneous joy. Robert Redford has Saturn square Jupiter in his chart, describing his career, promotional efforts, friendships, and subconscious desires. Robert has hedged his bet of success in Hollywood by building a ski resort in Provo, Utah, and an institute for filmmakers in Salt Lake City. He has expressed a distinct distaste for Hollywood lifestyle and society, and is definitely a loner. He is described as remote, cool, independent, and lonely.

Jamie Wyeth also has Saturn squaring Jupiter, with Jupiter posited in his second house of income, ruling home and lifestyle, and Saturn in the house of friendships and group associations and ruling his fifth house of creativity. Jamie is totally immersed in his work. He seems indifferent to distraction from social activities and is very modest and unassuming. His work is stark in its philosophical concepts. His paintings evoke tremendous emotion from their very simplicity and realism. His attention to detail is fine and accurate. The overall message is not joy, however, but sadness and sober reality. His paintings suggest that life is not a picnic, yet there is a life-affirming philosophical message underlying all.

Ted Turner has Saturn semisquare Jupiter, also indicative of conflicting voices between the two planets. Saturn in his chart is placed in the fourth house of home, land, property, but ruling the second house of money. Jupiter is in that house of income, ruling his personal life and personality. If Saturn were removed from his chart, Ted Turner might know no bounds, but with this natural caution describing his nature and all financial affairs, he is very frugal in spite of his flamboyance. He is a workaholic, expresses somewhat of a gloomy philosophy, and possesses a strong sense of personal discipline. It is said that Ted Turner has a sense of personal destiny. In spite of the potential to be a playboy, Ted is determined to express himself candidly and to make a contribution. He assumes a bit of a frosty exterior, which no doubt keeps most people at arm's length. Ted showed incredible stamina in starting an independent cable-news network in spite of public doubt and criticism. Cable Network News is not yet operating in the black, but the level of operation is of high quality and with serious intent.

ASPECTS TO URANUS

Uranus is the planet that describes anything that is inventive, unusual, avant-garde, or unique. The quality of energy associated with Uranus is electrical and highly charged. The energy is so spontaneous that it can also be impulsive, yet the end result of any activity associated with this planet can be brilliant and inspired. People who have this planet strongly aspected in their charts cannot do things in a routine or ordinary way. They may go to extremes and be very rebellious.

This planet was first discovered by Sir William Herschel on March 13, 1781. Herschel thought it was a comet. Four months later A. J. Lexell announced it was a planet. Uranus is the first of what astrologers term a "higher octave" planet, breaking the boundary of Saturn an "earthbound" planet. Its discovery came only a short five years after the United States rebelled and published the Declaration of Independence.

Uranus also describes anything that is electronic, musical, humanitarian, or healing. It rules science, astrology, radio, music, recordings, and anything associated with holistic medicine, biochemistry, or metaphysics. Uranus is the first of the higher-octave planets. Since Saturn describes the earth and earthbound activities, Uranus is the next step up into the stratosphere. It is an airy planet, describing anything that is intellectual or inspired. It is the etheric energy that may be beyond the awareness of more mundane, practical people.

Uranus is the planet that rules the sign of Aquarius. We are now on the threshold of the Aquarian Age, ready to work on a humanitarian level, willing to knock down former boundaries that existed between people. Saturn describes those boundaries, prejudices, and fears, whereas Uranus describes freedom. Freedom may be hard to take, however, unless one is prepared for it. Security comes with limitations, walls, judgments, rights and wrongs. When the freedom urge comes from the higher self and those energies begin to pour down into static conditions, it can be nerve-wracking indeed. The individual must open up to a higher voltage, which comes from enlightenment. The nervous system has to change patterns, relax, and be ready to receive inspiration. Uranus is light, the divine light. With Uranus aspects, one begins to touch upon the primordial essence of oneness. It is the spiritual energy that heals. If man can lift himself up to the pure light of spirit, all problems are seen in a different way. They become opportunity for enlightenment, inspiration, illumination. With difficult aspects to Uranus, the attention of the emotions, mind, love nature, and drive becomes too rooted in earth. The inpouring of the divine light of the spirit produces blockage of energy. Uranus rules the breath and the voice. Each person has a unique voice. Ultimate enlightenment has to do with finding the individual voice and blending it with the voice of the cosmos.

Uranus is found in the charts of everyone. It is the expression of universality. However, not everyone is ready to live on the higher plane of insight, risks, and inventiveness. The aspects in an individual chart indicate how easy it is for a person to live on that level. It may be that once a person has satisfied the practical, security needs, he is ready to tap into more universal consciousness. It is a matter of opening oneself up to higher forms of energy, instead of becoming scared and running away. Eventually, there is a need to work through the scare to allow more freedom of self-expression. Uranian energy is humanitarian in that it represents the principle of live and let live.

With Uranus, there is growth through crisis. It takes Uranus eighty-two years to complete its cycle through the zodiac. Periodically, that planet squares or opposes its own position in a natal chart. At approximately the ages of twenty or twenty-one, forty, and sixty, crisis situations can develop that test the willingness of the person to grow. Young adults have completed their school years by twenty-one and are contemplating their first work experiences and separation from home and family. Psychologists talk about midlife crisis. That coincides with the time that Uranus opposes its own position in the natal chart. More change comes at approximately the age of sixty or sixty-one, possibly around the time of retirement. At each one of these crisis times, the tendency is to be impulsive, rebellious, ready to kick over the traces. It can feel as though too much electricity is coursing through the system and the individual becomes nervous and erratic in his behavior. What was formerly acceptable is no longer tolerable or possible. He wants to make changes and may be compelled to do something drastic to bring more freedom into his life.

Since Uranus describes electricity, imagine an electrical device such as a computer. If one plugs that computer into the right socket, it accomplishes miracles in a short amount of time and produces fantastic results. But if one short-circuits that computer, it blows a fuse. However, the blown fuse protects the whole instrument from damage. Unless an individual finds the right outlet for some of his rebellious, but perhaps genius, potential, he continues to blow fuses within his own system. Perhaps he has an allergy attack, or develops a rash, runs away, takes premature action, or has a nervous breakdown. If he is aware of what is going on within his own system, both physically and psychologically, he can find an antidote. It may be that the higher self is saying something to him that he wants to ignore. So the person must be blasted out of a rut one way or another. Part of the self says, "Let's go for change." The other part is saying, "Yes, but I'm on familiar territory." The resulting dialogues can be extremely nerve-wracking.

One analogy for Uranus is "falling plaster." If a person decides to remodel his house, the resulting chaos is extremely difficult to live with. He may wish he had never started the whole project or that he could pull the plaster down faster to get the job over with sooner. Yet he must remain in the midst of the mess until all the old plaster is down and the plaster dust has settled. Only then can he see the results of the new conditions and environment. If he has a sense of humor and some perspective, he'll get through that difficult period of time with more ease. However, he may be sorely tempted to run away from the whole situation before it's completed or the new results emerge.

In psychological terms, these Uranus aspects describe times when it is necessary to work through the scare and be ready to take more chances with life. Timing is critical, however, because the individual may run away from progress and growth only to blow up a potentially fantastic opportunity prematurely. It is so important to keep something of a rein on impulses at that time, to allow oneself the freedom to investigate many new possibilities but refrain from any decisive action until the patterns emerge more clearly.

When Uranus rules or is posited in the first house in an individual's chart, the person can be unusually inventive, spontaneous, and ahead of his time. He is restless and quick, and may express genius potential. If Uranus is well aspected in the chart, he is able to express all of his unique humanitarian qualities with ease, but if just the opposite is true, he may be especially rebellious, nervous, high-strung, and sensitive. He can have a suicidal complex. He may not be serious about it or maudlin in any way; it is more of a flirtation with the idea. He has an inner voice that says, "Stop the world and let me off." He can want life to be so fast-moving that he flirts with the idea of running away permanently. He may have a primordial memory or association with Atlantis, where brilliant and advanced technologies ruled the day. In our civilization, we have not yet caught up with the highly advanced science that ruled that era. The person with Uranus strong in his chart feels different, apart from other people and perhaps bored with our slow development.

It is especially important to allow a child with this aspect the freedom he needs. If he is too regimented or pinned down, he may have allergy attacks, rashes, or learning disabilities. He could have crossed meridians, which causes a reaction similar to dyslexia. (In his fine book, *Touch for Health*, Dr. John F. Thie describes the problem of crossed meridians and prescribes simple remedial exercises.) The person with this aspect may have trouble with lungs or breathing. He needs a release for nervous energy that is constructive, stimulating, and exciting. He may be an electronics whiz, very musical, or have information that has been lost to civilizations for centuries. He is avant-garde and special, or if negative, an anarchist. He must be shown the way for release of high energy.

If Uranus affects the second house, the impulse, or genius, has to do with financial matters. Funds can run through his fingers, yet he may be able to earn income through inventive means. He will take risks with income that someone else might ignore or resist, if Uranus is well aspected, yet may be irresponsible if it is not well aspected. He may work better in free-lance areas than where he has to punch a time clock. Funds come in and go out rather spontaneously. He may have no sense of proportion with management of money. He may be rebellious on some level when it comes to financial situations. He probably needs to find a specialty that will satisfy the needs described by Uranus. He can be an impulse shopper, since spending money is a way to release all that extra electricity coming into his system. He usually has an uncanny split-second timing where income is concerned, if Uranus is well aspected. He may have to work through the scare where money is concerned if it is not well aspected. He will eventually learn where he can take risks and where he cannot. With his own special financial acumen, he may be especially brilliant in financial fields.

If Uranus rules or is positioned in the third house, the individual's ability to communicate is described by that planet. If Uranus is well aspected, he is spontaneous, inventive, and especially quick in early school years. He may have genius capacity. His speech patterns can be quite rapid and unusual, with quick reactions in his thought patterns. If Uranus is not well aspected, he may be erratic in thought and speech, dart from one subject to another, and feel nervous about expressing himself. He may have problems in traditional schools that would not be present where more freedom of learning is allowed. He could have speech defects. Dyslexia could cause him to reverse words or letters, or he may have other learning disabilities. In this instance, the simple exercise to uncross meridians can be very effective. Color healing may enable him to smooth out the energy moving through his body and brain. With the right encouragement and a school that allows for individual growth and that fosters a possibility of genius, rather than insisting on conformity, this person may reveal astonishing and special ability. With more freedom in the learning environment, difficulties can be mitigated. He may be simply too far ahead of others to learn in a traditional way. Relationships with siblings may be either spontaneous or very upsetting. He can never relate his own development to what he observes in brothers and sisters or in connection with his community of relatives or neighbors.

When this planet is related to the fourth house, the parent of the opposite sex may be especially unusual or inventive. If Uranus is badly aspected in the natal chart, that parent may have run away or otherwise behaved in an irresponsible manner. The child might be scared in the relationship with that parent. If that parent were able to channel the high potential into areas of productivity, such as music, inventions, or healing, the role model would give the child permission to release much of his inventiveness throughout his life, but particularly toward the latter part of life. If Uranus is not well aspected, the parent may have a tendency toward alcoholism. The parent's tendency would be to control and repress energy instead of utilizing it. The child would tend to copy the parent and try to calm the nervous system rather than find an outlet for the genius potential. The individual with this aspect may be quite rigid in his lifestyle if Uranus is not well aspected, as he can't stand chaos around him. He may dart in and out of his home, being unable to sit still for very long. He may want everything in its place so that he can find things quickly. If Uranus is well aspected, he may be more spontaneous about his lifestyle and may happily make changes for more exciting conditions at the base of his life. If Uranus is not well aspected, he may move impulsively, needing constantly new conditions around him, due to nerves and restlessness.

The fifth house in a chart describes creative expression, romance, children, and the gambling urges. If Uranus rules or is placed in this house, a person may be quite impulsive romantically, and find his greatest spark in life through creative outlets. A badly aspected Uranus can tempt the individual into unhealthy avant-garde relationships. He may be attracted to rebellious people or want unusual love affairs. He is not content to deal with traditional roles in love or with creativity. He may run away, attract unreliable situations, express his need for freedom in a dangerous way. Romance may not represent stability, due to the very type of person he chooses. If Uranus is well aspected, the greatest excitement comes through romance or creative expression. His children will be unusual, brilliant, ahead of the times. His greatest fear may be connected to self-expression or with children, however, if Uranus energy is not easily released. He may have to learn how to be more spontaneous with his gambling instincts. He could be a stock-market genius in some instances, with proper attunement to his impulses.

The sixth house in a chart describes service, work, health, relationships with co-workers, and dietary inclinations. When Uranus is well aspected and placed in this house, the individual will work rapidly, want the most innovative tools, and find an outlet for some unusual contribution with his work. He may be interested in health, especially in connection with holistic or metaphysical concepts, or he may have a somewhat scientific interest in diet and foods. In any case, he will not be cut out of the ordinary mold when it comes to health habits. He may have an unusual contribution to make through his work. If Uranus is not well aspected, nerves can be a health hazard. He may be impatient, impulsive, constantly upset with working situations, or have unpredictable success with his job unless he allows himself to work in avant-garde areas, or do free-lance work. He can express his genius in areas where he can be of service to mankind.

The seventh house describes relationships. It can be descriptive of marriage or business partnership. Whether Uranus is ruling this house or placed within it, the individual needs a great deal of freedom in partnership areas. If he is in touch with that basic need, he will look for a free soul, someone inventive, unusual, and with genius or fame potential. He will not be interested in anyone who is not somehow different. His marriage may take place suddenly. If Uranus is not well aspected, the individual may be impulsive about marriage. He may look for someone with a genius potential and be attracted instead to someone who has gone unhealthily awry, or find someone unpredictable who eventually runs away. With a badly aspected Uranus in the natal chart, he may look for someone who will ultimately behave in such a manner that he himself will want to run away. He may then be able to breathe a sigh of relief and say to himself, "I'm free again." He may have several impulsive mar-riages until he begins to express more of his own unique qualities. At that point he will be more able to attract someone to his side who is truly humanitarian, in touch with spontaneity and inventive-ness, and is a free soul.

The eighth house is descriptive of the way in which one gets his needs met; it can consequently be the quality of energy that one sends out to humanity at large. In traditional astrology, this is the house of death or inheritance, yet it describes a way in which one effects his own transformation in life. If Uranus is well aspected in the chart, unusual events bring in what the individual needs and wants. He may have last-second luck, or find unexpected funds through royalties, residuals, inheritance. He may be a risk taker, yet inventive when it comes to getting his needs met. If Uranus is not well aspected, the release may come from impulsively running up bills. He may be nervous about attention to details and be especially rebellious or nervous about getting his needs met. He may be afraid to take risks, yet the very working through the scare becomes the way of transformation. Spontaneity is important with extra funds or with expenditures. He may not be able to hang onto funds, so it is very important for him to understand that as freely as money flows out in his life, it flows in. If he feels that he is able to make a contribution to mankind, he will not hesitate to allow himself to take risks with income and expenditures. He can heal his own financial position, through expressing natural healing abilities.

The ninth house describes conditions related to travel, publicity, promotional efforts, legalities, and higher education. With Uranus describing this house, either by placement or rulership, the greatest release in life comes through travel, publishing, distribution of information, or simply risking the opening of the higher mind. This individual may encounter unexpected events in his life that propel him into entirely new conditions or into new territory. He is able to make a unique contribution through music, or through some unusual occupation. He may be on his soapbox to awaken mankind. If Uranus is well aspected, it is easy for him to be available for special tasks, or an unusual occupation that takes him into risky or uncharted territory. If Uranus is not well aspected, he may rebel or blow off steam by running away, only to find that uncertain conditions exist wherever he goes. A highly impulsive syndrome may eventually put him into the spotlight. He may be famous or infamous.

When Uranus describes the tenth house of career, the individual may have a need to do free-lance work or express his career potential through anything that is avant-garde or unusual. He may be musical, become famous or infamous, or have a messianic complex. His greatest gift comes through an ability to be a catalyst for other people. If he has a well-aspected Uranus, he enjoys the ability to put people and situations together and is well aware of his need for spontaneity in public endeavor. If Uranus is not well aspected, he may try to hang on to situations or conditions that are outmoded. Usually the parent of the same sex showed a brilliant potential whether in music, healing, or humanitarian concerns, or through inventions or science. Depending on his role model, this individual is willing to take risks with career matters and may actually have a degree of fame in his own life. He may seem unpredictable or unreliable in career areas, however, if Uranus is not well aspected. He may want to run away from career responsibilities. He needs an outlet for the high energy coursing through his system. He may always have to take risks with public endeavor and be in the vanguard with new information or techniques.

When Uranus is placed in or rules the eleventh house of friends, groups, or associations, he may have most unusual friendships. He will naturally be attracted to people who are walking to the beat of a different drummer. He can be especially humanitarian in group endeavors, be spontaneous and available to his friends, and make unique contributions through organizations or with group endeavors. Since Uranus rules music and inventions, he may join organizations that are humanitarian, musical, or dealing with metaphysical concepts. He may, if Uranus is not well aspected, look for unreliable people or unusual friendships through which to express his own rebellious nature. He may actually be surrounded by unsavory people or those with anarchistic tendencies.

The twelfth house is the house of the subconscious. If Uranus rules this house or is placed there, the individual may have very unusual psychic abilities. However, sometimes these flashes of brilliance may be especially scary. He may leave his body to do astral traveling, even if he is unaware of what he is doing. If Uranus is well aspected in the natal chart, he may be especially attuned to levels of awareness that produce genius ability. If he is able to listen to his inner messages, he is unusually inspired. If, however, that planet is not well aspected, the scare that he can experience on a subconscious level tempts him to do anything to tune out his messages. Drugs or alcohol can be especially damaging to an individual with this aspect. He may have to learn how to protect himself from psychic disturbances. He may be like a radio on a subconscious level. He can pick up frequencies, mistake them for his own inner voice, and blow a fuse, subconsciously, until he understands this high spiritual, psychic energy. When he can align himself to this energy, he can produce brilliant works, be especially inventive, and express genius potential.

URANUS CONJUNCT SUN

Uranus-Sun dialogues describe a quality of dynamic energy that may overshadow the quality of birth-sign energy. No matter what the birth sign may be, the planet Uranus can change or augment that particular quality. If a person with his Sun in Cancer or Taurus has the Sun conjunct (or sitting next to) Uranus, the inner soul quality will have a Uranian, as well as a Cancerian or a Taurean, characteristic. Depending on where the Sun and Uranus are placed in the chart, and how strongly they make connection with other planets, this combination can lead to unusual accomplishments. It can frequently lead to recognition from the public simply because the individual will be involved in situations or products that somehow set him apart from other people. Uranus describes a need for freedom and opportunity for unique self-expression. When Uranus is conjunct the Sun, the dialogue is so easy or harmonious that the person feels quite free inside and may have no need to prove anything. Uranus qualities can lead to investigation of anything new and different and ahead of the times, yet it may take a kicker from some other area of the chart to set it in motion.

Walt Disney had Uranus conjunct his Sun in Sagittarius. That conjunction is placed in the house of communications. It rules the sixth house of work, and the twelfth house of the subconscious mind. Walt Disney's genius extended into many areas of communications and led to an inventiveness that certainly set him apart from other people. He may have had psychic flashes that led to his ideas, but he was also able to spend time alone developing the techniques that led to his success. With that conjunction ruling the house of work, he would naturally want the fastest way of accomplishing tasks and have a profound ability to communicate and sell his ideas. Uranus is squaring his ascendant (or personality), leading to a rebellious quality that would force him to be somehow "different." His fame came almost secondary to the need for release of energy. Obviously Walt Disney was a man who did not wait for permission from others to do what he wanted to do. He said his inventions were primarily for his own pleasure. He loved his railroads as much as the millions of children who have benefited by his profound need for activity and self-expression.

Gary Collins also has this aspect in his chart. His Sun-Uranus conjunction is in the sign of Taurus and is placed in the tenth house of career activity. Uranus describes areas where an individual needs to blow off steam and release some of the pressure of his restless energy. Gary was asked if he missed the acting career, now that he is the host of a television show called "Hour Magazine." He replied that he just wanted to work. With such a strong aspect at the top of his chart, indicating an intense need for stimulation and freedom, with public activity, it is more than possible that Gary would have a hard time following the dictates of studio heads or putting himself in the hands of agents and others who would have control over a film career. A restless quality would make it extremely difficult for him to wait for jobs to appear.

Jim Diehl, a California psychic with a high degree of accuracy in his readings, seems to be on his way to fame. He has attracted so many stars as clients that a move to Los Angeles from Pennsylvania was dictated, and his reputation has already attracted attention from national magazines that deal with Hollywood and stardom. Jim has the Sun-Uranus conjunction placed in the ninth house of recognition, but ruling the sixth house of work, and the twelfth house of the psychic or subconscious. His work has to do with psychic and subconscious matters. I asked Jim if he felt fame was in the cards for him. He replied, "I feel that I will be pushed into it, that I have no control over that aspect of my life. My nervous system [sixth house] demands that I keep working and keep busy, or it is like overloading a circuit: if you don't feed it properly, you can burn it out. I feel freer on an inner level when I'm doing work on a higher spiral. As long as things keep moving, I think the nervous energy seems to smooth out on the inside." I asked him if he needed time alone. "I go off to the desert to tune in periodically. I feel I may have been in a monastery in a past life and I suspect my psychic ability comes from a time in the past when I was alone a great deal. Naturally, I have to have time alone now to prevent blowing out the circuits. I also need high spiritual energy to feed me. I work with the Bible in my readings and prescribe Psalms for my clients that I feel will be valuable for them. I get my messages in biblical phrases." Uranus has also been associated with a high spiritual quality of energy.

Shirley MacLaine has the Sun conjunct Uranus in her chart.

(Uranus is in the sign of Aries, and the Sun is in Taurus, but they are still conjunct.) This aspect is placed in her eighth house (transformation) and rules the eleventh house of friends, associations, and group activity. It also rules the fifth house of creativity. The eighth house describes the psychological "device" one employs to get his needs met. Sometimes this mode of obtaining aid, financing, or a flow of energy is entirely unconscious or automatic. It then describes the transformation in life and the ultimate gift one has to send out to humanity. Shirley is especially gifted musically and creatively. She has been able to easily express her talent. She has always seemed to gather people to her side who are unusual, inventive, and talented. Uranus describes the last-minute energy. It is interesting to note that Shirley's major step into the spotlight came very unexpectedly, when she was asked to replace someone on Broadway. Part of the necessity of working with this particular quality of energy is to be able to ride through nerve-wracking times to be ready when the spotlight comes around.

It is no secret that Shirley has a need for freedom. The fifth house rules children as well as creative activity. Shirley had a long but most unusual marriage, to a man who lived on the other side of the world from Shirley. Her daughter eventually went to live with her father, in Japan, while Shirley continued her career in the theater and in film. Shirley's daughter may also inherit her mother's talent, although she might express it in a very different manner. Shirley has taken her unique energies a step further with her investigation and writing about metaphysical matters. Her first book, *Don't Fall off the Mountain*, described her trip to the Himalayas, among other things. She was one of the first people to visit the tiny kingdom of Bhutan, a civilization based on astrology. Her latest book, *Out on a Limb*, deals with her long study of metaphysics. It may be that Shirley MacLaine's ultimate and greatest gift to people has to do with a healing energy, described by Uranus placed in the eighth house. Her name, reputation, and dramatic ability (described by the Sun) lend credence in some areas where another's approach would be unacceptable.

Glen Campbell also has Sun conjunct Uranus, as did singer Lawrence Tibbett. Glen Campbell has this aspect, describing music, in Taurus and placed in the sixth house of work. The aspect also rules his tenth house of career, and fourth house of home. He has an exciting public image in the music world which propelled him into the spotlight and has kept him there. He can work from home base, and will continue producing exciting music well into his later years. Since the fourth and tenth houses also describe parental influence, Glen's early programming was toward success and risk taking with work. Because of other aspects in his chart, he may have expressed a rebellion toward any feelings of limitation he saw in his parents' lives. He inherited talent from both his mother and his father.

Lawrence Tibbett, an internationally famous opera singer, had this aspect placed in the eighth house. It rules the sixth house of work, and the twelfth house of the subconscious. His was an inspired voice that put him on the roster of singers of the first order. Obviously he was a healer through his music and through his work.

In the political field, this planetary aspect can indicate an excitement that is extraordinary. Ron Ziegler, former White House press secretary, has this aspect in his chart. The Sun and Uranus are conjunct, or together, in the twelfth house, or the subconscious, psychic areas of mind, yet they rule his tenth house of career, and his fourth house of home. Ron was especially popular and well liked by the press corps. He was also criticized for being evasive, yet that very Uranian quality enabled him to show spontaneity and inventiveness in his public life. He was able to hold his share of the spotlight, give out information, yet wiggle out of tight situations with effectiveness and ease. With this aspect involved in a grand trine in his chart, he could develop a sudden, sixth sense about timing in his career. Divine protection will surely follow him in all high-risk areas of public life. He may have sudden bursts of fame throughout his life and be propelled into unusual situations rather suddenly.

Barry Goldwater also has Sun conjunct Uranus in his chart. This aspect is placed in his third house of communications, and rules the eleventh house of friendships, group situations, and dealings with organizations. It also rules the fifth house of creative expression. Barry Goldwater is an intellectual who shows genius potential and has a fantastic ability to campaign and promote. Yet even with so brilliant an ability to express himself, Uranus can describe a quality of energy that is so ephemeral that Goldwater may be just one step out of sync with the times. His ideas are innovative, his popularity strong, yet he seems to have only near misses with ultimate victory.

He also has the Sun-Uranus conjunction in a grand trine. That pattern is like a triangle of protective energy that can indicate too much ease and self-assurance. It can indicate a lack of enough challenge in the long run.

Joseph Alioto, former mayor of San Francisco, has this aspect, as does Walter Schirra, an astronaut. Walter Schirra was known to be quite mischievous as a child, with a penchant for pranks. But as a man of action, he was able to go through the rigid training demanded of him as an astronaut. The planet Uranus describes space programs and flight. This conjunction rules the sixth house in his chart, indicating high energy that must have an outlet in activity that is unique. The conjunction is placed in the seventh house of partnership. He would naturally have to work in close cooperative partnership on space flights. The partner also needs outlet for the expression of the Uranian quality described by that placement.

Joseph Alioto was described as being irrepressible. He was also tolerant about the hippy movement in San Francisco when he was mayor. It is interesting that the hippy movement coincided with the planet Uranus transiting the sign of Scorpio. It was a transformational, freeing time in history, as well as an extremely rebellious one.

URANUS IN HARD ASPECT TO THE SUN

When Uranus makes hard aspects to the Sun, the energy is even more dynamic than with a conjunction, simply because the dialogue is not easy. Uranus, in a less than positive sense, describes rebellion, whereas the Sun represents energy, ego, sense of self-worth, and authority. It would appear that individuals with hard aspects between the Sun and Uranus have a more difficult, therefore more dynamic, time in expressing the unique, free part of themselves. They may well need an authority figure to rebel against. Judy Garland had Uranus squaring her Sun. Uranus is placed at the zenith of her chart, describing a potential for fame through music or any unusual accomplishment. The Sun is in the twelfth house, indicating an inner need for time alone, away from the prying eyes of the public. Judy said that in her early life she never had enough time to sleep. The tenth house represents career, "bosses," and the parent of the same sex. Judy's mother, Gladys, was the driving force in

Judy's early life. Gladys was extremely musical and talented in her own right. Perhaps because of her own frustrations, she pushed Judy into the spotlight. When Judy Garland began to work in film, Louis B. Mayer took the place of the authority figure and gave her real cause to rebel. He made her mother look tame in comparison. Psychologically, Judy simply found a replacement authority figure that would give her a chance to rebel. Yet it was precisely because of that rebellious spirit, unique talent, and personality that she refused to be pigeonholed or categorized or regimented. She simply had to walk to the beat of a different drummer.

Indira Gandhi also had the Sun square Uranus in her chart. In this case, Uranus is placed in the sixth house of work, and the Sun is positioned in the house describing the father, the fourth house of the chart. With Leo rising, the Sun describes her personality. The identification with her father would be especially strong. Uranus is opposite her ascendant, giving a double-barreled kicker to the Sun in her chart. This is further complicated by Saturn, the planet of duty and destiny, placed in her subconscious, twelfth house, but conjunct her ascendant. She was born with a subconscious, deep sense of destiny that accompanied a fierce rebellion against the dictates of the times. Her energy would necessarily propel her to take up the sword where her father, Jawaharlal Nehru, left off. She had to rebel against the dictates of the times in more than one way. She found herself in a position of advocating freedom not only for India but inadvertently for women, and mankind, in all lands. She was a force ahead of her time, a leader and a fighter for the rights of humanity, the true Uranian trait.

When two planets are in opposition to each other, the energy is somewhat easier to resolve than when they are squared. A balance can be achieved that produces action from less friction. But wherever the planet Uranus is involved in a chart is where the greatest release comes. When it is in opposition to the Sun, the release comes with running away, taking risks, or through the nervous system. It seems the "electrical wiring" in the system is not quite properly aligned. A fuse must be blown in some way to give release. This can also indicate scattered energy and a tendency to be distracted, or slightly out of focus sometimes, and restlessness or impulsive behavior.

But primarily the rebellion is against authority or any situation, or person, who represents dominance. There is an inner need to integrate one's own sense of self-worth, dominance, and authority. If the individual is not recognized by the external world and is not given "permission" to be who he is, he becomes rebellious. He may actually be running away from himself, his own need to be dominant, in the executive position. He may ultimately need to give himself permission for self-expression without rebelling in order to do so. He was obviously made to feel that his genius or inventiveness was in some way less than desirable. But that unique quality must emerge. He learns to allow true freedom into his life, refuses to value himself by how others see him, and can be light-years ahead of the rest of the clan.

Carolyn is the producer of a theatre for children. She is married to Steve, a producer of many Broadway hits. Both have the Sun in opposition to Uranus in their charts, but the houses involved are quite different. Carolyn has Uranus conjunct her ascendant in Aries, describing a fiercely independent nature, with the Sun in Libra positioned in the seventh house of partnership. The inner Libran quality is balanced, in need of peace, harmony, love, affection, pleasure, and beauty—and she would look for a partner or mate to express and fulfill those qualities. Steve also has the Sun in Libra, so he naturally expresses the qualities Carolyn needs in a mate. Carolyn has the personality traits of the Aries with an Aquarian flavor thrown in. She is active, energetic, feisty, unique, and a very free soul. She described this quality of energy by saying, "When I was a child, instead of napping, I would be climbing on the furniture or swinging on the door. I had so much nervous energy I just couldn't sit still. I still can't sit still. If I'm supposed to be lying by the pool, pretty soon I'm up cleaning the pool, getting the pebbles out of the way or picking off the dead leaves from the bushes. I release a lot of that nervous energy athletically. As a child I would get on a horse and ride for hours by myself. It satisfied my need for freedom. I love openness. I just can't stand being closed in. For instance, I love the independence of skiing. You're not dependent on someone else to hit a ball back, it's just you. It gives me the feeling of flying. Skiing is like being a bird. The only sound you hear is that of your own breathing."

With Uranus opposite the Sun in partnership areas, Carolyn's first marriage was not a happy one. "I ran away from my first marriage or I think I would have had a nervous breakdown. Everything had to be under control. I think my husband was afraid of me and my ways. If I was bored—and I can't *stand* being bored—I would sit there for just a minute, then go looking for something to do. I have an almost compulsive restlessness. If I felt like climbing a cherry tree and eating Bing cherries with the kids, that's what I would do. I would ice down the streets so the city would have to block them off. Then the children would have someplace to ice-skate and I'd be out there with them. Sometimes I'd clean the house at 11 P.M. I have to do things when I feel like it.

"I also can't stand being told what to do, and I don't like having to report to anyone. I hate to get trapped in situations where I can't get up and leave if I want to. Sometimes I get so bored with dumb conversations, I just want to get up and leave."

Carolyn said that she felt much of her restless energy was due to unhappiness as a child. Psychologically, Uranus can describe fear, or "scare." People find many ways to work through the scare in life. Carolyn described it in this way, "The scare is part of the excitement. I would love to parachute out of airplanes, for instance. Most of all, I love that feeling of being a bird." The Uranian energy can also find great release through music. Carolyn played the piano and the violin as a child.

As an adult, Carolyn has created a tremendously exciting lifestyle. There is never a dull moment. Her work in the theatre and all the other projects she has in the works have to be sandwiched in between trips with Steve. They literally commute on an almost weekly and, sometimes, daily, basis between New York, Florida, New Orleans, Texas, California, and Aspen, Colorado. Because of her own exciting personality, Carolyn attracts the most unusual and inventive people to her side wherever she finds herself. With Uranus ruling the eleventh house of friendships, groups, and associations, she likes people who are ahead of the times. Uranus has been described as the planet of true friendship. Carolyn has proved to be one of the best friends one could hope to have.

Steve has the Uranus-Sun opposition ruling his tenth house of career, and fourth house of home. (The planet Uranus is posited in the fifth house of creative expression, and the Sun in the eleventh house of associations, groups, and friends.) This aspect is intensified by Jupiter conjunct Pluto in a square to both planets, creating a

T-square from the ninth house. Jupiter-Pluto is an extremely lucky aspect that creates special dynamic tension when it is hooked up with Uranus-Sun. Gambling instincts, the career, and group projects have propelled Steve into fame in the third portion of his life (approximately after the age of forty-nine), only after honoring many conflicting voices that had to be reconciled early in life. The ninth house in a chart describes travel, expansion, and dealing in countries away from the place of birth (Steve was born in Israel). If it is possible to do so, we will leave the Jupiter-Pluto portion of this situation to be discussed in another chapter. It is extremely difficult to isolate one factor from another, because energy can be intertwined in a person's life; yet, considering only the rebellious part of Steve's chart, it would appear that he would have to have free rein to express his own particular and unique concept of talent. Authority figures would indeed present a problem. Carolyn was very helpful in describing events of the past. "Steve stopped being a movie producer because of his need to be free to do what he feels. He just doesn't have the time to consult and report to others. He loves to have creative meetings with writers and directors. He gets especially excited about creating and writing. He is the best storyteller around." The fifth house describes entertainment, whether that is in the theater or creating entertaining evenings with friends. I volunteered that I thought much of Steve's brilliance as a producer was to do things that other people would simply overlook or ignore. Carolyn said, "He is very inventive about projects, but it's not just that he *thinks* about them. He can talk other people into things." Steve creates an excitement about his projects that can be contagious.

Steve's early life certainly provided opportunity to work through the scare. At the age of eighteen, he commanded a troop in the Israeli Army. Carolyn continued, "I suppose it's natural at that age to be unafraid, but he was a high risk taker even then. He would be on a motorcycle leading a convoy down a riverbed in the middle of the night many times. When he was twenty-seven, they called him the roadrunner. He never sat still. When I first met Steve, he had the kind of nervous energy that was like being on a pogo stick." It seems only natural that Steve won contests in Israel as the jitterbug champion of the area. He began to tap his special good fortune when he made his way to California to become an actor. Again the rebellion against authority came into play. He wasn't content to take direction from others, he had to heed the beat of his own inner instincts as far as the expression of talent went.

I asked Steve how that exciting energy feels on a day-to-day basis. "It is as if you prepare for something for a long time and nothing moves. The function of preparing appears as though you're not doing anything to those around you, yet there is a process of waiting that seems to be necessary. When the pieces fall into place, then you go into high gear. After what appears to be simply waiting, you take off at what is a backbreaking pace for everyone else around you. At that point you don't check to see if it is right or wrong. You simply move ahead, even recklessly. There is a great feeling of joy and exhilaration. If your risk fails, it can be devastating and you can be hurt very badly. When you fail, you fail, yet that burst of energy seems to come again and you plunge in the same way toward something else."

URANUS CONJUNCT THE MOON

When Uranian, electrical energy is connected to the Moon in a natal chart, the emotional nature is affected. Uranus-Moon aspects —whether hard, neutral, or soft—describe a quality of energy that is extremely sensitive, vulnerable, and sometimes unstable. They indicate a tendency to hysteria that can usually be traced to an early scare in life that scars the emotions. A person with this aspect feels for everyone and everything around him. He cannot be discriminating about his reactions. He can cry easily and may do so at the most inopportune times, yet that is, at least, a release for some of his excess feelings and emotions. He can be moved to cry at corny soap operas as well as the really emotional things around him.

The Moon describes mothering, nurturing feelings. When the Moon is conjunct Uranus, the resulting energy may be used to heal on an extremely sensitive level, or it can indicate a tendency to run away from emotional involvement and mothering. More than likely, there have been feelings of abandonment that have been too frightening to deal with in a rational manner. The person with this aspect may run away from people and situations, rather than stick around to resolve the condition. The positive side of this emotional quality is a profound ability to touch people on a subconscious level. His identification with pain in the life of someone else can be hard to deal with early in life, however, so the child with such an aspect may need special understanding and nurturing. He tends to take on the pain of other people and not realize it is not his own. He may need a special kind of outlet to release an unusually sensitive quality of emotional energy.

The individual with this aspect has an emotional antenna in the air. He can pick up static or beautiful music, but whatever the feelings, they can be very disturbing until he learns how to fine-tune his radio. He may be attracted to people who unconsciously transmit their pain onto him, simply because his sensitive nature is so receptive. The Moon describes rescuing tendencies in a chart. With a Uranus conjunction, the individual may go through agonizing phases of emotional imbalance and instability because of his inability to make everything all right for everyone. In terms of transactional analysis, the "rescue triangle" describes a situation in which the rescuer rescues the victim; the victim then becomes the persecuter and persecutes the rescuer. It becomes a vicious cycle. The person who had such an emotional scare that he wants to rescue other people from pain is persecuted, once again abandoned after his attempts, and left to deal with his emotional scare all over again.

Mercury is the antidote for the Moon. Mercury is the planet that describes analysis, mental activity, and objectivity. When the mind is put in gear to analyze an overly emotional reaction, the person with this aspect can decipher the situation clearly. He may observe that his feelings are the kind of feelings shared by many people. He may then be quite thankful for his quick ability to feel what is in the air. He elicits deep response from the public at large if he transmutes this quality of energy into productivity, rather than non-productive activity. Uranian energy needs an outlet. Otherwise it becomes rebellion.

Tears may provide a natural way to release some of the excess energy with this aspect. The person with this nature may need to blow a fuse on an emotional level to prevent a complete breakdown of the system. Music is also a way to channel feelings, as well as being involved with any activity described by Uranus, such as healing, astrology, inventions, electronics, and recordings. Writing is an excellent way to become more objective. It seems to be a matter of working through the emotional pain to identify with feelings of humanity on a more subconscious level.

Perhaps the best example of this quality of association with mankind at large is shown in the chart of Bing Crosby. There was hardly a star alive with a more incredible ability to wring out feelings and elicit strong emotion from the public than Bing, whether he was singing or acting. His music touched millions of people during his very active career. It seems quite sad that he could express such feelings to strangers through the medium of film, and yet may not have been able to express them within the confines of his own family. Bing is reported to have been cool to his older children. They did not seem to benefit from that nurturing potential. Since the Moon can be self-protective because of such vulnerability, he may have utilized his feelings in the field of communications, so he had little left to show to the people close to him.

Ellen Burstyn has the Moon conjunct Uranus in the sixth house of work, in her chart. Ellen is not only a brilliant and sensitive actress, she is very much involved in metaphysical practices and the teachings of the new Age of Aquarius. Her metaphysical work is as important as her work as an actress. Uranus rules the fourth house of home, in her chart. Ellen's home reflects her need for an environment that fosters positive energy. She has obviously learned how to tune her emotional antenna to very high sources of inspiration through meditation, proper food, and metaphysical disciplines.

Lisa has Moon conjunct Uranus in the third house of communications. That is the house that also rules siblings and other relatives. In a regression session, Lisa recounted a very traumatic experience she had as a tiny child. She was playing with her younger sister on a sliding board near their house at the beach. She was evidently left alone to look after her sister, who was a year younger than she. As her sister climbed up the slide to turn around at the top, she lost her balance, fell into the sand below, and struck the wooden edge, hitting a protruding nail in the process. Hearing the screams of both children, their mother came running out to see what had happened. The wound from the nail was so deep that the child had to be rushed to the hospital and was in critical condition for quite a while. Lisa became aware of her own feelings of inadequacy that she couldn't have prevented the accident. She was also aware that she was too young to really act as the mother in that situation and knew that the accident had terrified her. She felt a great distance from that sister in later years. With new awareness, she knew that perhaps she had run away from too close an involvement with her younger sister. She may have felt, on a deeply subconscious level, that she could protect her sister better from afar and with distance between them. Lisa described her reaction in this way. "I had a symbiosis with that sister that was frightening. I was afraid of killing a part of me if I got too close to her, so I shut down any emotions relating to her. I knew the thought forms and emotions of everyone as a child. I wasn't clear about that then, so I didn't know how to handle it. I have left my body when I was scared. I am afraid of being totally in that kind of symbiosis again for fear I won't come back to my body the next time.

"I have an addictive type of personality. I am actually a dry alcoholic. If I have too much sugar, for instance, I get a rush of energy. That high rush of energy is an addiction. It is thrill-seeking energy. I have learned that the nervous energy I experience is actually a lack of energy. At times I've tried to do more, running on nervous energy, and have collapsed mentally and physically. My thought processes get very confused when I don't follow my inner sense of timing."

Uranus rules the twelfth house of the subconscious mind, in Lisa's chart. When Uranus describes that kind of energy coming in "behind the scenes," it is high psychic attunement. The subconscious mind can become overloaded, and leaving the body is an escape route. Lisa's statement about being a dry alcoholic is very important, because many times a person turns to alcohol as a means of trying to calm down that high energy, without realizing what is really happening. The energy needs release, not repression.

The Moon rules the fifth house in Lisa's chart. This describes Lisa's relationship with her children. In discussing her feelings, she volunteered, "It's hard not to rescue my children. I try to set parameters and then allow them to make their own decisions. But I don't want my children to feel pain. I'd like to take away the pain completely, but I know that's impossible. I am aware of an impatient quality I possess. For instance, I am too impatient to stand in line at the grocery store. I definitely feel everything in my solar plexus." Since the fifth house also describes the creative process and the Moon can be associated with writing, anything Lisa can do to channel her subconscious information into creative projects, especially in connection with the communications fields, will regulate that quality of high energy into very productive activity.

I have Moon conjunct Uranus in Aries in the tenth house of career. That also describes my relationship with my beloved mother. My own experiences may shed some light on how that aspect is manifest in life. Since Cancer (the Moon) rules my ascendant, Uranus is a co-ruler because of that conjunction. My early-childhood experiences were especially emotionally frightening. I have become aware only recently that I have had a scared little emotional body as a result of feeling terribly abandoned as a baby. I was evidently traumatized at about the age of five months by identifying with and becoming aware of a terrifying thing that was happening in my mother's life. The events that began when I was five months old culminated when I was two. My mother was left a widow with two children to bring up alone. She was thrown into a state of shock that affected her health. She suffered from severe migraine headaches (Moon-Uranus conjunction in Aries, ruling the head) and lost her sense of smell. She had an extremely painful sinus condition as well. Naturally, she couldn't give me any feelings of security or safety.

One of my earliest conscious memories was that of seeing my mother faint. I was terrified that I would lose her. The way I chose to deal with her was to "run away." I lived away from her with my grandmother for each school year. My reaction to going away to school was both tremendous excitement and sadness. But I knew I was protecting my mother from any extra problems she might have encountered or that I might unwillingly impose. I took on the protective role of the mother at about the age of four. It has been rather obvious that I can deal with running away from emotional involvement more easily than getting close. The need for emotional freedom has resulted in rebellious action more often than not. The fear of loss is very strong, especially since my mother died when I was fourteen.

I can remember being very upset as a teenager when my freedom was taken away. I would sit at the piano for hours, cry, and make music. The combined effort would bring peace. Later I studied voice, not only because I love to sing, but because it was the best therapy I could find. As long as I sang, I was happy. Music has been very much a part of my life, as a performer and as an appreciator. When I began working with astrology, especially with writing, I felt less of a *need* for the music. Metaphysical practices and involvement with healing and meditation, as well as astrology and writing, have provided a positive outlet for the emotions.

The first house describes physical conditions. I am allergic to many things and am terribly sensitive to my environment. My tissues swell, like the Moon in its phases, with exposure to feathers, cigarette smoke, house dust, cats and dogs, sugar, and shellfish. I have an addictive personality, and like Lisa am a "dry alcoholic." I have no attraction to alcohol, but I could eat cake, candy, and ice cream without stopping if I didn't suffer so much from migraine headaches as a result. I have strong oral needs, especially if I'm upset about something. The feelings of abandonment described by Cancer rising may be associated with oral deprivation as an infant. My allergies to milk may have begun very early on. Uranus rules the nervous system in particular. Difficult Uranus aspects also seem to increase sensitivity to particular substances or in connection with specific parts of the body. With Uranus in Aries, I am particularly affected in the area of the head.

I have had to learn to pay attention to signals my body gives me. I have an antenna that picks up coming weather conditions. Just before a snowstorm or a rainstorm, I become very sensitive to the atmospheric pressure in the sinus or head area. I can have a headache, become very tired or even slightly depressed. If I can cry, whether I'm sad or not, it seems to relieve the excess pressure. As an actress, I could easily cry on cue. It is very important to maintain my emotional balance. I have a tendency to have very spontaneous feelings, and if my emotions are overstimulated, or I'm threatened with abandonment, they can then swing in the opposite way and I can become extremely upset.

I'm very restless and impatient. I hate to wait for people or things. I become terribly irritable. When I have to leave a place or a situation, I just have to leave. It has nothing to do with anything rational. I have an inner alarm clock that I must not ignore. I react badly when someone tries to tell me what to do. I suppose it is that extreme need for total emotional freedom—the right to think, feel or do whatever it is I feel I must at any given moment. I am a caring person, so I will never intentionally do any harm to anyone through my own needs. Just the opposite. It seems I feel I somehow protect them by retaining that spontaneous reaction and running away. It becomes difficult for people around me who care and who may not understand it. I seem to get my clues and sense of timing, as well as direction, from other sources. I can't ignore them, or my system kicks up a big fuss. I fight boredom constantly.

In a positive way, life can be very exciting. Spontaneous events bring such emotional joy that I can feel my heart swell up. I can become very "wired" and spirited, even mischievous. I love to be a catalyst for people and definitely have a messianic complex. I feel joyous when I express the nurturing and healing energies. My strongest sense of emotional freedom came from my grandmother. We had a psychic tie that was very spontaneous and strong. She gave me permission to express myself in whatever way was necessary, even if I rebelled against her. Nothing I could ever do or say would damage that love. That is the ultimate in freedom of emotional expression. I am always shocked when I discover I must keep a tight control on my reactions to avoid misunderstandings. Other people are not always so tolerant of my feisty emotional nature.

URANUS IN HARD ASPECT TO THE MOON

Joan has carved a special niche for herself in the film world by writing episodes for various TV hit series. She is a lovely, attractive, warm woman who lives in a charming storybook house in the hills above Los Angeles. Joan was able to shed light on the sensitivity of Uranus square the Moon by her willingness to describe what happened in her young life. Her normal emotional growth and security stopped at about the age of three. Joan's adored younger brother became terminally ill at that time. She recalls an incident that took place in the hospital where her brother was taken for treatment. "I think the worst thing that can happen to a child is abandonment of any kind. I was waiting in the reception room reading a book while my father was visiting my brother in his room. I was not allowed to see him, so I was waiting downstairs. I could see my father coming down the stairs crying. It was quite early in the morning, seven or eight o'clock, and I walked over to the stairs where my father was coming down. I felt very separate from the other children and I knew on some level that things were not right with my brother. I went to my father, not only to comfort him, but to receive some comfort from him. He walked right past me! This memory has stuck in my mind so much that I've had bad dreams about that hallway and reception desk. I felt that my father abandoned me. My mother told me later that it was probably when he first found out that my brother was going to die. I can still see my father's back as he continued walking out, away from me. I wanted to reach out to give and receive comfort. I was not even allowed to go in my brother's room. I used to hide in my room. I became deathly ill when I was a child and became allergic to everything. My father really hurt me when he didn't give me the comfort I needed when my brother died. He made me feel I didn't exist.

"I'm always late. Now, how can you be late as a child? There's nothing to keep you. You don't have to go to the grocery store or pay bills, but I was always late because I used to hide in my room. I finally figured out only last year that I'm not late because I'm an inconsiderate boob, it's that I'm afraid to leave the house. My house is a child's house. I have toys and dolls all around. I could just stay in my house all the time. I got quite sick last year. Friends suddenly ignored me. They didn't come to see me in the hospital or they said they were busy, and I got really hurt. Again it was like I didn't exist. I'm not saying 'poor me.' I'm just aware that I feel like that if someone doesn't acknowledge that I'm there."

Perhaps the most extreme and saddest example of Uranus square the Moon was exhibited in the early life of Ellen Wagner. Ellen has Uranus in the ninth house with the Moon in the sign of Leo in the twelfth house. Uranus rules the sixth house and the Moon rules the eleventh house of friends and associations. Ellen is an astrologer and is internationally recognized for her special talent and success in connection with business charts. She therefore has a wide circle of friends and acquaintances, but with this unpredictable aspect in her natal chart, some of those associations proved to be especially traumatic.

Ellen described her emotional reactions by saying, "It is very hard to express feelings. I've always kept things within myself. I must have felt abandoned even prenatally. I was the twelfth child, born in June, and my mother died at Christmas when I was only six months old. My mother actually died of pneumonia, but I'm sure she was diabetic and my birth must have weakened her. I was a huge baby, weighing almost twelve pounds. My father was naturally traumatized and I was left in the care of older siblings. Until I was about eighteen months old I was put in a dark room by myself and tied to a chair to keep me out of trouble. When my adoptive parents adopted me, I was judged to be mentally retarded. I couldn't talk and I had rickets from malnutrition. Thank God for my second mother and father, because very soon I could read whole books and my intelligence level was judged to be especially high. I've had lots of losses though. My sister was murdered and I've lost so many people I've loved. Life has not reassured me about trust on an emotional level."

Ellen described a recent event that seemed to cap her difficult experiences. "When I was under the midlife crisis of Uranus opposite its own position, I was brought to trial in Vermont on a drug conspiracy charge, based on a conversation I had with someone about a third person who was very heavily into cocaine. My telephone wire had been tapped and I was subpoenaed by the grand jury. It came totally out of the blue. When my lawyer told me I had been called for an arraignment before the U.S. Government, I was absolutely shocked. It was a nightmare. There was no evidence of anything. There were no drugs found, and in fact, no one ever came to the house to look for anything. The only evidence was the fact that I knew someone who was involved with drugs. It took a year and a half of court appearances. I had the local police chief testify as to my character as well as people from all over the world. But I had appeared as a witness in a trial four years previously where I protected someone innocent and a situation was set up where I could be entrapped. I was convicted with no evidence! I made an appeal in New York and won quite easily. In fact they looked at the case and just laughed. They said, 'But where is the money, where are the drugs, where is the proof of any deal? This woman was convicted on a conversation she had about someone she knew in Florida?' It was so bizarre, I almost lost my mind. I'm still paying off the legal fees and you can imagine what happened to my practice when the 'scandal' hit the newspapers."

Ellen described the awakening that always comes in the shock of Uranus aspects. With a hard aspect to the Moon, the awakening has to do with emotional reactions and especially the mothering instincts. "Throughout the trial, the man I have now married stayed

by my side. He was wonderful. Because Kevin was with me and was
such a pillar, I realized I could really trust him. After everything in
my life was exposed that I might have been afraid to reveal, for fear
it would push someone away, and he was still there, I realized he
was someone very special. The cleansing came through total humiliation. Some people were wonderful and others were terrible. But
finally, you must go on living. You have to eat and you have to go to
the supermarket." The happy ending to the story is that not only
were Ellen's emotions awakened as far as love in her life, but at the
age of forty-two, she has just had a beautiful baby daughter. She
can now fully release those latent mothering urges.

In each incident of Uranus-Moon aspects, the shock of early
childhood losses never quite seems to go away. Left to deal with
emotional reactions alone, at an age too early to analyze the situation properly, results in an especially scarred emotional body. The
adult is born, leaving the child behind all too soon. When the
aspect is in a conjunction, however, it appears that the blocked
emotional energy is easier to release and direct. In fact, the emotions cannot be contained. Both Lisa and I had children at an early
age to provide an outlet for the need to mother and nurture. Both of
us had an especially strong emotional attachment to our children,
but encouraged them to be independent and unique. With hard
aspects between Uranus and the Moon, it may be hard to feel safe
in a mothering capacity until some situation triggers the awakening
of that quality.

One way to heal the trauma of the feelings of abandonment is to
use visualization techniques. Seeing oneself as the infant or young
child deprived of nurturing can enable a person to give himself
some of that missing emotional support. Joan admitted to having a
bedroom full of dolls and toys that is like a child's room. Giving
oneself things that are symbols of love or emotional support that
may have been missing early in life can help the stymied, stunted
little child begin to grow and become more independent on an
emotional level.

URANUS CONJUNCT MERCURY

With this aspect, the highly charged Uranian energy goes into the
brain, describing an especially brilliant mental quality. Again, the

energy must be healthfully and fluidly utilized or the individual with this aspect can blow a fuse. Periodically, the person with this aspect may feel as though he is suffering a mental breakdown. He may or may not actually succumb to the urge to blow a fuse and give his mind a rest. He can become scattered in thoughts or speech. His mind seems to race on ahead of his tongue, and he may have unusual speech patterns. Much of the outer manifestation has to do with whether he finds a release for his intelligence; indeed, this can be his biggest challenge. A person with this aspect can have genius potential. He will be extremely quick and inventive. He may not be able to tolerate pedantic speech patterns in other people. His own thoughts come rapidly, but they may leave as quickly as they come. He has great difficulty turning off his mind.

With Uranus-Sun aspects, the person *is* spontaneous. Uranus-Moon aspects describe spontaneous emotions, and Uranus-Mercury aspects, spontaneous mentality. But Mercury can also be indicative of the voice quality. With Uranus-Mercury aspects, that quality can be exceptional, bringing fame. Harry Belafonte has this aspect in his chart. His singing and speaking voice is unique. His chart indicates that he would be impelled to find a style that would be exceptional, different, and electrical in energy. Wit is associated with the planet Mercury. Jackie Gleason has Mercury conjunct Uranus. He developed a most unusual comedy routine that provided a fabulous showcase for his special wit. Coco Chanel used her brilliant ideas in the world of fashion, and Hugh Hefner propelled a publishing empire into many unique ventures. Governor Edmund Brown of California used the energy in the political world, whereas Ethel Barrymore channeled her brilliance into the theater.

Susan Strasberg, with this exciting aspect in the tenth house of career, began her acting career as a teenager with her portrayal of Anne Frank in *The Diary of Anne Frank* on Broadway. The tenth house describes the relationship with the mother, in a woman's chart, which seems to predetermine the choice of career. This was certainly true in Susan's case. "My Mother was extraordinarily scattered. She was also a fabulous speaker and teacher, and she could have written, but she was so scattered she could never get it together. She couldn't do it for herself, but she could do it for me. She coached me and worked with me and would tell me what to do, so because I had a kind of overseer, I never learned how to do for myself. She was very critical. She would say, 'Slow down, you're talking too fast.' Even now, I've gotten the same comment in my acting, writing, and speaking. 'Susan, less is more.' I had timed my one-woman show for exactly an hour, which is what was called for. I ended up adding a little funny story and that led to something else, which led to something else. It was interesting and I could tell people were listening, but it was too much.

"Meditation techniques have saved my life. I was never able to turn my mind off, but with techniques, whether it's breathing or actual meditation or listening to a tape, I can control my thoughts. Even with that, I have ten different ways that work. Most people only have one way. I'm torn between trying to limit myself and having all these ideas, like seeds, that I want to give away. I don't have time for them all. Suddenly there are three similar projects all at once and I'm developing ideas for all of them. It's terribly eclectic. I love to put people together. It gives me so much pleasure and satisfaction.

"Now that I'm writing, I'm forced to ground all that energy. When I say it, I can't see it. If I can *see* it on paper, and then have to edit, every problem I've ever had is there in black and white. If I use one metaphor, I can use ten. My life has had that Chinese-menu aspect anyway. Pick one from column A and one from column B. In career areas, everything is always last-minute. Some people have commitments years ahead, but mine is always at the last. It's terribly aggravating, because I also have several things at once. I'm already living in a high-anxiety business, so I'd like to have a little more stability. But it has always been feast or famine, easy come and easy go, quixotic."

Uranus describes the seventh house in Susan's chart. She would therefore be attracted to partners who are unique, brilliant, famous, or avant-garde in some way. Susan described partnership in this manner: "Relationships always come and go the same way as career opportunities. I consider myself to be a very faithful person within one relationship. When I was younger, a relationship would get to a certain point and then a thunderbolt would hit me. Suddenly it was over. People may have advised me long before that time to get out of it, that it was no good, but it took that thunderbolt to make me see it. As quickly as it started, it could be over. Even now, when I start to run, I begin to count to ten, turn around to see what it is that I'm running from. I may be running away from a good thing. I pick men who have a brilliant kind of aspect, but who may have an inability to focus the brilliance of their mind. My ex-husband, Christopher Jones, was like that. In my book *Bittersweet*, our relationship may have sounded primarily destructive, but it was more than that. Christopher was a painter. He was a writer, too. He was more than an actor. I remember him reading books on acupuncture ten years before people accepted such things. He was ahead of his time. He would line people up to do acupuncture on them while looking at the book. Only when the drugs entered in did it really turn destructive." Uranus ruling the seventh house will always indicate someone rebellious or a potential healer; Susan will always have an attraction for someone different. But Uranus also describes areas where one can be scared. She might inadvertently pick the very person whom she would run away from instead of being able to work through that scare in a partnership relationship.

Since that same scared aspect rules her house of career, I asked her if she was ever nervous in public or in career areas. "I was very nervous in public. I was terrified. My voice would close up. When I did my second play, my whole voice changed. It constricted in a way that would cause reviewers to say, 'What happened to her voice?' It was like the throat clamped down and a part of me literally disconnected. It seemed that I was talking from another time and space, like from an echo chamber. It took me three or four years to get rid of that. Now when I feel that old clamping down, if I really examine it without going out of contact, I can transform that energy to make it free again.

"I never felt as though I was having a nervous breakdown, but all that energy had no place to go except to short-circuit me. I would just get disconnected from everything. Everything would seem to be racing, like a time warp. My whole life has been a series of lightning bolts. Even things that I plan come in faster or more unexpectedly than I can prepare for. I have replaced people onstage or in films a number of times and then don't have a chance to really get ready for it. I have to admit it's not boring. When I broke my ankle last year, a lot was happening. I was going back onstage, I started thinking about writing my second book, I was just beginning to do lectures, and I was on overload. I believe that breaking my ankle was my way of grounding myself. I had to start meditating to get over the pain, and it discharged some of that energy into a positive outlet."

In addition to all her other activities, Susan has now become very involved with unusual healing techniques. She has been lecturing at holistic health conferences with very special success.

URANUS IN HARD ASPECT TO MERCURY

When these two planets have an inharmonious dialogue between them, the voices must be reconciled in one way or another to have mental stability. Otherwise, some outer manifestation will plague the person, whether it be in speech patterns, on a mental level, or on the Uranian spiritual level. If we relate Uranus to faulty wiring in the system, a fire can be started if the leak of energy is ignored. With difficult Uranus-Mercury aspects, high energy is not funneled into the brain in a fluid manner, causing difficulty and erratic mental processes. Static electricity must be discharged on a mental level to avoid a breakdown of the system.

Just as individuals with Moon-Uranus aspects may have impulsive emotions and may live to regret sudden emotional reactions, Mercury-Uranus difficulties can cause one to say things impulsively and be sorry later. Stuttering may be a result of erratic thought patterns. There is certainly a mental restlessness that can be hard to release. Elsa Maxwell had Uranus square Mercury in her chart. Uranus was posited in the fourth house of home, with Mercury ruling that same house. She moved constantly. She actually had no home of her own, but stayed with acquaintances who lived high on the rungs of the social ladder. She was considered to be two-faced as well. Elsa may have known when to leave one situation just when her welcome was about to wear out. Her sharp tongue may have been the product of her mental restlessness. She was thought to betray secrets. With a bolt of electrical energy, she may have inadvertently blurted things out without prior intention.

Mary Astor had this square aspect describing the second house of income, the fifth house of creative ability, and ruling her tenth house of career, and eighth house of transformation. She was successful as an actress, making lots of money in the early days of film, but after several marriages was wiped out financially by her fourth husband. She drank, but did not admit to being an alcoholic until she was fifty years old. She was able to channel her energy into writing and produced six books.

The brilliant soprano Maria Callas had Uranus squaring Mercury ruling her third house of communication. Mercury posited in the first house enabled her to work hard and with great detail on her voice, starting in the early portion of her life. But she became rebellious, not content with her tremendous success, and dieted too strenuously at the height of her career. She lost her voice, blew up a glorious career, and died very suddenly at the age of fifty-four. Uranus aspects indicate an inability to tolerate the status quo, especially if they are difficult ones. Maria was also known for being quite outspoken and impulsively difficult in the negotiation of contracts.

Stanley was born with Uranus opposite Mercury in his natal chart. Uranus is posited in the fourth house describing his relationship with his mother, who is an astrologer, and Mercury resides in his tenth house of public activity and career. That tenth-house position of Mercury indicates the relationship with his father. Stanley said, "My mother and father gave me two extremes in the kinds of messages they transmitted, both verbally and on a more subtle level. My father was a Depression baby and has a heavy security complex. He said, 'Be practical.' My mother told me the opposite, being inclined to be more loose. She said, 'Don't be so hard on yourself. Do what you want to do.' They tend to disagree on the most trivial matters, but even if they are upset with each other, when something is important, they rise to the occasion. I tended to escape all that by playing in my mind as a little kid. I had stomach problems as a child, but I've seemed to outgrow all that. It may be that they argue for the sake of arguing. He could break her down and get an emotional reaction out of her, then they had an excuse for making up. It was just their way of communicating.

"I find that I come up with the most brilliant thoughts in the middle of the night, but in the morning, when I read what I wrote down, I feel very exposed and open to any kind of criticism, even my own. It is like I have two different kinds of mind. The thoughts that seem to be unleashed without reservation sound like things I couldn't possibly write. I feel then that I could leave myself open for complete annihilation by other people. Then I think it is pure rubbish. But I am learning to carry a notebook around with me, because sometimes in the middle of an ordinary task, I do come up with some pretty good ideas. If I don't capture them immediately, however, they leave as soon as they come in."

Sandra Sherrard has embarked on a new career since her children have grown and gone away to school. She always had a musical talent, playing the piano and studying voice for many years. However, she admitted to herself that she would never attain the perfection she wanted either with singing or in playing the piano. She discovered an enjoyment that exceeded anything else through composing music. After she began playing her own compositions quite easily, it was necessary to take some courses in harmony and composition so that she could record what she conceived. Sandra has Uranus square Mercury in her natal chart. Mercury is placed in the ninth house of recognition and Uranus is posited in the sixth house of work. Uranus rules the fourth house of home in Sandra's chart and describes the relationship with her father and subsequent feelings about her home and lifestyle. Sandra's father died when she was twelve years old and changes began occurring in her life and home conditions as a result. Mercury describes the eighth house, or the way in which needs are met. It also describes the inverse concept, or the gift one has to give to mankind. Evidently, Sandra's words, thoughts, and ideas are associated with her gift. The fourth house can also indicate the third or later portion of one's life. A latent musical talent and ability would emerge in Sandra's life as a result of awakening.

Sandra described the process of composing. She said, "I will be sitting at the piano working on a particular theme and trying variations to see what fits the overall mode when suddenly, the right notes and melody pop into my head. I get so excited that I momentarily lose the very inspiration that has occurred. I used to think that my memory was poor, but now I know that I have temporarily overloaded my mental circuits and I haven't lost it altogether. I must sit quietly and calmly, letting the mental energy settle down and then I can recall what I thought I had lost. My brain seems to jam when I am excited, even though I may just be in an especially stimulating conversation with someone. I have to stop trying to think and let my mind rest so that I can resume a normal discussion. It can be very frustrating. I seem to suddenly be so far ahead of my own thoughts I don't know where I am in the conversation."

URANUS CONJUNCT VENUS

Very special and unique beauty can be associated with this combination of planets. Some of the outstandingly gorgeous actresses have this interesting aspect. While the combination can make the appearance striking, it can also indicate havoc with the love nature. Love may come in suddenly and leave just as rapidly with difficult aspects. Restlessness, a need for variety, and rebellion in areas of love make this energy quite hard to handle in long-term relationships. Love may go out the window just as it is getting off the ground, unless a level of excitement can be maintained. Venus also describes artistry, whether that be with painting or work in the theater, in connection with design, fabrics, or beauty products. With good aspects to the conjunction of Venus-Uranus, special talent can be displayed in almost any artistic area. The end result would be most unusual and unique, however, for traditional techniques are not described by this aspect.

The quality of energy between Venus and Uranus can be at odds to begin with. Venus is the planet that describes harmony, desire for ease of living, and a pacific attitude. It is connected with pleasure. When Venus is badly aspected, the tendency is to take the easy way out for the sake of peace, harmony, and the status quo. Uranus is the planet of variety, spice, excitement, and spontaneity. The conflict with the two energies comes with the desire for exciting, spontaneous and unique love experiences, and a possibility of not wanting to make waves if things become too passive. The aspects in an individual chart can describe whether rebellion or passivity is stronger.

Elizabeth Taylor has Venus conjunct Uranus ruling her Libra ascendant but posited in the seventh house of marriage. Uranus rules the fifth house of creative expression, children, and romance. Elizabeth has a distinct possibility of maintaining romance in a marriage and seemed to achieve just that with Mike Todd, her true love. But Mike, a restless, Uranian type, was taken away from her by death. The Libra ascendant indicates a great need for companionship, and with the conjunction of Venus and Uranus in the romantic areas of her chart, she can be literally swept off her feet. Love might come out of the blue and most unexpectedly. She would look for her twin soul, someone as ardently in love and as exciting as she is.

Elizabeth's marriages have never been dull, have never been status quo, and have never been very long-lasting. The earlier marriages, to Nicky Hilton and Michael Wilding, may have been mere impulse. After Mike Todd, she was consoled and attracted by Eddie Fisher, a singer (Uranian in energy), but that marriage was accompanied by much notoriety, again a Uranian quality. Her tolerance and love must have been tested continuously by Richard Burton in many a drunken scene. No one, however, would dispute the electricity between them. John Warner fit the description of Venus-Uranus through his political career. He was in the spotlight (Uranus) and was quite diplomatic, tactful, and polished, all Venus traits. The relationship may not have been quite high-wire enough as time wore on, however.

With Uranian partnerships, excitement must go hand in hand with tension and sudden changes. Although creative outlet provides a release for Uranian energy in Elizabeth's chart, partnership is a must. Elizabeth could blow fuses physically without the stimulation of love in her life. That might account for many of the health problems she has endured. Energy can be directed inwardly unless enough release is found. The biggest danger with any Uranus aspect is to try to calm down this electricity through drinking or taking drugs. Elizabeth would be attracted to men with genius potential who would either drown it in some way or, in a positive sense, express it through fame or unique activity.

It is interesting to note that Elizabeth released much of her love through her children. She has never been criticized in relation to them. In fact, she expressed the humanitarian love qualities associated with Uranus by adopting Maria, who was crippled. She lavished love, great care, and attention on this child, even though she had several natural children.

Elizabeth Montgomery also has Venus conjunct Uranus posited in the seventh house of marriage, ruling her Libra ascendant. Elizabeth has been married only three times, cares mostly for her marriage and children, but has found an additional artistic release through art. She sells watercolors and wrote and illustrated a children's book entitled *Annabelle*. Other outstanding performers with this aspect are Pearl Bailey, Anita Bryant, Jayne Mansfield, and

Cher. Male actors with this aspect are Warren Beatty, Tyrone Power, and Spencer Tracy. Composer Giacomo Puccini wrote operas about tragedy in love, and Tennessee Williams wrote brilliantly about the lazy decadence of the southern ladies tippling out of teacups on the side. Adlai Stevenson and Bertrand Russell share this aspect.

Candice Bergen expresses her Venus-Uranus aspect in a very different way. This aspect is placed in the sixth house of work and service, and rules the career, creativity, and financial areas of her chart. Her beauty is particularly stunning, but she was far from content to allow that to dominate her life and career. She has been a forerunner for humanitarian causes through her photojournalism and also through active political involvement. She has been jailed for antiwar demonstrations and has selected "message" films to appear in that could further the cause of humanity. Candice has an unusual but free lifestyle and earns money easily, but seems more dedicated to breaking down barriers between people than to self-serving activities.

Steve McQueen and Feodor Dostoevsky share this aspect. Steve McQueen was a rebel, an iconoclast, and certainly different. Dostoevsky wrote about social justice and freedom. Venus in its highest form wants balance. On a universal level it can mean a desire for things being fair and right in the world. Coco Chanel had Venus-Uranus conjunction. Her fashions were unique in a classic way. Fame came to her through her talent as a designer, a Venusian occupation. Louis Pasteur had this aspect giving him the love nature, caring, and patience to conduct experiments that would benefit all mankind. Shirley Temple, the most famous child actress of all time, and certainly a beauty, also has Uranus conjunct Venus in her chart.

URANUS IN HARD ASPECT TO VENUS

Kathryn Grant Crosby has Uranus square Venus in her chart. She began her career in the film world after winning a beauty contest and obtaining a Hollywood contract, all by the age of twenty. Her films were not sensational, however, and when she met and married Bing Crosby, she abandoned her career as an actress altogether. Venus is posited in the second house of money, and rules the seventh house of partnership. Venus, when in difficult aspect, tends to get lazy, only because of a desire to keep things harmonious, whereas Uranus leads to taking premature action and running away unexpectedly. The energy is first directed toward keeping the peace, rather than creating new situations, then getting restless and doing something impulsive. In her marriage, she had no need for income of her own, but Uranian desires still had to be met. Uranus rules healing. With its position in her fifth house of creative expression, after a period of time during which she was devoted to marriage, she was impelled to become a registered nurse. Then she had a brief fling at doing an interview show. When Uranian energy is not well utilized, it becomes scattered. Her children also fall under the domain of Uranus in her chart, so that she was quite content to take care of her marriage and her children for a while before that restlessness set in. It is interesting to note that Bing's children by his first wife did not accept Kathryn so readily. Venus describing partnership and Uranus describing children would indicate a rebelliousness on the part of at least some of her children, with perhaps some indifference or overly pacifying attitude from a partner or mate.

Writer Anaïs Nin had Venus square Uranus ruling her personality, creativity, ability to communicate, and work. Venus is posited in the sixth house, describing a need to work in artistic areas. The Uranian flavor ruling her fifth house impelled her to find unique, brilliant, and certainly avant-garde outlets for self-expression and in areas of romance. Uranus is placed in the third house of communications. Her release point, and way of letting off excess steam, was to write diaries. During the seventy-four years of her life, she produced sixty volumes. But she refused to deal with publishers, taking huge risks and publishing her own works. She also had Uranus conjunct the Moon, giving her exceptional sensitivity, which enabled her to write on a deep level about the inner workings of a woman's mind, emotions, and soul. She seemed to attract almost a cult worship from her readers. With the Uranus-Moon aspect ruling the house of career, she would have an exceptional ability to sense the trends of the times and be willing to risk exposing her own pain in order to identify with women in general. She was able to channel her free spirit into productive work. However, Venus rules her eighth house of getting her needs met. Her refusal to work with established publishers and to ask for aid or contracts enabled her to keep a degree of personal freedom. She did not seem overly concerned about income from her books; perhaps this was her way of taking the easy way out associated with Venus. For Venus can indicate a quality of self-indulgence and hesitation to stir things up. Eventually it is nonproductive. When Uranus becomes activated, suddenly the overly pacifist tendency gives way to unexpected risk taking.

URANUS CONJUNCT MARS

The energy that is generated by this conjunction is hard to beat. Mars describes the sexual energy as well as the highest creative spark. It indicates pioneering ability, drive, ambition, resourcefulness, courage, daring, and impatience. When it is hooked up to the Uranian voltage, it is incredibly dynamic. Some of the most famous Hollywood sex symbols had this aspect in their charts. When this impulsive energy is not well directed, however, it can be described as an accident aspect. With impulsive, impetuous, and impatient energy playing off each other, the individual may trip over things, burn himself, cut himself, and be too impatient to wait for exciting things to happen in his life.

Mars describes ambition and the ability to deal in competitive areas. Actors and actresses must have a tremendous amount of daring, courage, and resourcefulness in order to survive and deal with such a competitive business as the stage and particularly the film world generate. The actors who have this extra "fame" aspect attached cannot remain in the ordinary ranks of actors. They must dare to tap a special creative potential and walk out into the spotlight. Events happen out of the blue.

Perhaps the most famous sex symbol of her time, Marilyn Monroe, was blessed or cursed by this aspect. Ava Gardner, Jean Harlow, and Mata Hari shared this aspect. One of the most unique and talented actresses in the history of show business is Katharine Hepburn. Perhaps it is her Mars-Uranus conjunction that enables her to be consistently one step ahead of competition. She has displayed the kind of courage that many people would like to emulate, by continuing to work in the face of illness and personal loss.

Hepburn has no sense of defeat. She is a star among stars in the Hollywood firmament.

It is interesting to note that in the case of Mata Hari, the sexuality led to prostitution and subversive activity. She was shot by a firing squad for being a spy. Yet she was certainly able to claim her share of the spotlight, dubious honor as that may have been. Her affairs were not ordinary ones. She included in her list of lovers the German crown prince and the son-in-law of the Kaiser. Aspects can never be judged completely out of the context of the whole chart. The trigger point in her case was a square to this Uranus-Mars conjunction from Pluto (see "Pluto in Hard Aspect to Mars" and "Pluto in Hard Aspect to Uranus"). The rage described by this square led to the destructive use of her energy.

Mars energy enables an individual to be in the forefront of any activity. When it is conjunct Uranus, it can produce brilliance or rebellion, resourcefulness or accidents. A person with this aspect strongly accentuated in his or her chart needs constant physical release, lots of exercise to prevent the electricity from being stored. Ambition is a distinct release for Mars energy. As long as the person has a "fight" on his hands, he can get rid of the excess drive. He needs something to present a competitive challenge.

Marilyn Monroe had Mars-Uranus conjunction in the eighth house of getting one's needs met. It ruled the ninth house of publicity, promotional matters, and agents. Marilyn was especially resourceful in her first efforts to attract attention in the highy competitive Hollywood world. She was one of many young, beautiful starlets sitting around a pool where important executives in the film world were in attendance. Frustrated in her attempts to be noticed, she went into the pool and pretended to get a cramp in her leg. One of the men who jumped to the rescue was a top agent. He worked consistently in her behalf, really taking chances and sticking his neck out for her. She finally got her big break and the rest is history.

If Marilyn had been able to gain more control of this aspect, she might have avoided all the bad publicity she received for being unpredictable and difficult. Uranus describes scare, as well as nervous energy. She became addicted to pills and alcohol, probably as a way of dealing with all that excess energy coming into her system. It can be very difficult to regulate the energy with this aspect. It doesn't course through the body in a consistent way. Marilyn's death was considered to be a result of an overdose of medication. Uranus rules accidents, but whether hers was self-inflicted or not has remained a mystery to this day. In the traditional interpretation of astrology, the eighth house is the house of death. Frustration may have been a motivation for suicide, or she may simply have overloaded the fuses in her system. The suspicion of foul play can also be described by that conjunction in the eighth house. Posthumous fame is a distinct possibility with Uranus in the eighth house.

Tony, a successful young television producer in California, is aware of this aspect in his chart in a very special way. Tony has this conjunction posited in the tenth house of career, ruling the sixth house of work and health, and the ninth house of travel, recognition, distribution, promotion. The tenth house also describes the father in a man's chart (the parent of the same sex). Tony's father died when he was three years old. Tony described the feeling of this conjunction by saying, "When I feel this rush of energy coming on, I need to escape in some way, no matter what I'm doing, whether it's a job or a production or even lining up a putt. I get this tremendous energetic rush anytime, anywhere, and it will compel me to walk away. But it has a positive side too. I get very energized. It's when I find myself in a situation where I am not in control that I have to get away. I have actually gotten up and walked out of a business meeting. Now I have learned how to program myself so that I don't allow people to bug me. I get itchy at work. Then I have to get up and walk around. I suffer terribly from boredom unless I'm in a situation where I'm challenged or constantly active. I have a twenty-foot cord on my telephone so that I can get up from my desk. I even walk when I am reading. But I have another kind of rush that enables me to do things that other people can't do without suffering, such as eating too much or staying out too late. I can get an energy rush that will pull me through. I think that is a result of having taken care of myself physically.

"For years and years I suffered from seizures caused by a blood clot in my brain. The blood does not flow smoothly into that area, so, needless to say, at times I would just black out. It could be construed as a form of epilepsy, but it isn't just pure epilepsy. I was told that I could have an operation to have that condition corrected, but there was a fifty-fifty chance of living. I decided to work on it mentally. At times, I would feel myself getting terribly, terribly nervous and getting short of air and oxygen. I would start to talk to myself no matter whether I was driving a car or in the middle of a meeting or involved in athletics. I could still pay attention to what I was doing and bring myself back down to this calm level. If I didn't do that, I knew the area would close and I would black out. I found that after a while, with a lot of practice, it would work. I don't take nearly as much medication as I used to. I have found that just by getting inside myself I can handle it better.

"I think a lot of this reaction was due to my not having a father. My older brother was very capable and caring. I really didn't have to do anything for myself. I'm not sure I was able to cope with things when I had to begin doing things for myself." Tony evidently had a terrible scare with his father's death that shook up his life in a very unexpected way. Marilyn Monroe also had terribly frightening things in her early life. In almost every case of Uranus energy describing childhood, the loss of someone by death was a strong factor in forming the rebellious tendencies. The scare reacts physically in different parts of the body, depending on the planet involved. In the case of Mars-Uranus, Mars rules the blood, the head. Tony may have blacked out to prevent ultimate overload and stress.

One of the most interesting situations in which Mars is conjunct Uranus in a natal chart has to do with the expression of the sexual energy. Christine Jorgensen, the first transsexual to bring her story to the public in an unashamed way, has this aspect in her chart. She used her own experiences to pave the way for other people in a similar plight. With the Uranus-Mars conjunction ruling her sixth house of work, and her eighth house of transformation, she worked through her own scare to take the risks, walk out into the spotlight, and dare to be courageous enough to change her sex. She has been quite articulate in the description of what it was like to be trapped in a body that seemed quite foreign. Christine has this aspect posited in the house of marriage. She was admittedly repulsed by homosexuality, but was attracted to men. She may not ever have the stable kind of "marriage" she might desire with this unpredictable aspect in her chart, but her health depends on the attempt to at least investigate exciting possibilities. She would need a tremendous amount of freedom with this aspect to fight for humanitarian rights of others. Uranus rules music as well as many other things.

Christine developed a nightclub act that enabled her to release and channel this energy constructively.

With any Mars-Uranus aspects, sexual energy may be quite unique. Impulsive attractions may not last long, yet impulsive attractions are the most exciting; unless there is a sudden spark, the individual is rarely very interested. A certain amount of sexual freedom would be desired, and the possibility of choosing someone avant-garde, unpredictable, or unique is very strong. In a conjunction or easy aspect, the probability of finding the right person may be easier than with a difficult aspect.

URANUS IN HARD ASPECT TO MARS

When Uranus is in difficult aspect to Mars, impulse can be the order of the day. A person may be able to channel the drive and ambition in a consistent manner, and then unpredictably be overloaded and walk away from what he fought so hard to obtain. The obvious sexual excitement is indicated with this aspect as well as in more harmonious aspect, but the energy might be more difficult for the individual to handle. Two of Hollywood's current sex symbols have a difficult Mars-Uranus aspect. Both John Travolta and Robert Redford have Mars sesquisquare Uranus, which may be even more difficult to reconcile than a mere square. They have both established extraordinary careers, but it is obvious that much of their appeal lies beyond the talent. Their sex appeal attracts a great deal of admiration from their female fans. This may make both of them quite nervous.

John Travolta has Mars in the fifth house of romance and creative expression, but ruling the tenth house of career. He must channel his strong creative urge toward career and public activity, but Uranus is placed in the twelfth house of privacy and subconscious activity. It rules the eighth house of transformation. When John has time to be by himself, he can heal himself and regulate this impulsive energy. He may have to work past his rebellious tendencies. John had an unusual relationship with Diana Hyland, many years his senior. When Diana died, John needed a great deal of time alone to get over his loss. With Mars ruling his romantic interests and in difficult aspect to Uranus, he would not only be attracted to unusual situations but have to deal with sudden changes or loss. He may need to keep his romantic life quite private and away from the spotlight of his career.

Gregory Peck has Mars opposing Uranus in his natal chart. He was also a sex symbol, and never fit into the California lifestyle that many actors fell into. Gregory has Uranus at the very zenith of his chart, describing a brilliant career, but with Mars in the third house of communications, ruling his personality, he may have been very upset about contracts, the vehicles he was given, and the money he was paid. However, with Mars ruling the twelfth house of secrecy, he may never have been able to express that anger or frustration overtly. He is known to be a very nice man, rather self-effacing, yet his chart indicates extreme frustration that might never emerge.

One of the most versatile actresses in the theater and film world is Shelley Winters. Shelley has been working at her craft since she was in her late teens. She has played every imaginable type in her screen roles, from the vulnerable factory worker in *An American Tragedy* to character roles as she grew older. Shelley has Mars square Uranus in her chart, describing conflict between marriage and a career. Mars is placed exactly on the cusp of her seventh house of marriage, opposing her ascendant, or personality, giving her an especially impatient but romantic quality. She would exhibit a dynamic but feisty quality and be attracted to the type of husband who would stir things up. Resultant conflict in her life would then impel her to turn to her career for release. In Shelley's case, the square is compounded by the Moon in the first house in square to Uranus and opposing Mars. Vulnerability and feelings of abandonment early in life produce a hysterical quality that would be especially volatile in a marital situation. It produces brilliance when it is channeled away from her personal life into the public arena, however. Shelley has written a bestseller about her life. That may have been the best release she could find for the overly emotional reaction and sensitivity inherent in her personality.

Shelley was married to Vittorio Gassman. The marriage was not only volatile but conducted across continents. Uranus rules the house of travel, promotional effort, publicity, and publishing in Shelley's chart. When Shelley needs to rebel, she may have to get on a plane and run away. Her marriage may have been just that kind of rebellion against the frustration of ordinary, everyday routine. She might inadvertently create conflict just to keep life high-wire and exciting. Impulsive behavior early in life might give Shelley much cause for reflection later in life. This determined aspect can keep her in the public eye for as long as she chooses.

It seems as though anyone with Uranus strongly placed in his chart has had to undergo the extremes of scare, uncertainty, loss, and constantly unpredictable situations in life. Yet the ultimate possibility is the awakening of the spiritual life. No one has done this more beautifully and effectively than Peggy Lee. Peggy has been the sweetheart of American song since she was a very young girl. Yet Peggy's personal life has only now been made public. Peggy had the courage to tell her story in song in her Broadway show, *Peg*. She was the victim of child abuse. One of her songs talks about "A Beating a Day."

Peggy's beloved mother died when she was a mere babe, and the stepmother that came into her life had no trace of love or affection for her new stepchild. She took out all her frustration and rage on Peggy and hit her constantly with whatever was handy at the time. Peggy has Mars sesquisquare Uranus, with Uranus placed in and ruling the sixth house of work. Her Mars is positioned in the second house of income. Mars rules the eighth house of transformation. The escape from all that torture was through her music and her work. Otherwise her health would have been badly affected. In later years of therapy, the stepmother was diagnosed as being sexually sadistic. With Mars ruling the eighth house, Peggy might have literally died from all that abuse. But with all her courage and pioneering spirit, Peggy discovered a way to heal herself. She is very involved in metaphysical work and thought. But Mars-Uranus describes the unexpected. Peggy was involved in an accident that nearly cost her her life. She was in the elevator of a very exclusive New York hotel, stepped out onto the marble lobby floor and was thrown into the air, twisted and dropped, landing flat on her back. Unbeknownst to her, a sand-filled ashtray had overturned onto the marble floor, making it perilous to walk on.

The people Peggy was with emerged from the elevator, slipped or fell but were not badly hurt. Peggy was rushed to the hospital and was in critical condition for some time. Mars-Uranus is an accident aspect. If Peggy had known her chart, perhaps she might have been very cautious. As far as she can tell, she was not particularly impetuous that day, but when Uranian aspects hit, they come out of the blue. With Mars describing financial matters in Peggy's chart, the accident cost a great deal of money, which was never recouped. But the beautiful ending to the story is that Peggy had no choice but to get in touch with her ultimate gift to the world, the transformation described by the eighth house. As an example to many and with the power of her mind, she performs constantly, where other people would give up and become invalids. I can attest to the fact that Peggy can heal on a powerful level. After a mere telephone conversation with her, I become aware of a charge of energy shooting through my system. She has a power to uplift and energize that is most unusual and special. I, for one, am grateful that she is in touch with that ability. She has transmuted her own tragedy into a spiritual light that shines brilliantly.

URANUS CONJUNCT JUPITER

Uranus conjunct Jupiter may be the best aspect one could have in a chart, because it indicates divine protection. It is so fortunate that it is also a cliff-hanger aspect; luck comes at the last split second. Nothing in life is free, so perhaps the price one has to pay for such a blessing is that it is unpredictable. The nature of the individual with this aspect is such that optimism seems quite natural. It is the trust and expectancy within that attracts the outer blessings. It can still be a bit nerve-wracking, because whenever Uranus aspects another planet it is the necessity to work through the scare that brings enlightenment. With this aspect it seems one has to hang by the fingernails, ready to drop off the cliff, before an angel swoops down to gather the individual to a higher mountain peak. Luck won't come without the risks.

Evan, an astrologer with a most unique approach, combines his knowledge with massage and healing practices. He is also a musician, having played drums with a professional group. He describes his reaction to this aspect in this way: "This is a very exciting aspect. When I'm on the road, I seem to get special attention. I don't go looking for it, but I luck out. The cook lets me go in the kitchen after hours or I get the room with the Jacuzzi. I feel that I'm treated in a special way. I have discovered that I can sell anyone anything. I am extravagant, but I have last-second luck with money and extras that come in from unexpected places. It always happens out of the blue. I just have windfalls. Even with travel, for instance, our band work would come at the last minute. Sometimes we'd do replacement work, so I must be prepared for almost anything. When I play music, I'm in another world, really in another world. And I can take people along with me too. That is what is really exciting about it."

Evan has this exciting aspect in the ninth house of travel, promotion, publicity, and publishing. The ninth house describes the higher mind as well. Jupiter is a planet that indicates philosophy, special optimism, and a religious quality. Jupiter also describes growth, expansion, and goals. Wherever Jupiter is placed in the chart indicates where the natural optimism lies, and where the individual wants constant growth and continued challenges. Jupiter rules sales, but it may be the quality of enthusiasm that is contagious, enabling the Jupiterian person to talk others into projects, or products. The Jupiter-Uranus indicates a very exciting "high on life." It is high spirituality that may attract its own level of benefits.

Evan went on to describe the events that led to his awareness of this special quality. "I was born in Europe. We moved all the time. I was very introverted in elementary school and just didn't fit in, because we were always on the go. When I was a little kid, I didn't tell anyone what I was thinking or feeling. I've always had these flashes of enlightenment, for this is a very high spiritual quality. I would just go off by myself to experience this electrical, joyous energy. I can just sit by myself and get off on those ideas, but it becomes a real problem to try to capture those ideas and do something with them. It's like a stream of consciousness. When I write, those ideas are gone, but at other times, the ideas just pour in.

"I used to have difficulty turning off my mind. Now that I'm involved in meditational practices, it's easier. The ideas begin to flood in, sometimes making sense and sometimes not. But if I allow enough space, a germ of an idea slips in."

The founder of the Theosophical Society was Helena P. Blavatsky. She began her search into the work of metaphysics after an unsuccessful marriage. She traveled far and wide to do her research and wrote *The Secret Doctrine*, which is to this day a book of great depth and information. She was a pioneer in the work that is unfolding more rapidly only now. The Theosophical Society, founded in 1875, became an international organization, teaching concepts that were not commonly known at the time. Madame Blavatsky had the courage and enthusiasm to share with many people the information she discovered through her research. She has Jupiter conjunct Uranus in the eighth house of transformation, ruling her work, and ninth house of travel, publication, distribution, and international affairs. The eighth house describes the way one gets needs met and then, with transformation, the quality of energy one can send out to the world. Uranus in this house describes a profound healing ability all by itself, which when coupled with the Jupiterian enthusiasm is especially abundant. It is through teaching that one can express the unique quality described by this aspect.

Evalyn Walsh McLean had Jupiter conjunct Uranus in her chart posited in the ninth house of legalities, travel, and publishing. Jupiter rules her ascendant and Uranus rules the second house of money, in her chart. Evalyn lived an extraordinarily lavish lifestyle in Washington, D.C., and became the most famous hostess of her time. She and her husband built a mansion in Washington that cost $835,000 in 1902. She also owned the two most famous diamonds, the Hope and the Star of the East, which together cost $275,000. She spent money lavishly but was also extremely generous, giving much of her fortune to the underprivileged. She and her husband owned and published the Washington *Star*, so although Evalyn never scrimped on extravagant living, she released much of that high-wire, lucky energy through ninth-house activities.

Jupiter-Uranus rules last-second luck. Evalyn was not born to such wealth. She lived in mining camps with her family until her father hit a silver mine and established the vast estate that passed on to Evalyn. Jupiter-Uranus always indicates protection financially, even though it may not be directly aspecting that sector of the chart, simply because the optimism and philosophy attract good conditions. But the energy is still electrical and must be released, or the wires burn up and fuses blow.

Zelda Fitzgerald also had Jupiter conjunct Uranus. That aspect was posited in the fourth and fifth houses in her chart, describing creativity, lifestyle, and ability to entertain. The conjunction ruled her seventh house of partnership, and the fifth house. She maintained a romantic marriage to Scott Fitzgerald in spite of early schizophrenia. Their lifestyle was exotic, extravagant, and lavish in the entertainment of friends, until Zelda finally was forced into sanitariums. When Uranus rules the house of marriage, the partner can be a genius, famous, rebellious, and avant-garde. Scott Fitzgerald fit all of those descriptions. Yet Uranus can describe alcoholism as well. Scott was a hard-drinking man. He may have been as unable to tolerate all that abundant electrical energy in his system. He and Zelda seemed to blow out all the fuses in their respective systems until there was nothing left but tragedy. Zelda also had Uranus in opposition to Mars in her chart, which can be an accident aspect. She died in a mental-hospital fire in 1947.

URANUS IN HARD ASPECT TO JUPITER

Mata Hari had Jupiter square Uranus in her chart. What may have seemed like good fortune to her at the time ended up as not such good luck in the long run. She had the opportunity to move in high circles of society, but rather than attracting fame, she became infamous. Clara Bow had Uranus inconjunct Jupiter, describing her personality and financial opportunity. Jupiter was placed in the fifth house of creativity and romance, and ruled her ascendant. Uranus was right on the ascendant in her chart, describing a high-wire rebellious, frenetic kind of energy. With a difficult aspect to Jupiter, it was augmented and intensified to a high degree. She was the hottest thing to hit Hollywood, becoming the "IT" girl in the 1920s. However, she burned herself out and ended up in sanitariums for the last twenty years of her life.

Dolores del Rio was born the same year as Clara Bow and only a few days later. She had the same aspect in her chart, but she chose to use it in a very different manner. Both Uranus and Jupiter ruled her house of home, with Uranus posited in that house and ruling health and work, and Jupiter placed in the ninth house of publicity, travel, and promotion. She also had an exciting Hollywood career, but chose to return to her native Mexico to work in the theater. She founded a nursery for children of working actresses, expressing her need to do something special and inadvertently releasing her teaching ability as well as humanitarian concerns. With Uranus ruling the house of health in her chart, she adopted unique routines, practicing yoga, eating healthfully, and sleeping twelve hours a night. She maintained her beauty well into her seventies and was noted for a special sparkle in her eyes. Louise and Bruno Huber describe an inconjunct as a growth aspect. If Clara Bow had chosen to grow instead of becoming static, she might have had the same wonderful lifestyle as did Dolores del Rio in her later years.

URANUS CONJUNCT SATURN

Once every forty or forty-five years, Saturn and Uranus are conjunct in the heavens. Therefore it is a *generational aspect,* present in the chart of every baby born at that time. It describes a period of history, reflected in the lives of individuals, that is decisive, important, and growth-oriented. More than likely, it also indicates a time of scare, upsets, and change. Traditional values, methods, and activity must give way to more humanitarian concerns, but the pull of the old is just as strong as the impetus of the new. As long as Uranus and Saturn are ten degrees apart, we can consider that they are in conjunction. The last Saturn-Uranus conjunction, starting in the sign of Taurus and culminating in Gemini, began in April 1941 and continued until June 1943. The conflict in the lives of individuals born at that time matches the conflict that was universally present, since it occurred during World War II. The next conjunction of these two planets will take place in December 1986 and culminate in October 1988. This time the conjunction will take place in the sign of Sagittarius. Although external conditions will not be exactly the same, a similar quality will be apparent in some way. Serious conditions may impel everyone to pull back, be more cautious and conservative in order to preserve the freedom inherent with any Uranus aspect. A pull can occur between the old and the new. However, with any Saturn aspect, growth through pain will bring new enlightenment, a sense of universality.

Saturn energy is diametrically opposed to Uranian energy. One represents tradition, boundaries, judgments, discipline, and self-concern, whereas the other describes enlightenment, freedom, avant-garde trends, and humanitarian concerns. Saturn represents earth, whereas Uranus represents heaven. The downpouring of spiritual energy and concepts can create havoc with earth-plane values, responsibilities, and cautious approaches. The conjunction can describe the white light of spirit flooding in to illuminate the darkness of earth conditions. But tradition, boundaries, and roots are hard to give up. When new forms of energy come into being, the tendency is to cling ever more tightly to what is familiar. The more clinging, the more difficult it is to hear the voice of the new.

The tarot card The Tower can illustrate the change that occurs when Uranus and Saturn meet. That card depicts lightning striking a tower. The chaos is shown as the tower is torn asunder. Uranus strikes just like lightning. The analogy of falling plaster is particularly valid when Uranus and Saturn are combined. In remodeling a room, the old walls must be torn down to make way for the new. The mess that occurs in a remodeling job can tempt one to postpone that change forever, but with persistence, working through that mess, the new conditions are well worth the effort.

The two voices present with this aspect are clearly defined. One says, "Change is exciting. Go with it. New conditions are in store." The other one says, "I don't want anything to change. Leave me alone." But Uranus must win eventually. The individual can make it easier by regulating his resistance somewhat. Progress and change come along on schedule, like a railroad train screaming in the silence, whether we want them or not. Saturn represents gravity. Without Saturn in a chart, there would be no sense of responsibility, no sense of boundaries or limits, no judgments. But a negative Saturn is overly judgmental, overly responsible, overly duty-bound. When the spiritual part of man feels that new growth is necessary, that karmic conditions have been satisfied, or that there is danger of an individual remaining in a rut, those Uranian conditions come like that bolt of lightning and strike out the dead wood. However, the individual may not always be ready.

When Saturnian pressures or routines and drudgery become too much to bear and when the individual has decided he has had enough of a masochistic attitude, he begins to grow. That growth is almost always born out of pain and suffering. With Uranus-Saturn aspects, however, the growth comes quickly, with tremendous spontaneity and some scare. Balance can occur when the individual is ready to take responsibility to consistently release inspiration and work on a higher level. He allows himself to learn a technique that will make him feel safe before he rebels and delves into scary but exciting areas. He learns how to be both grounded and inspired.

Elizabeth Karaman has Uranus conjunct Saturn in the sixth house of health and work. Saturn rules her second house of money, and Uranus rules the third house of communications. Elizabeth tried to work in the entertainment fields for many years. She was diligent in her search for work (Saturn), very disciplined and determined. However, she went on her rounds in a limousine (Uranus) and no one took her very seriously. She began to study astrology in order to have some clues about timing in her chart and discovered that in order to remain vital and energetic enough to continue her efforts, she would have to develop health routines such as proper diet and food to have enough stamina. Elizabeth became very knowledgeable about combinations of food and the right kind of exercise, and related that to her astrological knowledge. Elizabeth is now writing a unique book about health and astrology, enzymes and planets. She is working on the highest humanitarian level and is successful in the communications fields. She is also quite psychic. Elizabeth gets her strongest psychic messages by first becoming very nervous. As soon as she realizes that her nerves are not of her own making, she can tune in and come up with astounding revelations.

Amelia Earhart had Uranus conjunct Saturn in her chart. The conjunction is in the seventh house of marriage, but Saturn rules her midheaven and Uranus rules her eleventh house of friends, groups, organizations, and associations. With this aspect describing her career, Amelia could never be content with an ordinary career. She began to take flying lessons when she was in her early twenties and became the first woman in the world to be issued a pilot's license. She married George Putnam, her publisher, who supported her unusual endeavor, rather than squelching her. She made a transatlantic flight as a passenger and after that set many records with her own plane. She was killed over the South Pacific when she lost radio contact. Amelia Earhart never lost sight of the fact that her mission was to encourage other people, especially women, to take chances. She said that failure should work only as a challenge.

URANUS IN HARD ASPECT TO SATURN

Uranus squares Saturn generationally, just like the conjunction of these two planets. The most memorable square between these two planets was at the time of the Great Depression. Individuals born at that time have a difficult conflict within them that reflects those very frightening times in the world. In this instance, Saturn seems to act as the heavier voice, cautioning the person against too much risk. The condition of the environment was far from joyous in the early thirties, so the person born at that time may have a hard time allowing himself to express anything less than caution. He was not given permission to be extravagant, exuberant, or optimistic by the world around him. He may never quite get over the scare that was inflicted by his earliest views of the attitudes around him.

Clint Eastwood has this aspect in his chart. Saturn is placed in his second house of money, ruling the third house of communications. With Uranus placed in the fifth house of creativity, and ruling the fourth house, Clint would find freedom late in life. Financial stability might be a major motivation in his life. The release point for him comes through the gambling urges expressed by the fifth house. As Clint grows older, he might allow himself to take more risks, throw caution to the wind, and express more spontaneity. Clint lives in a very unostentatious house in spite of his success in the film world. He is very interested in conservation, a Saturnian concern, and has not seemed to express the stronger Uranian qualities. In a positive way, he has been able to maintain a solid family life amid the turmoil of Hollywood. His severe, stoic image would reflect the Saturnian qualities in this aspect, rather than the Uranian ones.

Kaylan Pickford, on the other hand, has taken great risks in her life to allow her own situation to act as an example for many women. Kaylan was also born at that dire time in history. Her Bostonian background prepared her for an especially conservative life, yet such was not to be for Kaylan. Uranus is posited in the seventh house of marriage, and rules the fifth house of romance. Saturn is placed in the fourth house of home, and also rules that fourth house. Saturn is involved in a particularly difficult aspect in her chart. It squares and opposes many planets, so the indication was that her programming was particularly conservative. In this instance, freedom came to Kaylan by way of a very romantic marriage. Her first marriage ended in divorce when she met Bill Pickford, the dream man in her life. She was no doubt swept off her feet by the Uranian romance and was extremely happy. A very short time after their marriage, Bill discovered he had cancer. Kaylan spent the three years of her marriage helping her beloved to die.

She was left with teenage children and not a great deal of resources after the expensive illness of her husband, so with Uranian impulse and excitement, she attacked the fashion world in New York as a model. She discovered before very long that in spite of her beauty and special quality, her age seemed to prevent her from working as much as she would have liked. Many people in the same situation would simply have given up, but Kaylan followed the Uranian impulse, rather than let Saturn hold her back. She has been on a campaign to convince advertising agencies that the older woman is just as much a consumer as the younger woman and needs representation in advertising. Kaylan has written a book with many gorgeous pictures of herself, even nude ones, to illustrate that women do not have to slink away into the closet after fifty. Kaylan is now invited to lecture to women's groups around the country and has been on national television shows, including the Donohue show, to tell her story. Far from letting the conservative messages of her past prevent her from expressing the humanitarian impulses, Kaylan has taken the risk and worked through the scare to go to bat for her fellow women. The conflicting voices of Uranus and Saturn can be reconciled in a positive way by taking responsibility for humanity on a broader scope. Once the need to be needed, expressed by Saturn, is realized on a higher level, the spiritual downpouring can lift the person to the heights. He can keep his feet on the ground while walking with angels.

ASPECTS TO NEPTUNE

THE PLANET NEPTUNE RELATES TO QUALITIES THAT ARE idealistic, visionary, and imaginative. It is the second of the higher-octave planets. John Couch Adams and U.J.J. Leverrier deduced the existence of a trans-Uranian planet in November 1845. It was finally seen in September 1846 by Johann Galle, J.F. Encke, and H.L. d'Arrest. Whereas Uranus describes highly charged energy like electricity, Neptune describes gas. Neptune describes things that cannot be seen, especially if intuitive qualities are brought into play. The lower, concrete mind must see, touch, be able to measure and calculate, but Neptune is the higher mind, which connects an individual with his dreams or subconscious process. Mercury relates to left-brain activity, whereas Neptune describes the right-brain, conceptual part of the mental faculty. Neptune describes fantasy and can also relate to the glamour world.

When Neptune is strong in a chart, the individual is very high on life, inspired, creative, idealistic, and sometimes naïve. The tendency may be to see only beauty; the innate desire is to see life on an idealistic level. The person is able to function with what he considers perfection. He may have a Don Quixote complex. He fights windmills, and sees Dulcinea—or his particular tarnished cause—as a virginal figure. He puts people and things on pedestals. He looks for a master or guide to look up to, to trust and put his faith in. He can frequently be disillusioned and let down. Life and people may turn out to be very different from what he conceived them to be. The disastrous awakening can be very hard to take. He can become totally devastated when his dreams fall apart. He therefore takes great pains to make sure such a thing will never happen by rarely facing the reality of a situation. He is not easily able to confront. He can actually be myopic.

Every quality of energy has a positive, or productive, expression in life and a negative, or nonproductive, one. Neptune in its most positive sense describes an individual or a quality that is broad in scope, extremely intuitive and aware. Perceptions are acute, the senses are heightened. A Neptunian person does not need proof, as a scientist might. He trusts his own concepts and instincts to give him information. He may be an artist, dealing with film, music, or the glamour world in particular. He can be highly spiritual, yet on a more inspirational, devotional level than on a practical plane. Neptunian energy can be especially effective in therapy. Since Neptune rules both film and therapy, it is very interesting to note that many therapists are frustrated artists or actors. Many actors must have a sixth sense, such as a therapist must have, to effectively portray roles.

Neptune describes the process of visualization. The aspects to Neptune in an individual chart indicate how easy it is for the person to trust people and his own instincts about people, and how easy it is for him to be idealistic and visionary. His trust may be a universal trust that enables him to see life in its purest form. He can then seem to attract only idealistic people and qualities around him, because that is what he expects. However, he can express a subtle form of tyranny because of his expectancy and idealism. His Neptunian energy says, "I expect you to fulfill all my expectations. Don't you dare let me down." A simple quality of naïveté can keep him going down the garden path, smelling only the roses and lilacs but never seeing that weeds are choking the earth underneath him. He doesn't want to see reality or ugliness. Pain and suffering are not qualities he can deal with, because in Utopia such things cannot exist. If the rose-colored glasses come off and lofty ideals come under the lower laws of the universe, it can be quite devastating. Dreams that are broken can almost never be put back together again.

In areas of love, this can be particularly traumatic. The object of devotion is seen as the knight in shining armor or the pure princess, untouched and living in a tower. The individual places all his trust in his fantasy of how the love object must be, and can be unaware of the real personality of his dream. If the object of his affection fails to live up to his expectations, he may be devastated. The hurt is rarely directed toward the individual who has been mortal and fallible, but toward himself for being a fool. He ultimately becomes aware that he has placed trust in the wrong person and may find it very difficult to forgive himself enough to trust again. He may have to go through this process of idealism and disillusion repeatedly to eventually find a balance. In an extreme sense, this swing is manic-depressive. The highs are very high, but the lows are terrible.

Confrontation can be especially important for someone with a strong Neptunian quality of energy in his chart. The paradox is that with confrontation comes a possibility of disillusion. But a careful look, up front, can prevent later disaster. Rather than act out an ostrich complex and hide the head in the sand, the willingness to see the concept and overview, while also checking out details, facts, and figures, can enable a person to find balance between right- and left-brain activity. Dream life and fantasy life are also extremely important for the mental health and creativity of the individual, especially if Neptune is strongly aspected.

Fortunately, much information is now coming to light concerning the functioning of the brain. The man on the street is aware that the two halves of his brain work in differing ways. Many people are now aware of differing energies on the two sides of the body, and of their correlation to the brain function. For instance, eyesight gives fantastic clues about imbalance. One eye may be stronger than the other. If the left eye is strong, the right brain is strong, or dominant. The right brain or conceptual mind may function easily. Very strong idealistic qualities lead the person to activity of an artistic or visionary nature. However, he may not be good with details. His weaker right eye, connected to the left brain, which rules the power of analysis, may not want to handle more practical matters. Conversely, if the left eye is weak, the person may not want to confront situations in his life that are less than ideal. He weakens his own vision. His strong right eye, connected to the left brain, is easily capable of dealing with minute details of daily activity, but he may miss some of the beauty of life. Dominant halves of the body give somewhat the same kind of information. There are exercises that can help correct the imbalance.

One such exercise is called the "cross crawl." When a baby learns to crawl, he is also exercising the two halves of his brain. If a child has somehow skipped that stage of development, he may have some learning disabilities. However, that activity can be simulated even in an adult by swinging the arms in the opposite direction to the lifting of the knees. Energy can begin to flow, and a better balance between the two halves of the brain can occur. As the left knee is brought up, the right arm is lifted. When the right knee is lifted, the left arm is brought up, almost like an exaggerated walking in place. Better concentration can occur as more energy is sent to both sides of the brain. The exercise is described in more detail in *Touch for Health* by Dr. John Thie.

The eminent psychologist Milton Erickson discovered that hypnotherapy could be most effective in getting past the blocks of the left brain to the more subtle receptivity of the right brain. He felt that most people walk around in trance, that is, unfocused between the two halves of the mind, and therefore continue patterns that have nothing much to do with consciousness and awareness of positive conditioning.

Metaphysical teachings stress the power of using the right-brain, intuitive mind to create the proper conditions in life. The right brain is constantly photographing situations and conditions that perpetuate patterns of behavior. The concepts that begin very early in life are the ones that continue till death, unless the pictures are changed and rearranged. If a man has a beautiful mother, his pictures of ideal womanhood naturally lean to beauty. He simply could not be attracted to an ugly woman. This is an oversimplification, however, for the photographs are on a much more subtle level. The right brain may catch, unconsciously, what the left brain does not see. The left brain can analyze a situation or person incorrectly because of the subconscious messages he receives from early pictures.

Therefore the analysis of Neptune in a chart can be extremely important to determine what the inner pictorial messages are saying. Those unfocused, unclear, perhaps naïve messages may not give good signals for constructive analysis and decisions later in life. The negatives may have to be retouched, or even rephotographed. This is what the therapeutic process is all about. In simple terms, Neptune is like planting a flower in a pot. If one plants a petunia, a petunia grows. If one plants a gardenia, that is the flower that emerges. But when Neptunian energy is diffused, one may plant a petunia, expecting to grow a gardenia. This unrealistic thought process will naturally lead to a big letdown when the wrong flower blooms. Unfortunately, when Neptune is not well aspected in a chart, this process goes on constantly. It is important to read the print on the seed packet and not simply *assume* the seeds are what one might want them to be. Assumption can be strongly connected to Neptunian energy.

Carl Jung expressed this idea in a different way. He said, "Any unrealized energy or potential exteriorizes as fate or destiny." Life is indeed a mirror of what an individual projects at any given moment. Therefore, if the person takes responsibility for what he is creating, mostly unconsciously, he can begin to manifest better conditions around him. Breaking patterns of old concepts can be quite difficult, however. That process seems to require the constant monitoring of thoughts so that the person is eventually able to replace old pictures with new ones. The literary market is full of books such as *The Power of Positive Thinking*, which have helped mankind become aware that this is indeed possible. Dr. Maxwell Maltz wrote *Psycho-cybernetics* to describe his observations on this subject. He arrived at his theories by observing the difference in the lives of women who had plastic surgery and felt better about themselves after a very slight change in appearance. The difference the operation made in their lives was more than slight in many cases. Maxwell Maltz was more than a plastic surgeon. He was concerned about changing outer conditions as well as outer appearance. It is no surprise that he was a Pisces, ruled by Neptune.

When Neptune is placed in or is ruling the first house, the individual may have adopted an ostrich complex early in his life to avoid dealing with less than perfect conditions around him. He becomes very idealistic and trusting as his safety against painful conditions. If he can't see them, they can't hurt him. He learns to look at life through rose-colored glasses. He may put people on a pedestal, be very trusting and idealistic, but perhaps very unrealistic. He tends to project onto other people and situations his concept of how they should be. He expresses a subtle form of tyranny by inadvertently saying, "Don't you dare let me down. You must be perfect for me." His safety depends on assuming that everything will be all right. He can be especially beautiful in appearance. He may look as though a soft-focus lens captured the aura that shines around the head, or as if he had been photographed through gauze. He can actually have a subtle halo around the head. Many film stars have this ascendant or aspect in their charts, and they photograph like a dream. The individual can be especially poetic and have a gift of prophecy. He may want to save the world. He is especially intuitive. However, he also attracts hero worship and discovers that a pedestal is a scary place on which to exist. A big letdown, by the reality of conditions and people around him, can force him to take a second look at the way he deals with life. Disillusionment is usually associated with childhood, or with his personal life and in areas of self-expression. He needs an activity such as film, photography, or therapy to release an excess of subtle conceptual energy. That can help him to be more effective in his own life. Otherwise, he may become quite disillusioned and blocked in his outlook. He can look for something artificial to replace his dreams and help him see beauty again.

In the most destructive expression of negative Neptunian disillusionment, the individual turns to drugs or excess drinking. He may be trying to reach that "high on life" again. He may simply try to blot out the right-brain pictures that form in his mind, for when he drinks or takes drugs, he can make the nightmares go away momentarily. Some of the most fragile, sensitive visionaries may have the most severe problem with alcoholism or drug dependency. Neptune can easily describe that delicate quality of energy when it is associated with the first house. The physical system can be upset in its balance by a mere aspirin.

Neptune rules the "etheric" web that surrounds the body. That web cannot be seen through a microscope. If it is damaged by drugs —heroin, cocaine, and in some cases marijuana—the holes cannot be easily repaired. The natural protective sheath cannot do its job, and all energies are absorbed, with no natural faculty of discrimination. The very darkness the individual wants to avoid comes creeping in. He needs more drugs or alcohol to blot out the terror he cannot confront. He may not be able to allow himself to dream at all. He continues the process of blotting out anything frightening or ugly, but creates a dissipation of everything positive in his life. In drug rehabilitation, the most difficult thing to deal with is the recurring sense of hopelessness that comes with a more realistic outlook. The unrealistic hopes and dreams must be replaced by concepts that provide a more tangible anchor. Mistrust has to give way to something tangible that will stand the test of time.

When Neptune rules or is placed in the second house, the individual may have an unrealistic attitude about money. He can be somewhat of a dreamer where his personal finances are concerned or be inspired and visionary in his earning capacity. He may have an overly idealistic concept in connection with security instead of a more practical viewpoint. He will best earn income in connection with Neptunian activities such as glamour products, film, therapy, gas and oil, or anything conceptual. He may not want to be especially practical when it comes to expenditures, preferring to trust (hope) that his financial life will somehow be what he expects it to be. His prime expenditures will concern activities that are idealistic, conceptual, or that keep him high on life and inspired. He can feed his soul and body through idealistic financial projects. He may have a particular ability to put himself on a mental salary; what he conceives as income for himself is exactly what he will attract in outer circumstances. Dreams and concepts can enrich him in many ways if Neptune is well aspected, yet he can become involved in unrealistic schemes if Neptune has more difficult aspects in his chart. He may believe financial propositions offered to him without proper investigation. He can lead himself down the proverbial garden path in connection with income.

The third house relates to siblings and other relatives, neighbors, communications, contracts, and the ability to learn. It basically describes the quality of interaction an individual has with other people in conversations or discussions. Movement from one place to the other is described by this house, as well as the kind of transportation a person would prefer. It rules community affairs and telephones. When Neptune rules this house, the individual can have his most creative thoughts when he is driving a car or running errands. He may put his siblings and relatives on a pedestal, and may learn almost intuitively. He expresses the idealistic part of himself in negotiations and may be willing to settle for a handshake agreement instead of getting contracts in writing. He may not want to deal with nitpicky details when it comes to the expression of his concepts. If Neptune is well aspected, all negotiations and discussions can be on a high level of intention. If Neptune is not well aspected, he may be unrealistic in evaluation of people and situations quite close to him. He may have to learn not to be naïve and overly trusting of things that remain unspoken. He can project into conversations and onto people things he thinks they may mean, rather than asking questions to clarify discussions and plans.

Since the fourth house describes home conditions, the parent of the opposite sex, and the way the individual feels about his environment, it also describes the quality of lifestyle a person attracts. When Neptune is the ruler of or is placed in this house, the individual may be a visionary when it comes to land, property, and his homelife. He can have tremendous instincts and intuition about ecology or land projects and products. Neptune rules oil and gas. When Neptune is well aspected, the individual may find property that produces oil and gas. The parent of the opposite sex may have been idealistic, inspired, and poetic. He may have glamorized that parent or put him or her on a pedestal, refusing to see the real person. If Neptune is not well aspected, the parent may have been disillusioned in his or her own life, or he or she may have been the cause of tremendous disillusion in the life of the individual. That parent may have wanted to protect the person against the harsh reality of life and actually have done a disservice to him.

If Neptune describes the fifth house of creativity, the potential for self-expression in creative fields is especially strong. If Neptune is well aspected, the person is so conceptual he will quite naturally veer toward areas related to film, photography, or investments in natural resources. Creativity comes in very idealistic forms. He may put his own children on a pedestal and have very beautiful, sensitive, idealistic offspring. But if Neptune is not well aspected, he can be disillusioned by his children. He may be disappointed with creative attempts or be fearful of expressing dreams and talent for fear of a letdown. He may need to be in love with a dream and find that no one can ever live up to his expectations.

The sixth house in the chart describes the kind of work one chooses, the way one feels about work, and the natural kinds of work opportunities that come one's way. It also describes health conditions, service orientation, and relationships with co-workers. When Neptune rules or is posited here, the individual wants his working conditions to be ideal. He may be unable to stand strife or anything less than perfection where his work is concerned. He can easily be attracted to the glamour world or to occupations that allow him to express his idealism. He can participate in film, therapy, or other areas where he might be able to save the world. He needs to be of service on a very high level and can be especially inspired in any working activity. Health and energy depend on his having an outlet for the expression of dreams and visions. He exudes a quality of energy that is inspiring to others. However, if Neptune is not well aspected, the probability of disillusion in connection with his work is strong. He may become involved in the glamour world, only to discover that it is not all that ideal. He may have dreams and concepts that he is afraid to reveal for fear that they are less than inspired. He may lower vitality through drugs or stimulants in an attempt to increase dreams and inspiration. If he places all his hopes and trust in working situations, he may be let down, causing illness to deal with that letdown.

When Neptune is posited in or rules the seventh house of partnership or marriage, the person looks for perfection and idealism in his marital relationship. He wants to walk hand in hand with his mate down the garden path of life toward the sunset. He may feel that marriage will be the dream come true and look for the princess in the tower, untouched and aloof. He may put his mate on a pedestal, refusing to allow that person to be who he or she really is, and consequently can be very disillusioned indeed. He can be attracted to someone glamorous or idealistic. If Neptune is well aspected in the chart, he may find that dream through partnership activities and marriage. If Neptune is not well aspected, this is the area of his life in which he can be most disillusioned. He may discover it is hard to live with a dream on a daily basis.

Since Neptune is the planet of illusion, fantasy can work in a positive or a negative way, especially when it concerns financial matters. The eighth house describes the ability to get one's needs met. It is also the quality of energy that is an individual's gift to humanity. Neptune ruling or posited in this house indicates a great desire to save the world. The gift the individual has for other people is the quality of inspiration and vision. He releases hope and trust in others. When he expresses his ideals on a large scale, the probability of his getting his own needs met easily is quite strong. He can make a profound contribution through any activity that is ephemeral, such as film, therapy, music, art, or any medium that allows for inspiration. His inspiration also extends to ways of attracting aid, worldly goods, or the specific vehicles and opportunities he needs to express that vision. He seems to have a particular quality of trust in the universe to provide him with what he needs in life. If Neptune is not well aspected, however, he may hide his head in the sand as far as the practical matters in life go. He may have to learn to confront issues involved with aid.

When Neptune rules the ninth house of travel, promotional matters, publicity, and the higher mind, the individual can be especially idealistic and conceptual on a broad scale. He can be uplifted by travel, show idealism in connection with promotional efforts or in publishing, or be on his soapbox to share the concepts in which he believes. He can find ideal conditions for the expression of concepts through film, therapy, and travel. When Neptune is not well aspected, he may be unrealistic about his own efforts to reach out for new horizons, or in connection with concepts that lead to the promotion or publication of his dreams. He may have a need to spread out toward new and higher areas of inspiration to keep himself uplifted and inspired. Teaching on a university level, lecturing, and being published can be ideal avenues for continued inspiration. He may need to learn to be realistic about travel matters, situations in other countries, or promotional efforts to avoid a major letdown, however.

The tenth house in a chart describes career activity, public orientation, social situations, and the parent of the same sex. Neptune describes dreams and illusions. The public may idealize and glamorize an individual with Neptune ruling or placed in this house. The person with such a placement may have been fortunate enough to have a parent who expressed idealism, vision, and inspiration. He may have put that parent on a pedestal. Since the visionary quality exhibited by that parent is his role model for all social conditions and career goals, he expresses his high ideals in social or public situations. If that planet is well aspected, he will be attracted to career projects that will allow him to express his conceptual, creative thoughts. Again, film and therapy are natural outlets for this need for expression of idealism. If Neptune is not well aspected, the individual may have worshiped his parent of the same sex, and more than likely, experiences total disillusionment from that parent. His own expectations may have been unrealistic. He may have photographed that parent the way he wanted him or her to be. The resulting crash of high expectations can be devastating, causing that person to have difficulty trusting anyone or anything in connection with public activity.

With Neptune ruling or placed in the eleventh house of friendships, the individual will attract either totally idealistic friends or associates or just the opposite. If Neptune is not well aspected, he may find people who are cynical or pessimistic with whom to associate. He may expect too much from his friends and be very disillusioned. His relationships will either be the area of great blessings or the area in which he is most sorely disappointed. In group activity, he may look for situations that allow expression of his ideals or where he can sink to the depths. Neptune in its most negative form describes drugs. The obvious attempt in use of drugs is to regain a high that has been lost naturally. The need for inspiration that won't come any other way may tempt a person with a strong Neptune to try to find it through artificial means. A relationship between the glamour world and drugs has been apparent for some time. People in need of constant high inspiration may fear its loss and become hooked on the substitute. In its most positive form, Neptune describes poetry and prophecy.

Since Neptune is the planet that rules the natural twelfth house in the zodiac, it is the natural subconscious planet. The twelfth house describes qualities associated with hidden matters or subconscious activity, or the quality of energy that is least obvious in its expression. It may describe repressed or blocked energy. When Neptune describes this house by placement or position, it means a doubly compounded psychic attunement. If that inner inspiration is accurate, described by a positively aspected Neptune, the person has high guidance on a subconscious or inner level. He can be particularly attuned when he is off by himself. If that planet is not well aspected, he can be disillusioned and defeated on a subconscious level. He may not be able to trust his own inner voices and may not be able to visualize. The hidden disillusionment can lead to drugs or drink in efforts to still that voice of despair.

NEPTUNE CONJUNCT SUN

When the Sun and Neptune are conjunct in a chart, the individual will have a Piscean quality to his ego energy. Idealism is at the very core of his existence no matter what his Sun sign may be, as he takes on an additional Neptunian color. He is inwardly a dreamer, conceptualizer, and fantasizer. He can be inspired or unrealistic on a soul level. The quality of energy that is natural to him will be heightened by anything that lifts him above the ordinary route of mortals, for he sees, intuitively, what others may not even begin to perceive. He may be lost in the clouds of his dreams or able to bring his inspired visions into practical manifestation. He may feel it is difficult to live in the material world when it is his inner, fantasy life that sustains him.

Neptune is basically the planet of the poet, whether he keeps his poetry within his very soul or is able to find a medium of expression. He is essentially a person born knowing how to bring dreams into the material world, dealing with the fragile birth of conditions that are what he needs and wants at any given moment. He seems to have the ear of the angels and the brotherhood of the communion of saints in his heart. He can be as pure as the driven snow, or he can be the angel who has gone astray and is lost in the world of materiality. If he has help, indicated by stronger planets in his chart, he accomplishes his mission in life with ease, taking no heed of the rules that less-inspired souls must live by. The higher mind quality gives him a head start on any condition in life that needs to be uplifted into the realm of inspiration.

When Neptune is coupled with the Sun, a strong executive ability coexists with the quality of inspiration. Arturo Toscanini was born with the Sun and Neptune in the sign of Aries. The third-house placement of this conjunction in his chart led to strong abilities to communicate his inspiration in the musical field. Along with a strong ego need to share that inner vision, he had an ability to command a whole symphony orchestra, no small executive task in itself. He could retain his inspiration while still executing orders. Louis Pasteur was born with the Sun conjunct Neptune in the sign of Capricorn. The placement in his chart was also in the third house. He indeed had great vision and a need to communicate what his higher mind revealed to him. Clara Barton founded the Red Cross. Her Sun-Neptune conjunction in Capricorn was placed in the tenth house of public activity, ruling her sixth house of work and service, and her twelfth house of the subconscious. Clara must have had an overview of special intuition which enabled her to harness that dominant, leadership, executive quality and set in motion an organization that to this day provides hope for millions of people.

Presidents James Polk and Franklin Pierce shared this aspect, as did G. W. Russell, the Irish poet known as A.E. Gustave Flaubert, and Édouard Manet also had Sun conjunct Neptune. Perhaps the epitome of a description of this aspect comes with the mere mention of the name of Horatio Alger, whose special dream could be translated into a story of a young man who made his dreams come true. Although Sun-Neptune is not a political aspect, when the individual chooses to utilize that quality of inspiration in service, the job is always well done. Shirley Hufstedler became Secretary of Education. The Virgo Sun and Neptune in Leo combination is placed in her twelfth house of the subconscious. She is said to quickly penetrate problems using words as her chosen weapon. Her fragility and disarming vulnerability may be the very qualities that enable her to accomplish things that might otherwise fall apart in the maze of political bureaucracy.

Trudy Adam, a vivacious, charming, tasteful Englishwoman, has this aspect in her chart. Trudy lives with her husband, Mac, on the island of Ibiza. Trudy has a new career, away from her homeland, as an actress. Her Sun-Neptune conjunction in Leo lies in the first house of personal life and self-expression. There is no doubt about Trudy's efficiency and organizational qualities. She is a lady who gets things done in an environment that does not necessarily foster that quality. Although Trudy's new profession is confined for the most part to local productions, she and her husband have appeared in many films that were shot on location in Ibiza. Trudy confessed that she would have enjoyed being an actress in England. I asked Trudy about her executive ability. She said, "Oh, I can put things together all right. I can visualize things. I look at something and know how it should be. I have very good perceptions, but I do have a hard time making up my mind. Things can appear a bit fuzzy in the beginning, only because I have too many things to think of. Everything can appear to be a bit out of focus before I get to the core of a situation." I asked Trudy how she makes decisions about important matters. She said, "When there is a problem to be solved, the answers just come to me. I must sit down and concentrate, almost on an intuitive level, and the answers appear. It always works. I simply trust that I will know what to do." When Sun and Neptune are in harmonious aspect, that sense of seeing the whole picture can be trusted unerringly, for there is a special quality of vision.

NEPTUNE IN HARD ASPECT TO THE SUN

When these two planets are in hard aspect to each other, whether that is in square or in opposition, there is a tendency to want to ignore the executive ability. Since Neptune describes the process of purification, it is the ego that comes under the microscope with this aspect. There is an unwillingness to look at the inner self with reality. A fuzzy approach to qualities of strength, dominance, and vitality can bring outer circumstances of disillusionment until the rose-colored glasses are removed. An individual may have subtle and unconscious expectations that life and other people will do and take care of everything for him. He may not want to make an effort to make life more ideal. Sometimes it is a matter of wanting accomplishments to remain in the land of dreams, rather than taking charge of manifestation in the material world for fear of later disillusionment. With any Neptune aspects there exists a wishful-thinking quality, even a sense that "life owes it to me," and with hard aspects, the individual has particular difficulty in dealing with what is necessary to make the dreams real.

With a letdown, however, experiences in life bring a new consciousness to purify the sense of self-worth, ego, and vitality. The ego can be lifted to new heights of awareness to bathe in the light of inspiration. Trust becomes honed to go inward instead of focused outwardly onto people and situations that can bring pain. Clear perspective then becomes more possible. When the person listens to his inner intuition, follows his inspiration, and expresses the strength of inner awareness, he attracts new external conditions that will live up to his expectations. He must, however, shift into a higher gear to climb up the mountain.

Estela Bence, a vibrant Aries with Leo rising, has the Sun in opposition to Neptune. The Sun is placed in the eighth house of getting her needs met, with Neptune in the second house of finance. The Sun rules her first-house personality and areas of self-expression. Neptune describes the kinds of partners she picks, since that idealistic planet rules the seventh house. Leo ascending describes a quality of strength, executive ability, and dominance that can be quite difficult for a female to deal with, especially if there are difficult aspects to the Sun. When Neptune is in opposition to the Sun and ruling the seventh house, rather than taking charge in a partnership situation, there may be some wishful thinking involved. Estela described this very clearly. She said, "In partnership situations, I get suckered in all the time. I pick people, whether in my business or in personal life, who are very sweet and idealistic, but I end up doing all the work. I always end up having to take charge, but then I might as well do it on my own. Sometimes it is as if they get all the glamorous part and become the stars and I have to take the responsibility. Even as a teenager, I felt this load. For instance, I learned to drive the car when my family was away. They were very proud of me, so I was given the car to do the shopping and errands, but I wasn't allowed to use the car for any fun. I was constantly expecting that people would do what is fair or what I expected them to do, and I would be constantly disappointed. When I realized what the game was, I refused to play anymore. I used to feel like a fool. In some relationships I felt I was very naïve. But not anymore."

Estela has had a great deal of therapy. She described how that helped her change patterns and perspective. "Before therapy I would jump in a lot. Now I have learned to wait and see. My instincts were correct all the time, but I didn't believe them. Now I'm able to know that what people are saying is not what they really feel. I listen for clues. Some tiny words escape and you learn to put them all together. The way I deal with people now is to let them go. I'll find out pretty soon whether they are going to be trustworthy or not. I discovered I have wasted a lot of time believing promises."

With this difficult aspect ruling partnership and aid from others, I asked Estela about those areas of her life. She was very clear: "When I'm in love and in a relationship, I'm on cloud nine. I don't even think about the reality of a situation. Partners tend to think I'm very fragile, but I'm not. I tend to put myself in the background, but sooner or later my strength begins to show itself. When I start seeing things clearly, I say to myself, 'Why did I pick this person?' Usually, I have felt the person needed help. Now that I'm aware of all of this, it is very difficult. I never find anyone who is strong enough. I really don't want to carry all the load. I suppose

I'm just not dependent enough. I accept help if it comes spontaneously, but if I have to ask, and then wonder whether or not someone will come through for me, it takes less time to just go out and
do it myself. This is terrible. I probably pick the kind of people
who are going to let me down, just so that I will motivate myself to
do things. Maybe I need something disappointing from outside to
trigger me to assume the responsible role."

Difficult Neptune aspects seem to indicate the need to learn to
trust one's inner voices and instincts, whether those voices give
information about emotions, love, or people. When Neptune and
the Sun are in adverse dialogues with each other, it may be essential to trust oneself first and foremost. This is an intensely personal
aspect, however. It may be difficult to know whether another person
goes through the process of naïve trust and eventual letdown unless
the individual is willing to reveal that information.

Jerry Lewis has Sun in an inconjunct aspect to Neptune in his
chart. The Sun is placed in the ninth house of promotional effort
and publicity, and rules the second house of income. Neptune is
placed in the second house of income, and rules the ninth house of
publicity and public relations. Jerry may have had to become more
realistic about income and expenditures. However, we can assume
that in one area of his life he trusted another person completely.
His partnership and friendship with Dean Martin was highly publicized. A dissolution of the partnership resulted in a painful disillusionment that was evidently very deep. Until very recently, Jerry
and Dean didn't even speak to each other. Whether financial matters were at the base of the dissolving of what had seemed like an
ideal partnership is something the public may never fully know. It
appears that Jerry had to go on to express his own executive capacity alone. It seems he has done that very well.

NEPTUNE CONJUNCT MOON

High idealism is connected with this aspect, especially on an emotional level. The Moon has been statistically proved to be strong in
the charts of writers. When it is working in harmony with the
idealism described by Neptune, the quality of emotional inspiration
is very high.

Charles Dickens had the Moon conjunct Neptune in the second

house of income, but ruling the ninth house of publishing, and the fifth house of creativity, children, and talent. The Moon describes a nurturing quality. In his case, Dickens wrote about less than ideal conditions for children. He expressed his concern and emotional reaction to conditions that were not confronted in his time. Robert Louis Stevenson had this conjunction in the first house of self-expression, ruling the fifth house of creativity, and the sixth house of work. His poetry was inspired by, and concerned with presenting, ideals of beauty.

Johann Sebastian Bach had the Moon conjunct Neptune at the very top of his chart. The Moon, ruling his ascendant and personality, was placed in the ninth house, whereas Neptune, ruling his tenth house of career, was also posited in that tenth house. With both Moon and Neptune in the sign of Pisces, the inspiration and idealism is stressed in many ways. Hector Berlioz had Moon conjunct Neptune placed in the sixth house of work, and ruling his career and ascendant. Franz Liszt had Moon conjunct Neptune placed in the fourth house of home and later life, describing a relationship with his mother, and ruling the eleventh house of friends, and the eighth house of getting his needs met. Liszt was one composer who seemed able to live a grand lifestyle while he also produced great music. Richard Strauss had Moon conjunct Neptune in the eleventh house of friends, ruling the tenth house of career and his cancer ascendant.

Edward White, the first American astronaut to emerge from an orbiting spacecraft, had this conjunction ruling his fifth house of creativity, and the ninth house, in this case representing space travel. With the placement in the tenth house of career, he might have chosen any number of outlets for this sensitive quality. The Moon also describes a sensitivity toward the needs of mankind and the ability to feed people on a mass level. His vision lifted the hearts of many people in the world to new horizons and possibilities. Dag Hammarskjöld also had this conjunction in his chart. The Moon was posited in the eleventh house of group association and organizations, describing the United Nations, with Neptune placed in the twelfth house of the subconscious and "secret" mind. Hammarskjöld wrote poetry that was not fully revealed until after his death.

Susan Hayward and Rita Hayworth had Moon conjunct Neptune

in their charts. Rita Hayworth was the glamorous pinup girl that captured the heart of a prince. With the conjunction posited in her seventh house, she married Aly Khan, one of the wealthiest men in the world, an international playboy, and on the surface, the most ideal, glamorous husband possible. After several years of marriage, Rita became very disillusioned and divorced her husband, leaving her so-called glamorous life behind. At times, such severe disillusion leads to the escape mechanism of drugs and alcohol; Rita has been continually battling alcoholism for many years. Susan Hayward had the Moon conjunct Neptune in the ninth house of publicity and travel, and ruling her fifth house of creative expression. Susan was noted for portraying very sensitive roles. She won the Academy Award twice for her roles in *I'll Cry Tomorrow* and *I Want to Live*. Both roles dealt with sadness, disillusionment, and emotional pain.

Whitney has the Moon conjunct Neptune in the fifth house of creativity, ruling the ninth house of travel, in his chart. Whitney expressed a special artistic ability, a strong musical sense, and an unusual quality of vision as a child. After his university days, he was hired by a major advertising agency in New York City and became the fair-haired boy, the creative genius, in that organization. When the Moon is placed in or is ruling that ninth house, a special sense of what people need and want can lead to success in advertising, also a ninth-house activity. Eventually, Whitney became vice president of a major hotel chain and began to travel for his work. He lived in the most expensive hotels in the United States and in Europe. He enjoyed the Neptunian glamour that is associated with that occupation. He was hired by another major hotel chain and personally supervised the especially exotic and highly publicized opening of their top hotel in New York City. With the Moon and Neptune in the fifth house of creativity and children, although Whitney had ample opportunity to express all facets of his talent, he was lacking the chance to show his mothering qualities. He wanted to have a child. It would appear that Whitney now has fulfilled many of his dreams through his work and is now the proud father of a beautiful daughter.

Alan, on the other hand, with Moon conjunct Neptune in his fifth house but ruling the tenth house of career, and describing the relationship with his father, had opposite experiences. He had asthma as a child and remembers his father sitting by his bed, assuming a very nurturing role. But Alan is aware of a turning point that came when he felt abandoned by his father, around the age of twelve. The family took a trip to Europe, allowing Alan's older sister to go, but leaving Alan at home with a younger brother. Alan was totally devastated and spent much of his adult life trying to do things that might win back his father's attention. Instead of living up to the high side of Neptunian idealism, he began drinking heavily, gambling at an early age, and experimenting with his romantic life in a less than savory way. He had an illegitimate child that he refused to acknowledge and looked for love that would represent his ideal. Although he had an opportunity to work in films and was quite a good actor, he took a job with a major betting system that became legal in a major eastern city. Alan had tremendous writing ability and wrote some poetry, which he kept to himself. He did not continue that form of creative expression. He chose to use his fifth-house aspect in the gambling world and began to race horses.

Alan's father had a high position as a pillar of his community, which compelled people to look up to him as a savior of sorts. But Alan was never able to confront his father and conversely was never given realistic treatment by him. He continued on a downward path, even tattooing "loser" on his arm. His father adopted somewhat of an ostrich complex in connection with his son, assuming that time would straighten things out. The lack of confrontation and real emotional rapport between father and son only continue the disillusionment and the dream that everything is all right. Alan may continue his self-destruction in hope of some confrontation and attention from his father. His father has confessed to a sense of helplessness where his son is concerned. Alan has also expressed a total unwillingness to accept responsibility for failure in his own life.

When the Moon is connected to such a visionary and idealistic planet in the chart, artistic outlet is imperative. A child with such an aspect needs encouragement with his fantasies to make them work for him instead of against him. The quality of energy can be released easily through writing and is also strong in music, work in films, with therapy, and in any nurturing capacity. Eva Marie Saint and Robert Redford are two film actors who share this aspect. Mary

Wells, founder of a major advertising agency in New York, also has the Moon conjunct Neptune in her chart. A realistic overview and practical idealism are the qualities that can make this aspect positive, for Neptune is the stuff dreams are made of.

NEPTUNE IN HARD ASPECT TO THE MOON

Purification of the emotional nature seems to be the prime lesson to be learned in connection with the Moon in hard aspect to Neptune. The swing of highs to lows can be difficult to manage with this aspect. Neptune can describe a manic high and expectancy that becomes the devastating letdown of disillusionment. When the emotional reaction is unrealistic, external situations are very sure to bring about a more realistic outlook. This process may be painful, however. There is a special need to look at the reality of all emotional reactions to be sure that glamour is stripped away. Strong nurturing feelings may also need outlet for expression; a practical course of action is very important.

Many presidents of the United States had the Moon in hard aspect to Neptune. Original ideals of being able to solve the problems of mankind may have been brought to the threshold of total despair when bureaucracy interfered with the dreams of these men. Andrew Johnson had the Moon in opposition to Neptune, as did Grover Cleveland. James Buchanan had the Moon square Neptune. William Howard Taft had the Moon inconjunct Neptune. Since this is not a political aspect, with such extreme sensitivity apparent, these men may have left office more realistic, but sadder and wiser.

Sigmund Freud had the Moon square Neptune in his chart. He was the pioneer in the whole new territory of psychoanalysis; yet, in his lifetime, his colleagues thought he was off base, lacking in traditional techniques, and somewhat unrealistic in his approach to his work. His societies were not well respected, his publications were criticized, and yet he was able to persist in his research. In his chart, the Moon is placed in the eighth house of getting his needs met, while Neptune is place in the fourth house of home, and rules the fifth house of creativity, romance, and children. The final disillusionment of his emotional life may have been having to leave his home and homeland to flee the Nazi threat in Vienna. To this day, Freud's works seem shrouded under a mysterious veil of misunderstanding. Only recently, the former projects director of the Sigmund Freud Archives has charged that Freud suppressed a key theory in order to protect himself from strong liability. He accuses Freud of corrupting psychoanalysis at the very beginning of his research and practice. Only Sigmund Freud himself could really tell where his emotional disillusionment lay, however.

Ludwig van Beethoven, Vincent van Gogh, Henry David Thoreau, Stephen Foster, and Maurice Chevalier had this aspect in their charts. Poet Paul Verlaine, violinist Yehudi Menuhin, and Louis XVI also had such a conflict in their charts. Liza Minnelli, Janis Joplin, and Mario Lanza have the Moon square Neptune in their charts. Although each person had a strong public image, on a personal level a letdown with the emotional reaction may have been very hard to take. In the case of Liza Minnelli, the Moon is placed in the third house of communications, but ruling the fourth house of home. Neptune is posited in the sixth house of work, ruling the twelfth house of the subconscious process. Lack of clear communication with both of her parents is a strong possibility in her chart. She may have had both parents on a pedestal but felt as though she could never confront them in direct conversations and hope to receive a straight answer. Her childhood and homelife were indeed tempestuous. She attended sixteen schools on two continents before she was sixteen years old. No matter what achievements Liza may have in her career, the fear of disillusionment may prevent her from trusting her emotional life too much. She may rely on drive, ambition, and technique to replace the idealism that is a potential in her chart. She could worry about being on a pedestal or about assuming anything in connection with discussions and agreements. Ironclad contracts would be a must for Liza to feel security in a situation. Liza has recently undergone treatment for the cure of alcoholism and drug dependency.

NEPTUNE CONJUNCT MERCURY

Neptune and Mercury are descriptive of the two sides of the brain, with Neptune ruling right-brain activity and Mercury ruling left-brain, detailed productivity. When these two planets are conjunct, the mental potential seems increased tremendously simply because of the balance that is achieved between the two halves of the mind.

Mercury describes a careful attention to what can be seen, proved, and researched, while Neptune indicates the potential to see the overview. The connection and harmonious dialogue is like being able to see the forest and also the trees. Detailed observation doesn't obscure the concept of the whole. A person with this aspect can find a way to bring his dreams into practical focus so that others can trust him on an intellectual level as well as on an idealistic basis. He is also able to trust his own ability to conceptualize and conceive, then find a practical way to bring about his plans. He can express on an intellectual level what he senses and intuits subconsciously.

Rudolf Steiner had Neptune conjunct Mercury in his chart. His theory of education is descriptive of how this aspect works in the individual life. Steiner felt that all subjects taught in school should relate to each other, to facilitate learning. He set up a curriculum so that a student would not have to deal with disparate information and facts that were never tied together or assimilated into experience. For instance, if history was the number one topic of a specific learning period, mathematics, science, art, music, and all other subjects taught would bear a relationship to that particular period of history that was being discussed. He was a forerunner to the idea of *Drawing with the Right Side of the Brain.* Steiner was an occultist who found a way to translate his concepts into practical manifestation. Rather than live in the ivory tower of ideas and dreams, Steiner practiced the true route of metaphysical knowledge by bringing inspiration into a more practical form that could be lived and experienced on a daily basis.

The Scottish playwright James M. Barrie also had Neptune conjunct Mercury in his chart. He created Peter Pan, a Neptunian figure of illusion and fantasy who could fly through the air. Yet Peter was also a paragon of practical wisdom that was always tinged with the whimsical magic of dreams. Cornelia Otis Skinner had this aspect in her chart. She had a wit that was subtle. She could describe extraordinary events that might occur in the lives of almost anyone and bring a new perspective to the tale. She could also relate unusual escapades in her own life and make them seem as if they could happen to anyone. She had a marvelous storytelling ability.

Martin Luther had Neptune in conjunction to Mercury in the

fourth house of his chart. The fourth house describes homelife and the latter part of one's life. In this case, the fourth house can describe the church that Luther founded as a result of being condemned as a heretic. Neptune rules the eighth house in his chart. When Neptune is placed in or rules that house of transformation, the person wants to save the world. If Neptune is not well aspected, the individual doubts his ability to be effective in view of such a large task. But when Mercury is in harmonious dialogue, the words of wisdom can inspire people to a more idealistic outlook on life. The Lutheran Church was founded in 1525. Luther, a former priest, married and began a pattern that is becoming more than a subject for discussion among many priests of today. He found a way to combine the idealism of spiritual concepts with mundane life.

NEPTUNE IN HARD ASPECT TO MERCURY

This conflicting dialogue between right and left brain may result in a blocking of fantasy life or a lack of ability to deal in concepts. Whenever the individual with this aspect begins to sense something that he cannot touch, measure, or feel, he can be on dangerous territory. His left-brain, analytical qualities leap to the fore to obfuscate the overview. He may have had early experiences that burned him so badly that he is unwilling to take a chance on anything less than practicality, mundane observation, and proof. He can hide his true inspiration behind a wall of fact and intellect. He may see an overview but then question the method of bringing intangible dreams into practical experience. He does not easily trust his ability to create the circumstances of his life without strong documentation to back him up.

The fear of disillusion is perhaps the major concern when this aspect is in an individual's chart. For if the person trusts his fantasy life and allows himself to dream, he wants to be sure those dreams will come true. So he hides behind the intellect and develops the concrete level of intelligence through education and through gaining facts and information from other people. Then he is relieved of the problem of crashing dreams and a possible letdown. He loves to ask questions, quote those he considers authorities, and pick the brain of someone he respects. He doesn't have to trust himself, as he finds sources of information who present proof of certain facts.

The purification of the process of intellect working in harmony with inspiration is important in this case. There is no doubt about the ability to deal in facts and figures, but trust may be sadly lacking in his experience. His actual vision can be impaired, with weakness in the left eye. Depth perception is lacking in this case, on both the literal and the figurative levels. He ignores the poetry of his imagination.

Neptune describes the potential of a situation, whereas Mercury indicates the reality. There can be disparities between the observation of that potential and the collection of data, when these two planets are in difficult aspect. The aspect can describe an either/or situation. The individual sees an ultimate potential and can be high on the idea, but when he researches the facts, he loses sight of the potential. It can also describe a wait-and-see attitude that frequently prevents the individual from taking action and making decisions that might create more ideal conditions around him. He can use the excuse of "the reality of the facts" to excuse himself from daring to follow a dream.

Milton Erickson devised a technique for use in his therapeutic practice that enables the therapist to get behind the practical mind to the subconscious. For the truth of many situations lies not with the observations, but in the realm of the right brain. During periods of trauma or shock, the left brain may be slightly out of focus, allowing for information to go into the subconscious that is not properly filtered. A person may not have access to that deeper concept of truth because of a barricaded intellect. Whereas Erickson uses hynotherapy to break down barriers, there are other methods to find the balance between the two halves of the mind that seems sadly lacking when Mercury and Neptune are in hard aspect to each other. Dreams can reveal much truth that is generally beyond perceptive reality. Gestaldt techniques of dream analysis demonstrate an ability to dialogue with the subconscious in a waking state. Dr. C. Crane, in Dallas, Texas, uses a chiropractic technique of adjustment that realigns the cranial position, enabling better balance between the two halves of the brain. He suggests ten minutes on a trampoline each day to help maintain alignment. He also uses a cassette tape to teach a centering exercise that focuses attention on the center of the forehead for better concentration and clarity of thought. Many people with concrete, practical intelligence have discovered that drugs enable them to go beyond the barriers of the mind. Unfortunately drugs are now in more common use than more healthful techniques. The level of awareness is elevated to the lower astral plane, where lots of pictures exist, yet that mode of reaching the fruitful imagination is still distorted. The mind is propelled totally away from the healthy balance of right and left brain. In its positive balance, the intellect acts as a healthy tool of discrimination.

This aspect is, again, an intensely personal one. Unless an individual is willing to acknowledge his lack of perception, there may be few outer clues to the existence of this aspect. If the individual were able to see more conceptually, he would be more aware of his lack of perception, so a paradox exists that is not easily unraveled. Some small clues exist in behavior when this aspect is present. Philip Roth has Neptune inconjunct Mercury in his chart. Neptune lies in the ninth house of publishing, but Mercury is placed in the third house of communications, ruling the sixth house of work. Neptune is a co-ruler of the third house, indicating the inspiration that lies behind the practical, written, or spoken word. Roth is known to be a very disciplined writer, but his works are more sardonic and ironic than idealistic. According to interviewers, he is obscene in sessions and exhibits speech patterns that are like a "thesaurus of ad-lib bits."

Gloria Steinem has Neptune in opposition to Mercury in her chart. Neptune is placed in the tenth house of career, indicating a glamour image in public, with Mercury placed in the fourth house of home, ruling the eleventh house of group associations, and the eighth house of getting needs met. Gloria's opposition describes relationships with her mother and father. Neptune rules the fifth house of romance, creativity, and talent. Gloria opted for reporting as her entree into the literary world, after a very difficult childhood. Her father evidently did not meet her needs, since he left home when Gloria was only twelve. Her mother, described by Neptune, may have been sadly disillusioned, setting the patterns that led Gloria to crusade for women's rights. With the founding of MS. magazine, Gloria was able to give out information (eighth house ruled by Mercury) that would benefit many associates. Gloria's information was not of the dream variety; she writes and publishes exposés and crusades of a more practical nature. Gloria may have few illusions left about life and love.

Mae West also had Neptune square Mercury. Her approach to romance, with Mercury in the fifth house and ruling it as well, was one of verbalization and a frank, open attitude. She never used profanity, but tongue-in-cheek wit suggested what she meant quite clearly. Her advice about love was "It's not the men in your life, it's the life in your men," not exactly a rosy-colored approach to the idea of dreamy romantic idylls. She never let illusion enter into her discussion or exhibition of her romantic life.

NEPTUNE CONJUNCT VENUS

Venus is the planet that describes the love nature, artistic ability, diplomatic qualities, and general need for peace and harmony in the individual's chart. The quality of that love nature and artistic ability is augmented when Neptune is next to Venus, in a conjunction. Vision and high inspiration combine with a tremendous need for harmony to bring about conditions that lift the individual to the heights of fantasy in connection with expression of love or artistry. But when Neptune propels the person onto the level of glamour and unrealistic idealism, the rose-colored glasses may have to come off with a sudden, devastating thud.

Since Venus is so strongly connected to the art world and to theater and design, it might seem likely that this conjunction would be strong in the charts of successful artists, musicians, actresses, and designers. Both Venus and Neptune are planets that describe passive energy, however. There are actually fewer well-known people with this aspect than might be expected. It could appear that the individual wants to keep his dreams of beauty all to himself, rather than to display or commercialize them. With strong stimulation for self-expression from another planet, there is more potential for the demonstration of the artistic nature in public areas. But, by and large, Venus energy describes a desire to keep the status quo and to simply enjoy the pleasures of life and social conditions.

Beauty and desire for love are never lacking when this aspect is found in a chart. The tendency is to look for an ideal in love or with art, talent, and social life. The individual can be especially gracious, sociable, and loving, but a letdown in connection with those

areas of life is more than possible if the person indulges in mere
fantasy, rather than a realistic approach to conditions. Paul Cézanne was one artist with this aspect in his chart who expressed the
ultimate quality of beauty and softness in his work, especially his
watercolors. Color and brush strokes must necessarily be gentle and
pastel. In his work, Cézanne frequently showed repose, rest, and
peace. Even his more vivid paintings suggested a gracious way of
life, rather than stark realism. His landscapes suggest a Neptunian,
dreamy, filmy quality that doesn't allow for the turmoil of wind and
weather.

Hélène Boucher had Neptune conjunct Venus in her chart. The
position in the eleventh house of group association, and ruling her
tenth house of career, and third house of communications, might
suggest a career in theater or areas where she could express her
social qualities. However, she was trained as a couturiere and
opened a shop in Paris. She dropped that career to become an
airplane pilot, specializing in aerobatics and breaking world
records. Mars was far stronger in her chart, with its conjunction to
Pluto, than the dreamy Neptune-Venus aspect. Perhaps when
Boucher was in the clouds, described by Neptune, she could tune in
to the beauty she longed for on earth. Her associations with people
could perhaps be on a more idealistic level of fantasy when she
discussed and shared ideas about flying.

Amelia Earhart also had this aspect in her chart. Venus ruled her
first house of personality and self-expression, with Taurus on the
ascendant, and Neptune ruled her twelfth house of the subconscious. The position of the conjunction was in the second house of
income, and also described the sixth house of work. Earhart was
also a strong worker for human rights and for the feminist movement, demonstrating her dream of ideal social conditions. Obviously, on her solo flights she was able to tune in to beautiful dreams
of harmony, with Neptune and Venus describing her subconscious
processes. She may have had dreams in a waking state high in the
air that kept her high on life. Venus can describe the air element,
but Neptune describes gas, clouds, and illusion. Amelia Earhart's
plane crashed into the South Pacific, causing her to disappear with
no trace. She may have continued to soar higher and higher while
her ship got lost at sea.

Swimmer Marilyn Bell has this aspect in her chart as well. Venus also rules her first house of self-expression, with Libra on the ascendant. The Venus-Neptune conjunction is placed in the eleventh and twelfth houses in her chart, with Neptune in the eleventh and Venus in the twelfth house of the subconscious. Neptune rules her sixth house of work, and Venus also rules the eighth house of getting her needs met. Marilyn Bell may have wanted to save the world and express the idealism and vision, of which she was so capable, on a broader scale. When she was a teenager, she taught children who were crippled by polio how to swim. In her natural element, water, Marilyn Bell swam the English Channel when she was seventeen years old and then went on to swim Lake Ontario, which had never been done before. Against all odds, she braved the icy waters for twenty-one hours. She was named Woman of the Year by the Canadian press. She proved that dreams can come true.

James Beard has Venus conjunct Neptune in his chart. Although his exact time of birth is unknown, James was born with the Sun in the sign of Taurus. With the ruler of his Sun (Venus) conjunct Neptune, James Beard obviously has great vision when it comes to expression of his particular art form, the preparation of food. Venusian qualities are always very gracious and sociable. James Beard can combine people in such a way that although they may be of different personalities and backgrounds, they would take great pleasure in the immediate social event while consuming his good food and enjoying his hospitality.

Since Neptune describes the very personal area of dreams, it is hard to know whether people with Neptune conjunct Venus are able to achieve idealism on a personal love level or not. It is possible that they can channel much of the dream-level and romantic fantasies into activity that can bring about a more realistic outlook in personal life. It is also possible, however, that people with this aspect put their loved ones on pedestals. Too much realism in an approach to love can often result in disillusion, for most of the "high" is gone without the rose-colored glasses. If, indeed, love is a source of pleasure in the life of one with this aspect, the probability is strong that the whole truth is not often confronted, for few people could ever really live up to the expectations of Venus conjoined with Neptune.

NEPTUNE IN HARD ASPECT TO VENUS

Leslie is a soft-spoken yet vibrant young lady with two teenage daughters. Leslie has Neptune square Venus in her chart. Venus is posited in the first house in her chart, with Neptune in the fourth house of home, ruling her relationship with her mother. Neptune rules Leslie's tenth house of career or public activity, and describes her relationship with her father. Venus also rules her fifth house of children, romance, and creative expression. Leslie began by saying, "I always see the potential of someone. I see the beautiful level of this human being that I'm relating to and the sad thing is, the person has insecurities that won't allow him to express this quality. I see him as having all this potential if I can only make him feel secure enough to be able to let it out. Unfortunately for me, I never want to look at the part that is insecure, and they are afraid to show the part that I see as the basic self, so they show an image. The beautiful side is always there too, for everyone has a beautiful side, but . . ." She went on to describe her second marriage, which was, in the beginning, her dream come true. "I became a martyr in that marriage. I didn't want to bring myself down to a bland level of observation, because I want to see people as gods and goddesses. My five years in the marriage were terrible. I was beaten up and I just took it. I was the martyr on the cross (a negative Neptunian trait). It was not my idea of love. I haven't lived with anyone since then, and it has been eight years. I have spent a lot of time since then plowing through things, seeing that I didn't have to be that martyr." I asked Leslie if she got even nicer in her behavior when she began to be disillusioned. She replied, "Yes, that's exactly what happened. I guess that I felt it was my fault for not being more perfect. I felt if I was *more* loving, then he would be able to be the way I thought he could be. I blamed myself, rather than seeing that he was just that way."

Leslie went on to describe her relationship with her father. "Naturally my father was a pattern for my second marriage. Both my father and my husband are very artistic. My father paints, but not as a profession. He opted for security, rather than follow his dreams. But I feel he has this special quality also. My father was not affectionate. He is very closed off and aloof. I still can't get to that special quality within him. Both my mother and father let me down around the time I was about eleven or twelve. I suppose I did idealize them, although I never have thought about that. The realization that they were mere mortals came when I wanted to go out and do things and they wouldn't let me."

Leslie designs sweaters and clothes as an outlet and form of self-expression. She said her real dream is to write something truly exceptional, however. She said, "I write all the time, but just for me. I find that if I try to make it for other people, it isn't satisfying. I don't want to have to structure it. The essential thing of writing, for me, is therapeutic. I'm not very ambitious, and it spoils the fun if I thought I had to write to be published."

Leslie also has the Moon in the first house, conjunct Venus, bringing in the artistic expression of writing. But with both these planets square Neptune, the desire is to keep artistic self-expression in the realm of dreams. Neptune describes the purification process. By writing, Leslie is clarifying her attitudes about love and going through the process of purification simply by her willingness to confront, even for herself alone. The veils of Neptunian mystery seem to have to come down little by little to avoid the total devastation of broken dreams that can lead to drugs and drinking as a way out of despair. But however strong is that process of confrontation, the temptation to see life as rosy is always present. As Leslie describes it so well, "I want to see reality while retaining my vision of goodness and hope."

Toulouse-Lautrec had Neptune square his Venus. His reputation as a womanizer was especially strong, yet his companions were, for the most part, the prostitutes of Montmarte. When he did fall in love, the ultimate rejection from the dancer he adored was almost more than he could take. Patricia Neal has Neptune in opposition to Venus in her chart. After years of tender loving care from her husband, she was left by him for another woman. Barbra Streisand also has Neptune in opposition to Venus in her chart. Neptune is posited in the sixth house of work, with Venus in the twelfth house of the subconscious. Neptune rules that twelfth house, and Venus is placed in the sign of Pisces. Finally, Venus rules her second house of income. These inharmonious dialogues between Neptune and Venus are not obvious in Barbra's chart, for they are buried in the twelfth house, which describes behind-the-scenes feelings and activity. On a personality level, Barbra expresses an aggressive, energetic Aries quality, as would be expected with her Aries ascendant. When she is all by herself, Barbra may be very gentle, peaceful, affectionate, and idealistic. Venus describes her partnership, with Libra ruling the seventh house of marriage. Barbra no doubt enjoys being with her mate in serene and beautiful surroundings, perhaps where they can be off quietly by themselves. Her first marriage, to Elliott Gould, may have brought the disillusion that is indicated by this square between Neptune and Venus. In her choice of former hairdresser Jon Peters, it might appear that Barbra has found her Venusian dream mate.

NEPTUNE CONJUNCT MARS

When dreamy Neptune is conjunct aggressive Mars in a chart, the conflict may be debilitating. Each voice is saying exactly the opposite thing to the other. Neptunian dialogue concerns keeping events and situations on a dreamy, idealistic plane of perfection. Mars voices stimulate a person to action and ambitious drive. The end result may be a watering down of the drives and resourcefulness. This aspect has been termed the "liars" aspect, for the individual may hesitate to confront situations that will later on appear to contain deception. The individual with this aspect in his chart assumes too much about people, projects, or events. When he discovers missing information, he can become very angry, yet the anger can be only toward himself for lack of realistic action. He may be told some pertinent facts about a situation but neglect to ask what he might *not* have been told. Information may emerge years later when it is too late to review decisions and change direction. The person with this aspect in his chart is left with feelings of anger and helplessness. He might have done something entirely different and prevented disillusionment in his life if he had known all the facts. Unwarranted assumptions can exist all around. The person responsible for the missing information may have no intention of deception, taking it for granted that the Mars-Neptune individual was aware of pertinent information. This can happen quite easily in family situations. It might be assumed that a child growing up would be aware of what was really going on in the family, yet the child can end up feeling deluded, because facts that perhaps should have been obvious were left unstated.

Neptune conjunct Mars can also describe an inner lack of ambition and drive that can bring a disillusioning situation eventually. Martha, a therapist, described it this way: "I have a hesitancy to confront up front for fear of dispelling the magic." It is necessary to harness energy carefully with this aspect. When it is too late to put the dreams back together, it is too late to say, "I wish I'd known." The person with this aspect needs to learn to remove the rose-colored glasses, ask questions, and then continue to investigate the facts for himself. He needs to take action to bring his dreams into manifestation and reality, rather than just assume a situation is what it appears to be at first glance.

Zelda Fitzgerald had this aspect in her chart. Her life with Scott was a whirlwind of fun, people, travel, variety, and publicity. Wherever they went, they were the center of the glamorous world. Scott and Zelda were the original beautiful people, the first "jet-setters," sought after and much admired. Yet Zelda ended up in a mental hospital after a diagnosis of schizophrenia. The conjunction in her chart was placed in the eleventh house of friends, associations, and groups. Both Mars and Neptune ruled the ninth house of travel, publicity, publication, and recognition. The eighth house of getting needs met was also ruled by this conjunction. In traditional astrology, the eighth house is described as the death process. Zelda's death was by fire in a mental hospital, Mars ruling fire and Neptune describing her out-of-touch mental faculties.

Zelda had a great deal of talent in her own right. She was a writer, artist, and dancer. When Scott's alcoholism was severe, Zelda finished many of his manuscripts. She may have had secret ambitions to be a fine dancer, yet within the confines of their lifestyle, it would have been impossible for Zelda to build her own career. Her reputation as an artist would always have fallen in the shadow of his triumphant success, so she was never really recognized for her own creative efforts or the part she played in his success. When Zelda was confined to hospitals, she danced furiously, as if she could banish the mirage of broken dreams through vigorous physical activity. She may have had a glorious success in her fantasy that she was never able to bring about in real life.

Alison has Mars conjunct Neptune in her second house of finance, ruling the fifth house of creativity, and the sixth house of work. This aspect was strongly stimulated one year in particular, enabling her to really understand her reaction to dealing with income. She said, "Everything I tried to do financially turned out disastrously. I did my best to confront situations and pin people down to contracts, yet in each case, there was a small loophole that allowed the person to get away with lack of payment. I also became aware of my tendency to assume that people meant what they said. Unfortunately, I had several financial dealings with friends who I would have trusted with my life. Because I had been burned before, I made sure we got everything very clear and in writing. Yet, I was still let down. I felt a tremendous disillusionment when my friends behaved within the legal limits but not very ethically. I became aware of my own unwillingness to work as hard as usual. I structured things in my mind that turned out to be unrealistic. I realized too late what I should have done. Much of the real letdown and disillusionment had to do with new perspective about my trust and belief system. It was obviously a lesson I had to learn sooner or later. I had been naïve up to that point."

Gordon Hyatt is a very successful television producer in New York. Gordon has Mars conjunct Neptune in the tenth house of career, describing his relationship with his father, and ruling the fourth house of home, describing his mother. He said that his relationship with his parents might have been ideal, yet he felt overly protected and unprepared for the real world. Gordon talked about how this parental programming affected his life. "I was introspective and a loner and to compensate for this, I learned to express my personality and humor through a stage presentation of magic (a Neptune-ruled activity) and with comedy. I found myself in the company of others (Mars competitive activity) who went on to devote their lives to performance—Stacy Keach and Orson Bean, to name two fellow prestidigitators. My fear was that I wouldn't know enough, and this led me to a compulsion to learn about the real world. I began to follow things that interested me, especially history and art, one describing our society and its formation, and the other leading toward a development of my visual senses. Combining these two perspectives led to my career, documentary films." Although Gordon may have chosen not to tangle in the competitive struggle with performance of his comedic and magical abilities, he did indeed engage in the naturally competitive world of film. Yet, his ability to find the niche that enabled him to express his true idealistic, visual talent is a prime example of how one can release energy, described by this aspect, in a positive way.

It is impossible to describe a Mars aspect without considering the sexual implications of the aspect. The Mars energy describes not only drive, ambition, resourcefulness, and aggressive energy, but basically the sexual, creative energy that is expressed overtly in many ways. When Mars is connected to Neptune in a difficult dialogue, eventual disillusionment in the quality and romance of the sexual energy can lead to lack of drive or to disappointment. In some instances, the individual may rely on drugs or drinking to simulate the quality of naïveté or romance that is missing, or to break down the barriers of inhibition caused by a desire for the ultimate of perfection. Fear of lack of attainment of that dream can prevent the individual to attempt to bring his sexual fantasies into reality. His dream life may be far richer than anything that could be attained on earth. He may inadvertently set up situations of disillusionment sexually in order to purify his own concept of sex. He can go to the opposite extreme and look to the sordid side of sex as a way of avoiding a letdown.

NEPTUNE IN HARD ASPECT TO MARS

Oscar Wilde had Neptune square Mars in his chart. At the pinnacle of his career, Wilde was accused and convicted of a homosexual affair. After two years in jail, Oscar was a broken man. His career was ruined and his reputation in Victorian England was completely lost. It is easy to see that the ultimate disillusionment in his life had to do with the sexual energy. No matter what were the outer circumstances, he could never have regained an idealistic outlook toward sex after such a scandal.

Oscar had Mars placed in the third house of communications, also describing writing and contractual arrangements. It ruled the eighth house of getting his needs met. That eighth house also indicates the major transformation, or turning point, in life. With Mars ruling this house, Wilde could well have been able to get what he needed from people and life through his ambition, resourcefulness, and drive. But with a strong watering down from Neptune, the probability exists that he was unable to go after what he wanted in life in a direct manner. He might have assumed he would get his needs met and he may have used sex as a way of satisfying some of those needs, assuming that whatever he did would be accepted.

Neptune rules the seventh house of marriage, in his chart. It is placed exactly opposite his ascendant in the house of work. He would have adopted an ostrich complex about his marriage and himself. He was married at the age of thirty and had two sons by that marriage. Yet he may have been terribly disillusioned about marriage or by his wife, as well as with some facets of his work. A great deal of naïveté existed about sex within the framework of marriage in Victorian England. The attitudes of the time did not lead to open, healthful confrontation and discussion about such subjects. When Neptune rules the seventh house, the person with Virgo rising tends to put the marriage partner on a pedestal in the first place. He then proceeds to box himself into a double bind. If that vision of perfection and goddess-like loveliness should stoop so low as to be a healthy, feeling, sexual creature, she can no longer live on her pedestal. If she does not respond to normal sexual exchange, she is cold and untouchable. Either way, the person with Virgo rising can be disillusioned. If, as in Wilde's case, Neptune is square Mars, the devastation is intensified because the person feels lied to. He may have assumed this goddess would be warm and responsive once marriage vows were exchanged. Or he may have felt betrayed that she slipped from her pedestal.

This aspect does not necessarily indicate homosexuality but, rather, a disillusionment with all forms of drive, ambition, sexuality, and aggressiveness. A purification process may have to do with the feelings about sexuality, drive, ambition, and all forms of combative energy. The swing between high ideals and the frustrations, aggravations, and conflicts necessary to fight for those ideals can be hard to integrate and tolerate. Mohandas Gandhi had Mars inconjunct Neptune. Mars rules the sixth house of work, and Neptune is posited in that house. Mars is placed in the first house of self-expression and personality. Gandhi was very idealistic and willing to go to bat for better conditions for India in a nonviolent way. However, after many years of progress at a snail's pace, he became disillusioned with his work. His health was broken through many fasts. At the end of his life, he had to be persuaded to arise once more to be the inspiration to his people. Gandhi may have wondered when enough was enough.

Katharine Hepburn had Neptune opposite Mars in her chart. In Hepburn's case, Mars is posited in the third house of communications, with Neptune placed in the ninth house of public relations and promotional effort. Neptune rules her fifth house of romance, and Mars rules her sixth house of work. The idealism of work in the most glamorous business in the world may have gone through a purification process in Hepburn's life. Her career went through many changes. The romantic idealism no doubt had to give way to the practical aspect of competition. Mars and Neptune in hard aspect also describes a possibility of some facts being concealed for the sake of protection; her romance with Spencer Tracy was an example of just that. She has been quoted as saying that she had the most perfect companionship possible with a "man among men." A true Neptunian romance, yet she could never marry Tracy. His strict Catholic upbringing would not allow him to divorce his wife. So her romance with him had to be carefully concealed from the public. If the facts of their relationship had been revealed in the days of her stardom, when such things were frowned upon, her film career and reputation might have been shattered, as well as Tracy's reputation. Katharine may have found herself in a position of living a lie, especially if she had to endure many public situations when she was in the company of Spencer and his wife, or when she had to continually assure the press that they were just good friends.

NEPTUNE CONJUNCT JUPITER

The combination of Neptune and Jupiter indicates tremendous enthusiasm and idealism. The level of anticipation and vision can be quite high. The expectation of reaching exciting goals makes life's prospects seem extraordinary and unusual. Since Jupiter indicates luck and Neptune describes concepts and dreams, when this energy is utilized in a practical way the potential is profound. Many especially successful film stars have this aspect in their charts. The qualities of expectation and enthusiasm can project onto film, attracting even more good fortune in the process. Jupiterian energy is especially contagious and hard to resist. It describes salesmanship as well as universal goodwill and joy. These are especially important in highly idealistic work. The individual must believe in himself or his product in order to convey that to others. With the handholding of Neptune, which describes trust, an almost naïve, Jupiterian faith in the laws of the universe brings in great good fortune.

If this fragile quality of naïve, trusting expectation is exposed to a blow from the less idealistic side of life, the trust and faith may never be the same again. An incident of rude awakening may come sooner or later in life, but at some point, purification of philosophy and expectation may be imperative. When such an event happens in the life of the individual with this aspect, if he can continue to have the same quality of enthusiasm, but with a more focused awareness, major growth is accomplished. Jupiterian energy is hard to repress, so the probability of a rebound into joy is very strong. At times, the bursting of dreams can bring devastation and an inability to deal with life. The temptation to turn to drugs or alcohol is quite strong. The desire to continue the feeling of being very high on life leads to artificial means if the natural high is missing.

The Duke of Windsor had this aspect in his chart. The conjunction was placed in the fourth house of home, ruling his first house of personality, and his tenth house of career. The aspect describes his relationship with his mother and father and his views about public life. Bertie was not cut out to be a king. Yet his sense of duty enabled him to rule for almost a year before he gave up the throne for the woman he loved. He may have expected the English people and especially his family to come to his aid in a far different manner. The letdown happened, however, and it was made quite clear that he was to give up his dream of love if he wished to continue on the throne. He didn't, yet spent the rest of his life living well, in association with glamorous international society. Neptune also describes the glamour world in general. Bertie enjoyed all the pleasure of his status without the responsibility of being king. His relationship with England and his family suffered tremendously, however.

This aspect describes a very trusting nature that can allow the person to be taken for the proverbial ride. Implied promises can be a lure and a trap to keep the person working on an idealistic level. For one young man, the devastation of discovering the reality of a situation resulted in his death. James had been working for a particular family-owned corporation and was led to believe that he was figuratively a member of the family. He believed and cherished that special position and gave his all to the business. When a power struggle ensued at the death of the father of the family, he realized with a rude awakening that indeed blood is thicker than water. He wasn't even a contender for a top position in the company he had helped to build. Because of the feeling of family membership, no agreements had been put into writing about his future with the company, but he assumed that his faithful loyalty would be rewarded. He discovered all too late that he had been building castles in the air of his imagination rather than looking at reality. He had neglected to take care of his position in a businesslike manner. This young man drove his car over a cliff after a long night of drinking to drown his sorrow. In similar situations, the individual has confessed to feeling like a fool. One's own naïveté may be the hardest thing to accept and reconcile.

Michael Tilson Thomas has Neptune conjunct Jupiter in his chart. Michael was the director of the Boston Symphony at the age of twenty-six. He had played piano by ear at age five and begun piano lessons at age ten. His career as a pianist had begun at eighteen and lasted six years, until be became assistant conductor of the Boston Symphony. The Neptune-Jupiter conjunction is placed in the eighth house of getting his needs met, and rules the second house of income, and the eleventh house of groups, associations, and organizations. The quality of high inspiration indicated by this aspect is released through his music. He fulfills the transformation indicated by the eighth house and sends that high-level energy to the world. Music is the medium of his message of hope and vision.

In extreme cases of mental unbalance, this conjoining of Neptune and Jupiter can describe a manic state. The individual may continue on a very precarious high without the people around him being aware of the unbalance. Usually a terrible crash comes, plummeting the individual to the depths. When Neptune and Jupiter rule the first house of personality in particular, the person may see himself as a savior of the world, a prophet, or a Christ reincarnation. People exist only to feed the dreams of his imagination. In many cases, this aspect describes a person who looks for a guru or religious figure he can worship. If he selects a true teacher, he will soon be led to search within for his own inspiration and connection. If, however, he finds a false prophet, he may discover all too painfully the feet of clay. He needs to find ways to express high anticipation in an imperfect world.

Laurence Olivier has this aspect in his chart, placed in the second house of income, and ruling the eleventh house of groups and friendships, as well as the seventh house of marriage. In working associations with film groups and with theater, he found an outlet for the ephemeral quality of this conjunction. His marriage to Vivien Leigh seemed to be the epitome of an ideal blending of two extraordinary people. Yet the disillusionment came when Vivien's mental illness became extreme and intolerable. Vivien fell in love with someone else. Since the aspect ruling his seventh house not only indicates what he looks for in a mate, but the quality of personality of that mate, it may have been Vivien who was disillusioned, naïve, and fragile. Their attempts to recapture the dream failed and led to the divorce. Sir Laurence was able to find another idealistic, fortunate partnership when he married Joan Plowright. He was then able to combine marriage with the friendship he really wanted and to create the ideal relationship.

Katharine Hepburn has this conjunction placed in two houses, the eighth and the ninth. Jupiter in the eighth house of getting her needs met, and Neptune in the ninth house of publicity, public relations, and recognition, are both in opposition to Mars and Uranus in the third house of communications. This balance of strongly aggressive planets would enable Hepburn to swing between her idealistic, visionary qualities and her need for spontaneity and aggression. High enthusiasm in her life is expressed creatively and in practical financial areas, with that conjunction ruling the fifth house of talent, and the second house of income. She may have had to learn to negotiate contracts and deal with money in a more aggressive fashion than would have been natural to her. She was certainly able to market her talent without losing her integrity.

This is also a generational aspect, occurring approximately every twelve or thirteen years in a different sign of the zodiac. It would seem that nature intends to bring forth conditions and people on an extremely high beam of inspiration, intuition, and vision to test the waters of new conditions. Unfortunately, Saturn also concurs with Neptune periodically to bring about a shift of perspective. Generationally, people can tend to swing from the highest of the high to the doubt of the Neptune-Saturn conjunction. It would seem that the very cycles of nature are designed to purify and restore balance between overly idealistic concepts (Neptune-Jupiter) and the negative, disillusionment (Neptune-Saturn).

One very personable man who seemed to find the balance of Jupiter and Neptune in his own life is Mac Adam. Mac, a former manager of newspapers in England, is now retired and living in Ibiza with his wife, Trudy. Mac and Trudy are involved in many local theatrical productions as well as the international films that are shot on location in Ibiza. Mac has Neptune conjunct Jupiter in the eleventh house of friends, and ruling his sixth house of work, and third house of communications. Mac has the contagious good humor that endears him to friends and associates and makes him a wonderful conversationalist. He described his feelings about these areas of his life in a very succinct manner. He said, "Every cloud has a silver lining. I'm not a pessimist. I'm a great believer in nature, not religion. I believe in history, not predestination. Human nature being what it is, I don't believe in perfection."

I asked Mac about the curiosity that is associated with Jupiterian energy, especially in connection with friendships. He replied, "I'm fascinated with people and what makes them tick, not from a psychological level, but from a curiosity level. Strangers are fun. Sometimes when I know people too well, they cease to interest me. If I've drained my curiosity, then they don't interest me unless they are *really* interesting. Sometimes good people may bore me more than bad ones! I'll actually make allowances for anything but a lack of imagination." Jupiter's placement in a chart indicates the need for new challenges. The thrill comes from going after what is out of reach.

Since this aspect also describes the kind of work Mac would want, or the quality of energy he would invest in his work, I asked him if he had been disillusioned in any way. He reluctantly admitted, "In business I lost a little interest in what I was doing. I was in the wrong job. I'm not a businessman, because I'm not hard enough. I hate haggling or bargaining. It can create bad blood. So I was in a position to argue about prices and contracts and it was not what was in my nature. I am not competitive or jealous. I'm content with what I have, but I do want to do things my way. I *hate* gratuitous advice. If I need something, I'll ask." I finally was able to have confirmation about my feelings of a big letdown in conjunction with this aspect. Mac said, "Yes, an injustice was done and I felt hard done by. I was doing my best. I like to do my best and be accepted. I don't react well to criticism." In Mac's case, the ability to bounce back has put him in a whole new lifestyle, with many unusual friendships for stimulation and a whole new field of work. He summed it all up with "I always hope for the best, but expect the worst, so I'm never disappointed. If it happens, great. If not, I didn't really expect it anyway."

NEPTUNE IN HARD ASPECT TO JUPITER

The square between these two planets can intensify the unrealistic approach to matters. One voice is giving directions about dreams, idealism, vision, and perfection, while the other voice is encouraging those dreams to higher and higher levels. The end result can be an almost manic high that is bound to result in major disillusionment and disappointment of some kind. This is the aspect that astrologer Lynne Palmer describes as the con-man aspect. The level of unreality can reach such proportions that the individual convinces, or cons, himself into believing his dreams. In the true manic state, he shuts out the world unless the circumstances augment his particular level of idealism. He will not tolerate negativity or cold water dropped on his dreams.

The conjunction between these two planets is easier to release in a direct fashion, although characteristics of the two aspects are basically similar. The additional color (described by the square or opposition) to an already existent state of visionary process can be quite difficult if the individual vacillates between the two extreme states of being high—the Neptunian, illusionary high and the Jupiterian, optimistic high. He may gild the lily, allow himself to trust unrealistically, and assume too much in his daily associations. The world and people can constantly let him down.

Both Puccini and Theodore Dreiser had Neptune square Jupiter in their charts. In the chart of Puccini, Jupiter is placed in the eighth house of transformation, with Neptune in the fifth house of creativity and romance. Jupiter rules his third house of communications. He was born into a musical family and continued the family heritage by producing great melodic operas that are still performed throughout the world. But his stories were tragic. Their common theme was the idealism of love and the tragedy of the disillusionment of romance. In *La Bohème*, the poverty of Rodolfo and Mimi leads to the breakup of a passionate love affair. *Madame Butterfly* tells the story of a delicate Japanese girl devoted to the American father of her child. She is sure that he will return to her and his baby. When he returns with an American bride, the devastation is too much and poor Butterfly kills herself.

Theodore Dreiser also wrote of the tragedy of love. In *An American Tragedy*, the Neptune-Jupiter aspect is represented by the hero, who falls in love with an heiress. Just as he discovers the world of wealth and dreams opening the bounty for him to taste and capture, his former factory-working girlfriend announces her pregnancy. He loses everything, including his own life, in an attempt to hold onto the vision. Dreiser must have had some such experiences in his own life, to be able to write so poignantly about the broken dreams. Jupiter was placed in the tenth house of public life and career. Neptune was posited in the seventh house of marriage. Jupiter rules his third house of communications, with Neptune ruling the house of work. He was able to use the very quality of energy indicated in his own chart through his work in areas of communication.

The most tragic example of Neptune in opposition to Jupiter in a chart can be seen in the life of Marilyn Monroe. Neptune is placed in her first house, describing a naïve, idealistic quality that was especially obvious in her personality. When Neptune is connected to the ascendant, the individual sees the world through rose-colored glasses, and the world may see the person through those same rosy glasses. Marilyn lived in a dream world to prevent the harsh reality of her childhood from creeping in. The mirage she wove in her head helped her deal with conditions that were nothing short of tragic. She actually created her place in the sun by veering toward the glamour world and films in particular. Her fragility of appearance was one the camera loved, for with Neptune on the ascendant, the camera does have a love affair with the person, yet it was only the mask to cover the perseverance and ambition that lay behind.

Jupiter, in Marilyn's chart, is placed in the seventh house of marriage or partnership, in opposition to her Neptune. The final glorious luck in her life seemed to lie with fortunate partnerships. With an opposition to Jupiterian luck, she was bound to be disap-

pointed or never satisfied. Her first marriage did not take her into
the magic kingdom she yearned for. Her second major love was for
her agent, who forced her down Hollywood's throats, then died just
as her success was assured. The suddenness of his death made the
marriage, which would have secured her life, impossible. Joe
DiMaggio took Marilyn on a whirlwind tour into another land of
magic, but as devoted as was Joe, the marriage was shattered. No
doubt the breakup of that relationship was one more major disappointment in what promised to be glorious and ideal. Then came
New York, Lee Strasberg, and Arthur Miller. Arthur represented
everything Marilyn seemed to be missing in her life. She must have
felt very naïve and a babe in the woods with such an erudite man.
He was brilliant, intellectual, successful, and aloof. Again a disappointment in partnership. With Neptune describing her eighth
house of death, that mystery is still not solved. Some say the reality
has been covered up by the CIA, while still others say it was a mere
overdose of sleeping pills. The underlying fact remains that
Marilyn's life was glamorous, a dream come true, and a mirage.
Arthur Miller wrote a play about his marriage to her. The title
describes the Neptune-Jupiter opposition perfectly. He called it *After the Fall.*

NEPTUNE CONJUNCT SATURN

Whenever Saturn is aspecting a planet, the probability is that the
weight of Saturn represses or squelches the energy described by the
other planet. In the case of Saturn and Neptune, the judgment
imposed by Saturn tends to negate the vision and hope of Neptune.
The result is a "What's the use?" attitude toward life or specific
situations. The external limitations described by Saturn prevent the
individual with this aspect from seeing the overview. Hope and
trust, vision and dreams give way to the unrelenting pressures of
restrictive conditions. In the case of a conjunction, however, there
is a wonderful possibility of turning the situation around to see the
beauty and idealism in a world of limitation. Usually it takes an
incident in life to enable the person to knock down the walls of his
playpen, take greater responsibility, and fly above what formerly
held him down.

Neptune describes the purification process. In the conjoining of

Saturn, that purification has to do with the quality of responsibility. When the individual accepts his or her *ultimate* responsibility, he or she is free to soar into the realms of idealism. There is no one more capable of bringing better conditions into the world than one with this aspect, once he has climbed out of the pit of Saturnian limitation. This choice belongs to the individual. When this kind of major commitment is made, the individual with Neptune conjunct Saturn can live firmly rooted in the traditional, earthbound existence while his head is in the clouds. He can find practical ways to bring concepts into reality. He purifies a self-defeating attitude of "You can't fight City Hall" into something visionary yet practical. He doesn't break the rules of tradition, he soars above them to find a more ideal way. He can deal with conformity, yet bring fresh inspiration into old methods.

Charles F. Luce did just that when he revitalized the staid image of Con Edison in New York City. He introduced more courteous service and better public relations into the existing system. His concerns go toward other social programs as well. In his chart, Neptune conjunct Saturn is found in the tenth house of career. Saturn rules the third house of communications, and Neptune rules the fifth house of investments, creativity, and the gambling instincts. Luce would not be able to express creativity or any gambling instincts unless he had taken the precaution to investigate the practicality of an investment of time, energy, or talent. He would naturally opt for heavy responsibilities in public life, rather than trusting creative instincts. After proving to himself his practical sense of responsibility, he could begin to deal with his concepts of the future. He could then begin to express more idealism in the career arena.

Betty Ford also has Neptune conjunct Saturn in her chart. The placement in her chart is in the eleventh house of friends, groups, and associations. Neptune rules her seventh house of partnership or marriage, and also the eighth house of income and transmutation. Saturn rules the fifth house of children, creativity, entertainment, talent. Betty was married for a short time before her marriage to Jerry Ford. If Betty had been working on the negative side of her chart, she might have felt duty-bound to stay in a marriage without romance or hope. As it was, she was divorced. She then met Jerry Ford and found the romantic marriage of her dreams. Their devotion and loyalty to each other was apparent in the short time Ford was President of the United States. The eighth house describes not only the way in which an individual gets his needs met, but the quality of his gift to humanity. When Neptune rules this house, the gift to give is that of uplifting, inspiring, giving hope for the future. Betty conquered cancer and an addiction to drugs and alcohol. She shared this with the world through interviews, television appearances, and personal talks so that she could inspire others to change their lives as well. Her message was one of inspiration: "If I can do it, so can you."

Dean Martin has Neptune conjunct Saturn in his chart. The placement is in his fifth house of creativity, children, talent, and gambling instincts. Saturn rules career activity and friends, with Neptune ruling the twelfth house of subconscious processes or behind-the-scenes activity. Although Dean is a singer and has appeared on stage much of his life, his television career has also kept him working behind the scenes. On his shows, Dean carried a coffee cup wherever he went; his frequent jokes about his cup made it obvious that it did not hold coffee. His attitude and humor are an indication of the inner message of bitterness hidden behind a façade of charm. Dean is never sober. His long-time friendship with Jerry Lewis has been terminated and his career steady but uninspired for quite a long time. With Saturn ruling the twelfth house, a deep karmic guilt may have induced a disillusioned attitude about many hopeful situations in life, even prenatally. He was able to rise above conditions imposed by family structure and express his talent, but it would seem that at some point, Dean simply gave up.

Jack Paar has the same aspect in his chart. His humor is negative and disparaging, especially after his bitter battle with the networks. The conjunction in his chart is placed in the sixth and seventh houses, exactly opposite his ascendant. Saturn is in the sixth house of work, and rules the first house of personality, and twelfth house of subconscious processes and behind-the-scenes activity. Neptune is the seventh house of partnership, and rules the second house of income. Jack had a very long-running show on television and was able to have an outlet for his unusual talent. Yet the sullenness began to come through the wit, and finally he gave up trying to cover up his defeatist attitude. In his case, he really was not able to fight City Hall or, in this case, the executives of NBC. If Jack had taken a different attitude toward his dispute, obviously financial, he might have found a resolution to the problem. In many cases, when a person is tired or unwilling to continue in a responsible position, he will find a special way to set it up so that he has an out and is relieved of his burden. The attitude of "What's the use?" is a wonderful way of preventing new conditions from prevailing.

NEPTUNE IN HARD ASPECT TO SATURN

In the hard aspect between Neptune and Saturn, the defeatist attitude can be especially strong. Life may seem to present a series of events to test the faith of one with this aspect. Again, there are two voices working against each other. Neptune's message is hope and trust, and Saturn's dialogue is practicality, diligence, and routine. Since Neptune describes a purification process, it may be necessary for the earthbound attitudes of Saturn to be lifted into the realm of new inspiration. With an outer test from the universe, an individual with this aspect has a chance to renew his faith in all the bounty of life, or give up and give in to despair. The original feelings of defeat may set these conditions into motion.

One person who has overcome devastating tests from life is Patricia Neal. Patricia has Neptune placed in the eighth house of getting her needs met and death, and ruling the third house of communications. Saturn, overshadowing this idealistic expectancy, is placed in the eleventh house of group activity, and rules her second house of income. Neptune, with its subtlety, is so personal that it is almost impossible to know what goes on in the inner workings of the mind of another. It is the planet of intuition. We can intuit from Patricia's chart that some major disillusionment with her ability to get her needs met, perhaps in connection with her film work, led to an original feeling of despair. She might have hesitated to ask for what she really wanted, and may have been terribly letdown when contracts did not provide what she deserved. But we can only assume that this is so.

What we know as fact is the series of events in her life that would have completely devastated another, less courageous human being. First, her son Theo was killed in an automobile accident. Her daughter Olivia then died of encephalitis. Finally, Patricia suffered a series of paralyzing strokes that left her without speech. She

spent two years relearning to walk and speak. To counterbalance
the disillusionment of her Neptune-Saturn square, Patricia has the
Sun conjunct Jupiter in her chart. Her optimism and need for challenges enabled her to completely recover and win an Oscar for her
role in *The Subject Was Roses.*

In psychological terms, the eighth house describes the gift one
has to give to humanity once the transformation in life is completed. With Neptune placed in this house, film is a natural medium
for whatever message Patricia needs to convey. With the square
between Neptune and Jupiter, Neal may have had to learn how to
accept help, and how to expect and trust that her needs would be
met, since she was totally helpless on her own. Eventually she was
able to say to the world, "It can be done. There is hope and fresh
inspiration no matter how devastating the circumstances in life."
Patricia never conveyed publicly how close she may have come to
giving up, but, again, we can assume it was not easy.

Paul Lynde also had Neptune square Saturn in his chart. Paul's
brand of humor was self-deprecating and negative to an extreme. In
his case, Neptune was posited in the first house of personality, and
ruling the ninth house of publicity and promotional efforts. Saturn
was placed in the fourth house of home, ruling the sixth house of
work and health. His messages of despair must have come from his
mother, even inadvertently. Her own life must have been much less
than ideal and glamorous. Paul was consumed by self-doubt. Possible early traumas in his life may have left him negative and without
hope. His humor reflected the "What's the use?" attitude. His
worry-wart tendencies made it very difficult for anyone to work with
him without taking on the role of encouraging him that indeed
everything would go well. The individual with this difficult dialogue
within is constantly looking for reassurance and permission to
hope. Yet he will never accept or totally believe it until he begins to
trust his own sense of perseverance and responsibility. He must
have an inner conviction that he is capable. Paul did not seem to be
able to make that transition during his lifetime. He died while still
at the peak of his career and life potential.

Anton Chekhov had Saturn inconjunct Neptune. This aspect is
called a growth aspect by astrologers Louise and Bruno Huber and
is considered by them to be especially important in a chart. Chekhov wrote simply and beautifully about poverty and despair. He

also portrayed the joy and hope that could be attained even under such conditions. In his own life, he observed the reality of the human condition. His plays and stories were not about defeat, but about life in its simplest form, the common denominator of humanity. Suffering on some level is not confined to the peasants of Russia. Survival is real, not always beautiful, but not always without hope. Chekhov's ultimate message may have been directed toward himself and his own struggle with that hope.

Gloria Swanson has Neptune in opposition to Saturn in her chart. Saturn is conjunct her ascendant, describing her personality, with Neptune in opposition in the house of marriage or partnership. Neptune rules her third house of communications, and Saturn rules her second house of income. After her first marriage had ended, Gloria's defeatist attitude showed itself in her feeling that she would never marry again. She adopted her second child. However, Gloria overcame her self-doubts about partnership matters and continued trying to find a perfect marriage until age seventy-seven, when she married her sixth husband, a man twenty years her junior. Gloria proved beyond doubt that the hard aspect between Neptune and Saturn can indeed be purified into constant new hope, for she finally found her ideal mate after many failed attempts. The balance is achieved through a practical look at the dreams and hopes of perfection and ideal conditions in life.

NEPTUNE CONJUNCT URANUS

Neptune and Uranus coincide in the heavens very rarely. The last conjunction was from 1817 until approximately 1826, and the next one will take place from late 1988 until 1998. Everyone born during those times had or will have that conjunction in their charts. The combination of high energy produced a group of especially inspired people in the early 1800s. They might be termed, in general, the geniuses of an age. The range of productivity covered fields of literature, science, and government. Many of the people born at this time were especially inspired. If we consider that Uranian energy is like electricity and Neptunian quality is gaseous, the combination is very charged. Uranus describes enlightenment, whereas Neptune describes inspiration. A flow of energy on inspirational levels seems to indicate an ability to tap the akashic records of time and space, where all thought and action are contained. Intuition and brilliance bring new inventions, new consciousness, and change on a humanistic level.

Karl Marx had this aspect. His philosophy of a truly humanitarian Utopia was bastardized into communism. Novelists Herman Melville, Emily Brontë, George Eliot, and Ivan Turgenev shared this aspect with Walt Whitman, Henry David Thoreau, and Charles Baudelaire. Feodor Dostoevsky and Gustave Flaubert also had Neptune conjunct Uranus in their charts. Clara Barton, founder of the Red Cross, Mary Baker Eddy, founder of Christian Science, and Queen Victoria had the aspect as well. English socialist and philosopher Herbert Spencer and German socialist Friedrich Engels shared the aspect with English adventurer Sir Richard Burton. Presidents Rutherford B. Hayes and Ulysses S. Grant had the conjunction in their charts as well as composers Johann Strauss and Stephen Foster. French scientist Louis Pasteur seems to epitomize the potential of this inspired combination with his major contribution to health.

When this aspect returns again to herald the incoming new century, the world will (it is hoped) have completed its transition into the Age of Aquarius. Exciting new concepts that are even now emerging will become realities among everyone on earth. Health, science, literature, and inspiration for the future will no doubt undergo major transformation. Such exciting concepts emerging from all sources and in all areas will change mankind's way of thinking to one of greater awareness. Negativity and doubt should be a pattern of past history. We can only lend our awareness of possibilities of a greater age by individual attunement to spiraling sources of inspiration.

NEPTUNE IN HARD ASPECT TO URANUS

Whenever Uranus makes a difficult aspect to another planet, it indicates a special time of awakening. That awakening process is never easy. It seems to arrive just when conditions seem settled and comfortable. It ultimately seems to blast away any slim chance of remaining in a comfortable rut. The aspect between Neptune and Uranus is no different. Old conditions must give way to the new, yet the scare connected with that birth process is strong, because the results of that change are unknown. With this particular aspect, Neptunian attunement and vision are in contradiction to the external conditions. The overview of Neptune seems to become obscured or diffused when Uranian shake-ups occur. If anything, the quality of inspiration seems to be filtered through a subtle, velvet, Neptunian fog that can distort the picture and contort the ease of bringing about new conditions. A subtle inner struggle about risks can make matters seem unclear. A mirage effect exists.

On a universal level, the new age that must soon be born from such a Neptune-square-Uranus aspect must go through the difficulties of that birth process. Old patterns must be broken so that enlightenment can pour forth, but resistance in this case is ephemeral. There can be a lack of confrontation that is harder to deal with than an actual disagreement. On the form side of life, that is, life on earth, conditions may be disillusioning, yet the desire for growth coincides with a vision and intuition and concern for new conditions that might replace what appears to be fact. An amount of trust in the senses and the conceptual realm may be necessary. People born with this aspect in their natal charts have a chance to be the enlightened showers of the way, but it is first necessary to work through the scare on an individual level to bring about what the inner vision dictates. It can be quite frightening to listen to inspiration when exterior conditions and people are distinctly upset about the results of what the awareness dictates. The person may hesitate to take the risk of trusting his or her right-brain concepts of heightened intuition. Eventually, it must be done. If not, stagnation of the person's creative juices can occur. Possible physical disabilities may even manifest from a lack of expression. The individual may try to develop an ostrich complex, hiding his head in the sand as far as the genius potential is concerned, yet ultimately conditions will force a look at the true potential.

This aspect is quite rare. Neptune and Uranus were in a square aspect to each other from mid 1865 until mid 1874 and not again until May 1951. The aspect lasted until August 1958. People born during these periods of time are especially unique, inventive, and futuristic. Marie Curie had this aspect in her chart. The struggle she endured to convince science of the powers of radiation are well documented. Her attunement to that inner vision led her through incredibly difficult times in her life when discouragement and lack of support from anyone but her husband must have tempted her to stop the experiments. Once she was able to bring forth the manifest proof of what her Neptunian inspiration told her, she was hailed as a genius and has been revered by everyone since that time. Orville and Wilbur Wright, also born with this aspect in their charts, had no easy time convincing people that man could fly. They were ridiculed and put through tests that would have stopped people with less vision.

Evangeline Adams also had this aspect in her chart. She was without doubt the person who changed the course of astrology in this century, through her own courage and vision. Evangeline went to trial in the courts of New York to prove that astrology was not fortunetelling. She insisted on a public trial in order to legalize astrology and its practice in New York. Astrologers can be grateful to her for lifting astrology onto a new level of acceptance. It must have been quite scary to go through such a test, even though she knew the power of her subject. Even now, many people, in ignorance and fear, look askance at astrology. How much more skepticism must have existed in her day! Evangeline had Neptune in her first house of personality, with Neptune ruling the same house. Uranus was placed in the fourth house of home, and described her relationship with her father as well as the conditions at the end of her life. Uranus ruled the twelfth house of the subconscious. She was born into a wealthy and proper Bostonian family who must have expected something quite different from their daughter. Her father, described by Uranus in her chart, may have paved the way for her on a subtle level, however. He was obviously a unique man in his own right. The fame that came to her was almost accidental. She was staying in a hotel in New York City and correctly predicted a fire that would take place. Thereafter she was swamped with clients, among whom was J. P. Morgan. The enlightenment and vision of this special woman brought about new conditions for a Uranian-ruled subject, astrology. The people born in the 1950s may have a similar task ahead of them. Whether that new level of consciousness will have to do with astrology, space travel, or science remains to be seen. A strong time of destiny for this generation will no doubt come when Neptune and Uranus are conjunct again, from 1988 until 1998.

Scott was born with this aspect in his chart. Neptune is placed in his fifth house of creativity, investments, and talent, and rules his first house of personality. Uranus is placed in the eighth house of getting needs met, and rules the twelfth house of the subconscious. Scott is aware of his psychic or intuitive processes, as he works in an area where hunches and intuition play a large part in the overall success. He is involved with the stock market and especially with commodities, which is the most speculative field of all. He described his sense of timing in this way. "Sometimes I say to myself, 'I know I have to do this. I know it's right,' but I very rarely follow that impulse. Then I miss out. I want to kick myself, but the problem is that even though I know it should have been done, I like to look through rose-colored glasses. If I was too slow the first time, then I decide to be quicker the next time. But sometimes when I'm quicker the next time, I should have been slower. Luckily in the stock market, many opportunities present themselves so that I may have five to eight opportunities in a day. The odds then balance out."

I talked to Scott about the tendency of a Pisces ascendant to avoid confrontation. Since Uranus is square the ruler of his ascendant, it could make him want to run away prematurely or become nervous about reaching out for his dreams. He was quite candid about his dreams and aspirations. He described it in this way: "I'm very happy with the status quo. If I'm content, then even when the grass looks greener on the other side, I won't necessarily jump in and give it a shot if I have to give up what I already have. It might be a fear of failure, but I see it as more of a Gatsby syndrome. After you dream about it for so long and you put so much effort into it, when you finally get there, it's not what you expected. I'd rather not take the chance." We discussed his choice of a career, for with the particular aspect in his chart, he might have focused talent on other areas. He agreed. "I tried to act and model for a summer, but it made me very nervous. I've always been nervous in front of people. I'm good with one or two people but not with crowds." I suggested that the fear of not being able to get his needs met or earn enough money might have had something to do with his avoiding films and acting. Yet the gambling impulse associated with the fifth house found its expression in his life through investments and the stock market. My feelings are that Scott may have extraordinary events in his life that will propel him into more awareness of that inner, intuitive power. He may yet discover a special talent that fulfills the promise of his ability to enlighten others through his own vision.

ASPECTS TO PLUTO

PLUTO DESCRIBES THE MOST PROFOUND ENERGY IN THE zodiac. It is the planet of transformation, although with each boost of dynamic energy described by any particular planet, the growth process can also be transforming. Growth through Saturn is slow and painful, through Uranus it is lightning-like and nerve-wracking, and through Neptune it is a process of clearing away the mists of illusion. But growth through Pluto is like an atomic blast—traumatic, and reaching from the depths to the heights. There are no in-between stages with Plutonian energy. When the rug is pulled out from under, a readjustment comes whether one is ready or not, for this is energy that works on a cosmic, universal level. It can feel like Moses wrestling with the angel on the mountain. Plutonian growth burns away the gross material in life in order to purify.

Pluto aspects can indicate the areas of life's ultimate testing ground. Periodically, the individual must again experience the lesson of the Garden of Eden. He sees the apple dangling before his very eyes, and it is beautiful and shiny, delicious and tempting. If he is hungry, he might do or give anything to take a bite of that apple, even knowing that a dangerous hook lurks inside. For if one succumbs to the temptation to compromise his principles, there is always a price to pay. If he decides the end justifies the means, he loses in one way or another. He may merely lose his soul. Yet with the resistance to that temptation—and the test is never an easy one —he rises to the mountaintop, where he can soar like an eagle. He rises from his belly to the skies.

Just as Saturn describes lead, Uranus describes electricity, and Neptune gas, Pluto describes plutonium. The analogy of the atomic bomb can effectively describe the Plutonian energy. The dropping of the atomic bomb on Nagasaki was terrible and drastic. The destruction was complete and agonizing. Yet the war ended. It may be a matter of history to determine whether that was the only way to put an end to destruction on a wider scale, but we now live in fear and in the shadow of the power of that destruction. Within the individual, a war can exist between the power of transformation and good intent and the negative or revengeful qualities. The higher self may have to drop an atom bomb within the life of the person to stop the negative, usually self-destructive tendencies. It can happen when the higher self decides it is time for the individual to transform his potential from destructive to the highest constructive energy.

Pluto describes cosmic consciousness. It is like the *kundalini*, or serpent fire, which is trapped, blocked, and locked inside each individual until he is ready to tap and transform that power. But just as in raising kundalini, the process can be dangerous. It must be integrated carefully—drop by drop of water on the stone of life. It is like being put in the furnace to make steel from iron; the searing pain may be too much to handle. It is only when the individual is willing to monitor each thought, action, and deed in his life to be sure of the highest motivation for the good of all that he is allowed finally to experience the brilliance of the kingdom of heaven within himself. If he wants to play games, manipulate, or compromise principles, he must remain fast to the inner rules of earth and the wheel of karma that keeps him bound.

If it were only possible to understand that the traumas in life are the most powerful opportunity to grow on a cosmic level, each individual might be begging for more tests, rather than more pleasure and ease of living. It is hard to see on that universal level when one exists on earth. Under difficult Pluto aspects, something may be taken away from the individual. The more he is willing to let go of that situation, the more room he makes in his life for bigger and better conditions. He may have to make room for dynamic new opportunities or circumstances, but the tendency is to want to hang on to the familiar and comfortable things he knows. He is like a child. He doesn't really know that the universe, or his higher self, has infinitely more-exquisite things in store for him if he'd only let go of what he has outgrown. He is unaware of the divine order of things that he cannot see, focusing instead on his own immediate desires. Since Pluto describes will, the ultimate transmutation is from willfulness to attunement with divine will.

The analogy of the child's ego state is particularly appropriate.

The child can be innocent or he can be manipulative, overly forceful, temperamental, and demanding of attention. He might prefer negative attention to positive strokes and good reward for his behavior. In terms of Transactional Analysis, the child ego is the most powerful. The message is in essence "I want what I want when I want it." The Plutonian energy has much the quality of that message. There is an intensity, a determination, that allows nothing to get in the way of what this person wants. He can be extremely potent, charismatic, and compulsive in his desires. There is no halfway effort associated with this energy. He may run over anyone or anything that is in the way of the attainment of his desires.

Pluto was the mythological god of the underworld. His domain was Hades. But the transformed Pluto is the angel that sits at the right hand of God. The dual symbology of Pluto is the serpent and the eagle. The quality of temptation that is described by this energy is life or death. When the pain is too great, the lower self gives up to the higher self. The transmutation is the phoenix rising from the ashes. The quality of energy is likened to a turbulent body of water that is either destructive in its force or can be harnessed to send electricity out to light up cities. Strong Pluto in an individual chart can produce the priestess-courtesan complex. One is never very far away from the other.

The planet Pluto has remained somewhat of a mystery as far as clear interpretation goes. Scorpio is a sign of mystery, for that transformation process is a mysterious one. The burning out of the lower fires is analogous to a death of sorts. The rebirth that is part of the process brings innocence, highest awareness, a sense of cosmic oneness. Scorpio rules the eighth house in natural progression. That has been described as the house of death. But in psychological terms the transcendence has to do with getting needs met. The eighth house in a chart indicates how the individual gets what he needs and wants from life, whether those needs are monetary or simply aid of some sort. With transformation on any level, the individual becomes less concerned about things for himself and becomes concerned with what is good for humanity or the group as a whole. Pluto's position in a particular house in the individual chart describes the area where that major transformation can occur, and the aspects indicate how easy it is to make that transformation.

Pluto describes the development of the child ego state. If Pluto is well aspected, it would appear that the child had no major traumas in early life, and therefore is more aware of his potency and effectiveness. He never forces a situation or a person. Yet if Pluto is not well aspected, the indication is that traumatic situations in early life led to an intensity that can sometimes be annoying and aggravating. In this instance, the determination and compulsive behavior can antagonize and push people away. His childhood methods continue, and he can still be traumatized by lack of proper response from people and situations around him.

Imagine two children at a party. One child may feel especially loved and assured of his safety. He is so adorable and charismatic that even if he sits in a corner and is absorbed in eating ice cream and cake, the people in the room will be attracted to him. He will probably have lots of pats on the head. The other child has been neglected, ignored, and has had early traumatic experiences. He is likely to yank on the skirts of the people at the party, saying in one way or another, "Please notice me." The adults will respond in a manner that brings the wrong kind of attention, and once again the child feels traumatized.

Prince Charles of England is a Scorpio. He has been taught responsibility, but, we can assume, has always had his needs met. He certainly knew as a child that he would go to the right schools, have the right friendships, toys, and opportunities. He would not be ignored. When Prince Charles grew up, he would be correct in assuming that life would continue to bring him what he needs and wants at the right time. He would therefore not be inclined to push a situation that seemed uncertain or involved people of dubious integrity. He would avoid shady activities, and have less reason to rebel than someone who did not have the same childhood conditions. If Prince Charles wanted to put together a major project, he would want only the right people in his group. His motivation would probably be for the good of all concerned, since he would have no reason for personal gain with that project. He would certainly be in a powerful position to affect the lives of people around him.

The child who has had the rug pulled out from under him goes into what transactional analysis calls the "little professor" ego state. He learns early on that unless he screams loudly, he may not get the attention he needs or may not even get fed. He then learns to scream loudly all through life. He may go "underground" and learn how to manipulate the situations and people around him. He plays games with Mommy and Daddy to get what he wants from them. He is not willing to assume that his needs will be met without his giving the situation a helping hand. Let's say his best friend has a new bicycle and he also wants a bicycle. He may be well aware of the difficulty in convincing his parents that he is old enough or that he deserves that toy. So he plays one parent against the other, is very effective, gets the bicycle—but is actually too young. When he tries to ride that new toy, he may fall off, break his arm, and then be in double pain, because he knows it is all his own fault. Chances are he will never enjoy riding that bicycle again. When Pluto is not well aspected in the natal chart, there is a tendency to go after a situation no matter what the consequences might be. It is like justifying the means by the end result. If the individual continues in this fashion all his life, eventually the games and manipulation catch up with him and he suffers a major trauma all over again. Finally, he is tired of the pain and learns to let go.

Letting go of a situation, especially if it is something terribly important to one, is not easy. Perhaps when the Plutonian situation is transmuted through a desire for the greatest good for all, the eagle can emerge where the serpent formerly existed. Another analogy for this energy has to do with a jigsaw puzzle: If a person pounds the wrong piece of the puzzle into place, he will only break up the whole puzzle. He must be content to let each piece of the puzzle turn up in time. He can then complete the picture.

Plutonian energy is also like a body of water, quite turbulent in its patterns. If a swollen river is allowed to flood the riverbanks, devastation follows; yet if that water is dammed, its energy can light up cities. The Plutonian energy must be conserved, dammed up, and channeled onto the highest level of activity for ultimate effectiveness. A child will not always be a child, yet the child ego state is the most powerful of all.

Pluto describes masses of people or major corporations. It also describes television. The television industry reaches masses of people and could be the most effective tool imaginable to change the lives of people who watch what is televised. Yet the compromises that exist in shows that are aired are quite obvious. TV is an effective method of communication, yet how much more so if only highly motivated shows were produced. The change in consciousness of the daily audience might be remarkable. In no way can one imply that the child ego or the highly motivated situations are dull. A child's need is to play. It is the way in which the child plays that is important. Pluto describes extremes. It can rule the underworld, yet it is an evangelical quality. It can describe a swing from the courtesan to the priestess. There are no halfway measures where Pluto is concerned.

When Pluto rules or is posited in the first house, it describes the personality, conditions in childhood, and viewpoint toward life. The survival issues are connected with the child's need for power. If Pluto is well aspected, the individual can be especially magnetic, charismatic, powerful, capable. He cannot do things in a half-hearted manner and may easily be able to put projects together. This is the natural placement for the producer. He is able to combine the right people for a major, effective outcome. He works well with groups and can literally transform situations around him by his magnetic quality. He may have a great need for play, but the world is his playground. He will always be a child at heart, and therefore retains a youthful appearance and zest for life. He seems to attract the right situations to himself without making much effort.

If Pluto is not well aspected, childhood may have been especially upsetting or traumatic. The individual may have had a traumatic disillusionment and learned early on how to "go underground" and manipulate. He can be overly forceful, sneaky, or game-playing. Pluto is one of the most rebellious qualities of energy when it is not well aspected. His underlying message, behind an intense countenance, is "I'll show you, I'll get even." He may be unaware of the intensity and forcefulness of his personality and be hurt when people back away from him. He will never go unnoticed, and eventually learns how to curb the tendency to force the situations around him. Any revengeful attitudes will only boomerang eventually.

When Pluto rules the second house or is situated therein, it describes a powerful ability to make money. One may also have a compulsive need to spend money, yet his expenditures are not on small "toys." He will save money carefully, then blow it on a major purchase. He may also be a compulsive spender, buying multiples of everything. He earns funds best through anything that is far-reaching or powerful, or through manufacturing or producing a major project. He may earn money through major organizations or through something like television. He needs to have fun where income is concerned. If Pluto is well aspected, he is especially potent in connection with income, but if it is not, he may play games with money or manipulate to obtain it. He can use the financial arena to "get even" or prove himself, or at least try to do so. His motivation may determine his potency with funds.

When that powerful planet describes the third house of communications, or is placed in that house, one is most effective in areas of communications. He can negotiate, discuss things that will be of powerful benefit to people around him, or be involved in activities that have a transformational effect. His siblings and other relatives are especially charismatic, effective people, and interrelationships in general are quite potent. He will make a great impact through activities that will reach many people, such as in television or the communications fields in general. He may have been especially powerful in early school years. In a positive way, he can put together big deals or powerful situations quite easily. People respond to his ideas, thoughts, and plans.

If Pluto is not well aspected, the individual may be tempted to manipulate conversations, be a compulsive talker, or become engaged in activities that are less than highly motivated. He would want to drive fast cars as a way of working off some of his compulsions and may be motivated to get even or show the people around him how rebellious and childlike he really is. He may say what he thinks other people want to hear and go right on doing just what he wants to do. Siblings may be manipulative, game-playing, or tricky, and compulsively childlike. His greatest lessons may come through traumatic interaction with people, through contracts or agreements that backfire.

The fourth house in an astrological chart rules the homelife, the parent of the opposite sex, and the conditions at the end of life. When Pluto rules or describes these conditions, the person wants to live a lavish lifestyle. He can be involved in major land deals, and his power has to do with property, building, real estate, or investment in land. The parent of the opposite sex may be quite magnetic, powerful, charismatic. The person might feel that his parent was really a child, but he would also be aware of the effectiveness of that individual. He might tend to emulate that parent, especially as he grows older. If Pluto is well aspected, the parent would have exhibited an especially transformational effect on people around him and would be a wonderful role model for the well-placed use of power. If, however, Pluto is not well aspected, the parent may have been overly forceful and manipulative, and the strongest message that came across would have been "Do what I say and don't ask any questions." The child may have felt tremendous power coming from that parent early in life and could be motivated by an unconscious desire to get even.

If Pluto is well aspected, the home life is lavish and magnificent, with lots of "toys" around to play with. He may have an estate or own property that houses many people, such as a hotel or a small community. He might be involved with land development or shopping centers. He could not do things on a small scale in connection with his lifestyle. If Pluto is not well aspected, he could want a magnificent display just to show off or to thumb his nose. He might be tempted to manipulate or play games with group projects or try to force matters in connection with property or lifestyle. He may have traumatic experiences connected to his homelife or with the parent of the opposite sex.

The fifth house in a chart represents the gambling instincts. It rules romance, children, entertainment, investments, and creative expression. It is a gamble to fall in love, a gamble to have children, a gamble to give a party, play the stock market, bet on horse races. When Pluto is associated with fifth-house energy, the gambles are extreme. The individual is willing to play for very high stakes, can hit the heights or reach the depths, win or lose all. He can become compulsive about any of these activities in his life. He may be a compulsive romantic, be compulsive about having children, or make investments that are dynamic in potential—or he can have the rug pulled out from under him in these same areas. These are the kinds of experience that can bring the greatest transformation in life, however.

With Pluto describing the creative area of life, his talent can be enormous. Relationships with loved ones and children will be intense, dynamic, and potent. He may want the kind of love interest that he can play with, and he will be playful with his children. Any association with groups of children could be a transforming experience that could go both ways. The fifth-house Pluto can show associations with schools as well as major organizations connected to children, such as orphanages or centers that encourage transformation and expression of talent.

When Pluto describes sixth-house activity, the quality of the work potential is exceptionally powerful. He may not easily work on a small level and may have to tap areas that will reach masses of people. He can be involved in projects that will have dynamic effect on the lives of others, can mass-produce things, be a producer, or work with television in any number of capacities. Group projects and major corporations can have special appeal. If Pluto is not well aspected, he may be a compulsive worker and can knock people over with the intensity of his determination. He has the opposite potential of being able to inspire people by setting a dynamic example. He may glow with health and energy if Pluto is well aspected, or he may push his energy unwisely and temporarily burn himself out. He will have tremendous rejuvenation and regenerative powers, however. Pluto describes will. His will can bring about miracles with health and any work projects.

When Pluto is posited in or rules the seventh house of marriage, one may have a compulsion for partnership. The individual with this placement of Pluto can easily rush into marriage at a very early age. It may be a charismatic attraction or his way of rebelling. He may jump from the frying pan into the fire, however. He can be attracted to someone with a childlike quality who is especially charismatic and powerful. If Pluto is well aspected, the probability of a dynamic association is strong. If Pluto is not well aspected, he may find himself in a situation in which lots of games are played and the partner adopts manipulative behavior. The seventh house can also mean business partnerships as well as personal partnerships. The partner may be the producer or coordinator of events who provides lots of stimulation through important activities.

When Pluto rules or is placed in the eighth house, the natural Scorpio house, the ability to get his needs met in life is exceptional. He may be the beneficiary of a major inheritance or have the potential to have a flood of financial benefits from his own efforts. He can ultimately be involved in projects that will transform the lives of many people. He can be the eagle or the serpent in getting what he needs and wants from life and the people around him. This placement can indicate a tendency to really go out on a limb financially, even manipulating to get the desired results. He may periodically thumb his nose at life or at certain individuals or situations, and play disastrous games that are sure to come home to haunt him. He can consciously or unconsciously want to get even with someone or some situation that was traumatic early in his life. He could make major purchases, run up huge charges only to find that he has to swallow his pride to pay for them himself. He may sabotage himself by compulsive behavior in getting what he wants the moment he wants it. He may have had early traumatic loss in connection with inheritance or simply in connection with the loss of his innocence or his childhood. If Pluto is well aspected, however, he may easily have income and opportunities that will eventually impel him to return the bounty to the universal good. He can have a powerful ability to transform many lives by showing the way for others. He may not have to do very much to affect people on a very deep level.

Pluto in the ninth house or ruling that sector of the chart can bring incredibly dynamic experiences through travel, legalities, or promotional effort. The individual may find that he is most effective in countries away from his place of birth, or in connection with international organizations or events. If Pluto is well aspected, he can be quite potent in advertising or promotional campaigns. He can deal with import and export, be effective in areas of distribution or as an agent. He can receive powerful publicity for his own efforts and activities or publicize the efforts of others.

The desire to "jet set" around the world can be especially strong with this placement of Pluto and, depending on the aspects, he can accomplish just that in his life. He will be able to live on an international level of luxury if Pluto is well aspected, but may suffer disillusionment in that connection if Pluto is not. If he is published, his works will have mass distribution, especially if his motivation is on a high level, or he can receive notoriety if he manipulates or plays games. With motivation for the good of all concerned, the person will have the kind of dynamic opportunities that he wants while he is working on a cause that will affect or reach many people. Television, advertising, promotion, and worldwide organizations are good outlets for a well-aspected Pluto in the ninth house. What the individual says and does will reach many people. He may have great power, or great potential to fall from grace.

A tenth-house placement of Pluto indicates a very potent ability to deal with public activity and career. It is in this area that the individual is able to be effective and "play" at the same time. He can work as a producer or coordinator and will have the greatest transforming experiences in connection with public life. He may form his own corporation, be associated with powerful groups in the career arena, and be incredibly charismatic in the public eye. The tenth house describes the parent of the same sex. If Pluto is well aspected in the chart, that parent would have an especially magnetic quality, acting like the eagle, rising above pettiness to do great things with his or her own life. That parent may have been involved in very powerful activity and can be a dynamic role model for the individual.

If Pluto is not well aspected, however, it may be in connection with public activities in which the individual uses cunning and manipulative techniques to get where he wants to be. He may have a compulsion to get even with the parent of the same sex, only creating conflict for himself in the process. Richard Nixon is a prime example of someone with Pluto in the tenth house who felt that the ends justified the means. An underlying compulsion to get to the top only to find himself at the bottom of public opinion is characteristic of Plutonian messages and experiences. At the bottom of what would seem to be innocence can be a self-destructive tendency that is in reality an attempt to get even with the parent who was manipulative, childlike, overly forceful, and damaging to the individual. When Pluto is badly aspected and is ruling or placed in either the tenth or the fourth house, one of the parents (same sex or opposite sex) can be described as the "witch parent." There may have been a tug of wills that is almost impossible to reconcile.

With an eleventh-house placement of Pluto, group situations can be especially dynamic, powerful, and potent. The individual with a well-aspected Pluto will associate himself with organizations that are motivated by the good of all concerned and will attract very powerful friends in his life. If Pluto is not well aspected, the individual may look for powerful associations and connections only to find that he can be manipulated more effectively than he could have imagined. He may have to learn to be especially discriminating about his associations. He can inadvertently get caught in the schemes or games of others, with his only crime a tendency to look the other way.

The placement of Pluto in the twelfth house or ruling that house indicates a more powerful ability to affect people with the mind than with any other placement in that house of the subconscious. The individual may have to learn how potent he is on the unconscious level to be able to utilize that power most effectively. He will be able to reach people without words whether he knows it or not. If Pluto is well aspected, he can transform and transmute circumstances in his own life and in the lives of the people he touches. He has a laser beam that reaches out of his deepest, most inner self to heal, if Pluto is well aspected, or to do just the opposite if it is not. It is as if this individual has been tapped by the spiritual hierarchy to be an instrument in the awakening of mankind. He can do this with the awareness of the cosmic level of his effectiveness.

If Pluto is badly aspected, he may have a subconscious desire to get even that can be terribly destructive. He may have to monitor his thoughts constantly to avoid the temptation toward using that laser beam destructively. He may not be aware that he can trip someone up thousands of miles away, but unless he becomes aware of that potency, he can do terrible damage. He will not escape the karmic penalty, however, because on his own highest level, he is aware of his power. He may not have to do or say anything out of the ordinary in his daily activity, yet his mere presence can affect people for good or for ill. This is power working on a universal level to uplift the state of the world, to bring it to the golden age of transcendency, or it is the blackest of black magic. It becomes the choice and the task of the individual to effect first the transformation in his own life in the areas described by Plutonian energy.

PLUTO CONJUNCT SUN

The Sun in a chart describes vitality, sense of self-worth, and ego identification. The placement of the Sun in a particular sign describes the quality of the vitality, and the aspects describe the ease of self-awareness or lack of ego strength. When the Sun is conjunct Pluto, an additional Scorpionic quality colors the vitality, sense of self-worth, and ego identification, no matter what sign holds the placement of the Sun. The Sun also describes the inner or soul quality, and when it is hooked up to Pluto, that planet's dynamic energy adds tremendous charisma and power on the ego level. If the individual is able to release that inner quality onto a high enough or potent enough level, his effectiveness is intense and powerful, but if he tries to remain unaware of that quality he can push people and situations away from him, play ego games, and show the destructive qualities of Pluto energy. He has an atom bomb ticking away inside of himself on a soul level and must find a constructive use for that energy.

Motivation seems to be the key to the transformation of Pluto, for it describes the little will or the will for the greater good. The eagle-like Plutonian energy never pushes anything. It simply soars above to the greatest heights in full majesty. But if the "little professor" ego state is allowed to remain on its lower level, the energy is like a child kicking its heels in a tantrum to get attention and what he wants at that instant. He can act as the producer or coordinator of a project simply to be at the center of attention.

Elisabeth Kübler-Ross is a Swiss psychologist who now travels around the world lecturing, teaching, and transforming the lives of the people around her. She works with terminally ill patients and has written a book, *On Death and Dying*, that is changing the way people deal with the whole idea of death. Elisabeth has strong Pluto aspects in her chart, among them Pluto conjunct the Sun. It is placed in the fifth house of creative potential, the "gambling" instincts, and investments. In this case Elisabeth invests her creative potential and energy in her cause. Pluto rules the ninth house in her chart, describing publishing, travel, international affairs. She has a powerful potential to transform the lives of many people through her power to touch the mass level. Her work on an individual level with her patients is potent enough, but her real dynamic quality is expressed in group endeavor and through lecturing and traveling.

When Elisabeth speaks to an audience, her voice is soft and low, yet she possesses such an intensity of purpose that her audience strains to hear every breath she takes. She speaks with quiet dignity and brings her audience to tears when she talks about her work. When she talks about the dying children that she has worked with, not a dry eye remains in an audience of perhaps many hundreds of people. Yet her intention is not to evoke pity but, rather, the dignity that a dying person deserves. She helps to liberate those patients from their conspiracy of silence. She gives them a chance to explore their fears, rage, isolation, and depression. Then comes the acceptance that brings the peace and serenity. Scorpio rules the eighth house of death and transformation, in the natural progression of signs and houses. What better way for Cancerian Elisabeth to use her additional Plutonian power than to work toward the transformation of that condition all of mankind eventually faces. She has an eagle-like purpose to her life and no time to waste on pettiness or negative energy. Elisabeth leaves the podium immediately after her talk. She has no time to hang around to answer questions but must be onward and upward with her task. She uplifts everyone she comes in contact with and is certainly no easygoing, charming, overly diplomatic lady. She magnetizes. She is intense and focused.

Tokyo Rose has her Cancer Sun also conjunct Pluto, in the twelfth house of the subconscious power. That conjunction also rules her fifth house of creative expression. It is interesting to see how each lady chose to use her energy. Iva Toguri D'Aquino was an American visiting Japan when the war broke out. She supported herself by broadcasting in English to the servicemen from her native land. Her propaganda was subtle and insidious. With the Pluto-Sun aspect she was in a position to influence many people, and she did. However, she was brought to the United States after the war and convicted of treason. Although she was one of thirteen "Roses," she was the only one who was punished. It was the exact same quality of powerful energy on a soul level as Elisabeth Kübler-Ross's, but misused and misdirected with selfishness and evil as motivation, instead of good. Motivation is the key to understanding the quality of Pluto.

Jane Russell also has the Sun conjunct Pluto placed in the twelfth house in her chart. Her Sun is in Gemini and rules the second house of income, while Pluto rules her fifth house of creative expression. Jane chose to direct her energy in the film world, where she reigned as queen of the sex goddesses of her time. She was filmed in such a torrid love scene in *The Outlaw* that the movie had censorship problems for over a year. She wore a specially designed bra in that film. Jane is still peddling bras through her work in television commercials today. The benefits to her second house seem assured with that activity. Eva Marie Saint has Pluto conjunct her Cancer Sun in the eighth house. It also rules her twelfth house as well as the ninth house of publicity, promotion, public relations. Both Jane and Eva Marie worked in films, described by the twelfth house. (That house describes not only the subconscious power, but activities connected with closed doors, or closed sets.) Whereas Jane exhibits the sensuous side of the Plutonian energy, Eva Marie has an innocent, childlike quality. She may not have tapped her true ability as yet, for with that powerful aspect ruling both the twelfth and the eighth houses, her potential to transform on a subconscious level can extend to the far corners of the earth.

Dean Martin has his Gemini Sun conjunct Pluto in Cancer. The Sun is in the third house of communications, whereas Pluto is in the fourth house of home. Dean Martin is close to his family but has a reputation for being most difficult, primarily because he is in a habitual state of inebriation. Milton Shapp had Pluto in Gemini and Sun in Cancer, conjunct and sitting on his ascendant. He founded his own company, was a self-made millionaire, and became governor of Pennsylvania. His Sun-Pluto conjunction rules the third house of communications, as does Dean Martin's conjunction, but it also rules the sixth house of work. He chose to upgrade the quality of his power to a higher level of mass responsibility. He was known to be humanitarian, philanthropic, and hardheaded politically. He was not easy with the usual back slapping that is associated with politics.

PLUTO IN HARD ASPECT TO THE SUN

Difficult aspects between Pluto and the Sun describe a quality of discordant inner power. The natural sense of self-worth and potency has been damaged through traumatic conditions that prevent the individual from having a clear vision of his childlike power. He may therefore utilize the negative child energy in a way that is really not effective. A faulty hookup between the child ego state and his inner vitality can keep him "yanking on skirts," creating a scene, when he would be more effective pulling back into a more dignified, reserved state of consciousness. He may be motivated by an unconscious desire to be noticed and recognized, but he may not know how to go about getting the ego strokes in a healthy way. He may even manipulate without being aware of that quality. He can be overly forceful and actually push away the people and conditions he'd like to attract. Ultimately, after many times of feeling that the rug has been pulled out from under, or after many traumatic experiences, humiliation transmutes the ego onto a purer level of self-worth and effectiveness.

Chris Sizemore is the real person behind the story of the *Three Faces of Eve*. Even after the book and the film were completed, an additional nineteen distinct personalities continued to emerge from this one small person. The square between Pluto and the Sun in Chris's chart does not describe the multiple personalities but, rather, the traumatic events that led to her inability to know herself. With this aspect, the ego is certainly disoriented but may not necessarily become split, as in her case. Chris has Leo rising with Pluto ruling the fourth house of home. Her Sun is posited in the eighth house of getting needs met, with Pluto in the eleventh house of friends and associates. Chris was a witness to two violent deaths before she was two years old. She evidently felt as though she struggled with death in her battles with the varying personalities within herself. Her homelife was a source of terrifying experiences, with the house itself seeming to be foreboding, dark, and dangerous. Chris's mother was the cause of much of the withdrawal, yet she may have felt as though her father, ruled by the fourth house, deserted or betrayed her by being childlike and refusing to recognize her plight. The transmuting power of Pluto enabled her to resolve her own dilemma. But the willingness to let her story be told may have been the ultimate gift she could give to humanity.

Debbie Reynolds was born with Pluto square the Sun in her chart. Pluto is posited in the tenth house of career, and the Sun in the seventh house of marriage. Debbie has the Sun in Aries conjunct Uranus, which only added to the energy of the trauma she experienced with her marriage. Debbie had a very public romance and marriage to Eddie Fisher. They seemed an idyllic couple until Eddie left Debbie and his daughter, Carrie, in order to marry Elizabeth Taylor. Her public humiliation was complete, as the triangle situation was reported daily in newspapers and magazines across the nation. Pluto square Sun takes away what may have been an ego prop and forces the person to develop inner strength. Debbie could do nothing except swallow her pride and keep a low profile. " 'Revenge is mine,' saith the Lord," and Eddie, in turn, had his own public humiliation when Liz left him to marry Richard Burton, for Pluto can create a boomerang situation. Although the way was cleared for another marriage for Debbie, she eventually divorced Harry Karl, a multimillionaire. No doubt Debbie's financial life went through transformation as well as her pride, partnership activity, and career. She certainly became a stronger, more transformed person as a result of her inner growth. Pluto's growth seems to come through trauma.

Marianne was an American girl who married an Arab and lived in his harem. She was also born with Pluto square the Sun. In her chart, Pluto is posited in the seventh house of marriage, and the Sun, again in Aries, in the third house of communications. She closed herself off from the outside world with no communication other than with the other women in the communal household. Without warning, and with no apparent reason, her husband divorced her. Marianne went to court to fight for her children and won a battle that was unheard of in Moslem law. She may also have paved the way, through her own traumatic experience, for the good of many. The Sun rules the eighth house of death and transformation. Through her experiences in a harem, where the ego would have to suffer, she found her strength and true inner quality of vitality.

Ryan O'Neal has the Sun square Pluto in his natal chart. Ryan shows the boyish, charming, childlike quality associated with any hookup between Sun and Pluto, but also periodically expresses the forceful, rebellious, arrogant quality. Ryan has the Sun in his fifth house of creativity and children. Pluto is in the eighth house, again describing the quality of transformation in a powerful way. Tatum O'Neal increased publicity to herself and Ryan through her work in films. Ryan could take great pride as a father in his daughter's accomplishments. But only recently Ryan, with his Sun ruling the ninth house of publicity, was involved in a dispute with his son and knocked out the son's front teeth in an effort to discipline him. He no doubt suffered a great deal of public humiliation through that situation. Ryan may tap his ultimate potential in creative areas simply because of hard lessons that will eventually hone and purify the inner qualities of strength. He will learn a deeper meaning of power and have that major transforming experience in his life indicated by Pluto. Pluto-square-Sun dialogues tend to bring one to one's knees on the ego level. From there it is possible only to rise to the heights and become transmuted like iron being forged into steel.

John Travolta has Pluto in opposition to his Sun, which may be an easier energy to resolve than Sun square Pluto; yet the transformation comes, just the same. In John's case, the Sun is posited in the eighth house of death, transformation, and getting ones needs met, and rules the second house of money through income. Pluto is posited in that second house, indicating a powerful ability to earn major sums of money. Pluto rules the fifth house of talent, creativity, and romance. One of the first traumas to hit this charismatic actor was the death of Diana Hyland. John hid away for a period of time to recuperate and then had several deaths in his own family. His dynamic career would necessarily have to undergo transformation as a result of his own experiences.

One young lady talked about how this aspect felt in her own life. We will call her Catherine. Catherine has Pluto on the ascendant in her chart ruling the fifth house of children. Her Sun is posited in the fourth house of home, and rules her second and eighth houses of money. Catherine's father committed suicide when she was only two years old. He had been very successful and lost everything at the time of the Depression. Catherine was in the next room when her father killed himself. She said, "I always thought I didn't know my father, but during a regression session, I became very aware of our relationship. I saw myself as being very powerful and very much in control at the time of his death. But my contempt for him was beyond description. I said to myself, 'Who needs you anyway? I can take care of things better than you could.' Of course at two years old, that simply wasn't true, and my life changed drastically. I was never able to tell anyone the circumstances of his death, because I was humiliated and even more humiliated at the plight of my family. I always affected great dignity. I may have unconsciously behaved arrogantly when that was far from the way I felt. Not only that, I convinced myself that I was still as independently wealthy as I would have been under different circumstances. That alone has wrought havoc with my financial life, for, on one level, I have no conception of not being able to buy anything I want at any time. I have gone overboard at times and had to pay dearly for my compulsions. The most drastic humiliation I can think of is to lose my home, however. I have a compulsion for my 'castle' but am terrified to even own land, for fear of having to go through that same traumatic loss again. The loss of lifestyle and home went hand in hand with the loss of my father.

"Perhaps the most profound result of all of this continued in the relationship with my children. I had an absolute compulsion to have children in order to provide them with the love and security that I didn't have. I again had the rug pulled out from under me by my husband, who left and refused to support his children, and by every other man in my life. After four engagements and four subsequent deaths, one by suicide, I don't trust myself in the romantic department. My father loved me dearly, but that didn't stop him from leaving. I have never lacked for love from men and my children, but in each case there has been something drastic that I have had to swallow. I have felt as though this was a process of being brought to my knees. They say pride goeth before a fall. If I could look to a higher reason for all of this, I would say I've had to be humbled in order to be motivated on a better level. Each time I was excessively proud of someone or something, it has been taken away drastically. I only hope that transformation can take place and I can make a contribution. Perhaps I'm just not meant to have anything tangible. I have learned not to force things. I only want what is best and right for my highest good. Otherwise, it will backfire. I certainly lost my childhood quickly, yet I feel like I am still a young girl, even though I am far from that now. I also still feel as though I can do almost anything that I want with my life. Perhaps a positive result is that I don't feel limitation with my creative potential." Catherine confessed to me that periodically she feels like being an irresponsible child and loves to get into mischief. She said she resists that impulse, for although the mischief might be innocent, it can cause pain on some level. She is involved in metaphysical practices and works to rise above negative, overly forceful, or manipulative behavior. She practices magnetizing only the right people and situations to herself, working with divine order in her life. Perhaps her story is not yet complete.

PLUTO CONJUNCT MOON

The Moon describes emotions, feelings, sensitivity, vulnerability, and a tremendous identification with mankind. It describes the qualities that we all have in common. When the Moon is strong in a chart, the feelings can lead to overreaction, vulnerability, and sensitivity, or can give a quality of mothering and nurturing. When the Moon is conjunct the powerful energy described by Pluto, those feelings are particularly deep. They can be directed inward or outward. They can be expressed on the highest level of identification with humanity, or give a quality of revenge on an intense emotional level. Again, the key to the transmutation of the overly emotional reactions can be motivation for the good of all concerned. Whatever is sent out will be returned in a magnified and powerful way. The Moon describes a particular ability to feed the needs of humanity which, when it is conjunct with Pluto, escalates into a potency that has the power of an atomic blast. That radioactive quality of feeling can be very destructive or very uplifting.

Michel and Françoise Gauquelin, perhaps the most prestigious scientific researchers in astrology, have come to the conclusion through extensive work that the Moon is the strongest planet found in the charts of writers. My own theory is that from the necessity of working through the pain associated with such strong feelings comes the ability to realize that many other people share the same experiences. When the individual is able to allow himself to feel and show his vulnerability, people around him feel permission to let down their own walls, and the drama that unfolds in humanity is revealed. The public responds to that with which it can identify. If a person protects his pain, hides his feelings, he does not allow the same interaction with people as the individual who stands naked. Whether the person with a Moon-Pluto aspect writes, plays baseball, or sings, he receives that depth and wave of response in return.

Next to Babe Ruth, Ted Williams may be the best-loved baseball player in history. Ted Williams could have a bad day, be moody, imperious, and willful, yet his loyal fans forgave him anything. Ted had Scorpio on the ascendant, with the Moon conjunct Pluto. The co-ruler of his ascendant is the Moon, and the Moon and Pluto also rule the ninth house of publicity, promotional matters, public relations. That conjunction is placed in the eighth house of transformation. Ted Williams had an influence over every young boy with inclinations toward sports, whether he was aware of it or not. It was by his own personality, actions, and feelings that Williams was able to affect people on a mass level.

Mark Twain had the powerful Moon-conjunct-Pluto aspect in his chart. With a Scorpio ascendant, that aspect ruled his personality and his ability to express himself, and is placed in the fifth house of creativity. The Moon, therefore Pluto, rules the ninth house of publishing, publicity, promotional efforts. Mark Twain's own life, as described in his writing, touched everyone in the country, for who has not read of the adventures of Tom Sawyer and his friends? Émile Zola has this aspect with a conjunction of the Sun as well. The placement in the fourth house of home, ruling the subconscious twelfth house, and the eighth and ninth houses, again describes this profound ability to reach masses of people, not just a few people here and there. No one could dispute his place in literary history.

Carl Jung had this conjunction in the third house of communications, ruling his tenth house of career, the sixth house of work, and the seventh house of partnership. This aspect in his chart not only describes his own depth of work and feelings, but the partnership he had with Sigmund Freud. Jung made an incredibly powerful contribution to the field of psychology by reaching into the field of metaphysics. Pluto describes cosmic consciousness when elevated, and Jung was indeed the pioneer in describing, on a profound level, the universal archetypes that all of mankind share.

And then we have Oscar Wilde. Oscar Wilde had this conjunction placed in the ninth house of publishing, reputation, promotional matters, distribution. It ruled the third house of communications, and the eleventh house of friendships; it described very clearly the choice an individual can make in the use of this aspect. Wilde wrote about transformation. His story of Dorian Gray is the ultimate in the expression of a manipulative child compromising principles in order to remain a youth. Dorian was charismatic, magnetic, and never wanted to stop playing. Oscar Wilde had the same desires. It was precisely that emotional compulsion used to get even, play games, or step into the Victorian forbidden world of sexual adventure that caused Wilde to lose his reputation and be found guilty of the sexual crime of sodomy. Wilde is now a cult hero of sorts among many heterosexual as well as homosexual people. Dorian Gray still represents the picture of transformation and the ultimate message of the price of compromise.

Gavin MacLeod has Pluto conjunct the Moon in his chart. With a Scorpio ascendant, Gavin expresses the additional Moon quality in his personality. That conjunction rules his ninth house of promotion, travel, and publicity, and is placed in the eighth house of getting his needs met. Gavin spent many years working as an actor in Hollywood, finally landing a long-term role as Murray on "The Mary Tyler Moore Show." His role was an integral one to the show but had little variety and may have lacked any challenge for an actor. But when that show folded, Gavin found his real niche. He portrays the captain on "The Love Boat," one of the most popular roles on a most popular television series. Gavin travels around the world for location cruises and works with some of the most famous stars of all time. Gavin has a most complex chart, with many aspects to Pluto, but it is clear that the major transformation in his life will have to do with setting an example through his own life. His first marriage ended with divorce when he met Patti Steele, who became his second wife. Yet after seven years with Patti, Gavin suddenly wanted his freedom. Minutes before he asked for a divorce, Gavin was on television with Patti, giving her credit for his path away from alcoholism and into success. Gavin has an incredible potential for eliciting public response. It is a matter of choice as to how each individual chooses to use that gift. Gavin may suddenly have decided he wanted to retain his youth and needed to shed reminders of his old life just as he shed many pounds. Plutonian energy always describes an ability to rejuvenate and change. The happy ending to the story is that, with his own transformation, Gavin and Patti are together again in their joyous, private love boat.

PLUTO IN HARD ASPECT TO THE MOON

When Pluto is in hard aspect to the Moon, the emotional quality can tempt the individual to lash out, when deeply hurt, with a childlike determination to get even. The inner dialogue seems to be a conflict between the emotions and the voice of the eagle. The traumatic events that come seem to be designed to transmute the feelings onto a higher level. After intense, searing emotional pain, the individual can become the eagle, but he must never take things personally or allow himself the luxury of self-indulgent reaction.

Pierre Curie had Pluto square the Moon. Pluto is posited in the twelfth house of subconscious activity, in opposition to the Moon in the house of work. An even stronger color of Plutonian energy comes with his Moon placed in Scorpio at birth. The discovery of radiation came after incredible hardship in the lives of the Curies. Through Pierre's chart, Marie Curie is described by Pluto, and she was born with the sun in Scorpio, ruled by Pluto. She also had Cancer rising, giving her the additional Moon quality as seen in his chart. Their partnership was made even closer by their highest desire to work for the good of mankind. With that difficult aspect in his chart, Pierre Curie may have been especially hurt by the lack of response from people toward their goal. The path may have been even more arduous because there was no public support until they had achieved the great victory of their discovery. Yet the powerful ability to care about the welfare of mankind above their own comfort eventually brought the world to their feet. Pierre Curie may never have experienced any of that gratitude in his lifetime.

A woman whom we shall call Anna is a very fascinating lady with a definite mind of her own. She was born to a woman who was not very interested in having children. Her father was not either; he never married her mother. At a very early age Anna went to live with an aunt and uncle and then a grandmother. Although she had a home and attention, she became independent as early as she could. She was quite beautiful and was soon involved with a very powerful theatrical producer. They lived together for fifteen years and were finally married just before his death. Although he was many years older than Anna, she never felt that he was a father figure to her. They traveled, had a very exciting lifestyle, and played together. When he died, he left her a sizable inheritance. Although Anna could have continued with his work, and she missed the excitement of the theater, she chose not to continue in that field. She became involved with a man closer to her age just a few months after she was widowed. This time, her mate was not wealthy, but industrious, energetic, and dynamic in his own way, and together they built a very successful business. Anna did not want to marry again.

Anna has the Moon in the first house, describing the early abandonment, and ruling the seventh house of partnership. Pluto is in opposition to the Moon and is placed in that seventh house, ruling her career. She first chose a man who was extremely dynamic but was like a child. He needed constant attention and care. She felt terribly abandoned when he died and said she jumped into the second relationship much too soon. During her years with her second partner, she was constantly embarrassed by his flirtations, and felt that she had been humiliated. For the sake of their business partnership, she let things that bothered her just slide by. Even though it was her money that enabled them to start the business, he pestered her like a child morning, noon, and night for a larger share of the profits. Finally she relented and suggested he just take what he wanted, even though the funds were in both their names. This changed the dynamic of their relationship, because Anna lost her independence, became more vulnerable, and felt totally manipulated. As long as they worked together, Anna had an outlet and balance for her Moon opposite Pluto. As soon as they sold their business, for a very large profit, she was confined to domesticity, which kept her in a state of upsetting boredom. Anna has a special ability to sense the trends of the times and can sense what people need and want. She needs an outlet for her powerful emotional nature. She can write or find some activity to nurture people to release the flood of feelings within herself. Otherwise those feelings back up inside and can cause overreaction, overemotion, tremendous vulnerability, and oversensitivity.

PLUTO CONJUNCT MERCURY

Mercury describes any intellectual activity and ability to speak, analyze, and collect data. When Mercury and Pluto are conjunct, the power of the mind is profound. The ability to influence people or situations is dynamic. Charles Evans Hughes was born with this aspect in his chart. With a Virgo ascendant, Pluto was a co-ruler of his personality. The conjunction in his chart is split between the eighth and ninth houses, ruling the tenth house of career, as well. After a successful law career, he became Chief Justice of the United

States and used his powerful mind to make decisions that would transform conditions on the highest level of justice. He could never have been content to remain a mere lawyer. What he said had a profound effect on the people around him; there was no higher authority in the country. His photographs reflect the intensity of his nature. His gaze is penetrating and deep.

Pluto has been described as the detective energy. Not much can escape the potency in getting to the bottom of things when Pluto is connected to a situation. Sir Arthur Conan Doyle wrote about Sherlock Holmes, the ultimate detective. Mercury conjunct Pluto are placed in the twelfth house of Sir Arthur's chart, ruling the ascendant, or area of viewpoint, and the fifth house of self-expression. Pluto rules the sixth house of work. He would quite naturally work behind the scenes, in connection with hidden or secret matters, and have a great need to express powerful creative potential. His Gemini ascendant would lead to a need for intellectual activity and collection of trivia, and Pluto, as a natural co-ruler, would describe an inclination to mystery, peering behind the scenes, and getting to the bottom of things. Sir Arthur did just that—and reached masses of people with his writing.

PLUTO IN HARD ASPECT TO MERCURY

Difficult Pluto-Mercury aspects may produce a compulsive talker. There can be contamination between the adult and child ego states, and it is with words that the child ego can get attention. He can overdo it and talk fast, for fear no one will really listen, and generally make a nuisance of himself, only to have much of what he says come home to roost. There is a tendency to manipulate with words, to say what the person thinks others want to hear. On a thinking level, he may outsmart himself with too much planning and plotting of what he will say. He eventually must become aware of the power of his words, be willing to put all his cards on the table, withholding nothing, with the willingness to walk away if his ideas are not accepted immediately. When he learns to say less, rather than more, he will find that people look to him for advice, planning, and ideas. He will find the right groups to work with if he is unwilling to compromise just to have his ideas accepted by someone.

Both Willie Nelson and Janis Paige have Pluto square Mercury, but, with the emphasis on the twelfth house, the probability is that thoughts are hard to turn off. Both are prolific performers. What goes on in the deepest recesses of their minds can only be speculation. Gloria Steinem has this aspect in sesquisquare, which is even more difficult to reconcile. Her Mercury is posited in the fourth house of home and of father, and rules the eighth house of getting her needs met. Pluto rules her first house of personality, and is placed in the ninth house of promotion and publicity. It may have taken a lot of fast talking and powerful arguments to launch the Women's Movement. Gloria's father left home when she was only twelve years old. She may have felt as though he pulled the rug out from under her and did not meet her needs. Gloria's relationships, and her vehemence, may have come from a subconscious desire to get even with him, and rectify the situation for many people. Her power lies in the eighth-house (ruled by Mercury) ability to give out potent information and transform the lives of others. It appears as though Gloria has done just that.

Patricia Neal has Mercury posited in her first house, opposing Pluto in her seventh house of marriage, with Mercury ruling that seventh house and ruling her ninth house of publicity, and the sixth house of work and health. Pluto rules her eleventh house of group association. Patricia established her reputation as an actress to reckon with when she won five awards for her performance in Lillian Hellman's play *Another Part of the Forest*. She won stronger recognition and is best remembered in connection with her performance in *Hud* with Paul Newman. When Patricia was thirty-nine years old, she suffered a stroke that paralyzed her and left her speechless. She was totally helpless as a result of that stroke.

Without the encouragement and perhaps nagging from her husband, Roald Dahl, she might never have walked or spoken again. But that powerful, dynamic, and forceful man cajoled, manipulated, and challenged her to recover. Her own strength enabled her to completely overcome any handicap and she relearned how to walk and speak. Her first film after that recovery was *The Subject Was Roses*, and she won her second Oscar. Patricia had more tragedy in her life when her daughter was killed, yet she and her husband remained firmly connected in their mutual fight against adversity. The love and devotion on his part was obvious in the television play about her struggle. Yet Pluto is the transformer. For reasons that have not been made public, Roald left Patricia when she was able to stand on her own, and married a much younger woman, so that after the traumatic times that bound them together in working toward her recovery, Pat suffered one more trauma. Many times in an opposition, it is the struggle that binds, whereas easy times present no challenge. Patricia Neal is now openly committed to working for more understanding for stroke victims. Her words now truly carry weight. Her message is "If I can do it, so can you!"

PLUTO CONJUNCT VENUS

Venus describes beauty, pleasure, sensuality, as well as a sense of social justice. In a positive way, Venus describes a need for harmony and pleasure, and in the negative, a tendency to take the easy way out or become lazy. When Venus is connected to the power of Plutonian energy, that same tendency becomes more forceful. The need for self-indulgence can be most important of all, but the ability to create social justice on a dynamic, potent level is assured. It is the love nature that must be transformed and purified eventually. For it is in connection with pleasures—whether of beauty, objects, or love—that the transformation occurs.

Raquel Welch may be the epitome of beauty and sensuality. She was on the covers of over a hundred magazines in one year and has been involved in films that depict primarily her beautiful figure and face. Raquel has the conjunction of Pluto and Venus in the fifth house of self-expression, romance, and children. She has a compulsion for children, love, and self-expression with such a powerful aspect in her chart. She has two children, and has had two marriages. Pluto-Venus rules her house of partnership and the eighth house of getting her needs met, as well as her second house of money. She has a dynamic potential to make money through partnership activities, investment, and self-expression. Raquel has the potential to upgrade public consciousness regarding matters of social justice, or with beauty. She has just written a book about health and beauty entitled *Raquel*. Whether she chooses to continue to use her energy in that way is up to her, of course.

Phyllis Schlafly has the same aspect in her chart in the second house of income, ruling the twelfth house of the subconscious, and the sixth house of work. Phyllis is all for keeping the status quo when it comes to fair play for women. Venus is the planet of the diplomat and lawyer, as well as the social politician. She has been accused of being a professional politician. She has campaigned tirelessly against women's rights and is a contradiction since she is engaged in more than housewifely duties. Phyllis may have found the ideal way of satisfying her particular need for income and pleasure.

Margot Fonteyn has Pluto conjunct Venus in the fifth house, ruling her profound artistic talent. This conjunction rules her ninth house of travel and publicity, as well as the third house of communications, and the eighth house of transformation. She has been dancing since she was four years old and made her professional debut at the age of fourteen. She is still dancing at the age of sixty-six while the usual end of the dancer's life comes at around thirty. Perhaps Dame Margot can transform the lives of other dancers who might automatically give up just because of chronological age. She has touched the hearts and brought enormous pleasure to anyone privileged enough to see her dance. She communicates artistry and pleasure through her own creative life, bringing harmony on a potent level.

Pierre Salinger also has this aspect in his chart, placed in the eighth house, ruling his personality and partnership activities. Pierre has a potent ability to express a charming, gracious, diplomatic part of his personality, making a great impact at the same time. He has wisdom and diligence and is noted for his complex but passionate energy. Bertrand Russell, noted English mathematician and philosopher, also had this conjunction ruling his personality, placed in the house of partnership and describing the twelfth house of the subconscious. He was also noted for his ability to speak out on many subjects in a powerful but gracious and diplomatic manner. He spoke out on controversial subjects but was primarily a defender of humanity and freedom of thought. Sigmund Freud, also with a Scorpio ascendant, and with his Pluto-conjunct-Venus aspect placed in the sixth house of work, and ruling the twelfth house, was powerful in his ability to delve into the subconscious mind. He developed psychoanalysis to enable man to understand his inner self. The impact of his work has been felt worldwide. His love of art and beauty is well known. He was almost too late in leaving Vienna to flee the Nazis because of a reluctance to make changes. (Venus can describe a tendency to take an easy way out, to opt for peace and harmony and pleasure.) Freud took opium to relieve the pain of cancer in his body. Health was a problem in his life, and perhaps a major transforming experience. The choice of opium as a pain reliever may have propelled him onto opiated pleasure levels that he felt unable to attain in other ways. It may also have been his way of attempting to bring peace to an intense and troubled life.

PLUTO IN HARD ASPECT TO VENUS

When Pluto and Venus are in adverse aspect to each other, the tendency to manipulate with charm, the love nature, and an overly diplomatic quality is very strong. The individual with this aspect may be very ingratiating in precisely the way that will serve his needs best; he may doubt his ability to be powerful without compromise of some sort. The sensual nature is pervasive and there may be a compulsion for love. In this case, transmutation must take place on a love level, for when this energy is utilized in a socially conscious way, the love nature is powerfully effective in all areas of life.

The individual with this aspect can be obsessive about pleasure. He tends to be very self-indulgent. He may not know the meaning of moderation with the affectionate nature or sensuality. He may compromise his principles early in his life, feeling that he must be overly nice to have attention or be effective. Whenever Venus is not well aspected, there is a tendency to be lazy in some way; the person may not *appear* to be lazy, but may lack discipline. Some areas of self-indulgence seem to compensate for the feeling of having had the rug pulled out from under him where love or pleasure is concerned.

Jennifer has Venus posited in the tenth house of career and mother, and ruling the fourth house of home and father. Pluto is squared that placement in the second house of income, and ruling the fifth house of creativity, investment, romance, and children. Jennifer is an artist and has specialized in jewelry design. She is very sociable, gracious, and attractive. She appears very energetic, but her special creative talent is lying dormant. After working for a major jewelry company as a production supervisor, she decided to design her own line of jewelry. Her taste is exquisite and her elegant pieces are not inexpensive. Jennifer takes individual orders from her friends and acquaintances but hasn't been able to produce her jewelry on a mass level. Her primary income is derived from working for other jewelry designers. She feels she doesn't have enough capital to start her business properly. While Jennifer's reasoning is obviously true, and she is stuck momentarily, there may be a deeper reason and a more subconscious factor involved.

Venus in a chart describes areas in which the individual wants peace and harmony. Jennifer's mother and father were divorced when she was about eleven years old. She loved both parents but wanted to live with her father. She adored him and had secret hopes of getting the family back together again. She was sure her mother would never let her go to live with her father, so she devised a Plutonian plan. She said, "I used to baby-sit a lot. I began doing things that I hoped would get back to my mother. I am ashamed to admit what I did. I compulsively ate all the cake or desserts or special food I would find in the house and when that failed to get back to her, I began to take money from purses or drawers. I didn't spend any of it. I hid it on my closet shelf. Finally, my employers told my mother that they were missing money and of course, she was very upset. I was very well brought up. My mother would never dream in a million years that I could do something like that. I wanted her to think that she couldn't handle me and give up on me so I could go to my father. My mother was beside herself and arranged to let me go.

"My little plan backfired, however, because I discovered that I didn't have my father all to myself. He was already involved with a girlfriend and had no intention of returning to my mother. My father and I lived on one side of the street and the girlfriend, Anita, lived on the other. Actually, I ended up living alone when I was twelve years old with a big dog for company, because my father stayed with Anita all the time. I would go across the street for lunch money in the morning before school and perhaps see him for a while in the evening for dinner. I didn't dare tell my mother what was going on, because I didn't want to upset her any more than she already was. I figured if I had gone to such extremes to get there, I had made my bed and I had to lie in it. After about six months of that, I finally went back to my mother's home. I didn't tell her what the situation was for many years, although she must have known I wasn't too happy.

"My adored father continued to play games with me all his life. Just before he died, he did the worst thing of all. He was alcoholic and very ill with a brain tumor, and I was the only member of the family on the West Coast, so I had to get him to the psychiatric ward by myself. He called me every filthy name in the book. I have had a hard time erasing that from my memory. He pulled the rug out from under me with money, too. He left everything to me, instead of dividing it up between his three children. It put me in a terrible position. I didn't know if he wanted me to be his executor or wanted me to have it all. It was just enough to cause trouble."

I asked Jennifer if she felt her mother and father had lived up to their potential, especially in a financial way. She said, "My father was brilliant and never a really successful lawyer. My mother is very creative, an artist, musician, and didn't really use her talent in a productive way." I suggested to Jennifer that perhaps her love for them prevented her from going beyond what they had done with their income potential, then showed her the other side of the coin. She said, "I really never thought that I might be paying them back because they didn't provide me with that funding I need to start my own business. Of course my mother worries about my financial state of affairs and I'm sure my father would be concerned as well." With Pluto in the second house of income, in a square to her Venus, Jennifer has the potential of transforming her love nature, artistic ability, and therefore her income by being motivated on a higher level. Pluto rules her fifth house of children, romance, and creativity. If she has to provide a home for children or someone she loves, she will rise like the eagle to do whatever is necessary for that loved one. The major change in her life can be connected to involvement with social justice, creation of beauty and harmony, or major projects connected to children.

Donald Ballard was the son of parents who founded a religious cult called the Mighty I Am. He began to manage the money for this organization and was convicted of mail fraud, conspiracy, and plagiarism when he was only twenty-two years old. Pluto is in his second house of money, but ruling the sixth house of work. Venus, placed in the eleventh house of friends, groups, and organizations, squares Pluto and rules the twelfth house of the subconscious mind.

The twelfth house describes any "hidden" areas of life, including jails. Donald may have tried to take the easy way out, manipulating funds, on that subconscious level. He ended up in jail with plenty of time for the transformation to take place. He may have needed solitary time free of unhealthy temptation so much that he was attracted to jail, completely unconsciously. Meditation and real metaphysical practices could have brought Donald to a position of noncompromise and to the higher path. His ultimate role might have been that of a diplomat or negotiator for peace.

Brooke Shields has Pluto square Venus in her chart. Venus is placed in the tenth house of career, describing her mother as well. Pluto is in the twelfth house of the subconscious, ruling the third house of communications. Brooke played a prostitute in her first film, *Pretty Baby*, with her mother's full consent and blessing. Brooke was only twelve years old. Her mother has managed her career since that time and has parlayed Brooke's beauty and talent into millions. Mars and Uranus are conjunct Pluto in Brooke's twelfth house of the subconscious, indicating rebellion and rage, added to the Plutonian power. While Brooke continues to protest her undying love and devotion for her mother, only time will tell whether she will finally rebel against her mother's companionship in her public life as well as in her social life. She may feel that her mother took the easy way out with her own career. The Moon is conjunct Venus in the ninth house of Brooke's chart, possibly describing her feeling of mothering her mother. She might show a totally protective quality publicly while feeling just the opposite privately.

Burt Reynolds, Harry Belafonte, and Warren Beatty may well represent the epitome of male pulchritude and sexual magnetism in Hollywood. All three of them have Pluto square Venus in their charts. Each one of them has a reputation for charm, graciousness, and a compulsive need for romance. The sensuous quality is quite pronounced in each man.

PLUTO CONJUNCT MARS

The Pluto-and-Mars combination may be, of all the aspects, descriptive of the most difficult energy in a chart. It is so explosively powerful that it is imperative to find a high enough outlet to release the energy. It describes drive, ambition, and power on an atomic level. But anger can also be volcanic, atomic, and potentially destructive. The individual may be unaware of what he might do with such potency if he internalizes all his energy. He could self-destruct on some level unless he channels such intense energy into projects with potentially big results. He needs to work in areas that will affect many people or concern mass production. He can be potent in connection with "big deals" or with major organizations. The person with such an aspect can look like an angel outwardly, and appear calm, kind, and easygoing. A closer look at the internal nature gives evidence of intense frustration.

Mars is the planet that describes drive, ambition, pioneering qualities, and especially the sexual energy. If that strong sexual energy, which is the prime force motivating the ambition and aggressive actions, is hooked up to powerful Pluto, it is like sitting on a nuclear power plant. The person may be hesitant to throw the switch and release that level of aggression, but if it backs up, it can be like a leak of nuclear energy into the system. The sexual nature can be especially powerful, and so intense the individual can hardly handle that drive. Pluto can describe the need for revenge. If this aspect is placed in a particular way in a chart, it can be linked to homosexuality. The motivation may be to get even with a person or situation, and that can be one way to thumb one's nose at society or a parent. The person may also feel more able to release the potency of the sexual energy with a person of the same sex. The Pluto-Mars combination does not describe homosexuality per se, but may be a way of "playing," being mischievous, or of getting even. An individual may choose another way of releasing the anger.

James was an especially brilliant man. He was a member of Mensa, with an extraordinarily high intelligence quotient, but left college before graduation because he was presented with an opportunity in business that was too good to miss. He was married soon after he went to work, but that first marriage ended in divorce with no children. He married again, this time to a college friend who had been the eternal beauty queen. Their children inherited both the brains and the beauty from their parents. They had a beautiful home in a major city and their lifestyle seemed quite luxurious and comfortable. James had everything he thought he wanted from life. Yet, behind the scenes, all was not so rosy. James was impotent very early in his life. His wife was diagnosed as schizophrenic and was hospitalized many times. Their children were brought up by a governess, for the most part.

The one area of his life that was productive was business. James was honored and respected in his field. He was made to feel like a family member and part owner of the corporation that employed him, even though such was not really the case. The only thorn in his side was the aged father of the owner of the company, who was quite active even though he was in his nineties. James tried to be diplomatic and step around the problems that were caused by his interference.

Suddenly, James's life began to change. His wife asked for a divorce. At the same time, he felt that he had been deceived in his business-family relationship and was tired of pacifying the older man. He allowed the man to drive quite a few miles out of the way to a meeting that had been canceled, and when the older man was understandably angry and threatened to have James fired over the incident, it seemed like the last straw. James went to his farm outside of the city and put a bullet into his brain.

James's astrological chart showed not only that homicidal rage but also a suicide complex. The Pluto-Mars conjunction was placed in the eighth house, which describes the way one gets his needs met, and the inheritance factor, as well as death. Mars ruled the third and fourth houses in his chart, describing his ability to negotiate contracts, communicate, and learn. The third house also describes relationships with siblings. The fourth house indicates lifestyle and the relationship with the parent of the opposite sex. Pluto ruled the eleventh house of groups, friends, associations, organizations. In all these areas James was very effective and dynamic. But James confessed that his relationships with his sister and mother were very difficult. It was in this area that his rage was indicated. His mother had been a musician, very talented, sexy, and dynamic. She had an incestuous relationship with her son from puberty until James was able to break away. His sister continued where his mother left off. James sublimated all that rage, and finally went into therapy. It was the incident in his business life that triggered the threat of loss of home and income that was the last straw. Then it all became too much for him. He killed himself beside his mother's grave, on the farm he loved so much.

The conjunction of Pluto-Mars is more easily released than other combinations of Pluto and Mars, however, for at least that powerful energy can be directed outwardly. The eagle-like potential is profound, but the quality of power must be directed upward and for the good of humanity in order to be transformed. Bertrand Russell and Pierre Salinger have this aspect, as did Douglas MacArthur. Robert Redford, Bruce Springsteen, and James Taylor share this conjunction. Two very dynamic and sexy ladies, Cher and Jane Russell, have this same aspect, as does Bette Midler. Although they may not be working on a particularly humanitarian level, show business demands so much energy they can at least direct that dynamic quality outward. Bette Midler's comedy routines are so sexually explicit that she has to delete much of her material if she is on television. Cher and Jane Russell don't have to say anything sexual; the aura they project (along with Robert Redford) shows their intense sexuality. If they were not able to work in competitive areas, they might be in psychological trouble. Mars is the "directors" planet. Acting may not be enough of a challenge for Robert Redford. He needs lots of physical exercise and the outlet of being a pioneer to release that nuclear power.

Eugene, with this powerful aspect in his chart, is a living, breathing example of this dynamic, charismatic energy in operation. Eugene, a former highly successful casting director in London, has Pluto conjunct Mars in the fifth house of creativity, gambles, and self-expression, with Mars ruling the ascendant, describing the personality and effectiveness, and Pluto ruling the seventh house of partnership, whether business or personal. The single-mindedness connected with this aspect can easily describe a directorial ability as well as that of a producer. Recently, Eugene was the stage manager of a production of *Oliver!* in the United States. His untiring efforts were key in the special success of the production. Eugene was especially effective when he worked with the children involved in the performance (fifth-house activity). It was his job to oversee the entire operation backstage once the performance began. It was clear that Eugene's professionalism enabled him to rise to the occasion even at times when emergencies demanded last-second solutions.

Eugene talked about his entry into the field of show business: "I really just got lucky. I got the first job I ever auditioned for, that as a dancer in a London show, and worked steadily in the same show for four years. After that, a friend asked if I could help out with casting, and as luck would have it, the owner of the agency was ill and I was left to do all the casting myself. I was so busy, I had to hire several girls to get everything done. I cast a multitude of commercials and films." After that, Eugene decided to work as an agent and took a tremendous cut in salary to gain the experience. Within a short period of time, it was suggested that he would be better off working alone and his own agency was born. Eugene described his working day: "The telephones started ringing as soon as the office was opened and didn't stop all day. I even catered lunch for the girls, because we were too busy for anyone to go out. Whereas most agents concluded the day's business at a normal hour and had their evenings free, most of my deals were made at nine o'clock at night. By that time of the evening, I was simply exhausted. It was not uncommon for the phone to ring at two o'clock in the morning with some casting emergency. One day, I simply woke up, looked out of the window, and said, 'That's it. Today it's all going,' and I sold the agency."

I asked Eugene to describe what it is like to have such an abundance of drive, ambition, and energy. He said, "I simply must be busy doing something or I get so terribly frustrated. I have to be busy doing something, even if it is only laundry or cleaning the house. Otherwise, I would simply go crazy. When I was working with *Oliver!* I would come home exhausted, but to do the show every night was lovely adrenalin." Since the fifth house describes entertainment such as giving a party, Eugene confirmed that even then he must do things in a big way. "I really go overboard, with ninety or a hundred people, tables and chairs, canopies, and the works. I can't mess around with little stuff. It has to be a real challenge for me. I rarely give up if I feel something is right. I always pursue it. I have a sixth sense that tells me a project is right." Eugene's green light and go-ahead signal seems once again set in motion. *Oliver!* seemed to whet his professional appetite, and plans are afoot to bring back two major recording artists into the spotlight again. Since Pluto is catalytic, powerful, and dynamic, I have no doubt Eugene's latest projects will be extremely successful.

PLUTO IN HARD ASPECT TO MARS

When these two planets are in hard aspect, they can describe the rage that is extremely difficult to release. Andy has Mars placed in his first house of personality, square Pluto placed in the tenth house of career, ruling Andy's relationship with his father. Andy's father was a "Plutonian," a dynamic businessman whose message was "Do what I say and don't ask questions." Andy chose to study ballet, a Mars activity which was far from what his father wanted from him. One incident in particular described the way the Plutonian child-father got even with Andy. When Andy's mother and father decided to sell their large, comfortable home to live in a smaller house, since their children were no longer at home, they planned to give each child some of the income from the sale, unbeknownst to the three children. Andy's two sisters announced that they were going to help their mother pack and move but that Andy was under no obligation to join them. They were quite willing to relieve him of that task. He was happy that they would do that for him. But Andy's father said, "The girls deserve more money because they helped us pack." Andy felt tremendously manipulated over the trivial incident. He knew very well it was his father's way of getting even with him over other things, and he had been working on that issue in his weekly therapy sessions. Andy came to an astrological-therapeutic workshop and brought up the issue of his sexuality, rather than the relationship with his father. When the hookup with money, the father, and his choice of career came to light, Andy felt that he finally knew how to deal with his father. He said, "I now know that I'll never win the eternal struggle with my father. He is very powerful and as long as he can keep me enraged, he has me right where he wants me. I must go up and around him, to go my way. Only in that way can I see things from a higher perspective. He is the child. I can't expect him to understand and I won't even try now. I can love him instead of being so angry that he manipulates me." Strenuous exercise (such as dance) is very essential for Andy so that he can work off excess frustration.

Muhammad Ali has Pluto square Mars in his chart. Mars is placed in the ninth house of publicity, with Pluto in the twelfth house of subconscious activity. Mars rules the ninth house and

Pluto rules the fourth house of home. Muhammad certainly showed his anger in interviews, especially in his early days of boxing, and through poetry and his vivid descriptions of what he intended to do to his opponents. He may have been motivated even more strongly on a subconscious level than the public knew. His need to release rage was especially strong. Many times this quality of rage is hidden behind what seems to be an easygoing personality, as if butter would melt in the mouth. Ali's poetry is gentle, only hinting at the rage beneath. Ali seems to have mellowed somewhat as he has come toward the victorious finale of his career. He may have worked out his frustrations long ago, or he may only now be really in touch with that inner motivation.

When Pluto and Mars are in opposition, the two voices can eventually balance, but the aspect is so intense that it may be next to impossible to find a healthy way to release the energy without undergoing some form of therapy. (Next to impossible, but not impossible.) Understanding of the rage can be the first step toward reducing it.

Jessica has this aspect in her chart. Jessica is a gorgeous Amazonian woman who juggles an active career as a therapist and the editorship of a magazine with marriage to a prominent physician. She was also involved in the founding of a university with her first husband. Her children and home are very much a part of her life. Jessica has Scorpio on the ascendant, with Pluto in her ninth house of publishing, higher education, and promotional efforts. Mars in her chart is in the third house of communications, siblings, and negotiations. Mars rules her sixth house of work. She was able to describe in detail how the Mars-Pluto aspect worked out in her life. "Before I understood my rage and began conscious work to reduce it, I was terrified of losing my temper, because I knew I could kill. I could physically feel it in my jaw. I could annihilate someone with my words, I could devastate people emotionally. I would come closer to violence with my son than with anyone, because he would bait me. I would literally hold his shoulders and shake him, and be scared of the rage I felt inside. I knew he wasn't the cause of that rage, he only stimulated it. Sometimes I would ask my husband to hold me very tight because I would just want to rip everything to shreds. He would literally restrain me.

"I've always had to hide who I am. You've talked about my

sitting on personal power and that's exactly what I've done. What I'm learning is that when I have to use struggling energy to make something happen, it's just not supposed to be. There is a higher organization in the universe that I'm in touch with a lot of the time. There is either a natural flow and things just fall into place or it's just not there. If it's not there, I've just got to let go. I'm learning patience, and also that I'm not in control. Internally, I now have far more energy, being in tune with a flowing of energy, than I did before. So I'm learning to release the rage.

Ten years ago I exploded a disk in my back. The disk was literally shattered when they operated on me. I know that what I was doing was backing up my energy and turning it inward. There are two new ways that I'm trying to reconcile what you call the homicidal rage. One of them is by working out physically. Nine months of the year, I work out three days a week starting at 6:30 A.M. I also swim and run. My body is different now. Another way that I'm dealing with this energy is in disciplined meditation: when I reach an altered state, I can let go much more easily.

"I did a regression session that was very revealing. I was not only aware of a birth struggle and trauma during the regression session, but I knew that right after birth I was tranquilized. That's how I became aware of repressing and building up that rage, because I was so angry and there was nothing that I could do about it at birth. So the process of my sitting on my power, energy, and rage began right away."

Richard Nixon has Pluto opposite Mars in his chart. Pluto is placed in the tenth house of career, with Mars in the fourth house of home. Sometimes this aspect can also describe a rationale that the end justifies the means. Nixon exhibited this quality over and over again. When he made his final speech from the White House before departing the humiliation of Watergate, he talked about his mother. The struggle between Nixon's mother and father may have kept him feeling impotent with rage. He was still publicly airing his feelings about his mother having the rug pulled out from under her during the worst crisis of his life. He may subconsciously have been getting even with his father even then. For in his public degradation, he could inwardly thumb his nose at his father and say, "If it hadn't been for you, this wouldn't have happened." If those early-childhood memories had not still been in his mind, he would never have brought his mother into the situation at all. Self-punishment can be the only way to work off the rage unless an individual becomes aware of what it is, where it came from, and how to transmute it away from unconscious self-torture.

Colleen is a very honest young woman who also has this aspect. She was quite willing to confirm what I saw in her chart. I said to her, "You could easily have had children as a protection against being a prostitute, if not literally, certainly subconsciously." She replied without hesitation, "You've got it. I have such a strong sex drive that I've always been terrified of it until recently. I'm married, but that simply isn't enough. I have such an intense sex drive that I have to have dynamic sex going for me all the time or I can feel the frustration settling in my body. Right now, I have four active lovers. You're so right. One of my deep-seated fears was of being a prostitute." She continued, "I'm much more confident about my marriage now, because I have an outlet for all the frustration. I'm willing to put in a lot of time and energy to make it happen in a way that is not destructive." I told Colleen that my description of Pluto-Mars is the priestess-courtesan complex.

I asked her if she would discuss the potentially homosexual side to this aspect. She replied, "I happen to choose men as my partners, but I have an emotional support from women that I don't have with men. It may have a sexual part and it may not. Women are physically nurturing. I don't act on sex with women, but it would be consistent with my emotions if I did."

Albert Schweitzer had Pluto opposite Mars in his chart. It is obvious that he chose to use the dynamic, atomic energy to pave the way for progress. His Pluto was placed in the eighth house of transformation, with Mars in the second house of money. Pluto also ruled that second house, with Mars ruling partnerships. Albert Schweitzer was a theologian, physician, and musician. He was a missionary and wrote about theology from a practical and practiced point of view. He not only won the Nobel Peace Prize, he touched the lives of people he came in contact with. He worked consistently to upgrade the quality of life and conditions for humanity. Albert Schweitzer's life is a positive example of how hard aspects, indicating growth potential, can be channeled and reconciled in an extremely positive way. Schweitzer was obviously motivated by concern for mankind.

PLUTO CONJUNCT JUPITER

The conjunction of Jupiter and Pluto is one of the most potent aspects in astrology. Jupiter describes luck, abundance, expansion, and optimism. When it is conjoined Pluto, the power of the luck is upgraded considerably. The charisma associated with Pluto is compounded by the humor and contagious enthusiasm that Jupiter exhibits. The individual with this aspect can sell anyone anything, but it is easier for him to work on a mass level than it is on an individual basis. The universe seems to have a hand in the affairs of a person with this aspect. He can be at the right place at the right time. His charisma and magnetism seem to attract situations and people to his side that enable him to put big deals together easily. He can be extremely successful in whatever he chooses to do. Since Jupiter rules not only enthusiasm and optimism, but a sense of curiosity about the workings of people and the universe, it is associated with religion and spiritual matters. It may not describe religion in a traditional or orthodox way, but more of a sense of universality. The transformation of the person's life has to do with the expression of his highest sense of humor, which is the cosmic humor connected to religious concepts.

Mahatma Gandhi had Jupiter conjunct Pluto in his chart. He transformed all of India with his moral strength, charisma, and religious joy. Over a hundred years after his birth, he was still evoking powerful feelings in the souls of mankind through an Academy Award-winning film about his life. His influence will extend far beyond his good works on earth, and well after his death his energy will continue to transform the lives of people who hear about him. Gandhi had Scorpio on the ascendant, with Jupiter ruling the second house of income. That powerful conjunction lay in the seventh house of partnership. It might be assumed that Gandhi would have been very wealthy with this dynamic aspect ruling the house of income. Gandhi was indeed extremely wealthy, but on a universal, cosmic level, rather than on an individual, greedy level. His concern was for the financial well-being of everyone else. Although Gandhi never had great wealth, he always got what he needed for his extended family as well as for his own real family. His life expressed that universal formula better than any other example.

When the motivation is for the good of all, blessings flow in with abundance. Gandhi never was motivated by selfish desires. Pluto describes the willingness to let go of anything that is not for the highest, greatest good. Gandhi let go of even the food he needed for his own sustenance to transform the lives of millions of hungry people. He did nothing forceful or manipulative. He showed by his own example what one lone man could do for humanity. That he was in touch with his own higher self and with the universal plan of mankind cannot be disputed. His strength seemed to come from sources beyond him. He was like a child in his clarity of intention and his singleminded commitment.

It is always necessary to stress in the study of astrology that the chart is a map only of potential. Mankind has free will. The beauty of that free will is that the same quality of energy can be utilized in many differing ways. The choice is with the individual. Jacqueline Susann also had Pluto conjunct Jupiter. Jackie reached millions of people with her books and films. To say that Jackie changed lives might be a gross exaggeration, but she was certainly effective; what she wrote could not be ignored. Jupiter conjunct Pluto in her chart was placed in the ninth house of publishing, distribution, and publicity. Jackie also had a Scorpio ascendant, with both Jupiter and Pluto ruling her personality and the second house of income. She made a great deal of money from her books as well as the film deals she put together. She was her own best producer.

People either liked Jacqueline Susann or they did not. She was warm, humorous, and fun if she was accepted for herself. She had a philosophical viewpoint that never allowed her to burden anyone else with her problems. Few people knew that Jackie had a retarded child. She never revealed that she had cancer to anyone but her very closest, most intimate friends. She was not the kind of person to indulge in self-pity. Jackie had a sense of philosophy that was extraordinary. She wrote metaphysical stories, one of which was published in book form after her death. But unfortunately Jackie did not live long enough to promote the book about her inner and real philosophy. She touched the lives of the people she came in contact with, but she may not have lived long enough to realize her ultimate potential.

V. I. Lenin had Pluto conjunct Jupiter in his chart. Pluto also ruled his first house of personality, as well as the twelfth house of the subconscious or secret activity. In his case, the conjunction was placed in the sixth house of work. Jupiter was a co-ruler of his personality. Lenin's philosophical ideal was far from what eventually manifested as communism. At the time of the Russian revolution, Lenin was in Germany, distressed that he could not be in his homeland to see the fruits of his labors. He had lived in abject poverty in Germany, struggling to publish his pamphlets about the sad plight of his beloved Russian countrymen. He was unable to raise money to finance his dream of political revolution and the end of corruption, until Germany entered into a negotiation that would allow Lenin to return safely to Russia through Germany with protection, to inspire the peasants to fight for what was right. Lenin was sneaked into Russia through the Finnish border. To his sorrow, he was met by the former palace guards, who would have killed him unless he made a deal with them. The deal was that they could switch sides and escort Lenin into Russia. These former palace guards became the dreaded Soviet secret police. Wherever Pluto is posited in a chart describes the necessity to uphold principles and refuse to compromise. If Lenin had been killed at the border, refusing to bastardize his dream of freedom for Russia, his martyrdom might have changed the course of history.

David Henesy was born with Pluto conjunct Jupiter in the fifth house of creative expression. It rules partnership and the eighth house of getting one's needs met. David was a child actor on Broadway at the age of eight. He was attending the Professional Children's School and became friendly with a child actor who was appearing with Mary Martin on Broadway in *Jenny*. David discovered that a part was available for him, understudying his friend, Brian, but also appearing in the performance in a small role. He made arrangements to see the director, on his own, and announced to his family that he was going to do a Broadway play. From there, he performed in the road company of *Oliver!* for nine months to return home and win the coveted role of David Collins in "Dark Shadows." This popular television soap opera featured Joan Bennett as the heroine of a drama full of vampires, ghosts, and chilling experiences. David was on this show for five years and acted in the *Dark Shadows* film. There was hardly a person from the age of eleven to perhaps fifteen who did not rush home from school to watch this unusual daytime drama. David's life changed drastically as a result of his popularity. He received tons of fan mail, was featured in national magazines, and was, of course, recognized on the streets—even in Mexico! Although David lost some privacy, the activity kept him very busy and out of trouble. When Jupiter is conjunct Pluto in the fifth house of romance, the romantic nature is quite powerful and abundant.

The fifth house also describes entertainment, investments, and the stock market. At the age of twenty-three, David opened his own restaurant, Punch, in New York City, and attracted many famous and interesting clients, making them feel at home. David is now involved in the commodities market, making deals for sales of food on an international basis. With this powerful conjunction ruling the eighth house of transformation, David may have only had rehearsals for his ultimate potential to affect the lives of many people through his own creativity, work with children, or investments of time, energy, or money.

PLUTO IN HARD ASPECT TO JUPITER

When Pluto and Jupiter are in hard aspect to each other, the individual is still incredibly dynamic and fortunate, but disappointment can come in unexpected ways. The person may overdo things, have overexpectations, and be compulsive at times. His enthusiasm knows no bounds, but he may be so enthusiastically potent that he sets himself up for a letdown. Drawn to his enthusiastic quality, people may promise more than they can deliver. The individual with this aspect may tend to do the same thing. He feels he can do almost anything and sometimes bites off more than he can chew. After a few major disappointments, he may hesitate to build up his hopes for fear of a letdown.

Moira is a very dynamic, attractive lady who described Pluto square Jupiter in her own chart by saying, "I feel very much like a free child in touch with the oneness of the universe. When I lift myself up to that level, the right things and conditions flow in; I experience tremendous synchronicity. But sometimes when I really focus that energy, it can be perceived by others as a laser beam that bores through them. I need to be aware of that quality and not focus too strongly on one person. I've been told that I was too intense. My marriage partners say, 'I can't handle your energy.'

That's why I'm not married now. I was too unknowing to realize that it wasn't a rejection."

Pluto is placed in the twelfth house in Moira's chart, ruling the fourth house of home and father, in square aspect to Jupiter in the third house of communications, ruling the fifth house of romance, creativity, and children. Moira is extremely intelligent, caring, loving, and aware, yet her youngest child is now in jail for repeated minor thefts. He was first convicted for being in possession of marijuana and was sent to a correction center. Moira can provide for her son very well, yet he persists in rebellious activity that backfires in his life. I suggested to her that he might be thumbing his nose at her in some way. The communication between them is very strong, yet he continues to do things that disappoint her. She may need to back off and let him find his own way.

Moira is extremely capable. She is easily able to handle details with ease and most gracefully, yet she may just do too much. She is very youthful in appearance and has a zest and energy that are exciting. She can devise systems for work that simplify things for others. For instance, she used a coding system of letters and numbers for a particular project that was incredibly effective. She went to graduate school after her children were born and said it was easy for her to handle everything at once. She had a full-time job, children, and a husband to look after. With this quality of energy, Moira must diversify on a mass level in order to avoid threatening people around her who are not so dynamic and capable. She described that wonderful flow of energy by saying, "I have an ability to be a child first and foremost. When I become attracted to a person or situation, I feel lit up. I feel a constant flow of energy. I am rarely blocked in that flow. I have occasionally lost contact with my parent and adult ego state and can feel the difference between that state and the one that I would call synergistic. Incredible things can happen if I just let go and let the energy work for me."

Hedy Lamarr has Pluto sesquisquare Jupiter in her chart. The conflict is the same as that described by a square, but a sesquisquare is a more difficult dialogue to reconcile. In Hedy's case, it describes conditions with money. Jupiter is placed in the eighth house of debts, bills, getting one's needs met, and transformation. Pluto rules the fifth house of creative ability and the gambling instincts, and is placed in the twelfth house of subconscious desires and activity. Hedy has an added difficult aspect with Saturn conjunct Pluto in that twelfth house. After many successful years as a Hollywood star with powerful magnetic qualities, Hedy started on a downward path. She had psychiatric problems, periods of illness (Jupiter rules the sixth house of health), and legal problems. She was arrested for shoplifting in the May Company in California. It is claimed that all her problems have cost $30 million. Hedy payed a high price for her compulsive tendencies.

Jayne Mansfield's daughter, Jayne Marie, has Pluto in opposition to Jupiter. Pluto is placed in the eighth house of inheritance, while Jupiter is placed in the second house of earned income. Jayne Marie is a *Playboy* model, easily able to earn large sums of money. She was brought up in lavish Hollywood surroundings and, by all rights, should have had a large inheritance from her mother. When Jayne Mansfield was killed in a tragic automobile accident, she left an estate of about $513,000 but no will. Jayne Marie and her four siblings had practically nothing from that sum after other claims were settled. Her mother's forty-room mansion sold for a paltry sum, considering the value of California real estate. Jayne Marie not only lost her mother when she was only seventeen years old, but any financial security that might have come from her mother's death.

PLUTO CONJUNCT SATURN

When slower-moving planets begin to aspect each other, many people share the same aspect, simply because it is generational. The aspects not only describe tendencies in an individual chart, they describe the outer-world conditions that can give overt cause for those tendencies. The combination of Pluto and Saturn can indicate a political ability. The involvement may not be in governmental politics, but in the politics of daily events as well. Pluto describes power, while Saturn describes responsibility. Together they describe a profound dedication to assume the ultimate potential. But just the opposite can be true. Saturn can describe limitation, fears, and pressures that prevent the expression of that power. Or it can indicate the possibility of squeezing out the power through gritted teeth and clenched fists, with a steely-eyed determination. The

choice of the individual determines the expression or the nonex-
pression of his most profound potential.

In terms of transactional analysis, Saturn represents the parent
while Pluto represents the child ego state. With this conjunction,
the judgments coming from parental messages or the judgments of
the environmental conditions prevent the free child from fully expressing his potentially dynamic energy. Child-ego-state activities
range from sexual activity to charismatic and universal projects.
Perhaps no age expresses as dramatically the conflict between the
child need to "play" and the parental judgments that say, "Thou
shalt not," as the Victorian Age. Queen Victoria was born with
Pluto conjunct Saturn in her chart. She seemed to epitomize both
sides of the conjunction. She was incredibly potent as a ruler, and
the positive effects of her reign were far-reaching. But the sublimation of sex during the Victorian Age led to underground expression
of its impulses, with flirtations, mistresses, and rampant venereal
disease. The outer form was cloaked with propriety from head to
toe, while the undergarments reeked of titilation, games, and manipulation. The lower classes had no problem in expressing their
voluptuous and passionate nature, but the upper classes were virtu-
ous in public and powerfully playful behind the scenes.

Queen Victoria had Pluto and Saturn in the eleventh house of
group activity. Pluto rules the sixth house of work, whereas the
ninth house rules international affairs, publicity, and reputation.
Her greatest power lay in expansion on a global level. The Sun
never set on the British Empire during her reign. She also led
Great Britain into a powerful time of industrial growth, described
by the conjunction in the eleventh house. She assumed the throne
of England when she was a mere eighteen years old. Duty-bound,
she never shirked her tasks, and she was a mighty example of
discipline, responsibility, and regimentation. She was not given to
any sort of frivolity. She left that final bursting forth of the rebellious child for generations to come. Her colonies did rebel, however, leaving England a smaller but perhaps less rigid country.

The control of Saturn in conjunction with Pluto is like a child
being kept quiet and so rigidly disciplined that when he is allowed
out into society he doesn't know how to behave. The parent ego
says in effect, "I don't trust you out from under my thumb. I know
just what you'll do if I even take my eyes away. You'll get into

trouble." That is exactly what England said to India, for instance. But that child ego is too strong to stay buried for long. When the child bursts forth, he is liable to run right into traffic and get hurt. In pain, he admits to the parent, "You're right. I'll be a good child and listen to you." However, the process repeats itself until the child is determined to take responsibility for himself and show his true nature in a healthy way. Thanks to Gandhi, India rebelled consistently, in a determined manner, and with responsibility.

Orson Welles had Pluto conjunct Saturn describing his personality and ruling the sixth house of work, and the eighth house of getting his needs met. Orson was able to get what he wanted from studio heads and could deal on a political level with the authorities who had the final word on his productions. He was a brilliant actor, but with such a potent aspect describing his personality, he became director, producer, and writer of many films. In his case, he was able to deal with heads of corporations without losing his own sense of identity. Orson was not ever known to compromise his principles or good taste to satisfy the demands of others. He was, however, a renegade in Hollywood. At times, the battle seemed to be too much to fight. Gregory Peck had this aspect, as did singer James Taylor and many other successful people. In a positive sense, it describes a determination that is unbeatable and simply will not give up. When the tendency to rigidity is balanced by allowing the potency to emerge in a consistent and responsible manner, the combination is ultimately the most powerful of all. For then the parent is supportive of the dynamic, charismatic child, with responsibility as the keystone of the flight of the eagle.

PLUTO IN HARD ASPECT TO SATURN

Frances was born at the time of the Depression in the United States. She was brought up by very strict parents and grandparents. She was constantly reminded that life was not all fun and games and that hard times had taken their toll on her family. She was taught responsibility and duty and above all to be aware of what the neighbors would think. She was an only child and led a very sheltered life. She has Pluto conjunct the ascendant in opposition to Saturn in the sixth house of work and health. She said, "The worst thing I can remember about my childhood is that I had no friends to play with. I was not allowed to go swimming with the other friends my age because of the fear of polio. I stayed at home playing with dolls, reading, and feeling very cut off and isolated. I was not even allowed to go to the movies, for fear that groups of any kind could harbor polio germs. I had a hard time learning how to relate to groups. I always felt very isolated. Finally, I realized that I was still living those early messages even as an adult. I tend to work hard and not allow myself to play. There was a time when I really rebelled and got into a bit of mischief, but then the pendulum would spring back and I would do nothing but work. I still am trying to find a balance. I love to entertain and have fun, but I find that it is difficult to work and play at the same time. I still tend to do one or the other. At least I've gotten rid of the guilt of having too much fun, but now any late hours or too much rich food and drink takes its toll on my health. Moderation seems essential in my life."

An overly strong sense of responsibility can be connected to this combination of planets, with the resulting fear of not being able to accomplish what is expected of one. Ted Kennedy has Saturn in Capricorn in the first house, in opposition to Pluto in the seventh house of marriage. Pluto rules his tenth house of career and father, and Saturn rules his Capricorn ascendant. Joe Kennedy began to groom his first son, Joe, Jr., for the presidency of the United States. Joe was killed in the Second World War, and the mantle of the presidency fell onto John's shoulders. The golden age of Camelot was brought to a screaming halt with the brutal death of the beloved President. Teddy's brother Bobby was also murdered. Now, after three deaths, the possibility remained that he might live up to the family expectations and take his place on the throne. With Saturn so heavily aspected in his personality, the sense of responsibility would be extreme, as well as the insecurity about being able to do a good job, especially with all that has gone on before him. But his powerful child-ego state found a way out for him. First, he "got even" with that powerful, forceful child-father who said, "Do what I say and don't ask any questions," by sullying his reputation publicly. He was involved in a tragic accident at Chappaquiddick, where a pretty young girl was killed. Whether Teddy was innocent or guilty of an affair is almost incidental at this point. No one will ever forget the incident. He was married to Joan, described by

Pluto in his chart, who consciously or unconsciously continued to besmirch his public image. She was an alcoholic, causing Ted some embarrassment, and then pulled the rug out from under him by establishing separate residence and getting a divorce. Ted is Catholic, under constant scrutiny, and might have a hard time winning the plum of the presidency after all that has happened to him. Which comes first, the chicken or the egg? Did Ted unconsciously set up conditions that would give him an out from the expectancy of his father? Did he attract, or even pick the very conditions that would embarrass his father? Did he win, get even with Joe Kennedy, only to have all those events backfire in his own life, causing more unhappiness than he might have asked for? Saturn can keep an individual under constant pressure, nose to the grindstone, but in an eventually limited or nonproductive way. Ted has a political career, but not to the extent that was expected from his programming and preconditioning. Saturn describes a need to be in control and can be, indeed, very controlling. Ted Kennedy may be exactly where he wants to be in life and politics.

PLUTO CONJUNCT URANUS

The individual may be thumbing his nose at society, the people close in his life, or at any restrictive condition he encounters. A deep-seated need to get even, for what he may not really know, compels him to show the world that no one can stop him from getting what he needs and wants. He may do it in a passive, resistant fashion as well as in a dynamic, active way. But that potent combination is like sending a rocket to the Moon. It is electrical and atomic energy ready to blast off at any moment. It can be very volatile and destructive.

This is a very powerful generational aspect. Children born between late September 1961 and November 1969 have these two planets in conjunction. They are particularly high-powered, talented, and unusual. They are the Aquarian Age babies, born at a time in history when old forms were breaking up with considerable speed. They are a product of the '60s and the "hippie generation." The environmental conditioning in the outer world was extremely rebellious and powerful in its sweeping force. This was the era of flower children living together in Utopian communes, but it was also the era of the Manson gang and the brutal and tragic murder of Sharon Tate. It was a time of rebellion on all levels of society. Young people left home at an alarming rate to wander dirty and unkempt, living from hand to mouth in search of a different life with different values. No matter what the consequences, they were unwilling to go on with life as they were brought up to expect it to be.

Uranus always describes awakening. It always comes with drastic and unexpected experiences until the individual or society is ready to accept change with humor and joy. The '60s generation changed more than the young. Older people began to let go of the traditional, earthbound, Saturnian way of life in order to feel more freedom. Grandmothers began to wear hip-high skirts, shedding prejudices along with their clothes. Patterns were broken forever. Some people suffered along the way, but others were able to bring more joy and meaning into their lives. The '60s flower children led the way. The Bible says, "and a little child shall lead them." When we consider the concept of Pluto as the child ego, that powerful quality of innocence can transmute negative conditions through lighter and higher perspective. When that quality is coupled with Uranian inspiration, the drastic change works well and easily. When motivation is not pure, or game-playing conditions exist, the results can be devastating and darkness can prevail.

During that period of Pluto conjunct Uranus, many birth defects occurred, but the era also produced exceptionally talented young people. It is probably too soon to see the full results of that possibility of talent. Lois Rodden cites several examples of birth defects, multiple births, and Siamese twins in her book *The American Book of Charts.* For instance, there were sets of Siamese twins born in 1961, 1962, and 1963. Only two of the six children survived surgery. The conjunctions were placed in differing sectors of their charts. Only one set of twins had this aspect describing the personality, and one set had the conjunction describing health.

There were also three sets of female multiple births at this time. Quadruplets were born to the Axe family in 1963, and quadruplets came to the Harkis family in the same year. Quintuplets were born to the Hanson family in 1969. All thirteen girls lived. There may be many more undocumented births that were unusual during this period of time. This was the era of drugs, but whether any of these births were drug-related or merely a reflection of the outer environmental conditioning is mere speculation. The trends of the times were certainly mirroring unusual and special qualities.

Jennifer Strasberg was born with this conjunction in her chart. Jennifer has these two planets in her first house of personality and self-expression. The first house also describes the physical condition and the birth-survival decisions. Jennifer was born with four holes in her heart. Her mother, charismatic actress Susan Strasberg, describes the conditions in her own life and the resulting decisions she made at the time of Jennifer's birth in her book *Bittersweet*. Jennifer had heart surgery that has corrected the heart defect. She is now a talented, unusual, and very perceptive young lady in her late teens. Jennifer has inherited the Strasberg family talent and has been writing brilliantly since she was a small child. However, Jennifer is her own person. She is highly intuitive, aware, and sensitive to people. She refuses to go along with conditions just to be amenable, because of her inner sense of awareness. Her true genius may still be totally unexplored, but Jennifer will never allow herself to get by on her family name. She may go beyond the accomplishments of her grandfather, mother, and uncle, but we can be sure that the outlet Jennifer chooses for herself will set her apart in some way or other.

The conjunction during the sixties was placed in the sign of Virgo. Virgo indicates mental activity, so we can expect the talent-oriented outcome of such a placement to be on a mental level, reflected in activities such as writing, speaking, acting, and decision making. Two young actresses born at this time who have reached stardom already are Brooke Shields and Tatum O'Neal. Both girls catapulted their careers into the limelight through mold-breaking roles. Brooke played a teenage prostitute at the age of twelve, shocking many people, and Tatum played the young companion of a con man. Both of them exuded a kind of innocence in their roles that set them apart. Pluto can be described as the ultimate gambler and the priestess-courtesan complex. The quality of innocence, charisma, and rebellion was the underlying characteristic of both roles, providing perfect vehicles for these young ladies to ride to fame. Uranus can describe fame, simply because the individual is willing to work through the scare to take risks that will set him apart. In both charts, the conjunction rules the twelfth house of the subconscious, and describes creative outlet for Tatum and work opportunity for Brooke.

Tracy Austin has this conjunction in her chart placed in the ninth house of publicity, promotional effort, and travel. She was the youngest tennis player allowed on the Virginia Slims tennis tour. The aspect also describes her twelfth house of subconscious process. It has been said that Tracy has an uncanny ability to sense her opponent's weakness and use it to her advantage. Amy Carter was catapulted into the limelight and the press with her father's election to the presidency. Amy was allowed at state dinners and was scrutinized constantly by everyone to see how she would handle such public notoriety. The aspect in her chart describes her father and homelife as well as the seventh house of partnership. It is not unlikely that Amy would see her father as brilliant, charismatic, and magnetic, a man ahead of the times. It would also be quite in line with psychological programming to expect Amy to want a marriage with someone equally as unusual in her eyes. The fourth house describes not only the father in a chart, but the latter part of the individual's life. Amy may find her own full potential and unique quality as she goes into her late forties. This aspect rules her eighth house of inheritance, and second house of money. Amy can already expect at least a portion of her father's land and property to come to her through gifts or inheritance. She is more than likely quite accustomed to living in most comfortable surroundings, and no doubt can expect to continue her lifestyle in that fashion, one way or another. Bruno and Louisa Huber describe Uranus as ruling the grandparents. Jimmy Carter's mother is indeed very avant-garde, charismatic, and a free soul. Perhaps Amy will grow up to be another Miss Lillian.

The last time this aspect was in existence was in the mid 1800s. That era produced some very interesting people. Pluto was conjunct Uranus in the sign of Aries at that time. Aries quality is exceptionally pioneering, daring, and courageous. It also must be manifest on a physically active level. Jesse James became notorious because of his defiance and rebellion toward society. It took physical courage to rob all those banks. Wyatt Earp, with the same aspect in his chart, chose the other side of the coin and became the defender of justice, with just as much or more courage demanded of him. Annie Besant, born with this aspect, was extremely pioneering. She was the forerunner of all the women's groups and women's reform issues of our present day and age. She was arrested and tried on a morals charge in the late 1800s for lecturing on and publishing birth-control information. Her life was dedicated to equal rights for women, intellectual freedom, and unions for the oppressed. She became a leader in the Theosophical Movement. When George Bernard Shaw gave her a book on Theosophy, she converted from atheism and became the president of the movement in India until her death.

Vincent van Gogh and Paul Gauguin rebelled against their upbringing, fleeing to spots where their genius might flourish unhampered. Vincent was a tormented soul, wringing out his art at the expense of his own ear. August Strindberg, Robert Louis Stevenson and Guy de Maupassant shared this aspect in their charts. Their works are as important now as they were when they were written. Strindberg showed his rebellion by writing about feelings and emotions that were not allowed to be expressed in his time. Those descriptive words of hidden passions are as valid now as then. He seemed to have universal knowledge about struggles indigenous to the human condition that continue throughout all generations.

PLUTO IN HARD ASPECT TO URANUS

Even more difficult to release than a conjunction is the hard aspect of a square or an opposition between Pluto and Uranus. For in this case, instead of standing side by side, the voices of rebellion are in conflict. The frustrations that are apparent when Pluto squares Uranus were mirrored by society with the Great Depression, of the thirties. The aspect started in mid-March 1929 and continued through September 1929, only to begin again in late January 1930 and continue through forward and retrograde phases until the peak square on April 21, 1932. That almost irreconcilable aspect continued again through forward and retrograde times until another exact square on March 8, 1933, when the planets finally began to move apart from their most fierce struggle. The aspect was still in existence, however, until Uranus was well into another sign, Taurus, in June 1935. It was not until that time that the country began to heal its wounds from original impulses that caused the stock market to crash in 1929.

One of the most interesting facts emerging from astrological research is the discovery that important events seem to be born from
conflict as well as from ease. In fact, it seems that the more conflict
is indicated in an individual chart or in a period of history, the
greater the possibility of greatness. And so in the connection with
the plight of the economic welfare of the nation, a generation was
born ready to transmute the quality of rebellion onto a more
healthy level. There have been former periods of history that also
exhibited this aspect. James Monroe was born at a time in history
before either Uranus or Pluto was actually discovered, but with the
square aspect in his chart nevertheless; he took first steps toward
humanitarian concern for the welfare of all the Americas with his
Monroe Doctrine. Pluto describes concern for the welfare of all. If
his motivation was truly on a cosmic level, the doctrine will stand
the test of time. Uranus describes humanitarian concerns or rebellion. He risked an avant-garde approach to preserve freedom within
our own country.

This square aspect was in effect for approximately five years
between 1874 and 1879, even though undiscovered. Many advanced people were born during that period of time, including Albert Schweitzer, Winston Churchill, Robert Frost, Carl Jung, Her-
mann Hesse, Carl Sandburg, Isadora Duncan, Albert Einstein,
Alice Bailey, and Edgar Cayce. Transformation came about in the
lives of many of these people after traumas occurred that seemed to
leave them no choice. Winston Churchill might easily have led the
life of a wealthy English playboy if he had not been forced into his
role because of world events. Edgar Cayce, brought up with traditional religious concepts, would have been content to sell books if
he had not lost his voice and been forced to become a photographer. With that change of profession came the deeper understanding of his ability to cure himself and restore his lost voice. From
there it was a small step to the curing of thousands of people by
putting himself into a trancelike state and diagnosing what was
wrong with the particular person. Throughout his life, Cayce kept
his motivation pure, even refusing to accept any additional income
from his healing work. He continued to earn money for his family
through photography, even though he might have helped his own
family's financial condition if he had charged only a small fee for
his time. His readings have been documented and are on file in

Virginia Beach, Virginia, to aid anyone who needs help to this day. Pluto describes the events that seem to pull the rug out from under a person at the time, but in retrospect, those fierce events release the higher form of energy. When Pluto is squared Uranus, transformation of the rebellious instincts leads to a more universal, humanitarian quality of energy.

PLUTO CONJUNCT NEPTUNE

This aspect has occurred only once, yet it was before Pluto was discovered. Percival Lowell predicted a trans-Neptunian planet in 1915. From approximately mid 1883 until mid 1899 these two planets were conjunct; however, since this occurred before Pluto's existence was actually confirmed by Clyde William Tombaugh on February 18, 1930, we can only make a guess as to the esoteric meaning of this unobserved conjunction. This period of history heralded the boom of the twentieth century. For Pluto always describes a major transformation, whereas Neptune indicates special inspiration. This period of time produced incredibly talented, magnetic, charismatic people as well as exceptional developments in industry, labor, and quality of lifestyle. Neptunian idealism wants to save the world and may not always be practical, but when it is in association with the potent energy of Pluto, accomplishments are not only inspired but far-reaching.

Jiddu Krishnamurti was born with Pluto conjunct Neptune in the fourth house of home, but ruling the first house of personality, and the ninth house of philosophy and travel, and the tenth house of career. He exuded an aura of power that transformed the lives of people around him without his doing anything at all. Edna Miller, a warm, wonderful woman now in her eighties, tells the story of her first exciting transatlantic voyage, when this dynamic man was also on board ship. She said he could not go unnoticed as he strode purposefully along the decks of the ship, his long, white hair flowing behind him. Krishnamurti was a theosophist who was a forerunner of modern-day gurus. His writings and teachings changed many ideas and concepts about religion and the purpose of life. With this aspect describing his early life, his career, and his later life, it would seem that he came into this world with a clear concept of what he was to do. That perception continued, growing and building to the very end. Another spiritual leader born with the same aspect in his chart was Archbishop Fulton J. Sheen. The conjunction is placed in the first house of personality, ruling the eleventh house of group activity or organizations, and the seventh house of partnership. His power was channeled into the Catholic Church and his marriage was to God. He was revered and respected by millions.

F. Scott Fitzgerald had such a following that he is almost a cult hero to this day. His reputation in the literary world is legendary and he is avidly read by American youth and adults alike. He epitomized an era gone by. After he wrote *This Side of Paradise*, in 1920, he sold everything he wrote. He and his wife, Zelda, lived a lifestyle that many envied. They traveled, lived abroad, and entertained lavishly. Money never seemed to stop flowing. Until the last days of Fitzgerald's life, when Zelda's illness and his own drinking took away his zest, he was blessed with an incredible creative flow. His income then came from writing films in Hollywood, but he was never happy working in that medium. Pluto describes transformation in the life. In the case of Fitzgerald, with Pluto-Neptune placed in the fourth and fifth houses, describing creativity and lifestyle as well as the last cycle of life and ruling his career, and the ninth house of publicity, promotion, traveling, and publishing, he had the potential to become more prolific and powerfully productive throughout his whole life. However, when the lower side of Pluto is lived to the exclusion of the eagle, the universe exacts a price. With the end of idealism, the sad result of the game-playing expression of the child ego is total disillusionment. When the glamour of Neptune is gone, many times the individual turns to drugs or drinking to restore the hope and illusion.

This quality of idealism can be very dangerous when linked to powerful Pluto. Adolf Hitler was born with this aspect in his chart in the eighth house. He was powerful in getting his needs met, to the sorrow of the world for generations and perhaps centuries to come. Nikita Khrushchev had this aspect, as did Mao Tse-tung, Charles de Gaulle, and Chiang Kai-shek. Jawaharlal Nehru and Dwight D. Eisenhower also shared this conjunction, with J. Edgar Hoover, J. Paul Getty, and Joseph and Rose Kennedy. The list of powerful people is endless. In all fields, a contribution was made that may still be acknowledged. The impact is strong for good or evil. Both Paramhansa Yogananda and Meher Baba had this idealistic dynamism in their charts.

Neptune describes the glamour world. The fine actors, dancers, and artists born in this time period excelled in their fields. Jack Benny, Fred Allen, Walter Brennan, Jimmy Durante, Edward G. Robinson, and Charles Chaplin were born with this aspect. Rudolph Valentino had Pluto conjunct Neptune in the third house of communications, posited in the twelfth house of the subconscious, ruling his eighth house of getting his needs met. The name Valentino still conjures up the epitome of the male sex symbol. Rudolph was said to be really unaware of the incredible charisma and magnetism that had women by the millions swooning at the mention of his name. Nijinsky may be the greatest dancer that ever lived. He also had this aspect in his chart.

The writers with Pluto conjunct Neptune conjure up a respect and awe unparalleled. Pearl Buck, Aldous Huxley, Eugene O'Neill, e. e. cummings, Edna St. Vincent Millay, Henry Miller, and Dashiell Hammett. Pianist Arthur Rubinstein, classical guitarist Andrés Segovia, and composers Cole Porter and Irving Berlin share the aspect. Painters Marc Chagall and Joan Miró and director John Ford are examples of this quality of talent. Three men born at this time in history made very important contributions to the field of astrology: astrologers everywhere in the world revere the names of Marc Edmund Jones, C. E. O. Carter, and the beloved Dane Rudhyar, who first wrote of the humanistic point of view in connection with astrology. We will not see this kind of high-powered idealistic energy again until four hundred years hence, in 2384, when these planets once again form a conjunction in the skies. Midway into the year 2000, we will see the first major hard aspect (a square) between these two planets.

It is obvious that civilization has reached a high level of knowledge, technological sophistication, and power. What we choose to do with this advantage can determine the future of mankind. It may be that during the year of the turning of the century, such choices will become even more apparent. It has been predicted by Nostradamus, Edgar Cayce, and almost everyone with vision that we are entering the Age of Enlightenment, described as the Age of Aquarius, in which people will work on a truly humanitarian level, become better friends to each other, and care about the welfare of their brothers. The struggle to attain the transformation on the most minute personal level is the first step in changing the world. If life is viewed from the highest perspective, it can be clear that daily difficulties, problems, and conflicts are really golden opportunities to pass some universal tests. Here's to the possibility of getting some "A's" in our individual initiation process.